PRACTICING STALINISM

PRACTICING STALINISM

BOLSHEVIKS, BOYARS,

AND THE PERSISTENCE

OF TRADITION

J. ARCH GETTY

Yale UNIVERSITY PRESS
New Haven and London

Published with assistance from the Louis Stern Memorial Fund.

Yale University Press books may be purchased in quantity for educational, business, or promotional use. For information, please e-mail sales.press@yale.edu (U.S. office) or sales @yaleup.co.uk (U.K. office).

Set in Sabon type by Westchester Book Group, Danbury, Connecticut.
Printed in the United States of America.

Library of Congress Cataloging-in-Publication Data

Getty, J. Arch (John Arch), 1950–, author.
Practicing Stalinism : Bolsheviks, boyars, and the persistence of tradition / J. Arch Getty.
  pages ;   cm
Includes bibliographical references and index.
ISBN 978-0-300-16929-4 (cloth : alkaline paper)   1. Politics, Practical—Soviet Union.   2. Politics, Practical—Social aspects—Soviet Union.   3. Soviet Union—Politics and government—1917–1936.   4. Soviet Union—Politics and government—1936–1953.   5. Kommunisticheskaia partiia Sovetskogo Soiuza—Party work.   I. Title.
JN6581.G48 2013
324.247'07509041—dc23
2013000343

A catalogue record for this book is available from the British Library.

This paper meets the requirements of ANSI/NISO Z39.48-1992 (Permanence of Paper).

10 9 8 7 6 5 4 3 2 1

Contents

Preface

For more than twenty years I sat first in Soviet libraries and then in Soviet and Russian archives studying the political history of Stalin's time. As was common at that time, I was trained in "Soviet studies" by a few historians and several political scientists. My peers and I cut our teeth on Merle Fainsod's *How Russia Is Ruled,* and we knew everything there was to know about the hierarchical pyramids and structures of the "pattern of political controls." Although my intellectual path eventually led me to reject much of the totalitarian approach of such works, I remained convinced that there was a modern rational structure to Stalinist and Soviet power and that understanding the organization and interaction of institutions could reveal that structure, much as it could for Western countries and my native USA.

I visited Russia every year from 1987 and, like a good political historian, I assiduously pored through Soviet books, journals, newspapers, and eventually archives looking for the keys to this strange but recognizably modern society. The research difficulties we faced in those early years at the hands of hostile archivists, discouraging rules, pointless surveillance, and restrictions on access to materials brought the well-known forbidding power of ubiquitous Soviet bureaucracy home to us every day. For those of us studying politics, that seemed to provide a daily confirmation of the importance of understanding the history of that bureaucracy.

But for many of us, there were other Soviet and Russian experiences that were just as important. After work, we relaxed with Russian friends, spending long evenings eating and drinking and talking in the cramped kitchens of Moscow apartments. On weekends we would walk around the city and continue our mutually curious conversations about our respective societies. Perhaps because work was so stressful, I made an unconscious but sharp separation between work and leisure. At work I spent time with long-dead bureaucrats; after hours I mixed with very much alive average people. For a long time, these two circles of "friends" seemed to have little in common, even though some of my after-hours friends were themselves Communist Party members.

From those friends, I learned about Russia. I understood for the first time what it meant to be part of a group, a "clan," an "us." I understood the importance and comfort of doing informal favors for friends in the group, watching their backs as they watched mine, and learned the hundreds of informal (and sometimes technically illegal) ways to get things done, ranging from hitching a ride, getting a good cut of meat, buying a TV, or getting one's child into a good school. In the Soviet and later Russian climates of shortage, such skills and connections were important both economically and morally, and more than once I found nourishment of every kind at dinner with friends when my dorm's café and most of the grocery stores in town inexplicably closed.

In Russia, one often makes friends sequentially in networks. My first colleague in Leningrad introduced me to his two best army buddies, who introduced me to their neighbors, who introduced me to their dacha friends, and so forth. My circle consisted not only or even mostly of academics. As people my age often were, they tended to be sarcastic and irreverent about many things, and as I spent more and more time with them, I noticed that they put their irreverence into practice. They spent a good deal of time and energy sneering at rules, not only ridiculing them, but actively avoiding and violating them. The obtuse and uncooperative official system was impossible to navigate legally, so everyone learned how to circumvent it. One bought a driver's license. One bribed a policeman to leave one alone. One drove into the suburbs at night and gave a password in a clearing to get gasoline for the car. In a covert economy one used whatever resources one had based on reciprocity, friendship, and everything except the law. Avoidance of the official was the culture, and you helped your friends (and they you) to maneuver in a kind of parallel society that intersected the public, pre-scribed, official one only occasionally and accidentally.

Such behaviors are not new and scholars and journalists have writ-ten about them many times. They belong to the world of "informal practices" that, depending on whom you talk to, either subvert the system or help it to function efficiently. In either case, the general assumption—which I shared—was that the line between informal so-cial and formal political practices was firm and belonged to the era of Soviet bureaucracy and economic shortages.

But the more time I spent with my friends, the less clear that line seemed. Gradually, I began to detect a surprising convergence between the lives of my dead archival Bolsheviks and my dear living friends. For me, certain memories stand out as catalysts that launched my thinking in a different direction.

For a time in the early 1990s, I worked informally in a Russian uni-versity helping to establish a computer laboratory for quantitative methods in historical research. I worked with friends who worked under professors who worked under deans who worked under a vice rector in the usual Soviet pyramid arrangement. At one point, as a result of an intrigue in high places, one of the vice rectors was forced out. Even though this struggle of titans was many levels above my humble work, it immediately touched me and my friends. I was told that I needed to resign immediately "at my own request." Why? Because I was con-nected to someone who was connected to someone who was connected to a client of the purged official. "This is the custom here," I was told. "Everybody goes; it's pointless to argue." I was a victim of the age-old Russian notion of collective responsibility (*krugovaia poruka,* explored in Chapter 1) and was reminded of the chains of clients who fell in tsarist or Muscovite times when a senior boyar or family lost position. Or when entire networks of people down to the lowest level were ar-rested when their senior Old Bolshevik patron fell to Stalin's purges. No rule, law, or regulation dictated such a root-and-branch purge; it was an informal, customary practice in both my bureaucratic and my nonbureaucratic worlds that seemed to transcend centuries. Could both those worlds operate according to the same rules?

Another memory is from a walk across Red Square with my friend Leonid sometime in the 1990s after the fall of the USSR. Leonid was al-ways amused at my studies, which he considered "very American" and therefore a bit naïve. That day as we walked, I asked Leonid what he thought of crime in Russia. He patiently explained to me that "organized crime" was a peculiarly Western expression. "When there are too many laws, what is crime? When everyone pays someone for protection, who is the criminal? We don't think much about ideas like 'state' or 'law' or 'crime' these days. We try to figure out who is who and how to get by."

Then I asked him about the famous Russian mafia. "Which one?" he said. "Let's see. In Moscow, there's the Chechen mafia that handles fruits and vegetables. If you want to do business in fruits and vegetables, you do it with them or they kill you. There is the Tambov gang that handles prostitution in most parts of the city. The Iaroslavl' boys are into extortion; very tough guys. Same as with the vegetables; if you want to do these things, you do them with the appropriate gang or they hurt you. "Oh," and he gestured to the Kremlin: "there's that mafia too. They do politics, and they are really big. Lots of guns. You want to do politics, you do it with them or else. The thing about all these mafias is that they are highly organized and secret, and you're either in or out."

In Leonid's view, there was no very great difference between the official and the informal. There were several "mafias," defined as tight groups of people, criminal or not, protecting each other. When I thought about and unpacked it over a very long time, I realized that he had given me a key to Russians' view of government, power, and institutions. Official institutions were just collections of people whose public façade was better than most at convincing people to obey them. Few people trusted or even believed in institutions; they believed in people. Everything was personal. There were only groups and organizations inside, outside, and overlapping the line between government and society.

The line that separated informal from formal practices was imaginary. They were the same thing, and one could say that age-old informal cultural practices in society also characterized the official world, regardless of what the latter's rules might say. After a while, as I continued to sit in my archives, I began to wonder if those archival folders were, in a sense, tricking me. Was the modern state, as in Pierre Bourdieu's suspicion, creating itself through my reading of it? Was I reading the state the way it wanted me to read it? Maybe a little Bourdieuian reflexive sociology was in order; maybe it was time to be aware of my own illusions because "when it comes to the state, one never doubts enough."

The archives, organized by hierarchical departments into folders containing official and logical-sounding papers, commend themselves to us as the artifacts of a well-organized and rational modern state. But the more I read them, the more I started to have my doubts about this, especially as I talked to Russians outside the archive. Was it really possible that a rational bureaucratic (not to say totalitarian) state presided over millions of anarchists determined to circumvent it? Or could it rather be that the informal and ancient traditional practices of Russian society contaminated, infiltrated, or even made up the basic fabric of a state that desperately pretended to be something else? If we pulled back the curtain, would we see that there was little difference between official and informal practices, between the traditional and the modern? Maybe there were just practices, high and low.

Another conversation with a different Russian friend brought up another quandary. It was the early 1990s. The Soviet regime was gone and some kind of wild market mechanisms were getting traction. It seemed to me at the time that the impact of money would erode if not destroy the traditional informal clan way of doing things. After all, surely the collapse of Communist Party and the creation of free elections would end elite nepotism? Surely how one got a job or a place in school would no longer depend on connections? Surely money would now become the key to access rather than circles of friends? Nikolai agreed, but only to a point. Much of what he called the "Russian collective spirit" would remain forever. "Your money [!] will never change that." Yes, he thought, money would play an increasing role, but still within the realm of informal practice: as bribery. Russian "black market" practices would become universal. Yes, he thought, cars and refrigerators and a variety of foods would be easier to get, in principle, but only if you had the money. If not, the old circle of connections would continue to operate. And gesturing with a nod in the direction of the Kremlin (which Russians do even if far across town), "over there, nothing will change. Nobles, tsars, and clans will always operate the same way over there."

Over the years, I have been fortunate to be able to work with a talented and experienced group of archivists in the Moscow party archive, and they have become close friends. When I start a new project, I customarily explain it to them over tea to get their advice. This time, I started by explaining that I wanted to study informal practices, patronage, and practices in the Stalin period. They listened politely, then looked at each other frowning and shaking their heads. I was sure my Russian was correct and that they knew what these words meant. But they said they just didn't understand. Only in our third conversation did one of them finally light up. She got it! "Oh!" she said, "You mean real life! But everybody knows that. How is that a research project?"

I think it is, and now I think they do too. I hope the reader will agree.

Acknowledgments

Research for this work was supported by the generosity of the John Simon Guggenheim Foundation, the American Philosophical Society, and the Academic Senate, the International Institute, and the Division of Social Sciences at UCLA. I am particularly grateful to my then-Dean Scott Waugh, who helped me when he didn't need to.

Colleagues at UCLA, Utrecht University, the University of Amsterdam, Leeds University, the Ecole des Hautes Etudes en Sciences Sociales and the Sorbonne in Paris listened patiently to my seminar presentations and made helpful comments and criticisms. My students at UCLA and Utrecht read parts of the work and offered fresh thoughts, and my research assistant Michaela Dion performed yeoman service.

I benefited from conversations about the work with many people, and especially with William Chase, James Harris, Oleg Vladimirovich Naumov, Vladimir Pavlovich Naumov, Peter Reill, Andrei Konstantinovich Sokolov, Leonid Vladimirovich Veintraub, and my wonderful graduate students at UCLA. My dear friend Gabor Rittersporn read the manuscript with his usual sharp eye and was a source of both new ideas and cautionary tales. This work stands on the shoulders of several giants and original thinkers. Even though I was not able to discuss this work with them, I owe intellectual debts to Sheila Fitzpatrick, Graeme Gill, Ken Jowitt, Edward Keenan, and T. H. Rigby, whose creativity inspired me to start the project. I wish Ken Bailes, Earl Getty, and Bob McNeal had lived long enough to read this book.

Special thanks go to Nadezhda Vladimirovna Muraveva at the Russian State Archive of Socio-Political History (Rossiiskii gosudarstvennyi arkhiv sotsial'no-politicheskoi istorii), the archive of the former Communist Party of the Soviet Union, for sharing with me her encyclopedic knowledge of the archive and of party traditions and etiquette, as well as her warm friendship.

Although each of those mentioned above deserves credit for pushing me in good directions, none shares responsibility for any mistakes or outrages in what follows.

From thinking about informal practices, to collecting tidbits here and there, to systematic research, to the final writing of this work was a span of many years. Throughout that time, I could always count on the love and support of several special people, including my children, as well as Nancy Getty, Anna Boorstin, Wiley Gibson, and Teo Ruiz. Like me, they believed in the project even when they didn't understand it, and they cheerfully tolerated my erratic behavior—episodes of mumbling and staring into space, and sudden expository, if not boring, outbursts—with good grace.

Soviet Organizational Acronyms and Abbreviations

ChK, VChK (Cheka)	Extraordinary Commission for Combating Counterrevolution and Sabotage (1918–22). Political police; predecessor of GPU, OGPU, NKVD, MGB, KGB
gorkom	City committee of the Communist Party
gubkom	Provincial committee of the Communist Party
GPU	State Political Directorate attached to the Council of People's Commissars (SNK) of the USSR. Successor to CHEKA and predecessor of OGPU (see CHEKA)
GUGB	Main Administration for State Security of the NKVD of the USSR
kolkhoz	Collective farm
Komsomol	All-Union Leninist Youth League (VLKSM) a party organization for young people in the USSR
KPK	Commission for Party Control attached to the Central Committee of the VKP(b)
Kp/o	Conflict Subdepartment of the Organizational Department

kraikom	Regional committee of the Communist Party
Narodnyi komissar (Narkom)	Head of a People's Commissariat; equivalent to minister
Narkomvnudel (NKVD)	People's Commissariat for Internal Affairs. Successor to OGPU and predecessor of MGB (see Cheka).
NEP	New Economic Policy (from 1921, a policy of mixed socialist/capitalist economy instituted by Lenin.)
NKZem	People's Commissariat of Agriculture
obkom	Provincial committee of the Communist Party
OGPU	Unified State Political Directorate attached to the Council of People's Commissars (SNK) of the USSR. Successor to GPU and predecessor of NKVD (see Cheka)
Orgburo TsK VKP(b)	Organizational Bureau of the Central Committee of the Communist Party
Orginstrukt	Organizational-Instructional (Personnel) Department of the Central Committee, 1919–24
Orgraspred	Organizational Distribution (Personnel) Department of the Central Committee
ORPO	Department of Leading Party Organs of the Central Committee of the Russian Communist Party (Bolsheviks)
Politburo TsK VKP(b)	Political Bureau of the Central Committee of the Communist Party
raikom	District committee of the Communist Party
Raspredotdel	Personnel Distribution Department of the Central Committee
RSFSR	Russian Soviet Federated Socialist Republic
SR	Social Revolutionary Party
TsIK	Central Executive Committee of Soviets
TsK	Central Committee of the Communist Party
TsKK	Central Control Commission of the Communist Party
VKP(b)	All-Union Communist Party (Bolsheviks)

Note on Transliteration and Party/Government Terms

In transliterating from Russian to English I use the Library of Congress system, except for common proper names (e.g., Trotsky, not Trotskii)

Below the level of the Central Committee, the party was divided into a hierarchy of regional party committees based on the territory (*krai*), province (*oblast'* or *guberniia*), district (*raion*), and place of work. These bodies also conducted meetings (*plena*) but the real work was usually done in an inner executive committee known as a *biuro*. (All these bodies appear in the text in English form, such as buro/buros, oblast/oblasts, raion/raions, plenum/plenums.)

The territorial structures and designations of the USSR can be confusing. The USSR was a union of republics, with each republic being the political organization of a nationality. The Russian Republic (RSFSR) and the Ukrainian Republic (USFSR) were the largest of a series of "states" that included Belorussians, Georgians, Armenians, Uzbeks, and the other constituent peoples of the USSR. The RSFSR was clearly the most powerful and its administration overlapped in general with that of the USSR.

Each republic was divided into regional units, each of which was known as an oblast or krai. Thus, in the 1930s, at various times the RSFSR consisted of between seventy-five and ninety provinces and territories. Although technically all republics were on an equal footing, in practice the status attached to a major province of the RSFSR was equal to that of a non-Russian republic. The next subdivision (of provinces and territories) was the raion. Raions could be rural or urban, perhaps roughly equivalent to counties or boroughs. Cities had separate administrations that fell between district and provincial or territorial level.

PRACTICING STALINISM

Introduction

*Reading these regulations, instructions, and ukases, you cannot rid your-
self of the impression that European Russia is growing from the debris of
the devastated past. . . . [But] from the half-faded pages of these documents, through the outer shell of the jargon, old Muscovite Russia gazes
upon you, having successfully stepped over the threshold . . . and settled
comfortably with the new framework.*

—A. A. Kizevetter

THERE IS NO CLEARER modernist architectural statement than
Lenin's mausoleum on Red Square. Architect A. V. Shchusev's design
is pure constructivism. In the tradition of the fin de siècle avant-garde,
this was the modern architectural art of the 1920s and was noted for
its simplicity of line and lack of decoration. It was the building as machine. Here we find none of the classical ornamentation, portraits, or
flowery archaic Russian script of traditional buildings and tombs. The
façade of Shchusev's simple ziggurat of marble and granite is marked
simply with the word "LENIN" in stark, straight lines.

As part of Red Square's architectural ensemble, the mausoleum at
first seems glaringly out of place in a field of Russian tradition. Behind
it is the Kremlin, a fifteenth-century Renaissance fortress with add-on
towers in the old Muscovite style. Turning to the left we see St. Basil's
Cathedral from the sixteenth century. Turning farther to the left, opposite the mausoleum, we see GUM, a typical nineteenth-century shop-
ping arcade. Again to the left, turning back toward the mausoleum, we
see the History Museum with its red brick traditional Moscow style. In
all this, the hypermodernist tomb seems not to belong.

But this combination of tradition and modernity somehow works.
Maybe it is because we are so used to the place? The Lenin Mausoleum
with (until 1993) its famous changing of the guard is a fixture, and the

architectural dissonance is just part of the familiar landscape. On another level, though, it is the argument of this book that tradition combined with modernity everywhere in Soviet Russia, and not always in
tension or conflict.

Looking more closely at the mausoleum itself, we can see the mixture on many layers. First, Lenin, an undecaying saintly relic, was preserved not by mystical forces but by science. Another layer comes
when this archaic blessed object was housed in the most modern architectural design of the time. A third, ancient, layer comes when on the
most sacred ceremonial occasions, the leadership of the self-proclaimed
most modern state physically stood on the body, like chieftains on the
grave mound of a legendary ancient progenitor, but with architectural
modernity between them and the past. This ancient/modern layering
should seem wildly contradictory and dissonant, but like the larger
Red Square ensemble, somehow it succeeds as a blend. This blending
of contradictory impulses to produce a synthesis in politics at large is
the subject of this book.

☆

What follows is a collection of related essays about certain Russian
elite informal and archaic political practices that include the personifi-
cation of power as reflected in political "clan" and "family circle" networks, elite oligarchy combined with autocracy, and a host of lesser
but strongly suggestive practices that, taken together, one could call
traditional, neotraditional, patrimonial, or charismatic.[1] Although our
focus is on the formative Stalin period, we will look both forward and
backward in time from there. These practices and understandings have
roots that go back hundreds of years in Russian history, and many of
them continue today. Their persistence will lead us to questions about
the continuities of "deep structures" in Russian history and about the
supposed watersheds in that history, both past and future.[2]

This study is not the first to highlight traditional and personalized
politics and practices in modern history or Soviet history. But previous
studies have nearly all seen such "informal" or "traditional" practices
as external to the system, whether the system be bureaucratic or dictatorial. Practices such as patrimonial clientelism have been see as anachronistic vestiges that would wither away, or as addenda or adjuncts to
the (main) modern system, making that bureaucratic system efficient

or tolerable. They have been characterized as evidence of an "undeveloped" or "low level" of institutionalization. They are also sometimes seen as deliberately chosen instruments of rule that Stalin or others selected. These varied interpretations have one thing in common: they all assume that personalized or archaic practices are exterior to or in contradiction with the essential modern state. They are assumed to add to, ease, or hold back the main administrative system as we conceive it, but to be separate from it. The rational bureaucratic dog wags an archaic vestigial tail, and an annoying old flea-bitten one at that.

But what if the tail was wagging the dog? This study will suggest that archaic, personalized political practices were always an integral part of the system; indeed they were its essence and not an external palliative, vestige, or contradiction. It was not just a question of persistence or of reinvention at various times. They were a system themselves, one of ancient lineage and one that exists today. Indeed, along with certain rational bureaucratic elements, they *were* the system. And precisely because of their ancient pedigree, they were not techniques that rulers selected from a menu of possible tactics of rule.

It is easy to dismiss various "premodern" holdovers as interesting (or uninteresting) matters of style rather than substance. The undecaying body of the sainted Lenin, the icons of Stalin that people carried in processions, the confessional rituals of a purge trial, or the catechistic rhythms of Stalinist political prose all recall an earlier age. Other examples of premodern, traditional, or archaic practices might include:

- an emphasis on the heroic, personal and voluntarist, more than the civic;
- a precise hierarchy of titles and awards that confer status ("ennobling");
- a moral economy based on gifts and gratitude more than money;
- charismatic organizations of the select, with rituals and a culture of secrecy, rather than egalitarian organizations of an open society;
- pervasive clientelist relations that replace or preempt structures of formal position;
- an understanding of political authority as patrimonial and personalized rather than derived from formal position or a rule-bound rational bureaucracy.[3]

The space of one book does not permit detailed analysis of each of these and other manifestations of traditional practice. Most of this book focuses on the last item above, the patrimonial personalization of power.[4] But all the others items on the list in one way or another reflect persons rather than institutions as the social reference point. A careless reading of Max Weber or Karl Marx would suggest that such atavisms would eventually wither away in the progress toward an impersonal modern rational society. A strict functionalist approach suggests the same conclusion because the lack of utility in such practices should doom them to eventual extinction in a modernizing world.

So it is worth wondering why such practices survive as long as they do in Russia, and why some of them outlive others. How are they changed or adapted by modern state influences and needs? We might also wonder if some of them have functions that we simply have not yet discovered. Or could it be that they signal or symbolize deeper fundamental or embedded cultural structures that stubbornly refuse to wither away?

Consider, for example, the persistence today of certain very old political conceptions, practices, and discourses about leadership. Here there are survivals of old practices aplenty. Even after Stalin, the clientelism of rulers Khrushchev, Brezhnev, and Putin recalled patterns not only under Stalin but from the nineteenth century and earlier.[5]

In the 1990s, the mayor of Moscow decided to enforce residential registration regardless of its banning in the post-Soviet Russian constitution, recalling a practice as old as Russia whereby a powerful person decides which laws will be enforced and which not. The personal battle (pretending to be a legal one) between titans Vladimir Putin and Mikhail Khodorkovsky recalled that between Stalin and Trotsky (so much that Putin, like Stalin, was anxious that it not be seen as a personal struggle) or between any number of tsars and pretenders. Boris Yeltsin's crushing of the Duma and writing of a new less democratic constitution recalled Nicholas II dispersing his Duma and changing the electoral law in 1906, if not Ivan IV's destruction of Novgorod's liberties in the sixteenth century. The dual portraits of Putin and Medvedev on sale in Moscow today recall the famous photos of Stalin sitting next to Lenin and of Nicholas II with his son Aleksei, and any number of iconic genealogical representations legitimizing succession from tsar to son throughout Russian history.[6]

Of course, Putin is not a tsar and the Politburo was not the boyar duma of old. The ideology of the Soviets was communism, not Christianity; it was transformational, not conservative. The rapid industrialization and economic change of the twentieth century permanently rearranged Russian society. Ideology and economy changed dramatically. But what about political practice?

It is the argument of this book that to understand Russian political practice today, it is necessary to examine in detail what happened to it at the beginning of the Soviet period. In the postrevolutionary era that evolved into Stalinism, the foundations of the political practice of the later Soviet and post-Soviet periods were laid. At that time, certain thoughts and practices were retained from the past; some discarded. Today's Russian rulers were yesterday's communists and their practices have a history that is comprehensible only by understanding how they were transmitted and assimilated by their party ancestors early in the twentieth century. The book explores the possibility that those practices would have been comprehensible to their great-grandfathers.

So, before we confidently dismiss traditional practices as the arbitrary personal tastes of a primitive Caucasian mountaineer, we might inquire a bit about traditions and wonder whether they are merely survivals or rather integral parts of more modern structures of practice. One way to do this would be to look at Soviet political practices in detail, rather than in passing, while suspending our faith in the march to modernity, and to ask simply why people did what they did.

☆

Like it or not, we are all Weberians, at least to the extent that we are accustomed to separating the premodern and modern, with an evolutionary path from the former to the latter. We often use Weber's three types of authority. Traditional authority (or "domination") is based on custom; things are done and explicitly justified because they have always been done this way. Charismatic authority is based on a leader, prophet, or hero who is seen to have a transcendent connection with a higher power. Under the impact of more permanent institutions and political self-interests of others, charisma would be "routinized" into either traditional authority or modern rational-bureaucratic forms.

In this third type of authority, administration is bound by rules of law, specified duties, and a depersonalized system in which position, not person, determines administration and behavior. Rule-bound rational bureaucratic institutions function predictably, regardless of persons occupying offices, and there is a strict separation between the public and private spheres. Such a bureaucracy is staffed by impersonal rulers and substitutable actors, with clear-cut spheres of competence, ordered hierarchies of procedures. It functions like a machine.

Somewhere in the interstices between the traditional and the charismatic, Weber discussed patrimonial authority. Patrimonialism is a form of traditional domination in which the personal household, dominated by a father, is the model for politics. It is the essence of personalized politics; the person *is* the state. Administrations and bureaucracies are merely the tools of the ruler in "a realm of free arbitrariness."[7] If, in rational bureaucratic systems, one's behavior is governed by institutional rules, in patrimonial systems "the power and identity of an institution is defined in terms of the leader's political identity and power."[8] Weber thought patrimonialism was a "special case" of patriarchy.[9]

The argument of this book is that politics under Stalin was patrimonial. Again, we are not the first to suggest this.[10] Previous treatments, however, have tended to limit its application to the special case of Stalin, his preferences or method of rule, or to see it, like traditional practices in general, as anachronistic or antithetical to proper modern institutionalization. Here we will mostly study a special case of patrimonialism—the personalization of politics—as something that, like other traditional practices, characterized the entire political (and social) system. We shall make no judgments about whether it survived and prospered at the expense of "proper" or the "more advanced" modernization described by Weber and carried out in the West. Rather, we shall try to show that it preceded and outlived Stalin, who like his rivals, predecessors, and successors merely followed the patrimonial tradition. We will show that insofar as it defined almost every aspect of political life, and continues to do so to a great extent, it can hardly be seen as vestigial or antithetical to a bureaucratic system. It still exists.

Weber thought that in modern bureaucratic systems, "in the place of the old-type ruler who is moved by sympathy, favor, grace, and gratitude, modern culture requires for its sustaining external apparatus the emotionally detached, and hence rigorously 'professional' expert." Bureaucracy needs to depersonalize itself.[11] People should "obey the law rather than the persons implementing it."[12] We will argue that although the Soviet political-administrative system did change with time, this is a poor description of it before and after Stalin, when powerful pre-modern elements and practices continued to characterize the system. Some things did not change very much.

Weber noted that ideal types nearly always occur in combination with each other.[13] Still, in line with nineteenth-century teleological ideas of progress, he (and his latter day followers) saw an evolution toward modern rational bureaucracy and his social science successors followed him in seeing a basic contradiction between state development (desirable, inevitable, modern) and (backward) traditional, neotraditional, or patrimonial practices that impede that evolution. "Weak bureaucracies" are "perfect habitats" for informal practices.[14] Where such practices are prevalent, states and institutions are "weak," "underdeveloped," "undermined," or "in decay."[15] Informal traditional practices "undermine rational planning." They prevent or preclude "institutionalization" and are ultimately contradictory to the modern state.[16]

But some have argued that the path to the rational bureaucratic "modern" state is not so direct, if it is a path at all. That old road from traditional to modern now includes several way-station categories of "underdeveloped state." These scholars are less allergic to informal practices and see them as potentially useful elements that can actually make the institutional system function more efficiently. Such "adjuncts" or "addenda" are additions to rational institutions whose deficiencies they remedy.[17] Sometimes traditional or personalized relationships can act as mediators between center and periphery, as palliatives between bureaucracy and population.[18] Sometimes "informal social relations are responsible for the metabolic processes required to keep the formal institution operating. . . . we discover that the formal table of organization is elegant indeed, but fails to work, unless informal mechanisms are found for its direct contravention, as in the network of *blat* (informal reciprocal favors and exchanges) among Soviet industrial managers."[19]

Whether or not clientelism and other traditional "informal practices" function as mediators or functional adjuncts, many social scientists no longer see these practices as necessarily opposed to modern bureaucracy in general. Informal traditional practices can coexist with rational bureaucracy in a variety of times and places. "Patron-client relations do not necessarily disappear with economic development or political modernization. . . . the centrality of patron-client relationships as a major mode of social control and of regulating institutional relations persists."[20] This book will examine this point of view, originally developed for underdeveloped states, in the modern Russian context.

Others have suggested parallels between the early Soviet Union and developing states later in the twentieth century.[21] Soviet specialists who have studied these matters also divide into two camps. For some, personalized practices preclude or restrict the development of institutions and are therefore inimical to the growth or functioning of a modern state. Personalized power ran directly counter to the "emergence of organizational institutionalism in formal bodies of the system" and was a sign of undeveloped or insufficient institutionalization.[22] For others, however, the state system could not have worked at all without informal practices that might seem inimical to state rules. These practices, including patronage, informal economic "fixers," and the like were said to help the system function more smoothly and make it bearable for the population.[23] In any case, the lack of autonomous (and/or representative) institutions in Russia is said to have left the field to autocracy and personalized, clan politics.

On the other hand, Stephen White decoupled Soviet political arrangements from Weberian or Parsonian theories of teleological modernization, arguing that empirical examination shows that political modernization—the development of democracy or representative institutions—did not necessarily follow socio-economic modernization.[24] More recently, some social scientists have articulated a concept of "neotraditionalism" to explain the apparent survivals of archaic practice in the modern Soviet context. Ken Jowitt wrote that "The striking amalgam of charismatic, traditional, and modern features in Soviet institutions finds expression in the central place of the "heroic" . . . the centrality of *blat* in social transactions, the secretive quality of Soviet political life and the organization of sociopolitical life around the *kollektiv*." For Jowitt, charismatic and traditional elements were "enmeshed" or "mixed up" in an apparently modern system.[25] After all, the figurehead president of the modern USSR, Mikhail Kalinin, was known as the "All-Union Elder" of the country.

With all this interest in the relationship between formal institutions and informal practices, it seems worthwhile to examine for the first time the relationship in detail in the formative Stalin period of Soviet history. We will do this with an analysis of some important elements of

Stalinist politics while neither anticipating their eventual disappearance nor minimizing them in the context of a modernizing ideology.

The persistence of archaic and personalized practices raises questions about periodization. We know that the Bolsheviks transformed Russia in important and radical ways. They self-consciously broke with nearly everything in old Russia. The tsarist political autocracy, the social domination of the nobility, the power of the Orthodox church, the subordinate status of workers and peasants, and existing norms of culture and art were all swept away. It seemed to many both inside and outside Russia that a new millennium was beginning, freed from the shackles of hidebound tradition and of everything that had held back human progress. For those living at the time, this was a watershed.

It seemed so as well as for observers later on. The first generation of Soviet specialists focused on the new nature of the dictatorship, and the resulting totalitarian model with its exclusive focus on efficient top-down control held sway for decades.[26] New scholarly approaches appeared in the 1970s that both questioned the efficiency of totalitarian controls and shifted the focus to social history.[27] Recent studies of subjectivity have asked important questions about the individual's relation to the regime, without much concern for the former political models or social histories.[28] These studies, regardless of their tendency or approach, agreed that with the USSR we were seeing something fundamentally new and different. Even students of modernity, who put the Soviet Union in a comparative framework of post-Enlightenment transformational regimes, were nevertheless impressed by the scale and novelty of the Soviet experiment, as it is now often called.

Historians love to periodize, and while they often bitterly criticize each other they tend to agree on the major watersheds of the Soviet era, each of which is said to have ushered in a new era. 1917 was the year of the Russian Revolutions when the Bolsheviks came to power. 1921 was the end of the bitter and radical Civil War and the beginning of the semicapitalist retreat of the New Economic Policy (NEP). 1929 saw Stalin's final defeat of his rivals for Lenin's succession and the beginning of the period that bears his name. It also marked the beginning of the Stalin Revolution which, through agricultural collectivization, forced state-controlled industrialization, and the rapid promotion of people from below, ended both pluralism and capitalism and set the pattern for much of Soviet history to come. It marked the end of the "experimental" 1920s and the beginning of the Great Retreat into social and cultural conservatism. 1937–39 marked the Great Purges in which the generation of Old Bolshevik revolutionaries was replaced by "new men." 1941–45 was the period of the Great Patriotic War, which saw unimaginable death and destruction along with a brief liberalization that quickly died. 1953 saw Stalin's death and the beginning of the de-Stalinization of the 1950s and 1960s. 1964 began the Brezhnev era of "stagnation" that lasted until Gorbachev's perestroika of 1985. The collapse of the regime at the end of 1991 was the last in the series of watersheds that ushered in new periods. These watersheds seem to demarcate periods so dramatic that one leading specialist referred to Soviet history as a series of different systems.[29]

Certainly the years 1917, 1921, 1929, 1937, 1953, and the others mark important, even earthshaking changes in society, government, and ideology. But through the lenses of practice, language, semiotics, political culture, and conscious and unconscious assumptions, we can see a series of continuities.

We have often taken Russian and Soviet leaders at their word about watersheds. Even before the 1917 Revolutions, we identified watersheds that corresponded to the reigns of tsars. In so doing, we followed the lead of the tsars themselves. As Richard Wortman noted, "Each reign resumed the Petrine cadence, opening with energetic demonstrative change, a discrediting, explicit or implicit of the predecessor, a new vision of the creative perspective of the autocrat. . . . The next monarch then follows the symbolic dynamic, repudiating the premises of his predecessors."[30]

In each of our watershed years of dramatic regime overthrow, leadership change, or policy adjustment, those in charge explicitly presented the new order as the negation of the previous one. For Lotman and Uspenskii, "Total eschatological change" was the norm and each new period "must be oriented toward a decisive break with what preceded it. . . . The deep structure formed in the preceding period is preserved but completely renamed, while all the fundamental structural contours of the old are preserved. In this case, *new texts* are created while the archaic cultural frame is preserved."[31]

The discourse of 1917 was to denounce imperial Russia. The Stalin Revolution had to negate NEP. The postpurge leaders were the successors to "enemies." Stalin had to be de-Stalinized. Brezhnev had to denounce Khrushchev's "harebrained schemes." Gorbachev in turn negated the Brezhnev "stagnation," and Putin negates Gorbachev's "chaos." This practice reflects, as Lotman and Uspenskii put it, traditional Russian binary understandings of good (us, now) and bad (them, then). These persistent binaries, presenting themselves as *discontinuities,* are themselves a powerful cultural *continuity.*

We will use a new lens to look for preserved "archaic cultural frames" and practices that seem to ignore the famous turning points. We are interested in the archaic "texts" behind the new ones, at the watersheds that perhaps didn't "shed" as much as we might think.

To take one example, the "Great Retreat" from the 1920s to the 1930s is seen as Stalin's transformation of the USSR from a land of free experimentation in the 1920s to one of ponderous Russian conservatism of the 1930s in everything from art to historical evaluations to education to family policy. Although some scholars have questioned the black-and-white characterization of the differences between the decades,[32] it is true that in many areas there seemed to be a new period, especially in the arts and literature. Much of this perception may come from privileging cultural matters of interest to intellectuals like ourselves. But aside from the dubious assumptions that this was all Stalin's doing (or that any one person could so transform a culture), many important things—like elite political practices—did not change. There was no retreat, "Great" or otherwise, in political praxis, in the crucial area of the means by which the elite governed the country. The clientelism, clan-based politics, and personalized patrimonial understandings of government that the Bolsheviks inherited from Russian history persisted without retreat, advance, or much change from the 1920s to the 1930s and beyond.

Although the historiographical trend has clearly been to focus on watersheds and to frame and write our studies about them, some scholars did call attention to various continuities. More than seventy years ago, Boris Souvarine described Stalin's rule as the "historical atavism of ancient Muscovy."[33] More recently, Robert C. Tucker saw Stalin as an old-fashioned Russian nationalist who deliberately shaped the Soviet Union along archaic traditional lines. Because Stalin admired Ivan the Terrible, he patterned his policy and purges after him.[34]

Likewise, Richard Hellie wrote of three "service revolutions" that were reactions to foreign threats and that spanned Russian history, and of which "the elements of continuity are evident" across 1917. One, in the sixteenth century, created a garrison state defended by service cavalrymen. A second, in the early eighteenth century, bound the population to state service for the sake of the army. The third, in the late 1920s to early 1930s, sought modernization and created a new service class in the name of national defense. With each revolution, a key element (serfdom, collectivization) bound the population to the needs of the elite. And each time, once the crisis had passed, the new service elite tried to retain power and privilege but eventually faced insurmountable problems of legitimacy.[35]

For Robert Daniels, the "post-revolutionary political regime in the USSR was not only compatible with Russian political culture but was powerfully shaped by it."[36] V. A. Kozlov wrote of "the archaic social practices of Soviet life, the standing water of everyday Russian existence, which was capable of extinguishing the waves of political and economic transformations."[37] Richard Pipes finds it "inconceivable that on a single day, October 25, 1917, the course of a thousand-year-old history of a vast and populous country could undergo complete transformation . . . Only by viewing human beings as inert matter entirely molded by the environment could such an absurdity even be entertained."[38] This book will build on these insights through a systematic study of continuities in political practice in the Soviet period.

Other scholars have sought continuities not in the tastes of a single individual or the strategic choices of an elite facing military threat, but in broader and "deeper" culture. In a seminal article to which this book owes much, Edward Keenan wrote: "Soviet political culture . . . reestablished a number of underlying features of traditional political culture that have characterized Russian political culture for centuries."[39]

Political elites always face similar problems in governing. Whether or not they have ideological or transformational agendas, to remain in power they must maintain stability against both foreign threats and challenges to domestic order. They must develop control over the population to prevent revolt and disorder, extract wealth from that population in order to support themselves and their regime, and mobilize it or compel it in times of crisis or major national efforts. Over the centuries, Russia's rulers faced particularly severe versions of these imperatives.

Russia's elite always faced a harsh environment. Its position astride the world's main migratory pathway—the great Eurasian plain—

meant that foreign invasion was a constant threat. Until the sixteenth century, nomadic hordes from Asia repeatedly invaded, and after that Russia faced invasions from the great powers of central and northern Europe. Defending a dispersed state with poor roads, bad communications, and only a few fortified towns was no easy task. Here, survival was always tenuous.

From the time groups of armed Vikings imposed their rule over the Slavs of the Dnieper valley in the ninth century, old Russia was ruled by soldiers and autocratic centralized power. Old Russia's princes and nobles were the glorious armed cavalrymen who fought at the call of the grand prince. Organized into protofeudal networks of clans and clients, members of the elite swore to come with their arms and serving men and fight for their patron. In turn, they received the military loyalty of those below them, all in return for patronage protection.[40]

In peacetime, this knightly organization quite naturally became a political, clan-based oligarchy, as it did elsewhere in Europe. In Russia, an expanding class of princes and great boyar families competed for a limited national wealth (Russia had few subsurface minerals and poor agriculture) and for political power and prominence.[41] Princely and noble clans protected and promoted their own, arranged useful marriages, amassed and retained wealth, and jostled each other in constant alliances and intrigues. A garrison state dominated by professional fighting men competing for power and for scarce resources was a recipe for civil war and chaos. Kievan Rus was already torn apart by fratricidal wars long before the Mongol invasion in the thirteenth century. When the Mongols arrived, they found a patchwork of small quarrelsome kingdoms, each ruled by a princeling supported by his clan and those of his boyar noble retainers. A disastrous civil war in the fifteenth century saw rival coalitions of princes and clans further tear each other apart.

One response to chaos was a monarch, a unifying figure in the person of the grand prince of Moscow, who would rule together with the lesser princes and great boyars. For the fractious oligarchic boyars, such a person provided a much-needed referee, a judge. They were in fact the most vocal about pronouncing his power, extravagantly (and inaccurately) referring to themselves as his "slaves." In Russia, a powerful princely and boyar nobility coexisted happily and profitably with a supreme monarch.[42] Unlike Louis XIII in France, the Muscovite prince never faced rebellious aristocratic *frondeurs*.

The Moscow prince became a divinely anointed, theoretically supreme leader with what we would call today a "cult of personality" guaranteeing his legitimacy. There were to be no *parlements* or other competing institutions or possible limitations on his power, and this suited the elite. Making the prince the only legitimate political power saved the unity of the state from oligarchic competition. In Russia, "the ruler did not act politically as the 'monarchical' branch of government, continually battling the corporate estates or institutions; rather he ruled through his charisma, commanding total loyalty and favoring selected men with personal relationships as advisers to him. Together with these counselors, the boyars, the sovereign ruled patrimonially."[43] Absolutism plus oligarchy was Russia's structural and functional response to domestic anarchy. This combination also served the imperative of staying in power. The image of a divinely sanctioned monarch in a country with only one church provided a powerful social cement for the population, especially given patrimonial ideas of politics as personal and the state as the ruler's property. The prince needed the boyars, and they needed him.

Despite the boyars' loud acclamation and worship of the ruler and the glittering court ceremonies, behind the scenes old Russia had many of the characteristics of strong oligarchy. Before the time of Ivan IV, boyar clans at court ran the country at least as much as the prince did. A Muscovite prince or tsar defied powerful clan alliances of them at his peril. A strong ruler like Peter I or Catherine II could sometimes get the upper hand and tip the balance toward the throne. At other times, things went the other way, and oligarchic court factions could dominate a weak tsar or tsarina, as when nobles pressed their demands on a newly installed Empress Anna in 1730. They could also find it necessary to dispose of a troublesome prince or tsar (as in the assassinations of Ivan VI, Peter III, and Paul I) but these actions were about individuals rather than the institution of royal rule. Generally the balance held, and laws were promulgated by "the prince along with his boyars" in council.

Sometimes the balance of monarchs and grandees came apart when strong personalities upset the balance. In the sixteenth century, Ivan IV (the "Terrible") felt that his rightful prerogatives and powers were being usurped by powerful boyar clans. He broke the rules of the game, symbolically "resigning" as tsar to become another oligarch, and leaving the state to the boyars who sought to run it. He then launched a "private" reign of terror, the *Oprichnina,* slaughtering his enemies in a chaotic civil war that recalled that of the fifteenth century. Ironically, by resigning as monarch he sought to become an absolute monarch in reality—not just a referee or symbol—by reminding the boyars what chaos and lawlessness was like without a strong monarch. Eventually, the "people of Moscow" (read here the survivors who counted, the boyars) "asked" him to return, which he did with enhanced powers.

The boyar clans' politics at court—alliances and competitions with other clans, power measured by clan proximity to the throne—were all personal, nonideological matters. All this fit quite conveniently on top of peasant social organization out in the forests, where the patriarchal family was the basic social unit, and families banded together into village units whose patrimonial leaders took care of everybody.

As with the early Russian elite, many of the elements of Stalinist and post-Stalinist political practice can be seen as responses to the environment in which the Bolsheviks and their heirs found themselves. The Russian Revolution and especially the Civil War of 1918–21 tore the country apart and even when things calmed down, there was an abiding fear of chaos, both in the country and within the party. Survival hung by a thread, as it always had in Russia.

When the leading Old Bolsheviks came to govern the country, they also thought of themselves as the elite, as a corporate group and privileged breed apart. They closed ranks and created their own inner culture and society, married among themselves, and controlled acceptable thought and hunted heresy, just as their noble and churchmen forebears had done.

They preserved the bones of their charismatic warrior founder and put them on display for the commoners to see. They created a cult of the monarch with transcendental legitimacy to provide a referee, a public symbol to camouflage their maneuvers.[44] They nurtured and protected their own political clans. To avoid chaos, they found it necessary to create an oligarchic/absolutist systemic balance functionally not unlike that in Russian history for centuries. And the balance generally worked to ward off chaos.

Old Bolshevik oligarchs were the loudest in their praise of the monarch Stalin and his glories. Like the clientelist boyar clans of old who hid behind a glittering façade of court ceremony and high-sounding offices, the Old Bolshevik nobles worked in a vigorously enforced secrecy, hiding their personal maneuvers behind just as glittering a façade: the powerful Soviet state with its wise leader.

Like their forebears, the Bolsheviks, despite their seemingly iron control, were chronically afraid of all kinds of threats.[45] They kept the benighted "dark masses" out of politics, except rhetorically. As a kind of conquering nobility, they were also a fractious and quarrelsome lot when it came to precedence, clan interests, and ideology. Like their ancient forebears, as a corporate group they feared war amongst themselves in a hostile environment that threatened their hold on power. Everything always seemed to hang by a thread. A series of resolutions and strictures about party unity and discipline (whose repetition testifies to their impotence) failed to prevent "oppositions" and other factionalism. Patrimonial oligarchy, presided over by a prince and operating in secrecy, suited them.

But such systems have historically been characterized by decentralizing tendencies and a struggle for power between center and periphery, another feature of Stalinism (and of the later Soviet period).[46] "When these office-holders become local dignitaries who constitute themselves as a status group of notables, they may be able to prevail over the ruler and his personal dependents. . . . The decline of central authority is also furthered by the officials' physical distance from the center of authority. . . . Patrimonial rulers, however, do not accept such fragmentation of their authority without resistance."[47]

The oligarch/monarch balance worked until the 1930s when Stalin came to feel that the noble clans around him were becoming too powerful, that they were running things as a true oligarchy. Like Ivan IV, he struggled against them in various ways in an attempt to reduce their power and enhance his own. He wanted to be absolute in reality, not only in myth or symbolism. Finally, he launched his own *Oprichnina,* the Great Purges, in which his clan went to war against the others. And like Ivan, Stalin found that one could kill clan leaders in Russia but not the idea of patrimonial clan rule.

The Bolshevik autocracy/oligarchy arrangement after the Civil War seemed to recall the accommodation of an earlier age. In both cases, the functional responses to chaos were oligarchic arrangements presided over by a supreme leader. In both cases, noble elites set themselves apart, maintaining their "otherness" with status genealogies, social conventions, and self-constructing ideologies. In both cases, the understanding and practice of politics was patrimonial and personal.

At this point, one could easily say, "so what?" Isn't it a commonplace of modern history for revolutionaries to start with a powerful transformational mission but to degenerate after taking power into privileged bureaucrats and even hereditary elites. Indeed, this was Lev Trotsky's characterization of the Russian Revolution in *The Revolution Betrayed,* and nothing is easier than to see the aftermath of that revolution as a garden variety decay of idealism or a textbook case of power corrupting.

Similarly, an anthropologist or sociologist, unimpressed with the Bolsheviks' professed modern transformational verbiage, would immediately see the functions carried out by the specific self-aware culture of an elect group. One could look at the relative backwardness of Russian economic and political development in the early twentieth century and imagine these elite practices as entirely appropriate in many times and places, quite regardless of what the Bolshevik revolutionaries said. Again, one could point to many historical cases in which a self-conscious modernizing elite consciously uses certain tools to effect a transformation. In many modernizing Asian, African, and Latin American countries, the army fulfills the same functions. It educates, socializes, provides a cohesive organization, and anoints itself the natural leader of society. Throughout history, elites have done very similar things.

This approach has many merits, among them an emphasis on function and practice, and an agnosticism about what elites said (or even thought) they were doing. It also insists on looking at practices in their living contexts (or "fields" as Bourdieu would have it) at different times and places, rather than assuming their rise and fall according to some proffered teleology. But the strength of these continuities in this case suggests that there is something deeper here, in addition to systemic functionalism.

When we study societies over long spans of time, we often find that ancient practices may once have been specifically functional; they met a particular need. With time, however, when that particular need passed, they remained as part of the culture. They became embedded somehow in the general repertoire of practices, in the social and political culture of the society. Richard Hellie's fifteenth-century bow-and-arrow cavalrymen were a response to foreign military threats. Later on in the seventeenth century, they managed to keep their privileges and even formally bind the peasants to them at precisely the time they were being made militarily obsolete. No longer important as cavalrymen, they were nevertheless not uselessly vestigial because they became seamless and important parts of the political culture and practice.

As we shall see, the same can be said of archaic styles of letter writing, medals and awards, collective criminal responsibility, and clan politics, as well as of the understanding of politics as personal and patrimonial rather than institutional or legal. When raw and intentional (if it was ever that) functionalism becomes part of culture, we find a Russian specificity.

Although our subject is not social control per se, Pierre Bourdieu's reflections on "habitus" seem relevant here. A certain behavior or set of practices becomes part of the social structure even when its original purpose is no longer recalled. The practices of habitus function in a deep, unconscious way. This "genesis amnesia" is part of "schemes of thought and expression."[48]

Over the centuries, the symbiosis between ruler and oligarchs and their clans, self-conscious oligarchic identity, an understanding and practice of personalized politics, and scorn of rule-bound bureaucracy stopped being episodic functional responses. The symbiosis between throne and nobility was continuous over the centuries; the breakdowns forced by Ivan IV and Stalin were only the extreme cases of this enduring relationship. At some point in time, this form of traditional rule ceased to be a conscious choice or response, if it ever was. It lost its cause-and-effect character and melded into a seamless, unconscious set of practices, an enduring structure. It ceased being conscious or an unconscious functional response to a situation and became habit, familiar practice, and therefore culture.

Other political strategies or forms of organization might be more utilitarian and functional, but the old ones persist. The Bolsheviks could have chosen modern, bureaucratic tools of rule, but they didn't. For risk-averse elites, whether princes or party secretaries, Bolsheviks or boyars, these ancient practices were the ones they automatically followed, probably without parsing individual threats of chaos and choosing individual practical responses. In terms of practice, they set things up in ways that seemed natural to them. These practices were long-term conditioned reflexes or, as Edward Keenan called them, "deep structures" of Russian politics. Functionalism was not everything when post-Stalin leaders down to Vladimir Putin, who did not face anything like the crises of the fifteenth century or the Russian Revolution, continued political practices based on these deep structures. In everything from the design of Lenin's tomb to social and political conventions, to party personnel policy, to center-periphery struggles, practice was always about patronage, politics, was personal. These understandings and practices were embedded in Russian history, whatever the prevailing ideology, religion, or state program.

☆

It's time for a few caveats. Some historians may find that this approach is generally topical rather than chronological. The book intends to look back from the Stalin period to find precedents and antecedents, not to provide a continuous historical narrative of Russian political practices, which would be a different (and much larger) study altogether. Many of the precedents we find come from the Muscovite period, although we will have occasion to note imperial period continuities as well. It was in the rise of Muscovy that many of the contours of Russian politics (a strong militarized state, personal autocracy, binding farmers to the land, and others) were first laid down, so it does not seem unreasonable to investigate political practices in the twentieth (and twenty-first) century state in light of those prevalent when the state began. Others have found the comparison useful. Tucker's comparison of Stalin with Ivan the Terrible and Boris Souvarine's depiction of Stalinism as "Muscovy's revenge" are examples.[49] Of course, comparing practices in the 1930s with those of the 1920s, not to mention comparing elements of Stalinist Russia with old Muscovy, runs the risk of ignoring the social, economic, and other contexts of the different periods. Yet if political practices were very similar in widely separated times, that in itself would be telling. And it would not imply privileging practice over social, economic, or ideological history; it would merely imply separating it from them.[50]

Thus, for example, we will not treat ideology here to any extent because we seek to emphasize other factors as a kind of balance to historiography that has recently privileged ideology and culture. One of the reasons recent historians have overlooked the effects of political "deep structures" of Russian practice on the Soviet period has been a focus on the ideology of the modern, taking Bolsheviks at their word that they were in fact modern, even unprecedented. Studies have seen the USSR in terms of modernity, sharing many features with contemporaneous modern societies in the West, including the European democracies, Nazi Germany, and the United States after World War I. All had state police forces that carried out surveillance over their populations. Everywhere, there was a bigger role for government which, in the tradition of science and the Enlightenment, sought to plan, count, control, and ultimately perfect populations based on modern ideology.[51] While providing interesting comparative meta-insights, this approach is less able to explain traditional and charismatic elements in Soviet politics and practice.

One thesis of the book is that objects and practices that were originally functional eventually become embedded parts of culture even when their original function is forgotten. Such practices later become traditions or customs that can take on a variety of new functions or symbolisms, an idea that is not new to anthropologists. Yet although this study owes much to anthropological insights and theory, it is rather a somewhat old-fashioned empirical work of history based on a close reading of mostly archival sources. There is little attempt to support or criticize existing social theory, nor are there numerous references to theoretical literature. Some readers will find this approach "undertheorized," which is a currently fashionable criticism of historical works. Those readers interested in theory will already know the voluminous theoretical literature and can apply theory to this study if they wish. Other readers can read it as political history without being burdened or distracted by sometimes abstract theoretical jargon.

Certainly, the Bolsheviks were ideologues in their bones. Molotov tells us that he, Stalin, and the other Politburo members debated ideology in their private moments.[52] For us, studying Marxist-Leninist-Stalinist ideology is an important endeavor, as is its reception among individuals in society. Although one can find no shortage of professional Soviet ideologues and litterateurs who preached about perfecting the New Soviet Person, it is very rare to find such concerns among the top leaders of the party who made policy, validated or forbade actions, and created the authorized discourse. Except for occasional reflections about propaganda, Stalin and his associates almost never discussed transforming or perfecting citizens.

Stalin and the party elite acted more pragmatically than ideologically. Make no mistake, they were convinced communists who did what they did in order to build a modern communist utopia. Reaching that overall goal meant rapid industrialization, agricultural collectivization, and a kind of state-building. But the sources clearly show that the day-to-day practical decisions they took in this case were dictated by the need to help friends, destroy enemies, industrialize the country, and simply stay in power, all of which was ideologically justified after the fact. Flexible ideology could even be put to service explaining reverses in strategy and tactics and method.

It would be incautious to characterize an epoch in any country as "modern" when so much else remains traditional and charismatic. A "modern ideology" does not guarantee modernity. There are many examples. North Korea has a majority urban population (60 percent). Two-thirds of the population works in industry or services.[53] It has a gigantic, modern-equipped military and launches rockets. Other modern elements include a developed and rigid bureaucracy and Marxist-Leninist ideology. Yet in terms of political practice, it is a hereditary monarchy where senior officials are patriarchally designated "father," "uncle," "brother," and so forth.

Besides, in Russia, a modernizing ideology and a premodern set of practices were never incompatible and can be separated for purposes of discussion. Russian Marxism mediated between the premodern and the modern and contained elements of both. Marxist-Leninist-Stalinist ideology could accommodate such ancient Russian beliefs as a sacramental cult of the leader's personality, the notion of government as inalterable truth, the intolerant belief in opposition as sinful heresy, and the utopian belief in a future millennium.[54] The prevailing ideology could not only accommodate but actually encourage contradictory elements of patronage and venality, a hierarchy of bureaucratic dictatorships, and a fundamentally personalized view of politics. All of these, and many other practices and beliefs discussed below, were traditional parts and practices of Russian culture that were either put in the service of modernization or followed as "subterranean and largely unconscious" norms or rituals.[55]

Some caveats on terminology are in order. In the pages that follow, I shall frequently refer to Soviet provincial party secretaries as "nobles," "barons," "grandees," "boyars," and the like. Of course, in some ways—class origins most notably—Old Bolsheviks and old Russian nobles were a social world apart. But for reasons I spell out in Chapter 1, in *functional* terms the practices they deployed were not so different. I am not the first to make the connection. As Daniel Orlovsky wrote of Soviet officials, "Though the men and their class origin may have been different, the institutional structure, patterns of organization and above all the nature of clientelism remained strikingly similar to the patterns we have observed during the last years of the old regime."[56] We will also see similarities in self-image, repute in society, and political practice of party officials that more than recalls ancient nobility. Ken Jowitt wrote about the "party cadre's 'noble' disposition towards economic pursuits."[57] Graeme Gill called the party elite "grandees" and "notables" who thought of themselves as "the chosen ones.[58]

I will also compare the strategies of Charlemagne, Louis XIV, Ivan the Terrible, and Stalin. Again, aside from their separation by many centuries, these rulers could not be more different in many ways. Still, though, if we found that faced with similar political situations they implemented very similar practices, it would be worth studying. Practice matters.

With full recognition of the narrow specificity of the term "clan" to denote kinship, I shall use the word to describe what Merle Fainsod called "family circles" of officials.[59] These were political machines typically grouped around a dominant personality, the members of which protected each other, promoted each other, and ran things like a patronage machine.

These political clans had many of the functional characteristics of old Russian kinship clans going back centuries: patriarchal systems of authority, personalized rather than institutional politics, collective responsibility (*krugovaia poruka*). Moreover, "clan" was used often by contemporaries in the Stalin period and later to describe patron-client political circles. It is in especially common use today to describe the family circles below Putin.[60]

I am not the first to associate these Soviet political machines with old Russian clans based on kinship. Fifty years ago, Fainsod's "family circle" term was of course suggestive. Edward Keenan wrote that within the Communist Party, "the channels of informal power and influence, those that traditionally linked members of a clan or client/patron group, operate," and speaking of Muscovite boyars, "proximity to powerful persons, rather than ostensible officeholding, "was both the warrant and the objective of political activity ... successive outer rings were composed of client groups and/or other constituencies of the members of inner rings. . . . In modern times, they were to become bureaucratic and interest groups."[61]

The comparison of the Soviet bureaucracy with kin groups was also common at the time. As Stalin said, "both in the center and in the localities, decisions are made, not infrequently, in a familial way, as in the home, so to speak."[62] In a 1937 Central Committee meeting, A. A. Zhdanov and others decried "familyness" (*semeistvennost'*) in which everything was decided behind closed doors by small groups having common interests, among them self-protection. Stalin agreed, interjecting "It is a deal (*sgovor*)."[63]

Studies that attempt to get at informal practices in high politics, especially in a society characterized by personal relations, secrecy, and oral traditions, face problems with sources. Nevertheless, with due regard to problems of bias, one can find gems everywhere.

This study focuses on the Soviet Communist Party, the ruling group in politics, and is archive-based. Our main sources come from RGASPI (*Rossiiskii gosudarstvennyi arkhiv sotsial'no-politicheskoi istorii*), the archive of the former Soviet Communist Party. Specifically the archival collections of the Politburo, the Orgburo, and the Secretariat, along with the personal archives of Stalin and his leading lieutenants, Kaganovich, Molotov, Zhdanov, and Ezhov. Despite the possibly misleading way they introduce themselves to us as documentary organized reflections of an ordered structure that may or may not exist, they provide a voluminous record of the workings of the Communist Party. Like other sources, they must be used with care and, it must be said, not without occasional tedium. One can read through a hundred pages of formal Orgburo routine before finding documents that open the window a bit and let us peer inside. When a routine matter for some reason became an issue or investigation (which was not uncommon), a paper trail opens that shows us who the players were and how things really worked behind the scenes. To take another example, at various times in the Stalin period, an anti-bureaucratic Stalin speech or some national scandal opened a discursive window in which, at least until the window closed, we can see party officials and members from top to bottom speaking frankly about how politics really worked on the ground. Besides, if we can find evidence of informal, traditional practices in a source purporting to represent a rational bureaucracy, that would be something in its own right.

1   The Old and the New

A living culture always gives rise to structurally and functionally new systems and texts. But—and here is the important part for us—it cannot fail to contain within itself a memory of the past.
> —Iurii M. Lotman and Boris A. Uspenskii, 1985

IF THE LENIN MAUSOLEUM can be read as a kind of text combining ancient and modern messages, then we can see the same fusion, or continuity, in a variety of Soviet practices. Intriguing carryovers are everywhere, even in one's own experience, once one starts thinking about them. In Muscovite times, "great difficulties also confronted all foreigners who wished to enter Russia. Frontier guards were under strict orders to turn away any foreigner lacking an entry permit. . . . Even those who had the necessary documents were narrowly limited in their choice of residence and length of stay." Those who tried to get visas to visit the Soviet Union, or until recently post-Soviet Russia, will recognize this tradition. Older readers will also remember what a brave thing it was as late as the Brezhnev period for a Soviet colleague to invite a foreigner to dinner. It was the same ages ago, when "natives were discouraged from establishing contact with visitors from abroad: All conversations between [Muscovite] Russians and foreigners exposed the former to serious suspicion not only concerning their loyalty to native religion and customs, but also their politics."[1]

This chapter examines a perhaps eclectic selection of such practices and behaviors that suggest both the continuity of "deep structures" of Russian practice and the personalization of politics. We will look at the implications of letter writing, awards and medals, the value of collective rather than individual responsibility (*krugovaia poruka*), and elite social roles. All these practices have deep roots in Russian culture and consciously or unconsciously continued into the Soviet period and beyond.

TEXTS

We might start by considering unofficial texts and genres.[2] Throughout the Soviet period, citizens sought help and redress by writing letters to those in power. The archival files of Stalin, Kalinin, Molotov and others are filled with these letters, often including a "resolution" by the addressee.[3] Here, however, we are less concerned with the letter's result than with its voice, genre, and content.

For centuries before the Bolsheviks, Russians had written (or paid someone to write) petitions to powerful persons seeking favors or redress of grievances. One can clearly see ritualistic forms of patronage and patriarchal relations in these letters.[4] Known as *chelobitnye*, literally "beating the ground with one's forehead," these petitions closely followed traditional forms and consistent rhetorical features. In general, they were upward allocutions from the lowly to the powerful—exaltation combined with abasement and entreaty. Russians seem to have adopted literal head-beating as a court ceremony from the Mongols, who in turn had borrowed it from ancient Chinese practice from the time of the first Mongol emperor of China, Kublai. *Chelobitnye* is a calque of the Chinese *ke-tou*, or kowtow, literally, knocking or bumping the head.[5]

These letters had a three-part structure. First, an introductory formula fulsomely saluted the addressee and introduced the writer. A second section enumerated the writer's grievances or requests, and a third requested intercession and relief.

The introductory first section immediately established the relationship between the writer and reader. It typically contained praise for the powerful recipient combined with abasement of the writer, who was nearly always identified as "your slave" or an "orphan who petitions you":

> To the Tsar, Lord and Grand Prince Aleksei Mikhailovich, Great Sovereign of Great, Little, and White Russias, your orphan Tarasko Mikiforov beats his head before [petitions] you.[6]

The introduction often included an apology for disturbing or troubling the reader with the petty problems of a slave.

The second section, by far the most lengthy, contained the actual complaint. Its narrative elements included a chain of misfortune and unjust misdeeds of others. These elements were exaggerated in order to intensify the magnitude of the writer's suffering and cast the villains in the worst possible light. In the cases of requests for favors without blaming malefactors, this section consisted of endless descriptions of misfortune accompanied by flattery of the reader.

The third and final section contained the plea for intercession, often with additional persuasion to dispose the lord in the petitioner's favor and to demonstrate the righteousness of the lord. Here we also find some statement of the basis for a favorable intercession that might include justice, some advantage for the lord (a favorable result "will allow me to continue to serve"), or most often a simple appeal for mercy.

Golfo Alexopoulos has shown that there were two "styles of presentation" in Soviet-era letters to Bolshevik leaders. One was distinctly Soviet, in which the writer used officially approved language and terminology and made the appeal based on Soviet criteria having to do with useful labor and class. In the other, which she called the "ritual lament," one presented oneself against a backdrop of misfortune. As with the ancient Greek lamentation rituals performed at times of mourning, this was a "crying of one's fate." In the ritual lament, one presented oneself as the victim of unfortunate circumstances, injustice, or misfortune and as pitiful, weak, and helpless.[7]

There are certainly differences between types of Soviet letters, depending on the author and the type of request. Nevertheless, there are striking parallels and continuities between the ancient letters and both types used by Soviet citizens, whether the language was political or personal. Soviet letters come in an array of styles and languages. Some of them are direct and institutional; letters to newspapers and journals come into this category. But the vast majority of letters written to persons reflect patrimonial understandings of power. Stalin is the "giver of all good."[8]

First of all, we can note that the very act of petitioning an important person betrays an understanding of power as personal, regardless of the century. Although Soviet citizens could appeal to bureaucratic departments and entities and sometimes did, their reflex was the same as their ancestors': to write to a powerful person. They did so either because bureaucratic avenues had failed or because they had not even been tried. Power was personalized, as it always had been. People got things done, not offices. "Another implication of personalization was that people tried to avoid bureaucracies and formal channels, if possible. The informal ways of dealing with the system were perceived as the most natural, simple and efficient."[9] But the importance of the person rather than the bureaucracy was broader than the practices of ordinary citizens. It was at the center of the political system itself for centuries.

The structure of Soviet-era letters was nearly the same as in those from the seventeenth century and before. The vast majority of letters written to persons and preserved in the archives are addressed to either Mikhail Kalinin (chairman of the governmental Central Executive Committee of Soviets, later the Supreme Soviet) or to Stalin. Kalinin was an obvious choice as titular head of government. Just as important were his peasant origins and nickname "All-Union Elder" of the country; throughout Russian history one turned to the elder for help. At least figuratively, plebeians wrote to their village elder, and in some cases the writers used the familiar "ty" (you) as one might address a fellow villager. In the case of letters addressed to Stalin (as well as many to Kalinin), the powerful recipient was often called "father."

The introductory section flattered the reader and identified the writer as a "little person," thus establishing the writer's supplicant status and the reader's power. Even a Stalin Prize winner followed the patriarchal forms:

> Dear Comrade Stalin! My father! I write this to you with blood from my heart. All my hopes are on you.[10]

A simple collective farm woman wrote:

> Dear and Kindred Father Iosif Vissarionovich! Our beloved father, for me such a situation has arisen that required me to turn to you with a sincere request and to take away your beloved attention for a second, because my fate depends upon that second.[11]

A member of the Academy of Sciences was no less traditional:

> Dear Boundlessly Respected Iosif Vissarionovich! I take it upon myself to write to you, our teacher and leader, father, and protector of our glorious youth, always ready to devote your strength and life to the interests of our country.[12]

Others followed the same style of salutation:

> Profoundly Esteemed Viacheslav Mikhailovich [Molotov]. Forgive the effrontery with which I permitted myself to decide to write to you, lacking the strength to keep silent.[13]

And . . .

> Dear Viacheslav Mikhailovich! I did not want to disturb you, but in the Commissariat of Light Industry things have driven me to the point that nothing remained but to write to you.[14]

Sometimes letter writers were aware of some dissonance between patrimonial salutations and the approved businesslike Soviet style, and tried to avoid or even parody an obsequious tone. But they couldn't help themselves. They ended up exaggerating the traditional self-effacing and supplicant character of the first section:

> My Favorite Iosif Vissarionovich! You have received and receive thousands of telegrams and statements of love to you, of loyalty to you. Iosif Vissarionovich! My beloved leader. You are used to this. It's become a cliché, a tradition, a custom, an obligation. You are a sufficiently wise person to understand this. . . . I am writing this letter to you not out of tradition or obligation. I love you, I love my country, I love my people, although behind them are a great many mistakes, and I write to you not because it's necessary to summon up tradition and obligation but because my soul demands it. . . . I come from a worker's family and worked myself as a lathe operator in a metals factory for nine years. . . . My dear leader! I do not claim to be a genius, nor even talented or wise. I simply love my country and my people. . . . I participated in the war [World War II] under arms and destroyed around 30 Hitlerites. . . . Dear Iosif Vissarionvich! I don't claim anything and don't want anything. . . . [15]

Others also pretended that they did not want anything, before asking for it:

> Please forgive me if my letter tears you away from a more important matter. I was inspired to sit down and write you personally by a circumstance I can find no way out of. I believe you can give me a clear reply which will be beneficial not only to me but also to my work, to which I am devoted totally. . . . My own personal interests can be postponed, put off to the distant future.[16]

One difference between old Russian and Soviet letters had to do with self-identifications. While effacing himself before the powerful person, frequently the Soviet writer also spelled out his Soviet bona fides either in a heading or in the text of the introductory section itself. Party members provided the date of their admission and pointed out that they had never been in the oppositions or been reprimanded. Prize winners noted their awards, longtime proletarians discussed their work records, Red Army men (especially veterans of the Civil War) described their service.

In the case of party members, the allocution was not entirely upward, but more lateral: party comrade to party comrade in a tone reflecting party egalitarian tradition, etiquette, justice, shared hardship, and mission. The party comrade approach carried risks because party members were held to a higher standard of behavior: they were supposed to do their duty and not whine about personal problems. They carried the burden of needing to prove that the problem they were complaining of was objectively wrong.

It might seem that the pride displayed in the comrade-to-comrade approach was at odds with the generally obsequious nature of these introductions, but as with the powerless-to-powerful trope, the purpose here was to improve the chances of a favorable resolution. Both the little-person-orphan and the I-am-somebody tactics were ways to approach a powerful person, to portray oneself as clean and without sin and therefore deserving of help and mercy. Moreover, whether one took the "orphan" or "party comrade" discursive path (sometimes both), the very fact of writing to a powerful patriarchal personality established the subordinate status of the writer and affirmed the personal nature of political power.

The second section spelled out the injustice or problem and asked for resolution. As with the ancient versions, this section was long, detailed and full of "swollen enumerations."[17] It was necessary both to anticipate any objection and to make the case seem as convincing as possible. Letter writers provided chains of behaviors, an entire history of their problems including every related event and detail. Even when the writers concluded with "I am closing now" (perhaps to encourage the readers to continue following the litany) they rarely did so and instead continued at length, often repeating points they had made. In both ancient and modern eras, the petitioner told a long story. Whether

about mistreatment at the hands of a noble, party secretary, or bureau-
crat, the letter involved "forming, shaping, and molding elements: the
crafting of a narrative."[18] This section also bore close resemblance to
old Russian texts with a ritual lament of life hardships.

> I, the undersigned kolkhoz farmer, have decided to write you a letter and
> tell you about my life. I have a very hard life. Every spring there is not
> enough bread. I have two sons, the first sixteen years old, the second five.
> It is very hard for me to raise them. I have no husband. He died . . . my
> son stopped going to school because he wasn't eating enough . . . he had
> no boots, and he had no warm overcoat either. . . . A widowed kolkhoz
> farmer, half starved, I write and wash myself in tears.[19]

Similarly:

> I am the mother of four sons who gave their lives for their country. My
> last son was killed on 5 August near Belgorod. This was a great loss
> that finally knocked me off my feet. . . . I am 83 years old, living with
> my daughter whose husband is also fighting. . . . Now I beg you, Iosif
> Vissarionovich, not to refuse my plea and not to leave me in my old
> years without attention, but to help me get a pension. . . . I have no
> other protection or help, all my sons are dead. I ask you, as my own
> son, not to abandon me in my old age.[20]

The Soviet letters sought the same kind of relief as their ancestors. Res-
toration of their positions (job or party membership) after slander and
injustice, redress of wrongdoing or mistreatment at the hands of evil
officials, or simply mercy and charity in hard times. But most typically,
as with the ancient letters, evildoers were ultimately to blame. These
might be neighbors or spouses, but more typically they were high-
handed or corrupt bureaucrats or nobles. And accused officials could
fight back. As V. A. Kozlov put it, "If the denouncer frequently relied on
'a few words about myself' to strengthen his case, the refutation of the
denunciation offered a mirror image of the same ploy. The denouncer,
pointing to his services to the regime, tried to show that he was right
because he was 'one of our own' (svoi), while the bureaucrats tried to
show that he was wrong because he was an 'outsider' (chuzhoi)."[21]
    Compare a seventeenth-century petition . . .

> We petition . . . with many bloody tears, that the powerful oath-
> breakers, torturers of the common people, blood-sucking thieves, and

our destroyers who are ruling the country and ruining us by all possible means and are employing violence and injustice . . . [22]

. . . with one from the 1950s written to Molotov:

I beg you to defend us, simple people, from the terror of disgusting and high-handed thieves who steal in broad daylight and strut around. . . . We ask you to issue a law ordering thieves to have five fingers of their left hand cut off.[23]

The final section of a petition contained the actual request for redress or intervention, and in both ancient and modern versions, the same criteria were adduced. Most often, a favorable result should follow from elementary justice, religious-moral avoidance of sin, class entitlement, or mercy. Although appeals to mercy were more common in the old Russian petitions, they were an element of modern ones as well. Because of the ostensible egalitarianism of Soviet culture, the letter reader was not a merciful tsar so the appeal to mercy was often implicit rather than direct.

Other incentives or criteria for granting the request were promises that righting the wrong would allow the petitioner to serve or work better. The tsar should show mercy so "that I, thy royal slave, should not perish in the end and should not fail in thy royal service."[24] Soviet letters also often contained apocalyptic language ("I am ending my life!") as well as assurances like "I am writing to you, as to a natural father, not as complaint but as a letter and promise you that I will devote my knowledge and talent and life to the service of our great people."[25] Or: "I suffer terribly because of my illness, but still I won't give up working and await your reply to my letter. No matter what form it's in, your reply will be the supreme reward."[26]

The consistent format of these petitions over the centuries shows a powerful continuity that links the modern to the ancient. It demonstrates an understanding of politics as personal, a subject treated in detail in subsequent chapters. One sought redress via favor from powerful persons rather than institutions. That redress, if it came, was based on justice combined with the bestowing of personal favor, and was understood more as a gift from on high than one's civic due or transactional right.[27]

We do not have access to letters written to Yeltsin or Putin, but we can note a modern analogue to the process, the televised call-in shows that Putin hosts. In a format pioneered by former Moscow mayor Iurii Lushkov, these broadcasts often last several hours, and feature Putin receiving comments and requests from ordinary citizens. Like the historical letters, these are allocutions from low to high, although some of them have an indignant tone. Many of these are personal requests for relief from dire circumstances or the evildoing of bureaucrats, and sometimes the callers go on at length with their laments and have to be politely interrupted so Putin can respond. In a modern technological analogue to Stalin's notes in the margins of letters ordering resolution of a case, Putin often responds sympathetically, siding with the appellant against bureaucrats. Frequently he bestows a decision to rectify the problem immediately and personally, cutting through all the red tape and bypassing institutional channels. The positive decisions therefore show justice coming from a person, as a gift based on mercy and power.

Letters of appeal were not the only texts containing modern content in an ancient genre. In popular culture there are numerous examples of ancient forms that were filled with new content in the Soviet period. Thus, battle tales were updated with modern heroes and images. A traditional tale about an ancient Russian hero fighting the Mongols became a story of Civil War hero Chapaev. A sword became a machine gun; the Mongols became the White armies. But the elements of the traditional tale remained: saddling the warrior's horse, the arming of the hero, going out to battle against an enemy multitude, the battle morning to night, and the beating and tossing of the enemy.

> He arrayed himself in heroic attire,
> He put on him twelve tight saddle girths,
> And a thirteenth for strength, not beauty,
> For the hero's journey.
> He puts on his Damascene steel armor,
> His fighting armor,
> He takes with him his sharp sword,
> He takes with him his heavy club,
> He takes with him his steel knife,
> His machine gun, his Maxim gun.
> His horse struck the earth with his leg,
> Mother damp earth trembled,
> The trees in the dark forests swayed,
> The water in the sea overflowed in a wave.
> Behind him a countless force,
> Behind him forty generals, forty colonels
> Behind him forty captains, forty lieutenants

Behind him hordes and hordes of highwaymen.
He fought from morning to night,
He fought the whole dark night till early morn,
Not eating and not drinking,
He began walking around the force,
He began to beat the whole White force,
He tossed and threw the whole White force
Hither and yon.[28]

The folkloric image of the nation's leader arming himself to lead the struggle against the enemy continues today:

O Russia you have never turned
From foes most gruesome in the fray
O, soldiers all and generals all
Join in the motherland's array!
At crossroads, nation, do not pause,
Come morning we will join the fight!
Onward, O Vladimir Putin!
In the attack we're at your side. . . .
And Russia, she will rise renewed,
Our country will be new in full . . .
Its awesome power and great might
Will be revealed to each and all.
O Fatherland, you crave the real,
You stand for reason in all lands
Onward, O Vladimir Putin!
With you the Russian nation stands.[29]

In other cases, traditional songs were simply updated.[30] A seventeenth- or eighteenth-century song began:

That's how it was in our Moscow, the city of stone,
A great misfortune has occurred there,
Moscow, the city of stone is all in tears.

. . . and became:

That's how it was in our Moscow:
At midnight, the bells began ringing,
And our Moscow merchants burst into tears.

A popular funeral lament began:

But whither are you journeying?
And whither have you fitted yourself out to go?
And what way and road are you taking?

. . . and became:

> And whither is he journeying,
> On what way, and on what road?
> When he went away from us, he disappeared here,
> Like a mighty leader, our dear comrade,
> But still Lenin was the father of all Russia,
> Still Vladimir Ilich was our light.

A famous cycle of old ditties, the "little apple" *chastushki,* all began with the lines

> Oh little apple,
> Whither are you rolling.

A standard version was:

> Oh little apple,
> Whither you may roll,
> Give me in marriage, papa,
> Wherever I may wish.

. . . which became,

> Oh little apple,
> You have rolled away.
> The power of the Cadet Party
> Has been overthrown.

Sometimes, this happened more or less officially, from the top down, as regime representatives and employees simply rewrote old songs, ditties, and stories, adding propaganda content.[31] But as ethnographic studies showed, often the modern content was housed in ancient forms from below, seamlessly as part of traditional culture.[32] But whether adapted from above or below, the important point is the tradition producing or supporting the folklore.

AWARDS AND TITLES

The persistence of ancient person-centered practices also shows itself in the symbolism of identity and authority. Most modern societies have more or less similar ways to confer status and power. Monetary wealth is, of course, always related to power. In politics, office holding is a tool of status and power, given the power and authority of an institutional office in a rational bureaucratic society.

But in noncapitalist or premodern societies, entirely different criteria apply as both markers and tools of power and status. Privileges are often nonmonetary and institutional membership is a symbol more than an activity or power. Thus the Grand Chamberlain did not actually dress the king as his job description might suggest. In old Russia, the title *dumnyi d'iak*, literally Clerk of the Duma, was an important official who had nothing to do with clerical details. It was the honor that counted, and the title conferred power and authority far above those who might be richer or higher bred. In return, as we shall see, the personal honor and power that came with it resulted from proximity to the supreme personality.

Old Russia, along with many traditional societies, was characterized by a precise hierarchy of titles and awards that conferred or changed status. From Peter the Great's time, one's place in the Table of Ranks determined one's entire status, and even before that, the system of *mestnichestvo* established a system of precedence.[33] One's very identity depended on one's precise rank, and on titles and awards that in some cases could ennoble a person.

Titles were only loosely associated with institutions. Thus, at the top of society, those holding the rank of *boyar, okol'nichy (Courtier), dumnyi dvorianin (Courtier of the Duma)* and *dumnyi d'iak* were entitled to membership in the top boyar ranks. But it was the honor, the rank that mattered, and whether the institution ever met or acted on anything was irrelevant to the "badge" of rank that membership carried. Awards and conferred ranks indeed functioned like badges and were often advertised on one's clothing.

More importantly, an award or conferred title actually changed the person. A recipient of an order or ennoblement was now functionally a new person. Identity, therefore, in old Russia was bestowed, not inherent as in modern citizenship. A person receiving an order or award related to others in society both above and below him from a new and specific position, and in formal correspondence often listed his titles and awards.

Status could be inherent in the person. Those of princely or boyar rank held that status by birth. But most other titles and status markers were conferred by the tsar, who within loose boundaries of tradition, could give titles and take them away. Status and authority, therefore, were matters neither of accident of birth nor of office holding. They were largely about symbolic titles, whose number and distribution were strictly controlled by the central power and which were advertised by the person and recognized by those around him.

With few exceptions, nonmonetary criteria were also extremely important throughout the Soviet period. A precise array of awards, orders, and titles ranging from the Order of Lenin to the holder of the Stalin Prize to Outstanding Swinebreeder to Honored Archivist were taken very seriously and literally worn as badges of rank. Even now, more than twenty years after the end of the USSR, it is not uncommon to see people on the street wearing medals.

As in old Russia, institutional membership was a mechanism of power, but more important was the status it conferred as an identity. Like a pedigree, an official Soviet short biography included a list of positions and memberships that were honorifics more than levers of power. After listing a person's past and present positions, the biography cited the important honorifics, such as "delegate to 12th–18th Party Congresses, member of the Central Executive Committee of Soviets of 5th–9th convocations, etc." even though these bodies rarely met and never did anything substantive. Next came the awards, perhaps Order of Lenin, Hero of Socialist Labor, Order of the Red Banner, etc. which were the functional equivalents of office holding in bodies that rarely met.[34]

Such listings were an obligatory and significant part of one's biography, one's social and political personhood. When one wrote a letter to a person in authority with an appeal or complaint, one always listed one's awards either as a preamble or as a postscript (often with the date of joining the party), to indicate one's degree and "quality." And such a letter tended to get a response from the top leaders because a special person was the author.

Like princely or aristocratic status, Old Bolshevik status was immutable and permanent. Below that, however, the central leadership controlled awards and status. As in old Russia, identity was bestowed from above, by Stalin. The leadership took awards and medals as seriously as the general population. Important awards were matters for Politburo discussion and often for Stalin's personal decision. He thought medals had "moral force." In 1931, he wrote to the Politburo: "The Politburo decision to award the Order of Lenin to various people gives a bad impression. You have started to award medals too easily. If this continues, the medal will be cheapened and will lose all of its moral force. This cannot be allowed to happen under any circumstances!"[35]

When Commissar of Defense Voroshilov wanted to give awards to a cavalry division, Stalin wrote: "I don't know the Second Chernigov Cavalry Division and cannot vote either for or against the award."[36] In 1934, the Politburo proposed giving psychologist I. P. Pavlov an order and establishing a Pavlov Prize of twenty thousand rubles and five scholarships for young academics, along with providing a million rubles for Pavlov's biological station. Stalin replied the next day, "Pavlov, of course, is not Michurin. Michurin is ours politically and Pavlov is not ours (*ne nash*). It's necessary not to blur the difference in the press. Give him no orders, even if he wants one. I agree with the rest."[37]

Like the Russian population at large, Stalin took such things seriously. So did his successors. A Putin decree of 2010 listed well over a hundred titles and orders, along with the criteria for awarding them.[38] The president of Tatarstan was awarded The Kind Angel of Peace and other medals. The president of Udmurtia received medals for Statehood and the titles Outstanding Builder, Honored Academician, and others.[39]

COLLECTIVE RESPONSIBILITY

If the Bolsheviks (and the population they ruled) had a rather traditional view of status and honorifics, their attitude toward criminal responsibility had even deeper historical roots. Most modern societies tend to fix civic and criminal responsibility on individuals and, at least in principle, to apply the law equally. But Bolshevik practice, although apparently modern and transformational, was in reality quite ancient.

From the beginning of the Soviet period, the Bolsheviks used terror not only against individuals, but against groups. In the Red Terror of the Civil War, hostages were taken and executed as a matter of policy. If a few peasants held up a food train, their entire village was held responsible. During collectivization in the early 1930s, peasants who opposed collectivization were deported en masse, and from that time non-Russian populations were deported or moved from province to province. During World War II, entire nationalities (Chechens, Crimean Tatars, and others) were deported when only a percentage of them had collaborated with the Germans.

Such mass actions seem to imply a kind of social engineering in which a modern state seeks to remove "weeds" from its garden. Some scholars have pointed out that modern states seek to perfect their populations by counting, regulating, indoctrinating, controlling, and sorting good from bad amongst them.[40] Yet, we can also see these practices as continuations of ancient Russian "collective responsibility," by which groups were held liable and punished for the sins of a few of their members. From 1934, family members of military men who fled abroad were liable for punishment and could be sentenced to ten years in prison for abetting an escape or up to five years even if they did not know of a defection.[41] During the Great Purges of 1937–38, family members were routinely arrested when the head of household fell, just as a senior official's entourage always faced arrest when he was arrested.

In Stalin's time and well after, the relatives of "enemies of the people," even if they had been children at the time of a parent's arrest, faced stigmas. Their access to higher education, good jobs, and even party membership was sharply restricted. Similarly, to the end of the Soviet period, one could not travel abroad without leaving family members behind in the USSR as a kind of collective surety that one would return.

In a toast on the twentieth anniversary of the Bolshevik revolution, Stalin explicitly put the case for collective responsibility in a starkly premodern way: "And we will destroy each such enemy, be he Old Bolshevik or not, we will destroy his kin, his family. Anyone who by his actions and thoughts, yes, his thoughts encroaches on the unity of the socialist state we will destroy. To the destruction of all enemies to the very end, them and their kin!"[42]

One might compare Stalin's sentiments with those of Genghis Khan: "Everyone who does not submit and attempts to resist shall perish, along with his wife, children, relatives and those close to him!"[43] Genghis's Tatar descendants who ruled Russia certainly shared this view. Entire towns were destroyed and their populations massacred at the slightest resistance.

The Stalinists practiced a concept of "objective guilt" that extended collective culpability beyond any particular act or even conspiracy. Expressed most clearly in Arthur Koestler's *Darkness at Noon*, the idea was that even one's private doubts about official policy were tanta-mount to treason through their objective effect. Russian Orthodox tra-dition also recognized "sins of thought."[44] Thinking about overthrowing the state was as bad as actually plotting to do it. According to the Bol-shevik "algebra" of guilt, anyone who opposed the Bolsheviks was ob-jectively and by definition opposing the revolution, opposing socialism, and opposing human welfare, regardless of that person's subjective intent. Belonging to a group critical of the regime or sharing critical thoughts with others was considered as criminal as a treasonous act, as was knowing about such a "conspiracy" and not reporting it.

NKVD chief N. I. Ezhov, in his book manuscript "From Factional-ism to Open Counterrevolution (On the Zinovievist Counterrevolu-tionary Organization)," maintained that continued opposition to the party line inevitably led to counterrevolution and terrorism by inspir-ing others, even if the inspirers were not the direct organizers of such deeds.[45] Kotolynov, one of the defendants tried in 1934 for organizing Kirov's assassination even though he did not know of terrorist plans, said that the "algebra" of any such an organization was such that oth-ers would be encouraged to take criminal action.[46]

Some anti-Stalinist Bolsheviks initially resisted the criminality of objective guilt. During his interrogation, G. E. Zinoviev at first argued with his interrogator:

> ZINOVIEV: Nevertheless there is a difference when people happen to spend the night with each other and being in an organization. . . . People were associated with each other for years without carrying out any counterrevolutionary work. You can't mix them all up into one club.
> INTERROGATOR: Your answer is not serious.[47]

In his speech to the TsK plenum in December 1936, N. I. Bukharin said:

> I don't deny that some members of the Central Committee were at my apartment. They were. But should one deduce from this fact that I am affiliated with foreign states, that I have placed my name as a candi-date for the government, that I am helping those sons-of-bitches to kill the workers in the mining shafts?[48]

At the February 1937 Plenum, A. I. Rykov also insisted that his culpa-bility was only for things he had actually done.

I ought to be punished for that which I did, but I shouldn't be punished for that which I didn't do. . . . And there is no disgrace greater than the fact that many people perpetrated these revolting deeds by modeling themselves on me—this is a horrible thing. But it does not at all follow from this, on the basis of this one ought not to accuse me of knowing that Trotskyists talked to Hess, that they conceded the Ukraine to Germany, that they handed over the Primorskii Region to the Japanese, that they systematically practiced spying and sabotage on the widest possible scale. And if you think that I knew about this, then it's clear that such people ought to be annihilated. But I am innocent in this.[49]

Eventually, under pressure of interrogation or because of change of heart, the accused recognized the validity of objective guilt. In "A Deserved Sentence," a 540 page manuscript that Zinoviev wrote in prison shortly before his execution, he stated: "There is no question about it. . . . It is a fact. Whoever plays with the idea of "opposition" to the socialist state plays with the idea of counterrevolutionary terror . . ."[50]

At their show trials, Zinoviev, Bukharin, and Rykov all confessed to treason. For his part, Zinoviev admitted to being an "active organizer" of terror. Bukharin, while continuing to deny any details of a treasonous personal role, admitted that his "moral responsibility" was tantamount to treason.

An important corollary of *krugovaia poruka* and its latter-day version, "objective guilt," was the idea that knowing of a conspiracy and not reporting it to the authorities was tantamount to participating in the conspiracy and thus, to treason. As even Rykov admitted, "There can be no middle ground because if these traitors and turncoats had spoken to me about treason and I had not worked for them but only knew about it, then their fate would have been in my hands."[51] Although Bukharin continued to deny the technical details of his "treason" at his show trial, in a private letter to Stalin shortly before his death he admitted that he knew of a conspiracy but failed to report it:

Aikhenval'd told me in passing, *post factum* as we walked on the street about the conference which I knew nothing about (nor did I know anything about the Riutin platform) ("the gang has met, and a report was read")—or something of the sort. And, yes, I concealed this fact, feeling pity for the "gang." I was also guilty of engaging in duplicity . . . in my relations with my "followers," believing sincerely that I would thereby win them back wholly to the Party.[52]

This Stalinist practice effectively converted everyone into an obligatory informer and can be seen as the action of a modern totalitarian state—or of Stalin personally—creating unprecedented powers of surveillance to control a population.

But how new was all this? Stalin and the Bolsheviks did not invent collective guilt, nor did Stalin simply copy Ivan IV.[53] The practice of collective responsibility and punishment (*krugovaia poruka*) has a long tradition in Russian history well before modern times.

Even before the Tatar-Mongol invasion, the first Russian law code in the eleventh century, the *Russkaia pravda,* held communities collectively responsible for crime. During the Tatar period, tax collection was made a collective responsibility at the national, town, and communal levels as groups were collectively charged to come up with the payments. If we go back (and east) even further, we find that the Tatars learned collective responsibility from the Chinese. As far back as the Qin dynasty (230–206 B.C.E.), groups of homesteads were held collectively responsible for each others' crimes, and families were wiped out for the treason of a single member. By the thirteenth century, Genghis's son Ogotai decreed that if a single family took in a criminal or runaway, the entire city or commune was liable to execution. Ogotai's adviser Ye Lu Chu Cai convinced his khan to make households and villages, not individuals, the units of taxation so that if a taxpayer ran away, his remaining fellows were liable for his taxes.[54]

Similar provisions, along with communal responsibility for providing soldiers, would remain in Russian (and Soviet) practice for centuries. By at least the time of Ivan III in the late fifteenth century, *krugovaia poruka* was well developed and formalized. It was extended from peasant taxation to criminal responsibility of members of the elite, with written sureties according to which signatories were liable for the actions of a single individual. Ivan IV's massacre of entire families in his *Oprichnina* and the bloodbath he inflicted on Novgorod because of the disloyalty of a few are graphic examples.[55]

The responsibility to inform had deep roots in Russian history, and members of the elite were always expected to inform on each other's deeds and conversations. Prince Kholmskii promised Ivan III in writing "to serve my sovereign, Grand Prince Ivan Vasilievich, and his sons, and to report to them anything that anyone else said, favorable or unfavorable, pertaining to the Grand Prince and his sons."[56] In 1527,

Princes Bel'skii and Shuiskii promised not to join persons wishing harm to the sovereign "in any way, by any deeds or any guile," and to report anything they heard about the sovereign "for good or for evil."[57]

By the sixteenth century, "Moscow had extended the old communal suretyship in criminal and fiscal matters to another sphere—political 'loyalty.' A boyar's peasants and household serfs could be held collectively responsible for their master's faithful service. They were to eavesdrop on his conversation and keep track of his conduct, reporting anything that seemed amiss." Higher-ranking people who had transgressed or were under suspicion had to offer find sureties who would pledge to be responsible for "their conduct."[58] Even the Stalinist idea of "objective guilt" was not new. In the seventeenth century, intending to commit a crime against the sovereign was the same as committing it.[59]

Krugovaia poruka became embedded in Russian political thinking.[60] It continued to operate in the imperial period as it had since Muscovite times. For example, when Emperor Peter II died, Princess Dolgorukaia observed, "I knew enough about the customs of our country to know that when Emperors fall, all favorites follow." Dolgorukaia continued by describing how Ernst Biron, the favorite of the new ruler, Empress Anna Ivanovna, "began by calling in the very people who had been our friends . . . questioning them about the kind of life we lived and whether we had ever offended anyone or taken bribes."[61]

Krugovaia poruka spanned the centuries right up to today's Russia, and as one scholar pointed out, it is a subject that surely deserves much fuller study.[62] It is another example of an originally functional practice that became permanently embedded in political culture to be used later as a political tool or, perhaps, as a response to functional needs entirely different from the original ones. Originally a tax collection method applied to peasants, when applied to the elite it became a tool of the throne to breed distrust in kinship and political clans. Both Ivan III and Stalin insisted that clan and group members inform on one another and punished the group if a single member sinned. Both the Law Code (*Ulozhenie*) of 1649 and Article 58 of the Stalin-era criminal code made citizens, even family members, liable for not reporting the treason of friends or relatives.[63] This mode of *krugovaia poruka* benefited the ruler insofar as it made groups police themselves when the state could not reliably penetrate personal groups, and Stalin would use it as a weapon to fragment rival clans by encouraging denunciation and mistrust.

At the same time, *krugovaia poruka* could also be a practice to promote trust: to protect clans and "family circles" from the throne. Collective responsibility also meant collective security: group members watched each others' backs and practiced various forms of group self-protection. Thus, until the 1930s many Soviet government organizations were governed by "collegian" in which decisions were taken collectively. Soviet factories were governed by the "triangle" of management, party, and trade union officials. When things went wrong, the collegiums or the triangle prevented any single individual from taking all the responsibility or blame. When in 1930–31 Stalin decreed "one-man management" in industry, he fixed responsibility on the factory director, thus separating him from the collective protection and refuge of triangle and collegiums. Factory directors knew this, of course, and despite the growth in their personal authority, opposed the change.[64] Stalin struck a blow against one form of *krugovaia poruka,* while at the same time using another form of it as collective political punishment.

Later, in the post-Stalin period, *krugovaia poruka* meant group members' watching each other's backs, covering up each other's faults, saving each other from threats of all kinds. It became the basis for the resurrection and continued vitality of political "family circles" of officials that were so much a part of Soviet life.[65]

Krugovaia poruka, like all originally functional measures that become embedded cultural and political practices, could play contradictory roles and have various interpretations. Divorced from its original function to collect taxes from peasants, it had become part of the political landscape, part of the culture. Despite its contested uses and understandings, one basic understanding continued through the years: one rose or fell with one's group. Politics (and in some ways, survival) was therefore a matter of helping your friends and resisting your (and your friends') enemies. Although arrest and execution of entire political clans ended, it was still the case that the fall of one meant the fall of that person's entire group, and as we shall see, this understanding continues under Putin.[66]

SOCIAL ROLES: A NEW NOBILITY

In the name of creating a hyperrational scientific state, the Bolsheviks employed archaic practices and assumed traditional privileged social roles. Confronted with this apparent paradox, Bolshevik notables would surely have denied any continuity or connection with nobles of the past. But even as they spent their lives fighting Russian noble elites, they assumed many of the characteristics, prerogatives, and functions of those same elites.[67] As Molotov recalled, "all of us had such weaknesses, to live like a lord. We got used to that lifestyle, there is no denying it. Everything was prepared for us, all our wishes were attended to."[68]

Years ago, Don Rowney showed that despite dramatic changes in class and personnel, certain social roles bridged the 1917 divide. In industry and technology, both before and after the revolution, there were engineers, foremen, and industrial administrators with specific functions and levels. Faces, discourse, and ideology changed but positions and roles did not.[69]

Much like the Normans conquering England, or the Mongols conquering China, when the Vikings took over the Slavic lands they were foreigners and created a foreign dynasty. But over the years, the conquerors fused with or were subsumed by the conquered culture. In Russia, the Vikings came to speak Slavic, used Slavic names and practiced Slavic culture. This combined Viking-Russian oligarchic nobility, however, never considered itself to have anything in common with the ordinary people. Noble was noble, and through the generations the elite fostered an image of "otherness." Both to themselves and to the peasants, they were a breed apart, with their own culture, society, family structure, and political and military monopoly. That "otherness," among other things, was certified by genealogy and family history.

Bolsheviks were not boyars and it would be foolish to equate the two. But seen from the vantage point of sociology and anthropology, parallels between Old Bolsheviks and the old Russian aristocracy can tell us something about social groups and their roles as neotraditionalist elements of the Soviet system. In Soviet society, Old Bolsheviks enjoyed a prestige and status equal to that of the old Russian princely aristocracy. Admiring schoolchildren were taught about them. They were recognized and applauded at meetings. They had their own veteran societies. And, for the first twenty years after the 1917 Revolutions, as a corporate group they dominated Soviet politics as senior statesmen and powerful regional governors. As with princely aristocrats, eligibility was limited and their ranks were closed to new members.

They thought of themselves as a breed apart, with privileges and immunities and a special vision, almost equivalent to a birthright, an "otherness" that gave them the duty to govern.

Even before 1917 one can see signs that Old Bolshevik party members began to think of themselves as the elect, as special people with special knowledge and tasks. Although Lenin's ideas of a small militarized party with strict discipline were often breached, they said something about what a Bolshevik was. He was part of a small brotherhood and one of the few who understood the flow of history as Lenin had outlined it. Because of this special knowledge, the Old Bolsheviks consciously thought of themselves as "midwives of history," the enlightened group that would lead the workers and peasants to the earthly socialist paradise.[70]

The parallels with priesthoods are fairly obvious here, but for the moment we are more interested in the corporate identity and psychology of the Old Bolsheviks. Their special knowledge, shared underground hardship, common cause, and web of personal trust and connection made for a powerful corporate self-image. Although they frequently disagreed among themselves, the Bolshevik brotherhood closed ranks against outside threats, the general population, and even sometimes against rank-and-file party members.[71] As special and chosen ones, they were suspicious and fearful of those outside their quasi-aristocratic caste.

Within their caste, the Old Bolsheviks' sense of themselves as a group apart was reflected in their inner society. They knew and socialized with each other. They lived together in fortified places, the Kremlin being only one of their guarded castles. They had their own revolutionary veterans' societies and publications. Their sons and daughters attended the same schools, and married the daughters and sons of other Old Bolsheviks with whom they grew up. Kinship even played a role (although not nearly to the extent it had with nobles in the past): Trotsky, Zinoviev, Kamenev, Bukharin, Molotov, and Stalin, to name only a few, married other Old Bolsheviks or their offspring, and the first three were directly related by marriage as in-laws. Parents passed judgment on proper marriages for their children, and it was very rare to marry outside the caste. Old Bolsheviks entrusted their children's futures to each other, and customarily adopted the orphaned children of their deceased comrades, a practice that was followed by almost all the senior leaders in Stalin's time.

Given their shared revolutionary background and experiences it would have been unusual for them not to socialize exclusively with each other. Nevertheless, these habits contributed to the closed, insular culture of the Old Bolshevik notables who, like their aristocratic counterparts, almost never met a commoner unless it was a maid or cook. Lenin used to tell a story about the first time he met a worker. After a long conversation, he invited his first proletarian home for tea. While he was making the tea, the worker made off with his overcoat.

Nineteen seventeen soon became a mythic, heroic event in the discourse of the new regime and the Old Bolsheviks naturally assumed the role of the wise fighting heroes who brought it about. In the years after the revolution, various encyclopedias and other publications extolled their biographies and exploits.[72] They were the veterans, often called the "Bolshevik Knights" (*Bol'shevistskie rytsary*) whose brave exploits were the stuff of legend. This glorification could not help but emphasize their existing self-image as the chosen ones, those who fought when it was hard, those with special qualities who had made a revolution, in a process no less difficult and every bit as self-congratulatory as that of knights conquering a new land. They had struggled together against enormous odds, taken risks, braved dangers together, all of which gave them a real esprit de corps. They thought they had a responsibility and right to rule.[73] Their understanding of themselves as breed apart conflicted with their image as the "vanguard of the proletariat," and publicly they were at pains to avoid making the distinction between the elite and the masses of the party. In 1921, Comrade Medvedev was expelled from the party for a speech touching "on the question of 'highers and lowers'" (*verkhakh i nizakh*).[74]

Old Bolshevik grandees even built "castles" for their personal use. Although Stalin generally refrained from public criticism of his fellow Old Bolsheviks, their lavish lifestyles irked him. For example, he complained that many of them "had built themselves grandiose dacha-palaces of 15–20 or more rooms, where they luxuriated and frittered away the peoples' money, thus demonstrating their complete dissipation (*razlozhenie*) and degeneration (*pererozhdenie*)."[75]

Old Bolshevik status, like princely birth, was immutable but access to other ranks of the elite could be (and had to be) controlled and regulated. As the Bolsheviks took over control of the vast territory of the former Russian Empire, they needed large numbers of administrators, particularly to govern the regions. There were simply not enough Old Bolsheviks to go around, so a way had to be found to create a new stratum in the elite, one of administrators of the party apparatus: service nobles (*pomeshchiki,* in olden times). As we move into the 1920s, these *apparatchiki* become part of the new nobility, ranking somewhere between rank-and-file party members and the Old Bolshevik princes. These new Bolshevik petty nobles were defined by the top elite in terms of their *stazh,* or *partstazh:* their years in the party, usually since 1917.

Old Russian nobles and their clans were always in competition with each other for precedence which was the source of political power, as well as access to resources and patronage. Complicated genealogical calculations formed the basis for noble status and hierarchy, with members of the most ancient families receiving the best positions, favors, and military commands. Genealogy could be modified or at times even replaced by proximity to the monarch (i.e., his relatives or others he personally favored) to make up the *mestnichestvo* order that nobles and monarchs generally followed. *Mestnichestvo* also helped regulate conflict among the noble clans. There was natural competition among them, and the rankings of *mestnichestvo* established everyone's place, and therefore his access to prime positions, military commands, and economic monopolies. It was a functional response to the problem of elite competition.

The Old Bolsheviks also established a system to control who could be part of the elite. Ancient nobles had made precise *mestnichestvo* calculations of lineage and ancestral descent to determine prestige, power, and the right to position and office holding. This was a serious and contentious part of corporate membership, and the Bolsheviks took it no less seriously. In Bolshevik *mestnichestvo, partstazh* was a proxy for aristocratic blood ancestry, serving as both a marker of status and noble membership, and determining eligibility for office holding. Membership in their closed caste was strictly defined by calculating one's length of service in the party. Fine distinctions were made between those who joined the party before 1905, before 1917, and then between the precise months of joining in 1917 (before the February Revolution, during the summer's declining Bolshevik fortunes, before October). Documents were combed and compared, witnesses polled. Beginning in the early 1920s, central party personnel assignment paperwork recorded the geographic level (*masshtab*) of one's position:

national, provincial, district or village.[76] In this 1926 *mestnichestvo,* of full-time "responsible" party officials, only 2 percent were ranked for national-level positions.

Thus, a system was created whereby a party secretary at a given level (cell, factory, district, up to province) had to have a specific number of years' service in the party to qualify for rank and status.[77] Continuing our metaphor of years in the party for noble blood, these noble new-comers were not of ancient lineage and service, but neither were they commoner newcomers. Reserving certain positions for certain qualities of people had been traditional in Russia. The Muscovite system of *mestnichestvo* and, later, the Table of Ranks had codified the practice, and the Old Bolsheviks followed this example. Their party's leading organs, the Politburo, Orgburo, and Secretariat (discussed below) were mainly concerned with personnel appointments, and the techni-cal office for those appointments (at various times known as *uchraspred, orgraspred, orgotdel,* or *raspredotdel*) was at the heart of the party apparatus. Moreover, beginning in 1923, the party established a for-mal system of *nomenklatura:* a series of lists of positions appointment to which required confirmation by various groups of senior grandees. Bolsheviks were creating "a closed and minutely graded caste . . . in direct line of succession from the Muscovite service class." In some re-spects, this was the Bolshevik *mestnichestvo,* because "advancement to the highest ranks was rewarded with inclusion in the rolls of the no-menklatura, which carried entitlements beyond the reach of ordinary servitors . . . the Communist equivalent of a service nobility."[78]

These knights of the revolution monopolized the key positions in party, state, and economic administration, as well as in the provincial party committees that ran the territories.[79] As the victorious group in the revolution, it was only natural that they should hold the top positions in the new regime. But in this case, there was more than a little sense of entitlement and mission. They were the elect who had fought the hard fight and knew where history should go. Such people feared losing their monopoly of positions of power, and until the growing need for new administrators forced the matter, it did not occur to them to do so.

At lower levels, the Old Bolshevik princes also carefully controlled admission into the broader ranks of the party. During the revolutions and the Civil War (1918–21), the ranks had expanded dramatically. From fewer than twenty thousand at the beginning of 1917, the party had swollen to three quarters of a million members by 1921, despite periodic purges and wartime casualties. It would hit a million by 1926.[80] Party membership brought with it privileges and status, and it was a possible door to the larger elite. Although a huge Communist Party might be something to celebrate, the Old Bolsheviks were worried. Facing a massive influx of recruits (which they needed) into the ranks of the winning party, these Communist grandees feared dilution or redefining of their noble status, as well as loss of control of administrative positions and ideology.

The millions of new recruits from the working-class, peasant, and white-collar strata had none of the common experiences of the Old Bolsheviks. They had not been in the underground, had not been arrested or exiled (an important bonding experience for the Old Bolsheviks). They had no political experience, no knowledge of the history of the revolutionary struggle, and very little idea about Leninist ideology. They lacked the "special knowledge" of the Bolshevik knights. As late as 1927, 25 percent of party members had completed fewer than four years of school; 2.4 percent of them were illiterate. Some new party members had to ask what the Politburo was.[81] Like Russian nobles, the Old Bolsheviks could not but think of these *nouveaux* as "them" who were not at all like "us."

So the Old Bolsheviks established a strict screening system to limit admission to the party. One's class origins were important; the Bolsheviks were less frightened of workers than of peasants and white-collar employees. Lenin was frank about the dangers of mass admissions and loss of control by the "Old Guard" of the party, going so far as to use control by the elite as a rather bizarre proxy for proletarian social origins: "It must be borne in mind that the temptation to join the ruling party at the present time is very great. . . . the types who have been carried away by the political successes of the Bolsheviks are very remote from everything proletarian. . . . If we do not close our eyes to reality we must admit that at the present time the proletarian policy of the Party is not determined by the character of its membership, but by the enormous undivided prestige enjoyed by the small group which might be called the Old Guard of the Party."[82]

Again reflecting traditions of personal connections, applicants had to have recommendations from longtime party members who could vouch for them. To make sure the party's ranks remained clean, beginning in 1921 the party leadership also established a cycle of membership screenings [*chistki*, or cleanings or purges] to weed out crooks, enemies, bureaucrats abusing their positions, and general hangers-on.[83]

Like earlier elites, the Old Bolsheviks—with some fighting among themselves—established a system of ideological, if not religious orthodoxy. The disputes among Stalin, Trotsky, Zinoviev, and Bukharin for the correct reading of Lenin's heritage are well known. "Leninism" became the standard to adhere to, and "anti-Leninist" the sign of wrong belief, heresy or worse, and like all historical heresies it was defined by those in charge. Certainly these disputes had much to do with the struggle among these senior leaders for Lenin's mantle after his death in early 1924; one weapon in the struggle with a competitor was adherence to correct ideology and accusations of heresy. But here it is important to recognize that although senior Old Bolsheviks disagreed about what was proper Leninism (and individuals among them changed their minds from time to time about what that was), there was consensus in this elite that ideological conformity and control, as a principle, was a way to uniformly educate and socialize the masses of new party members.

The parallel with control of belief and obsession with rooting out heresy in ancient times is striking. Old Bolshevik obsession with heresy would have been familiar to any elite in history: it was necessary to show a common front, one face, to the population. For the population to accept the correct beliefs, it was necessary to present them with a single canon, sanctified by faith and belief and unanimously upheld by the nobility. This need for unanimity was particularly strong among the Bolsheviks. All the priests and nobles must stand together before the peasants, even as these grandees stabbed each other in the back in private. Lenin had taught that party unity was paramount and that a split in the party would be a disaster: "A slight conflict within this group [the "Old Guard"] will be enough, if not to destroy this prestige, at all events to weaken the group to such a degree as to rob it of its power to determine policy."[84] Stalin would later use this fear of a split for his own purposes to marginalize his opponents, but he could do so precisely because no matter what ideological differences they may have had with each other, the one thing all Bolsheviks shared was a fear of letting the public see disputes among their betters. It was important to keep their story straight in front of the children. Otherwise, they risked being overthrown or splitting the party.

Old Bolshevik control of party membership, ideology, and top institutional positions reflected not only universal control tactics of a new regime. The fact that they arrogated to themselves the power, the duty to do these things speaks further to their exclusive quasi-aristocratic self-image as a breed apart. "We" have things we must do to save the revolution. They became a closed caste of special people, equal to each other but with knowledge and mission superior to rank-and-file party members and the public at large. They thought of themselves as the gatekeepers and guides of the commoners.

The Old Bolsheviks also had among themselves a specific political/personal culture, reflecting their traditions, status, and privileges. That culture was reflected in both language and practice. For example, one prerevolutionary tradition and understanding was that each Bolshevik was to an extent autonomous, an individual knight. Despite Lenin's calls for party discipline and obedience, the actual situation was one in which before 1917 a TsK with a fluid and unelected composition could not and did not give binding orders to party committees and members. Lenin's TsK could and did recommend and suggest and could send emissaries with suggestions and recommendations, but before the revolution it was understood that neither the TsK nor Lenin himself could "order" anyone to do anything. As nascent grandees, the underground Old Bolsheviks were largely independent. After the revolution, this culture continued. Even the Politburo generally "recommended" and "suggested" what senior party members should do. Rarely did it "oblige" or "order."

In 1925, in the name of the Politburo, Stalin wrote to Anastas Mikoian, at that time first secretary of the North Caucasus party committee, asking Mikoian to release one of his lieutenants:

> In Ivanovo-Voznesensk it turns out that we have a situation where it is absolutely necessary to send Kolotilov there as first secretary of the City Party Committee. Please don't object.

Kolotilov worked for Mikoian, who did in fact object. Stalin:

> The Politburo confirmed the Orgburo decision about sending Kolotilov to Ivanovo-Voznesensk. The TsK suggests in a week's time, and not later than the 12th, to send Kolotilov.

Mikoian again differed. Stalin:

> I beg you not to insist. Today we voted for the second time to confirm the decision about Kolotilov. There is no other way out, considering the situation.[85]

Eleven years later, in 1936, knightly etiquette required Stalin to write politely to Genrikh Iagoda, disgraced and recently removed as head of the NKVD police, to "ask" [*proshu*] that he accept demotion to the post of commissar of communications.[86] These were simply the ways one noble treated another, at least rhetorically.

Like elites at all times and places, the Old Bolsheviks were jealous and protective of their status. For centuries before 1917, "the tsar was besieged with petitions from servitors who objected to being put in command positions below their rightful 'places' (*mesta*)."[87] As in the tsarist past, if a Bolshevik received a position that his "quality" did not permit, there were complaints from both his betters and his inferiors in both personal and corporate hierarchies. Lazar Kaganovich remembered how in the 1920s, staffers tried to build personnel files on Old Bolsheviks that involved putting each of them on a "grid" that recorded qualifications, geographic level of 'experience, and consequent suitability for assignment. "In the localities, arguments and even conflicts (*skloki*) often arose from affronts related to dissatisfaction about where we put them on the qualifications grid, and what level of work [*masshtab:* national, provincial, local, etc.] was specified."[88]

It was common in the 1920s and even in the 1930s for a Bolshevik to indignantly reject an assignment he considered beneath his status. In 1922 and 1923, Lev Trotsky refused appointment as Lenin's deputy at the Council of People's Commissars (running either the Council of National Economy or Gosplan) because he considered a position as deputy was beneath his station; it would end his career as a Soviet functionary.[89]

One's place in Soviet *mestnichestvo* was partly a function of one's proximity to the ruling elite and, as in ancient times, the prince could determine one's place. Nadezhda Mandelshtam recalls how "the state encouraged people to behave like the boyars in medieval Russia who fought each other over their place at the Czar's table, always reserving to itself the final decision as to who should sit at the top. . . . It used the ancient system of *mestnichestvo* and itself named people to first places."[90] In Soviet documents, regional party committees were often explicitly said to be run on the basis of *mestnichestvo,* with calculations of precedence becoming part of rivalries between local Bolshevik notables.[91]

Patrimonial patronage politics was the métier of the elite in old Russia. Each senior prince or boyar stood at the apex of a network of clients, relatives, and supporters who protected and promoted each other, and loyalty was given to those above and protection to those below at all levels of the clan. Nobles, especially the princes and boyars, headed clans whose fortunes rose and fell with those of their senior members.[92] In the times before ideology (and maybe even after), politics consisted of competition, intrigue, and maneuver with other clans and with the tsar, the goals being prestige, accumulation of offices and patronage, and making sure "ours" got as large a piece of the pie as possible. "Government . . . was conspiratorial: clans conspired against one another to expand their power; they conspired with other clans to preserve the political system against the potentially destabilizing consequences of their competition."[93]

After the revolution, the Old Bolsheviks also organized themselves into networks of clients centered around a senior patron.[94] These clans or "family circles" are discussed elsewhere in this book, but for now we note the resemblance to aristocratic clan networks of the past. Those networks were often based on family and kin, although they came to include nonrelative creatures as members. Both Old Bolshevik and noble patron-client network members protected and promoted each other. They depended on senior patrons for political protection at court and elsewhere, and as sources of office holding. In both eras, these networks were generally nonideological but rather based on resource allocation, power, and pure patronage.

Much of politics in both eras consisted of interclan intrigues and maneuvers. Much of Muscovite and imperial period Russian history is the story of competition among senior nobles and their clans. Similarly, nobody who studies Soviet history can avoid the omnipresent intrigues, thrusts and parries, and constant competition among groups. The literature is full of descriptions of court life under Stalin where senior Old Bolshevik nobles—each of whom stood at the head of a network of "his people"—jockeyed for position in constant intrigues that could and did sometimes end in the deaths of nobles who lost the contest or fell out of favor. They, along with their clients, were exiled or demonstratively killed as groups, with the winning groups taking the spoils. After their rival Zhdanov died of a heart attack, Malenkov and Beria annihilating their late adversary's clan in the Leningrad Affair of 1948–49 is a good example.[95] One post–World War II interviewee was asked, "'suppose a Malenkov man gets the job of first secretary of an obkom [provincial party committee]. What can the Zhdanov people do about this?' The respondent replied that Zhdanov would collect material on this first secretary through other secretaries in the obkom, such as, for example, the secretary responsible for industry and use this material to discredit the first secretary and eventually get him removed from his post. In reply to a question, the respondent added that the same system worked out at the obkom level of the Party, repeating itself almost exactly."[96]

The prince or tsar often mediated between and among the elite and their clans, but insisted on the last word. When the boyars got out of line, the tsar punished them with exile, confiscation, or as in the time of Ivan the Terrible, with death. Here it is perhaps not out of place to observe what Stalin said of his regional boyars. In 1934, he referred to provincial Old Bolshevik chief as "feudal princes" who felt that central decisions "were not written for them, but for fools." He noted that local officials did their best "to hide the real situation in the countryside" from Moscow, and complained that local officials did not fulfill central directives. "These overconceited bigwigs think that they are irreplaceable, and that they can violate the decisions of the leading bodies with impunity."[97]

Old Bolshevik practices also resembled those of aristocrats and nobles in their everyday practice. Our current access to archival documents gives us a good picture of how a Bolshevik worked. If we look not at sensational documentary revelations but rather at more mundane day-to-day workflow in the Politburo, Orgburo, Secretariat, and below, we see that Soviet politicians spent much of their time refereeing, judging, and choosing among options submitted to them from below.

Indeed, one's formal rank, one's level in the office-holding hierarchy, was really about the level of dispute one was authorized to resolve, and that in turn was based on one's personal prestige or proximity to a powerful grandee. Senior TsK department heads could resolve some of these, if the prestige of those involved was at their level or below. More serious disputes, or those involving participants of higher rank, went to the Orgburo. Sometimes, because of the power of the contestants or the complexity of the dispute, some matters could not be resolved short of the "supreme court," the Politburo, and that body's protocols are full of sessions in which judging disputes was the main activity.[98]

Refereeing disputes submitted from below is of course not specific to Russia; executives in the contemporary business world do the same thing. But in modern systems, procedures and policymaking tend to follow patterns of established impersonal rules to a far greater extent than in either old or modern Russia, where it seems that dispute resolution occupied officials far more than elsewhere.

Judging, of course, is the most ancient form of political leadership. Before they became administrators or governors, ancient tribal chieftains and then kings were basically judges who resolved disputes among their followers. Later, the rendering of noble justice depended on the standing of the claimants and the power of the judge. The first Russian law code, Iaroslav the Wise's *Russkaia Pravda,* was a guide to judging, a writing down of practices whereby disputes between and among claimants of various stations should be resolved. As Max Weber put it of an earlier age, "administrative officials are at the same time judges, and the prince himself, intervening at will into the administration. . . . The boundaries between law and ethics are then torn down just as those between legal coercion and paternal monition, and between legislative motives, ends, and techniques."[99] That Old Bolsheviks engaged in a similar system of dispute resolution again suggests parallels with aristocracies and nobilities.

Personal and personnel disputes worked their way up the network of senior politicians to be refereed and adjudicated. Informal "Party Courts" resolved slights, insults, and slanders between Old Bolsheviks. As we shall see, personnel disputes arose between a current boss (who might not want to release a subordinate) and the future boss to whom the person was to be reassigned. Depending on the ranks of those involved, such disputes percolated up to an appropriate level where, given the ranks of those involved, an appropriately senior Old Bolshevik could resolve them.

Despite Lenin's famous plan in *What is to Be Done?,* the fact of the matter was that Bolsheviks—especially senior ones—had always worked more or less independently or as ad hoc collections of militants on specific tasks. The knights of the revolution did what they wanted, or what they thought necessary, when they wanted. They were unused to showing up at someone's order or obeying the missives of some far-away committee of their aristocratic peers. They understood orders as requests or suggestions and took on new jobs only if they agreed with them, or if the request came from someone they liked, respected, or trusted. This sense of personal privilege was built into the party personnel assignment system.[100]

We saw above how Trotsky refused a position beneath his station. From the beginning it was understood that party members, especially ranking ones but not only they, had a "right of refusal." In fact, there was a line on the personnel department's worksheet for each appointment for "Agreement of the comrade to the transfer?"[101] And often the comrade did not agree.

Oppositionists are best known for defying and refusing the assignments of the TsK. Trotsky was famous for reading novels in Politburo meetings and refusing to participate there.[102] In 1921, Alexander Shliapnikov of the Workers' Opposition stated to the Orgburo "that he will not submit to the Orgburo, that he will not go to work in food production."[103] Rank-and-file Communists resented senior oppositionist princes refusing assignments and expecting permanent tenure [*nesmeniaemost'*] in their current positions. In 1923, Stalin spoke for them at the end of his account of Trotsky's refusal of a deputy appointment on the grounds that this would finish him as a Soviet worker:

> "Of course, comrades, it's a matter of taste, but I don't think that Comrades Rykov, Tsiurupa, Kamenev were finished as Soviet workers when they became deputies of Sovnarkom, but Comrade Trotsky thinks otherwise, and in any case, the TsK was not responsible [*ni pri chem*]. Evidently, Comrade Trotsky has some motive, some understanding that prevents him from accepting nonmilitary work, however difficult it may be. I repeat, the TsK is not the problem.[104]

Refusing to be transferred outside Moscow, Trotskyist Ivan Smil'ga remained there in Gosplan. Trotsky showed up only twice per month at the Council of National Economy. Later, at the Chief Concessions Committee which he headed, he stayed at home, using the 'committee's secretariat to gather materials for the Opposition.[105] Stalin noted at the 12th Party Congress that if oppositionist grandees declined to accept new positions, there was little the TsK could do about it.[106]

As the Stalin Revolution took off in the early 1930s, the enthusiasm and militancy of the modernization drive reduced refusals, as party duty was more and more emphasized. But refusals still happened, for the shortage of experienced cadres meant that bureaucratic veterans were typically offered their choice of positions, along with the right of refusal.

In general, Old Bolsheviks were prima donnas, quick to take offense and quick to defend their honor in ways that appear anachronistic among people who considered themselves the most modern and democratic. They postured, posed, and wrote florid letters about why their accomplishments and opinions were important, why they should not be subordinated to various persons or committees, or how they had been subjected to insupportable slights and unbearable insults from other comrades. This was party culture; everything was personal. Even at the height of the Civil War, when the regime was in danger, slights and insults that might have resulted in duels in an earlier age actually occupied the time of senior party bodies, as Bolshevik notables defended their honor and vigorously challenged slights against it.

Much of the time of senior party committees was taken up judging these spats. Entire party organizations were created for the sole purposes of resolving feuds and personal slights between and among party members. At senior levels, feuds found their way to the agendas of top party bodies for personal and reputational adjudication at the highest levels of the organization, even when it was fighting a civil war for survival.

Iakov Sverdlov, his wife Klavdiia Nogorodtseva, N. Krestinskii, and M. Vladimirskii began meeting informally in January 1919 as an "organizational buro." Already at their second meeting, they had to deal with a "personal conflict" between Comrades Piliaev and Rapoport. Krestinskii was charged with preparing a report and letter on the matter.[107]

In April of 1919, as a Polish offensive was chasing the Red Army out of Vilnius, A. I. Rykov informed the Orgburo that despite orders to do so, he could not possibly move out of his current apartment until renovation of the new one was completed. Considering the matter, the Orgburo ordered Comrade Mal'kov to repair the windows and doors of Rykov's flat.[108]

In 1920, as Wrangel's forces were still pressing the Red Army, Elena Stasova found it personally insulting to be transferred from Baku, obliging the Orgburo to take the time to "communicate to Comrade Stasova that the TsK's transfer of her from Baku does not reflect any lack of confidence."[109] That same summer, a few days after the Poles once again stormed Vilnius, the Orgburo had to take time to "express confidence" in a group of Mikhail Frunze's assistants who felt "morally insulted" at the indignity of being searched on a train.[110] Precisely when peasant uprisings and ferment at the Kronstadt naval base were threatening the new regime, Comrade Angarskii nevertheless found it intolerably insulting when in a speech Bukharin referred to Angarskii's previous expulsion from the party, even though he had been readmitted. Spending precious time investigating Bukharin's speech and Angarskii's record, the Orgburo decided that Bukharin had indeed been "tactless."[111]

As with the Orgburo and Politburo, the files of the Central Control Commission (TsKK) in 1920–24 are filled with accusations of personal insult, pique, complaint, and countercomplaint.[112] In April and May of 1921, among many other cases, the TsKK Presidium considered the fact that Comrade Malyshev made "rude remarks" about Comrade Avanesov, the "Statement of Comrade Kaidanovskii that Comrade Mrachkovskii slandered him," and the "Statement of a whole series of comrades about the rude references of Comrade Kuziakov."[113] Comrade Smil'ga was obliged to take back a complaint against Iaroslavskii's remarks in a speech, while Iaroslavskii had to admit that his remarks about Smil'ga had been "too sharp."[114]

In 1924, Mel'nichanskii accused Semkov of "political careerism," but the TsKK hearing found no evidence of it. Comrade Bogashevskaia denounced Meshcheriakov for "uncommunist conduct" but the TsKK hearing board could find "no facts to support it."[115] In 1923, the national party journal *Izvestiia TsK VKP(b)* devoted an entire column to Comrade Sosnovskii's assertion that Comrade Meerzon, Responsible Party Secretary in Tula, was a "chance element" in the party. Eventually three high-ranking commissions dealt with the charge and finally concluded that Meerzon "deserved the confidence of the party and was an honest member."[116]

While most Old Bolsheviks had a strong sense of honor and pride, some were more touchy, and others were simply poseurs. In 1920, Karl Radek took up the Orgburo's time with a statement that he could not take upon himself the editing of *Vestnik propagandy i agitatsii* without immediately receiving an office in the Kremlin and a secretary.[117] The following year, he accused trade representative Stomoniakov of currency speculation, personal business trading and "for 15 years having nothing in common with the workers' movement." After hearing from Radek, Stomoniakov, Krasikov, and other senior Bolsheviks, the TsKK Presidium concluded that there was nothing shady about Stomoniakov, and that "as far as Radek is concerned, he exercised a total lack of care in passing around false information and making completely baseless accusations."[118] In April 1921, Radek again demanded from the TsK Secretariat a new office, secretary, and stenographer; he would not fulfill the TsK's orders unless he got them. The Secretariat agreed to find him an office, but "recognized Comrade Radek's declaration as an impermissible ultimatum."[119] Later that year, the TsKK demanded "written explanations" from Radek about his possible slander of Zinoviev in criticizing the latter's speech on the German Revolution.[120] Alexander Shliapnikov's comparison of the methods of the political police (GPU) with those of the tsarist Okhrana was taken as a personal slander against GPU chief Feliks Dzerzhinskii, and Shliapnikov was forced to apologize.[121]

Sometimes honor was injured not by the words of a fellow noble but by an entire organization. In 1919, the Orgburo considered "the declaration of Comrade Roslavets that he considers it impossible to continue political work for the Moscow Cheka in view of the fact that the Moscow Committee declined his candidacy as a member of the Moscow Cheka collegium." (The Orgburo expressed "full confidence" in Roslavets and begged him to continue. He did.)[122] In 1921, the Orgburo refereed the request of the Samara Gubkom to recall Comrade Khataevich and with Solomonic wisdom decided

> a. to explain to Comrade Khataevich that in his criticism of the work of the Gubkom he did not properly stay within the bounds of party rules and discipline;
> b. To explain to the Samara Gubkom that the TsK does not see sufficient grounds to recall him only because he criticized the Gubkom from within the party organization.[123]

In Ivanovo-Voznesensk, an old revolutionary stronghold, local Old Bolshevik underground veterans were offended when gubkom party secretary Zorin mismanaged the funeral of Comrade Balashev, one of their number. Eventually, dozens of them signed a letter accusing Zorin of "not paying the necessary attention to Old Bolsheviks . . . which does not correspond to the historical and customary traditions of the

Ivanovo-Voznesensk organization." A three-man team led by Kaganov-ich had to come from Moscow to referee the matter. It recommended quickly and quietly removing Zorin before the matter spread to lower ranks. The Orgburo approved.[124]

When the Caucasus Buro of the party reversed a decision of Rostov-on-Don Responsible Secretary Alexander Beloborodov, his pride was so injured that he insisted on being transferred: "Such a situation puts me in an impossibly weak position if I remain in Rostov to work. . . . every future step I would take would be regarded as a continuation of previous mistakes. Naturally, in such a situation it would make no sense to leave me in Rostov for party work." In the same letter, inveter-ate complainer Beloborodov took the opportunity to chastise Zinoviev for an insult the latter had uttered in a speech about the Soviet Labor Army Beloborodov helped run.

> This characterization, based on completely false information, has so far not been disavowed and apparently will not be. Obviously, to re-main further in my post as Deputy Chairman of the Labor Army is impossible for me . . .
> On the basis of all this, I ask the TsK to reexamine the question of my statement and order me to the Wrangel front where I agree to take up any useful post.

The Orgburo decided instead to approve a one-month vacation for Beloborodov. When he returned, Beloborodov tried again to get out of Rostov, asking to be sent to the Urals. Two months later, he asked to be sent to Crimea. The Orgburo declined both requests and left him in Rostov. He renewed his attempt to get out of Rostov in March 1921, and only succeeded in getting transferred out eight months later.[125]

Old Bolshevik grandees' thin skins were accompanied by what might appear to be hypochondria. Beloborodov was famous for such com-plaints. In 1924, he actually produced a doctor's note stating that his refusal to take a proffered position would injure his health.[126] Trotsky's bouts with "nerves," which prevented him from attending crucial party meetings, like Beloborodov's complaints, may or may not have been simply diplomatic. Still, it was common for Old Bolsheviks to com-plain of "liver pains," angina, sciatica, and a variety of other ailments.

It is true that senior Old Bolsheviks worked themselves hard, day and night. It is not surprising, therefore, that such grandees were entitled to one or two months' vacation per year to be approved in each case by the Orgburo or Politburo. So many of them liked to take "treatments" and "cures" abroad that the Orgburo ordered that without exception, TsK approval for such treatment would be given only to those who were really ill.[127]

But given the propensity to complain about their health, it was hard to know. One comrade couldn't do his job because of self-diagnosed "most extreme illnesses (Siberian ulcer, a bloated liver, and expanded spleen)."[128] N. I. Ezhov, known to be a hard worker and not a complainer, nevertheless said that he suffered from "almost [?] 7 illnesses." At various times he had been treated for tuberculosis, anemia, malnutrition, angina, sciatica, exhaustion, and colitis.[129]

In 1934, while on holiday in Vienna, Ezhov was treated by a Dr. Noorden, who prescribed radioactive baths for a variety of ailments. Ezhov reported that after the treatment, he felt poorly at first, but then better.[130] Rather than being labeled a quack, Dr. Noorden became all the rage among health-conscious Politburo members. In 1936, he was invited to bring his cure to Moscow to treat ailing senior grandees.[131] The Politburo ordered Noorden treatments for Chubar', Ordzhonikidze, Ezhov, Kosior, Dmitrov, Gamarnik, Badaev, Piatnitskii, and others.[132]

The prevalence of dispute and disagreement among touchy Old Bolsheviks was so much a part of the system that dispute mechanisms were always part of the charter of an organization. The founding charters (often call *polozhenie*) of the Orgburo, Secretariat, TsKK, Orgraspred, and other bodies obligatorily contained explicit points about how to resolve disagreements and procedures for appeal to higher instances. Disputes were thus considered inevitable and rules for adjudicating them were an essential part of an organization's founding. The Bolsheviks even created a special separate agency, the Conflict Department, to handle the volume of disputes.

Neither the Politburo nor the Orgburo had been created to referee the wounded pride of Old Bolsheviks, but they soon found themselves doing just that. So much so, that a Central Control Commission (TsKK) was established by the 10th Party Congress in 1921 to handle disputes, accusations, and charges of ethical violations. According to its charter,

Control commissions are being established in order to strengthen the unity and authority of the party and their tasks include combating bureaucratism and careerism ... abuse by party members of their party and soviet positions, infringement of comradely relations in the party, dissemination of unfounded and unsubstantiated rumors and insinuations which bring disgrace ... to individual members.[133]

The TsKK is best known as a weapon Stalin used later in the 1920s against ideological opponents on the left: Trotskyists, Zinovievists and others. But as its charter indicates, it was also originally intended to deal with cases in which party members put their individual personal interests above comradely relations by committing crimes or spreading rumors or accusations that disgraced their peers. We shall see below, however, that there was no contradiction between the two. At the time, party members equated "opposition" with unprincipled personal attacks and intrigues.

From the beginning, the agendas of the Politburo, Orgburo, and TsKK were crowded with affronts to honor. To handle the volume, the TsK created a separate department in 1920, the Conflict Subdepartment of the Organizational Department (*Konfliktnyi pod/otdel,* or Kp/o], with regional affiliates, to deal with personal accusations.[134] Thus, Comrade Kaidanovskii's accusation that Comrade Mrachkovskii had slandered him was referred by the TsKK to the Kp/o. Comrade Kovylkin's "protest" that Comrade Smil'ga had wrongly arrested him was also sent there.[135]

For the few months in 1920–21 for which we have data, it is clear that the Kp/o was itself swamped. One to two hundred new cases arrived each month, joining the steady backlog of two to three hundred cases still unresolved. The Kp/o was not able to process even the new cases each month, and fell further and further behind.[136]

But the chief problem with the Conflict Subdepartment was turf confusion and status consciousness. Rather than taking upon itself the mass of honor accusations and violations, it rather became simply the fourth body to deal with them, along with the Politburo, Orgburo, and TsKK. The lines between and among these competencies were never spelled out. While Kaidanovskii's and Kovylkin's accusations were referred to the Kp/o, when higher dignitaries were involved the matter went straight to higher bodies. Beloborodov's and Zinoviev's mutual attacks, for instance, went straight to the Orgburo.

This made it easy for party members and organizations to simply ignore the Kp/o, since it seemed the least authoritative of the bodies dealing with personal slights and offenses. Forms were printed up under the letterhead of the TsK to impress the recipient:

Second Notice

Immediately communicate why our order No. _____ of [date] on Comrade _____ has not been implemented.

[signed] Chief of Orgotdel
[signed] Chief of Kp/o[137]

Not even the highest party bodies had a clear idea what kind of complaint, appeal or slight should go where.

Surely someone other than the Presidium of the TsKK should have heard the appeal of "Uncle Vania" of Eisk, out in Krasnodar. Uncle Vania ("his real name is Dobrei") complained that the Eisk party organization had wrongly expelled him for theft. He asked for readmission. Instead, the TsKK decided to expel Dobrei ("he is Uncle Vania") for good, without the right to reapply, and to put him under police surveillance.[138]

In November 1920, the Orgburo sent to the TsKK a "communication about the Orgburo's impressions of the dividing line between the work of the Kp/o and the TsKK" and asked for clarification. Along with its communication, the Orgburo sent Comrade Preobrazhenskii to discuss the matter. The TsKK's eventual reply was vague, noting that "all complaints directed to the TsK or the TsKK should go directly to the TsKK. All remaining materials were to be transferred to the Kp/o of the TsK RKP(b)." This was not particularly helpful; because complaints were almost always directed to the TsK or the TsKK, it was not clear what the "remaining materials" would be.

Moreover, the TsKK itself frequently referred complaints to the Kp/o without apparent rhyme or reason.[139] In early 1921, the TsKK's order "On the activities of the Conflict Subdepartment" instructed TsKK inspector Chelishev to acquaint himself with files inside and outside the Kp/o's competence.[140] The confusion continued for nearly a year after that, until January 1922 when the Orgburo set up a commission to study the continued existence of the Kp/o. The commission recommended abolishing Kp/os in the regions and returning to the former system whereby party committees and control commissions refereed the disputes.[141] Soon thereafter, the Kp/o was disbanded.

The Kp/o failed because of the personalized nature of noble Old Bolshevik culture. No grandee was interested in being judged by some committee of who-knew-what kind of clerks. Senior boyars insisted on being judged by their peers, and no institution was going to tell them what to do. That meant continuing to refer such matters to the Secretariat, Orgburo, and Politburo, as well as to the TsKK whose top bodies (Presidium and Collegium) contained grandees of appropriate rank to judge their equals.

☆

Soviet communism's debt to the past is not a new idea. Nikolai Berdyaev and others have described the connection of communist ideology to religion, and particularly to Russian Orthodoxy. For Berdyaev, even as the communists were "controlled by motives which belong to the world of ideas; they are inspired by their own religious faith. . . . The best type of communist . . . is a possibility only as the result of the Christian training of the human spirit."[142] Even as they violently stamped out religion, they created a communist one.[143] Similarly, Stephen White suggests that when it came to power "the new Bolshevik government was scarcely likely to relinquish the extensive controls of its predecessor when the lives of its leaders were in danger and its very existence was at stake."[144]

Of course, there is a danger in overstressing continuities. Many Soviet practices had no antecedents in Russian history and many traditional practices did not survive 1917. Yves Cohen is right to warn that "an entire explanation cannot be reached by simply referring to ancient forms already known under tsarism, be they religious or political or both. The intersection of government acts and popular practices . . . was produced in a particular historical moment. Each practice in its own right was itself partially a political interpretation of tradition in context. People borrowed some aspects of traditional forms while rejecting others, their selection being governed by actual exigencies in the situation at hand."[145]

On the other hand, it would be equally improbable to imagine the Stalinists consciously picking and choosing from a menu of traditional practices. Obviously, as Stephen White suggests, the new Bolshevik regime realized that some of the imperial political tools (like a centralized state and a secret police) were useful. But the Old Bolsheviks did not choose to become heirs to Russian nobility and would hotly deny that they had done so. That personalized system was embedded in Russian history and their adherence to it was not self-reflective.

An oligarchy mindful of an elite mission and fearful of chaos would likely organize itself a certain way, mindfully or not, especially if that way came from familiar culture. This was simply the way one governed, and it is easy to imagine the Bolsheviks stepping into continuities without giving conscious thought to choosing among them. The original functional purpose of the oligarchy + tsar practice—to militarily defend an open plain and keep the peace among the grandees—no longer existed. But the practice had become embedded in Russian political culture. For the Bolsheviks, it was not so much a matter of selecting a tool. As Bourdieu put it, "What is essential *goes without saying because it comes without saying:* the tradition is silent, not least about itself as tradition."[146]

Few of the Old Bolsheviks were more than one generation from the Russian village with its traditional practices, and the language and genres of their texts, the importance they attached to and the control they exercised over awards, their sense of collective responsibility and of elite roles were often unconscious inheritances. In one way or another, these practices and forms of social organization were therefore unconsciously functional. Patrimonialism, oligarchic privilege, and the like were a logical response to the fear of chaos, as well as to a fear of losing power.

Indeed, for an anthropologist, it would be surprising if Bolsheviks (and Russians) in 1917 suddenly transformed themselves completely, stepping out of their thousand-year-old culture and functional practices and looking at themselves from outside. We should not leap to the conclusion that they could dispense with these practices, or chose to do so, just because of their futurist political outlook. They were the heirs, if not prisoners, of centuries of assumptions, among these an understanding of politics—and indeed of the state itself—as personal, and it is to this that we now turn.

2 Cults and Personalities, Politics and Bodies

It goes without saying that neither we nor our comrades wanted to make a relic of the remains of V. I. Lenin by means of which we could popularize or maintain the memory of Vladimir Ilich.

—*Avel Enukidze, 1924*

I'm not Stalin. Stalin is Soviet power. Stalin is what he is in the newspapers and portraits, not you, no, not even me.

—*Stalin, to his son*

THE CULTS OF both Lenin and Stalin followed Russian traditions of seeing the body of the ruler as the direct embodiment of the state. But comparing them, we see key differences. Lenin's cult began spontaneously, while Stalin's was much more a deliberate political tool of the leadership from the beginning. Both cults, however, were quickly accepted by the population. These were not the only cults in the Soviet Union; leadership "cultism" penetrated all levels of the elite. Our attention is therefore drawn not only to the manufacture and reception of cults, but to their role as "communication between ruler and ruled," and in particular to how they symbolized a "culture of paternalism" in Russian history.[1] We shall see that personality cults not only were a symbol or reflection of a personalized understanding of politics, but were inherent in and a necessary product of them. This chapter asks why political cults of leadership found such fertile soil in Russia.

☆

We might begin with the notion of permanently preserving Lenin's body and making it accessible to the public. There was no precedent for this in Bolshevik thinking. Insofar as there was a party tradition, it was spelled out by Old Bolshevik M. S. Ol'minskii: "I am a long time supporter of the funeral ritual which the Party advocates. I think that all survivals of religious practice (coffins, funerals, the leave-taking from the corpse or cremation and all that) are nonsense. It is more pleasant for me to think that my body will be used more rationally. It should be sent to a factory without any ritual, and in the factory the fat should be used for technical purposes and the rest for fertilizer. I beg the Central Committee most seriously on this matter."[2] Agreeing with Ol'minskii, another comrade willed his body to a soap factory.[3] For its part, Russian Orthodox tradition rejected cremation and prescribed burial in the earth, but did allow for perpetual display of body relics of saints. In spite of their anticlericalism, however, Bolsheviks simply could not bear to see Lenin under the dirt.

So how did the Bolsheviks arrive at the unique solution we know today? The final result owes more to Russian tradition than to ashes or soap factories, or even to monuments in principle. Here, the archaic past intrudes. Russian Orthodox (and earlier pagan traditions) saw the undecayed body as a magical sign of holiness. Vladimir Putin has said that embalming Lenin was consistent with Russian traditions: "Go to the Kiev Caves Monastery, or take the Pskov Monastery or Mount Athos. There are relics of sacred people there, and in this sense the Communists captured tradition."[4] Orthodox saints' bodies do not decay, and through the centuries accidental disinterment of a body that had not decayed was sufficient reason for canonization. To the traditional Russian unconscious, therefore, Saint Lenin's undecayed remains naturally and unconsciously represented a connection to something transcendental—and something political.

Lenin's mausoleum is a strange combination of the ancient and the modern. Of course, relics of a saint and especially of a head of state need to be housed properly, and visitors to the mausoleum in Soviet times will remember the reverent atmosphere. There was no more sacred space in the USSR, and it recalled nothing so much as a traditional Orthodox church. In a generally darkened room where you could not see the corners—and therefore the limits—of the sacred space, as in a cathedral, the body was lit by modern floodlights that correspond to the ancient lighting of candles in a sanctuary that directed light to holy icons.

In the old days, the front door to the mausoleum was a bit ajar. The other Russian type of door left intentionally just a bit ajar is the sacred door in a church's iconostasis on holy days, a door that leads to a sacred space that can only be entered by priests. Moreover, as one child told me, "Lenin might need to get out." In fact, in the myth of "Clever Lenin" (based on a similar fable about the deceased Alexander I) Lenin periodically wakes up and wanders the Russian land checking on how things are going.[5]

While the radically modern Bolsheviks were renouncing religion and spiritual belief, they were making an ancient statement about immortality. Keeping the body preserved and on display somehow negated time, and therefore death. Every Soviet schoolchild was taught the slogan, "Lenin lived, Lenin lives, Lenin will live." In death, therefore, Lenin became a charismatic figure with a connection to the transcendent, the immortal.[6]

For the body itself, the traditional gave way to the modern. Aside from the constructivist architecture chosen to house the saint, the modern requirements of security blended seamlessly with religious reverence and respect: as in church, one could not put one's hands in one's pockets. The traditional magic of physical preservation was replaced by a chemical process invented in a laboratory. The undecayed relics of the saint were housed not only in the most modernist structure of its time, but directly above an underground pathology laboratory with the latest equipment.

How did this semiotic mixture come about? Were the Bolsheviks aware of the dissonance between ancient and modern?

Nothing would be easier and more obvious than to imagine that upon Lenin's death his successors—with Stalin in the lead—quickly gathered in a back room and immediately understood the utility of preserving, displaying, and worshiping his body. A top-down manufactured cult of Lenin would then provide a substitute religion for the peasants, complete with the sainted founder's relics, to replace the Russian Orthodoxy they were trying to destroy. It would enhance the legitimacy of Lenin's successors and of the regime in general by tracing that regime's descent from a founder, who was rapidly and intentionally becoming a mythical progenitor on whose pyramid the successor acolytes would stand to demonstrate their lineage.

This was certainly the final result; Lenin was branded and marketed by the regime as a useful symbol.[7] But this does not mean that the

Bolsheviks freely picked and chose among ancient and modern symbols from the beginning for a utilitarian purpose. This would assume that they were aware of the dissonance between their futuristic transformational goals and the archaic means they were using and didn't care about it. This idea, which is not uncommon in the scholarly literature, assumes that the Bolsheviks had a plan. This question—did they know what they were doing when they used ancient practices in the pursuit of modernist goals—is one we will ask again in the course of our analysis. And, as with all questions about the intentions of historical figures, there are no easy or definite answers. Here it seems that there was no plan, no major role for Stalin but rather a series of contradictory, ad hoc, and contested proposals reflecting input both from below and above. Lenin's successors stumbled and bumbled for a long time about what to do with his body.

First of all, it seems that Stalin had little if anything to do with the decision to permanently display Lenin. He was not on the Lenin Funeral Commission, chaired by Feliks Dzerzhinskii, where such decisions were made, and his associate Kliment Voroshilov, who was a member, bitterly opposed the idea. Stalin was a member of the Politburo, which, as it turned out, approved all the recommendations of the commission, but he seems to have played no active role in the decision. According to rumors that surfaced decades later (in the 1960s), Stalin had been the initiator of the idea to mummify Lenin even before Lenin died, having supposedly suggested it at an informal meeting of Politburo members in 1923, at which time Trotsky vehemently opposed the idea. This story is quite improbable on its face. The idea that such a careful political tactician as Stalin would openly talk about disposing of Ilich's body while the latter was still alive, and in the presence of his arch-rival Trotsky, borders on the ridiculous. The senior leaders would consider it unpardonably crude to have such a discussion while their dear Lenin lived, and Stalin would certainly not have handed Trotsky such a faux pas on a platter.[8]

It is clear that in later years the Lenin cult was deliberately and instrumentally cultivated for utilitarian purposes by Stalin and others. But at the time of Lenin's death, the archival record is not so clear about the origins and presumed planned nature of the cult.

The original idea was to bury Lenin. On 24 January 1924, the Politburo decided to inter him next to Iakov Sverdlov near the Kremlin wall.[9] On 26 January, Bukharin told the Congress of Soviets that soon

Lenin would go "into the grave."[10] At Lenin's funeral the next day, chief orator G. Evdokimov said "we are burying Lenin," and at the end of the ceremony radio stations across the country reported that "Ilich is being lowered into his grave."[11]

The decision to preserve and display Lenin's body was taken incrementally over a period of years, and it was not until 1929–30 that his resting place was finalized in the stone mausoleum. At first, on 24 January 1924, Lenin was put in the Kremlin's Hall of Columns for viewing by the public. Professor Abrikosov embalmed the body in customary fashion so it would last the three days until the funeral and burial. Nobody contemplated a longer viewing. Two days later, the huge crowds obliged the Politburo to order moving the display to Red Square near the Kremlin wall.[12] Architect A. V. Shchusev was quickly conscripted to design and build a temporary structure there which was thrown together by 27 January. The crowds kept coming, and soon Shchusev was charged with designing a larger structure that was completed some weeks later. But it was not made to last. It was a wooden structure called the "temporary mausoleum."

Meanwhile, during the extended viewing period, "time did its work,"[13] and Lenin's body began to decay. The Dzerzhinskii Commission was consequently faced with making a longer-term decision about the body.[14] In February, commission member and engineer Leonid Krasin claimed that he could preserve the body through freezing, and on the seventh the commission authorized him to buy expensive German machinery for that purpose.[15] By 14 March, the body continued to deteriorate and although Krasin continued to defend the freezing idea, the commission brought in Professors Zbarskii and Vorob'ev with a new chemical procedure for long-term preservation.[16] It was not until 26 July that the commission made the final decision to embalm and display Lenin forever, based on Zbarskii and Vorob'ev's procedure.[17]

Already while Lenin had been in the Hall of Columns, rumors were circulating that popular pressure and the opinions of some Bolsheviks favored preserving the body "for some time and to build a crypt or vault."[18] But when the question came up in the Dzerzhinskii Commission, at first in the form of whether or not even to have an open casket, there was sharp debate which A. Enukidze later euphemistically called "fluster about preserving V. I.'s body. . . . There was a lot of hesitation and doubt among members of the Commission."[19] Thus at its meeting of

23 January, senior Bolsheviks T. Sapronov and K. V. Voroshilov took sharp issue with N. I. Muralov's suggestion to display the body. According to Voroshilov, "We must not resort to canonization. That would be SR-like. . . . [20] We would stop being Marxist-Leninists. If Lenin heard Muralov's speech, he would hardly compliment him. Really, cultured people would cremate the body and put the ashes in an urn." Otherwise, Voroshilov said, we would be hypocrites: peasants would note that we were destroying their god and replacing it with our own sacred relics.[21]

Rather than take a firm decision on preserving Lenin, commission members Dzerzhinskii and K. Avanesov avoided taking a principled stand. As Dzerzhinskii put it, "To be principled in this question is to be principled in quotation marks." Would Lenin have approved? Probably not, Dzerzhinskii admitted, because he was a person of exceptional modesty. But he's not here; we have only one Lenin who is not here to judge, and the question is what to do with his body. He brushed aside deep questions, noting that everybody loved Lenin. Pictures of him were treasured; everyone wanted to see him. Lenin was a truly special person. "He is so dear to us that if we can preserve the body and see it, then why not do it?" "If science can really preserve the body for a long time, then why not do it?" "If it is impossible, then we won't do it." For Dzerzhinskii, the question was not "why" but "why not?"[22] Although the Voroshilov faction was still unhappy, the Dzerzhinskii group won the day and reported this "why not?" recommendation to the Politburo, which approved it.

Dzerzhinskii's avoidance of a stand on principle is the closest we have to a specific time and place where a decision was made and justified about preserving Lenin's body. It was rather an incremental process. Step by step, the Bolsheviks adopted traditional if not archaic means, combining them with modern aspects and goals. Did they sense this dissonance? Sometimes they did. It was almost as if the party was somehow schizophrenic, arguing with itself, rationalizing, reassuring itself, and compromising.

And there were arguments. Protests against these archaic practices were met with counterarguments that seemed strained. In reply to those who feared SR-like focus on a personality, Dzerzhinskii made the hair-splitting claim that "this is not a cult of personality, but to a certain extent a cult of Vladimir Ilich." Voroshilov, as we saw above, was afraid of the hypocrisy and person-worship that preservation of the body would involve. He feared creating religious "relics." Dzerzhinskii replied that they couldn't be relics because "relics were about magic and miracles and this was different."[23] But was it?

When Muralov suggested that preserving the body and displaying it could be advantageous (*vygodno*) to the regime, Voroshilov exploded. Muralov's idea was "nonsense" (*chepukha*), and "disgraceful" (*pozor*).[24] Voroshilov had been to London and seen Marx's grave, which had touched him although "nobody saw his face which was completely unnecessary." When someone suggested that such a monument would enhance the memory of Lenin, Enukidze replied with yet more casuistry, "It goes without saying that neither *we* nor our comrades wanted to make a relic of the remains of V. I. Lenin by means of which *we* could popularize or maintain the memory of Vladimir Ilich. The memory of this great man is great enough all over the world." "We want to preserve Lenin not to simply popularize his name but rather to attach great meaning to preserving the face, the image (*oblik*) of this great leader for the next generation and for future generations and also for those hundreds of thousands and maybe millions of people who would be made happy to see the face of this person."[25]

Other Bolsheviks, like Dzerzhinskii, preferred not to think about the contradictions too much, or rather thought that Lenin was such a special case as to not provoke such reflections. They just did what instinctively seemed natural at the moment: "why not?" They ended up creating a religious space, complete with sacred relic and monumental tomb, but even in their private counsels furiously denied to each other that they were doing that. When some took it that way, the elite continued to deny the religious aspect.

Of ten members of the commission, eight were village born, as were more than half of the members of the Central Committee. It is not so difficult to imagine internal conflict between their newly acquired positivism and the culture they grew up in. When they or some among them had doubts about what seemed natural, about contradicting the scientific rationalism they claimed, they went ahead and did the natural thing, the intuitive thing, the thing that combined science and superstition, while at the same time denying—even to themselves—they were doing it. Somewhere in the back of their minds, Lenin was a saint.

Another conflicted example is the odd practice whereby for decades the Politburo stood on Lenin's tomb—literally on his body—and thus faced the public on ceremonial occasions. Here the body receded into the background (as if it could), and the discourse was about meetings, not bodies. For Bolsheviks the mausoleum was said to have a "living feel" instead of a dead character (as if it could) and the mausoleum became a "proletarian tribune," a *place d'armes* of the revolution" and a presidium for mass meetings on Red Square.[26] While standing on the body, they tried to think of it as just another speakers' stand. One wonders if they really could.

The "temporary" wooden mausoleum stood from spring 1924 to 1929 when the final permanent structure we know today was built. Nobody could decide what to do. Committee after committee of architects, artists, and officials from the Commissariat of Enlightenment studied and debated sketches and proposals for years.[27] There was a scandal about architect Shchusev being a member of the jury to pick the final project.[28] The composition of the jury changed constantly before a decision could be reached. As late as 6 May 1929, the leadership decided to reconstitute the jury because many of its original members were dead or working elsewhere.[29]

The same kind of schizophrenia that characterized their thoughts on the body also plagued them when it came to "monumentalism" itself. Many thought that it ill suited a proletarian state to build lavish monuments to individuals. Even Lenin's widow N. K. Krupskaia resisted the idea, famously writing in *Pravda,* "Do not build memorials to him, palaces named after him. Do not hold celebrations in his memory etc. . . . If you want to honor the name of Vladimir Ilich, build day care centers, kindergartens, homes, schools, and most importantly try in all things to fulfill his legacy."[30]

As with preserving the body, the resistance to traditional monuments was strong and Bolshevik, so arguments for them also had to be rather inventive. In October–November 1924, senior Bolsheviks Lunacharskii and Krasin made the case for monuments. "The question of monuments should be seen from the point of view of the demands of the revolutionary people." The proletariat, they argued, has a solid sense of history and connection to the past. Proletarian monuments, unlike bourgeois ones, are not mere idols or signposts. Proletarian monuments are "sources of strength taken from the revolutionary masses. . . . A revolutionary monument is an active thing; it is a centralizer and transformer of social strength. . . . Revolutionary society does great deeds and therefore has a need to immortalize itself." "Lenin's tomb has already become a magnetic center for the masses, who visit it and whose literal voices of millions of people show that it answers a profound need of the masses."

They used strained historical analogies. Noting that the Napoleonic era in France was a time of great monuments, Lunacharskii and Krasin attributed that to the earlier revolutionary period. Napoleonic style "organically follows from the style set down in the previous revolutionary era, that is, a uniquely transformed antique." Even further back, pharaohs and other "ancient despotisms" (with which the proletariat would appear to have little affinity) built pyramids and other monuments. As it turned out, however, those regimes were actually "collectivist" [!] groups of a ruling class. "We are an organic unified class doing great things and therefore naturally monumental." The embalmed body of King Tut had been discovered at Luxor a few months before the deliberations about embalming Lenin. No explicit connection was made between the disposition of Lenin's body and ancient mummification, but it must have run through puzzled and conflicted Bolshevik heads. Positioning themselves between the individual-worshiping SRs and the leaderless anarchists, they concluded "We are not anarchists. We have great and brilliant leaders. So we conclude that monuments and monumentalism are completely natural in our revolutionary life."[31] Voroshilov, who resisted displaying the body, thought monuments were fine to maintain memory. After all, he had been to London to see Marx's grave.

So the Bolsheviks convinced themselves that it was acceptable to have a monument to Lenin, either to accommodate crowds or in response to conflicted impulses they themselves could not sort out. But why did they do it the way they did, with the preserved body? Why wouldn't a monument do? They were sometimes aware of and troubled by the archaic elements of Lenin's preservation, but they moved ahead without much questioning; they did what seemed right and natural at each moment.

Although the Bolsheviks were sometime aware of the dissonance between their modern theory and archaic practice, they were almost certainly not aware of what seems the main driving force in their unconscious. They were not aware of the "deep structures" that guided their decision. That decision was part of what Pierre Bourdieu called their *habitus:* the "cognitive and motivating structures" that operate as second nature, "unconsciously, since the history of the habitus is concealed under its subjective nature." Decisions go without saying "because subjects do not, strictly speaking, know what they are doing and that what they do has more meaning than they know."[32]

Why was everything focused on the body rather than a more traditional monumentalism? In remembering his visit to Marx's grave, Voroshilov said that there was no body to look at there, and that a regular monument could produce emotions and maintain memory just as well. To do that, he said, "It's not about a body."

But he was wrong. Of course it was. He just didn't recognize it.

It was not so much about Lenin's body (the contradictions surrounding which they often saw) but about the body in general in Russian political understanding.

In the beginning, of course, an impulse to the official Lenin cult was given when the leadership decided to preserve and display his body to the public in a lavish (and politically useful) monument. At the same time, though, from the very beginning a popular impulse and input stimulated, if not caused and created, the official actions. Thousands of unsolicited condolence letters and telegrams spontaneously poured in.[33] The very decision to move Lenin's body from the Hall of Columns to Red Square had to do with crowd control and was the result of thousands of requests from the public, especially from those unable to reach Moscow in time to see the body during the viewing period originally planned.[34] The decision to build the second, "temporary" wooden and then the third permanent stone mausoleum had similar causes: the people kept coming, more than a hundred thousand in the first six weeks, despite bitter cold.

Much of the cult came from below. Without demands from the leadership, proposals poured in from the provinces to build local monuments to Lenin and to name all kinds of things for him.[35] Without permission, in Cheboksarai they build an exact replica of the mausoleum to be used as a bookselling kiosk. This caused much consternation in Moscow.[36] Sailing in the wake of popular action, the regime quickly understood that they needed to get control of this process, and arrogated to themselves the right to approve or disapprove such requests; nothing could be built without their approval. Subsequently much of the work of the Dzerzhinskii Commission consisted of approving (but mostly disapproving) these proposals, which included everything from a proposal for an electrified mausoleum, complete with lightning bolts, to renaming the calendar months because as one letter-writer said, "Lenin was savior of the world more than Jesus."[37]

Before his death, Lenin was already a "charismatic" leader and his associates bit their rational Marxist tongues to make the connection: "Marx was a prophet with Mosaic tablets and Lenin is the greatest executor of the testaments" (Trotsky). Lenin was "our sun," "a god-sent leader, one of those who is born to mankind once in a thousand years" (Zinoviev). "A prophet of the proletariat" (Bonch-Bruevich).[38]

But it didn't take much coaching for the Russian people to consider Lenin's body to be holy. Upon seeing Lenin's body, "some bowed at the waist, others fell to their knees. . . . Many made vows at the coffin."[39] Letters to the commission complained of "profaning" the mausoleum by selling postcards of it. One worker thought that viewing Lenin's body could have curative powers: "If you were to join the party opposition, you would go to the crypt of Lenin and immediately enter the correct path."[40]

Sociologists have noted a universal human tendency to anthropomorphize political power. Edward Shils thought that it "is rooted in the neural constitution of the human organism" and that its intensity from place to place is based on the prevailing culture.[41] Weber's "charismatic authority" derives from a leader, a prophet, with almost magical powers, whose authority is based on a connection with the transcendent.[42] But Shils showed that in modern times the nonrational "sacred" exists in a mixture with rational-legal authority and is not necessarily linked to or the product of revolution and crisis.[43]

The Lenin cult had deep roots in Russian culture.[44] This cultural upswelling was met from the top not only by the crass manufacture and use of the Lenin cult as a tool, but by a section of the Bolshevik elite, the "God Builders," who believed in an eventual new religion in which humankind would become godlike and immortal. Peasants and some Bolsheviks thought or hoped that Lenin had transcended death. The fight inside the party between the positivist Leninists and the God Builders reflected in macrocosm the inner struggle of Bolsheviks in 1924 about what to do with Lenin's body. It took all these independent inputs to produce the cult.[45]

One of the key identifications for both Bolsheviks and peasants was the connection between the person-body and the state. Throughout Russian history the physical body of the ruler not only symbolized the state; in a real sense it was the state. Louis XIV's claim that he was the state pales in comparison to Russian understanding of the tsar. For centuries, Russians could not comprehend the idea of a state not headed by a person ruling for life with divine sanction. Although they often carried notions of radical reform, social justice, or nostalgia, every revolt and revolution through the centuries had to be led by or fought in favor of a "true tsar," a *person* who by rights should be the ruler. This association was closely bound up with the physical body of the tsar. According to one Russian tradition, the "true tsar" had a "royal mark" on his physical body, be he on the throne or not.[46] Sovereignty, and therefore the rightful power of the "state" was therefore inseparable from the body.

The state was not an idea that could be changed or casually restaffed; it was a matter of the right *person* "sitting." Injustice was the result of either an incorrect ruler or the proper ruler being deceived by evil courtiers. To a great extent, the state was the body and the body was the state. Preserving Lenin's body was presenting and preserving the state, almost as a kind of symbolic continuity—of practice and understanding—with a past the Bolsheviks were simultaneously renouncing.

A statue or simple monument somehow wouldn't do. In a famous analysis of the personal aspects of kingship, Ernst Kantorowicz wrote of the distinction between the "king's two bodies." One of these was his corporeal body, the other his person as head and symbol of the state.[47] Upon his death, his physical body went into the tomb, while his state body continued, perhaps as a statue. As Richard Wortman pointed out, in Russia the king did not have two bodies: a physical one and a political one. In Russia they were the same, or at least the identity was so close as to be imperceptible.[48] When one tsar died, there was no state continuity until a new tsar ruled. Even some emblems of the Soviet state carried Lenin's image, and it took a long time to separate them.

Historically, the body/person of the Russian ruler was always a peculiar fusion of the sacred, the benevolent paternal, the state, and the Russian land. The state could not be an abstraction, a thing in its own right with the tsar as custodian, but rather an object, the tsar's property to do with as he pleased.[49] We can readily see this fusion in Russian terminology and etymology.

The Russian word for "state," *gosudarstvo,* comes from the word *gosudar'* and before it in ancient Slavic, *gospodar',* both meaning master of a household. There is a clear sense of ownership here, with the master owning his household as property. Property without an owner made little sense, and therefore the state was inconceivable as a thing without a person. Similarly, a ruler sacralized by God made no sense without land and people. "The concepts of belonging to *gosudar'* and *gosudarstvo* completely overlapped. The state and state interest were thought of only as concretely embodied in the living person of the *gosudar'* and his affairs."[50] Even in the revolutionary tumult of 1917 when the tsar had fallen and all kinds of authority were questioned, soldiers refused to swear loyalty to the state (*gosudarstvo*) by saying, *net gosudaria, net i gosudarstva,* meaning "there is no master, so there can be no state."[51]

In Russia, the body of the ruler was understood not only in a sacred way but a paternal one. In this sense, rulers were like fathers, who settled disputes and provided protection and security. There was a blending of the ideas of the state and the family; the head of the Soviet state, like the tsar, was a "father." The Russian word for country or homeland is *otechestvo,* which derives from *otets* (father).[52] For centuries Russian peasants called the emperor *tsar-batiushka,* or "little father tsar" and in 1936, one Politburo member could write to another calling Stalin their "wise father" using the rather archaic word *roditel'.*[53] The USSR was a federation of different nationalities, peoples. But in popular usage, Stalin was the "father of the peoples," the patriarch of a patrimonial state. In some perceptual sense, therefore, the person of Stalin *was* the patriarchal state.[54]

The tsar was good, and disasters were not of his making. This "naïve monarchism" was no less genuine for being naïve, and was reflected everywhere. The Kronstadt sailors, even while rising up against Lenin's Bolshevik regime, "spoke of Lenin as a tsar whose wicked boyars prevented him from acting on behalf of the *narod* [people]."[55]

Like a tsar, Lenin and then Stalin was a "wise father." Boris Mironov has called attention to the resemblance between these patriarchal administrations and the Russian family: "There is one elder in the household and all must obey him. This is one of the distinctive characteristics of the Russian people. To look upon this little patriarchal administration is to see in embryo the unquestioning obedience of the Russian people to those in power, as if they were sent by God."[56] The father-ruler was also a provider, and economic relationships were represented as parts of a moral economy in which gifts were exchanged between persons. When Soviet citizens received coal, bread, jobs, or education they regarded them not as the rational benefits of a state but as personal gifts from Comrade Stalin.[57]

The Russian ruler was necessarily sacred, either anointed by God or somehow connected to something eternal and transcendent. During the age of kingship, divine right and otherwise, kings and gods were connected. The king either represented a god or was considered divine himself.[58] In Soviet times, that transcendence could be the laws of history, the prophet Marx, or his disciples Lenin and Stalin and their bodies. No one who has visited Lenin's tomb can escape a feeling of mysticism. Relating political charisma to symbolism, Clifford Geertz suggested that symbolic trappings become reality. "The difference between the symbolic trappings of rule and its substance are transformed into each other. The gravity of high politics and the solemnity of high worship spring from similar impulses."[59]

The transcendent aspects of the political order were inseparable from the tsar's physical body, and the identity was affirmed in various ceremonies, performances, and rituals.[60] Even images of the ruler were sacred. One of Peter the Great's soldiers worshiped Peter's icon.[61] Taking photographs of Lenin's holy body was forbidden from the beginning but guards at Lenin's temporary mausoleum sensed blasphemy and had begun to arrest people for even trying to photograph the mausoleum itself.[62] Stalin's picture, symbolizing his body and person, were sacred images, and people were arrested for even accidentally defacing them. Even today, icons of Stalin periodically appear in Russian churches.[63] In painting Stalin, it was important to follow a formula about his eyes and gaze, just as with the prescriptions for icons. His gaze "was invariably directed at a focal point outside the picture."[64] Today, a sect in the Nizhnyi Novgorod region worships an icon of Vladimir Putin.[65] These sacred images are the tangible symbols of the person-state in Russia.

The identification of the ruler with the state is not unique to Russia, although among "modern" states it persisted the longest there. When the Roman Empire replaced the republic, the person of the emperor was the state, and insults to him personally were considered treason to the state. Later in medieval times, the Roman *laesa maiestas* became *lèse-majesté,* and such insults continued to be regarded as attempts to upset the state, personified by and identified with the ruler. The personal part of the concept died out in western Europe, being transformed into *lèse-nation,* but it persisted in Russia where it was used as a legal basis to persecute outspoken revolutionaries and newspapers. As late as 1910, M. Purishkevich reminded the Russian Duma that insults to the person of Tsar Nicholas II, which Purishkevich called *lèse-majesté,* were punishable by terms of eight years in the galleys.[66] In the Stalin period, insulting the dictator (even by disrespecting his portrait) was chargeable at least as "anti-Soviet agitation," at most as "terrorism." In our more vegetarian times, such draconian punishments have vanished, but the concept of personal insult to the leader as a special crime remains. When activists invaded Putin's reception office in 2004, they were accused of trying to overthrow the state and received prison terms. In December 2011, penalties for insulting Russian officials were doubled, while those for insulting citizens reduced.[67]

Looking back in Russian history, we find a mass of evidence of the importance of the sacred/paternal/stateholder person of the ruler for Russians' understanding of politics, power, and the state. As elsewhere, the prince or tsar held his position "by the grace of God," but in Russia the ruler and polity had long been inseparable. His person, and even images of his person were sacred and powerful, connected as they were to a transcendent power. In the Kievan period, of fourteen grand princes of Kiev, ten were saints. Later, the Riurikid dynasty's Moscow branch ruled Russia for three hundred years, from the early fourteenth to the end of the sixteenth centuries. Of the twelve Moscow rulers, seven were saints. As Mikhail Cherniavsky put it, the state was not an independent abstraction; it received its legitimacy and reality from the holy person of the prince.[68]

When the Riurikid dynasty died out at the end of the sixteenth century with the deaths of Ivan the Terrible's sons, the state in fact ceased to exist, plunging the country into the anarchic Time of Troubles that ended only with the installation of a new person, a proper body, on the throne.[69] We might compare this with the combined chaos and grief surrounding Stalin's death in 1953, when it also seemed that the entire political order of the state might vanish and the authorities feared mass disorder.[70] Tanks guarded the streets. As at the coronation of Nicholas II in 1896, in 1953 people were trampled to death in an attempt to be close to the holy ruling person. In both cases, it was not only a matter of seeking security and order in the continuation of the state that the person embodied; it was a question of wanting to be near the sacred body of the father.

During the Time of Troubles, a series of "False Dmitris" appeared, each claiming to be the son of Ivan IV. The real Dmitri had died under suspicious circumstances in 1591. Because the state made no sense outside the person of a rightful ruler, any group trying to capture political power had to have such a rightful ruler at its helm. The First False Dmitri was followed by the Second False Dmitri, each backed by coalitions of boyars, nobles, and Cossacks. Even those raising revolts against these impostors had their own "true tsars," and by 1608 there were more than twenty of them claiming the state.[71] It was indisputable that the social, political, cultural, and religious aspects of Russian civilization—as well as the state itself—were bound up in the person of the prince or tsar. Without a rightful tsar, there could be no state and chaos and misfortune would surely follow. "Without the tsar, the land is a widow. Without the tsar the people are an orphan," as the Russian saying goes.

From the sixteenth to the nineteenth century, every rebellion had to account for the problem of the "true tsar." Advocating a new social or political order was inconceivable outside the embodiment of that order in a rightful person. Even the most radical rebels could not imagine a state separate from its rightful ruler. That their cause was just was in itself insufficient without the personal leadership of the proper tsar. And because the ruler was by definition holy, if things were amiss in the country there were only a few available answers.

One answer was naïve monarchism. "Rebels in the name of the tsar" fought on the tsar's behalf against evil boyars and great lords.[72] The seventeenth-century Cossack rebel Stenka Razin, like Bolotnikov before him in the sixteenth, fought for the "rightful sovereign."

Another answer was that the person on the throne was an impostor or illegitimate. Because the tsar was holy, bad conditions meant a false tsar on the throne. Although Razin fought for the true tsar on the throne, he kept two impostors in reserve: one was purportedly the tsarevich, the true heir to the throne. The other was a patriarch impostor.[73] In 1705, Moscow soldiers, disgruntled for various reasons, sent letters to Cossacks saying that Tsar Peter the Great was really a changeling, substituted at birth. Another story was that Peter had died or been killed on his European journey and been replaced by a German changeling.[74]

In the eighteenth century, rebel leader Emelian Pugachev claimed to be the rightful Tsar Paul III, and named his lieutenants after Catherine the Great's courtiers. The tradition of pretendership continued down to the nineteenth century. In the seventeenth century there were twenty-three "rightful tsar" pretenders; forty-four in the eighteenth century, eight of whom claimed to be Peter the Great's son Aleksei and sixteen of whom were Peter III, miraculously saved from assassination.[75] There was no state without a tsar, a royal body.[76]

In this patrimonial understanding of government, the prince (later, tsar) was owner of the country as his inheritable patrimonial estate (*votchina*), and bureaucracy, such as it was, consisted of those understood to be his household servitors. Muscovite princes thought of their holdings, parts of which they had seized, inherited, or purchased, as their *votchina,* and they so designated Muscovy in their wills and testaments.[77] According to Vasilii Kliuchevskii, just as Russian law identified "the owner of the house with the house," "the notion of the state was identified with the person of the Tsar." Kliuchevskii believed that Peter the Great, however, made a distinction between the ideas of the state and the person of the tsar.[78]

In the eighteenth century, Peter the Great did sometimes draw a distinction between his personal patrimony and the state, stating on several occasions that even he owed service to the latter. But this concept was constantly undermined by his use of traditional personal mechanisms of domination. For all his talk of the state, he ultimately saw the state as his personal patrimony, rather than as a self-standing impersonal abstraction. This is clearly demonstrated by his insistence on personally determining who would inherit the throne, which was his *votchina* to pass down.[79] Recent research suggests that Peter's was a distinction without a difference.[80]

Even much later, when filling out the 1897 census, Tsar Nicholas II wrote *khoziain* (owner, proprietor, landlord) of the Russian lands as his occupation. Historians as diverse as Richard Pipes and Geoffrey Hosking agree that the tsarist system was a "patrimonial regime."[81]

Of course, nobody thought that Lenin or Stalin literally owned the state or the people in it. Nevertheless, in a very real way their persons embodied that state. Returning to the revealing, if vestigial and figurative uses of language, we note that Stalin's lieutenants often referred to him as *khoziain.*[82]

In patrimonial systems, officials are seen as personal representatives of the ruler, from his "household" as it were. As we saw earlier, at least since Mongol times, the formulaic language of petitions included *b'et chelom kholop tvoi,* or "your slave beats his head in obeisance." At least since the time of Ivan III in the fifteenth century, formal salutations to the prince were patrimonial in nature, referring to the prince as "master" and subjects—even high-ranking ones—as "slaves." It is not clear whether ranking aristocrats actually considered themselves to be slaves, and certainly that changed over time into a formality for the elite, but it is all but certain that everyone else did.[83]

Perhaps because Khrushchev named it such in his "secret speech," the classic Russian cult of personality is Stalin's. There seems little need here to describe the heights (or depths) of the Stalin cult. "The father of the peoples," the "best friend" of nearly everyone, and the "greatest human being who ever lived" was the center of an officially manufactured personality cult. Beginning with Stalin's fiftieth birthday in 1929, but already in evidence before that, a series of official publications and iconographic images about "the greatest, most brilliant contemporary person" began to appear with great frequency.[84] Like Lenin's, Stalin's cult also had a popular worship component, but unlike Lenin's it began at the top as a well-managed political campaign.

The history and specificities of the term "cult of personality" have been analyzed in detail.[85] Most famously, in his psychohistorical study of Stalin, Robert C. Tucker spoke for many when he located the origins of the Stalin cult in the dictator's own self-image, which was characterized by feelings of inferiority, megalomania, and a consequent need to be better and more revered than other, more intellectual and accomplished Bolsheviks of his generation.[86]

On the other hand, several scholars have noted that Stalin's relationship to his cult was, like Lenin's, not so much psychologically invested as complicated.[87] There is the oft-cited but perhaps apocryphal story of a Stalin conversation with his son, who said, "But I am a Stalin too." Stalin is said to have replied, "No, you're not. . . . You're not Stalin and I'm not Stalin," and pointing to a portrait of himself, "That is Stalin."[88] According to a variant of the tale, Stalin instead said, "I'm not Stalin. Stalin is Soviet power. Stalin is what he is in the newspapers and portraits, not you, no, not even me."[89]

Of a proposed exhibition about his life, Stalin said that the "'cult of personality' ... is harmful and inconsistent with the spirit of our party."[90] In 1940, he wrote to Emelian Iaroslavskii against people who "want to advance themselves with excessive and nauseating flattery of the leaders. ... it is our duty to stop these shameful and groveling feelings ... sycophancy is not compatible with scientific history."[91] Another time, he dismissed the obsession with details of his life as "vulgar rubbish."[92] When a Soviet journalist sent him an account of an interview with his mother, the dictator scrawled across the top of the page, "I won't get involved. Neither confirm nor deny. Not my business."[93] He once returned the manuscript of a biography of him with the notation, "no time to look at it."[94]

Even though he thought great men were important in history, more than once Stalin described such leader-worship (as Voroshilov had about Lenin) as an "SR theory," by which he meant a primary focus on leaders rather than class.[95] He wrote to the Children's Publishing House (in a letter that was published only after his death) that a proposed children's book about him "abounds in a mass of factual improbabilities, alterations, and unearned praise. The theory of "heroes" and masses is not a Bolshevist theory. I recommend burning the book."[96] In this he followed Lenin who had been annoyed with the cult developing around him. "It is shameful to read. ... They exaggerate everything, call me a genius, some kind of special person. ... All our lives we have waged an ideological struggle against the glorification of the personality ... long ago we settled the problem of heroes. And suddenly here again is a glorification of the individual!"[97]

Despite his revulsion at his cult, Lenin saw the practical uses of it and allowed himself to be photographed professionally and otherwise marketed.[98] So did Stalin. Like Lenin, Stalin was annoyed by the excesses of the cult, but also took a functional, utilitarian attitude toward it. In private conversation with German writer Lion Feuchtwanger, he dismissed his cult as a "foolish" thing to give workers and peasants a unifying force.[99] Of course, expressions of modesty and denial of the cult itself can be seen as useful and expected supports for that cult: "The cult was denied in speech precisely so that it could be better constructed under the cover of denial."[100] On the other hand, Stalin's denials were not released for broad public consumption; most of them became known only after his death. Nothing could be allowed to blemish the image.

It is not difficult to see pragmatic and functional uses of the cult for the regime. By linking Stalin to Lenin (as "comrade in arms" or "best pupil") the Stalin cult provided legitimacy for Stalin, his entourage and ideology. One scholar wrote that the cult is "best seen as a desperate attempt to mobilize a society that was too poorly educated to grasp the philosophical tenets of the Party line."[101] It also served as a symbol of unity that hid divisions in that leadership and offered a peasant population a substitute apostle and eventually a god to worship.[102]

Although we know a good deal about the construction(s) of these cults, we still have an incomplete picture. Tucker's focus on Stalin's self-image as creator of the cult cannot explain his apparent revulsion at the cult. Nor can it explain the appearance of patrimonial cults of party leaders at all levels. They also became centers of their own personality cults, and unless we imagine that the entire party apparatus suffered from individual insecurity complexes, we must look further for an explanation.

The approaches that focus on how and why a useful cult evolved or was manufactured at the top for consumption below also cannot get at what must be an important question: Why did it work so well in Russia? It is not enough to quote Stalin, "the people need a tsar." The question is why? As we saw above, the answer seems to have much to do with deep structures in Russian culture about the sacralized person of the ruler. There is a temptation to characterize these twentieth-century cults as modern because they were directed at the masses in an age of mass politics, because they used modern mass media, and because the bureaucratic regime producing them was secular.[103] But the ancient tsar cults, like icons, were also meant for the common people, and the charismatic connection they made did not depend on religion.[104] The messages they sent and the popular consciousness they responded to were ancient and archaic, even when they were delivered by modern printing presses rather than solitary portrait or icon painters.[105]

Likewise, the cults of regional and even local leaders reflected patrimonial personalized rule if not the charismatic connections of the Lenin and Stalin cult. In early Soviet times these local cults were about leaders as patrons of the arts, friends of the little person, and patriarchal protectors, thereby putting them on a pedestal. Their birthdays were celebrated in the regional press, their speeches published in full, no matter how bland. At certain times, such cults were criticized and we find out about them through that criticism:

> Comrade Kuznetsov was supposed to speak at the meeting. Everyone was told beforehand to strongly applaud and shout *ura* when he appeared. A list of slogans was typed up to shout. . . . At 10:00, Savinov first spotted Kuznetsov coming into the hall and ran to the presidium to tell Kutirov, who passed out the slogans and yelled "Long live chairman Comrade Kuznetsov!"[106]

In one curious and revealing exchange in Kara-Kalpak, First Secretary Aliev even referred to himself in the third person, much as Stalin did to his son while pointing to his portrait:

> PANKRATOV: We always write to "Comrade Aliev," and "I write to you as the leader (*vozhd'*) of our party organization."
> ALIEV: Comrade Aliev is not responsible for that.[107]

Often, these local notables gave their names to geographical features, thus enshrining themselves in the physical landscape. Pankratov went on, "Take the boats named after Alexander Lunev, the cutter Grigorii Kvachev, take the tens of collective farms named Aliev, or Saparov, or Alimov or Kurbanov, Loginov, and others. Or how about the unending announcements of successes?"[108]

In Dagestan, "we have collective farms named after Mamedbekov, Tagiev, Saidov. They even give names of people expelled from the party and then forget to review them. Everybody thinks that he ought to have several collective farms named for him. If a secretary works in a district for 4 years, why shouldn't he have 4 collective farms named for him?"[109] In Kazakhstan, party First Secretary L. I. Mirzoian's public portraits were larger than those of Stalin. When mountain climbers named a "Stalin Peak," they were advised to name the next one for Mirzoian.[110]

In Smolensk, First Secretary I. P. Rumiantsev had skilled toadies promoting his image and it seems that he liked it:

> Kulikov succeeded in renaming it Rumiantsev Raion. And that's not all. In the district he established the practice that when anyone forgot the new name and used the old name, he was fined 5 rubles. Furthermore, he bought 500 portraits of Rumiantsev at 65 kopeks plus 20 portraits from Leningrad at 75 kopeks. When the portraits arrived

from Leningrad and it was time to pay for them, he summoned the secretary of the district ispolkom and told him to pay. He refused to pay, saying that this was illegal. Then Kulikov stormed at him and took away his party card.

Geertz noted the relationship between powerful charismatic politicians and the territories they ruled. "When kings journey around the countryside, making appearances, attending fetes, conferring honors, exchanging gifts, or defying rivals, they mark it, like some wolf or tiger spreading his scent through his territory, as almost physically part of them."[111] Lacking Stalin's modesty, Smolensk party First Secretary Rumiantsev marked his territory with his scent just like a tsar progressing through the realm or a nobleman visiting his estates:

> When Rumiantsev came to the district, Young Pioneers met him at the border of the district. Rumiantsev brought a supply of 25 rubles in change, which coins he threw to the children. The children threw themselves on the money in a free-for-all. When people noted that this was unseemly, Rumiantsev said "they should know who is driving through."[112]

These local cults of the party first secretary were part of the formation of "family circles": political clans and networks centering on a powerful personage and based on patronage and mutual self-protection. We will discuss these local political machines at some length below, but for now we are mainly interested in their cultic features. In most cases, the local dignitary's authority was said to derive from his comradeship with or proximity to Stalin, and the connection was made in many ways. In Dagestan,

> They organized a national ensemble, a good thing to listen to, a nice performance to watch, a good thing, but I don't understand why it was necessary to name it the Samurskii Ensemble. . . . What does the ensemble sing? I went to hear them and they sang the "Internationale," and then "Hymn to Stalin." So far so good. But then after "Hymn to Stalin" they sang a "Hymn to Samurskii." They couldn't do without it."[113]

Of course, there is a difference between charismatic cults of personality and more secular cults of leaders. Stalin was both transcendent in his own right as well as being the anointed apostolic successor to Lenin and Marx. Stalin's Soviet-era successors, lacking the dictator's power and authority, relied on a chain of apostolic succession from Lenin (in the cases of Khrushchev and Gorbachev, bypassing the now-illegitimate Stalin) and ratification by the Communist Party.

Long ago, scholars noted the characterization of Stalin as Lenin's "pupil," "loyal follower," "continuer of the cause of the immortal Lenin." He was also frequently characterized as "teacher," an image not inconsistent with the apostolic image.[114] The famous "anointing" photographs of Stalin alongside Lenin recall those of Nicholas II alongside his son Aleksei and preview those for sale today in Moscow of Putin skiing and chatting with Medvedev.[115]

Anthropologists have noted the universal aspects of charismatic authority in many places and times. All these personality or leadership cults were deliberately controlled and manipulated, if not invented, by leadership groups with functional goals. This was done over the centuries with coronation ceremonials, various rituals, religion, myths, and stories and, closer to our days, through what we now call branding and marketing. In the Soviet case, the authority the cults carried could be individually charismatically transcendent (Stalin), based on apostolic succession (Stalin and subsequent Soviet leaders), media-manufactured (Putin), and/or reproduced at lower levels.

Like the apostolic cults, those like Putin's which are based on an individual person have a structural component as well: They tend to exist to some extent at all levels of the system, with proximity to the supreme leader as the source of authority for local leaders. For regional officials under Stalin, for Khrushchev through Putin, proximity substituted for personal charisma.

In Russia, the relationship of officials to those above and below them always existed through the sinews of patron-client relations and personal connections.[116] This ancient patrimonial politics was renewed by Lenin, whose personal authority was "completely at odds with the notion of regularized authority based upon stable institutional structures." Political institutions were in fact the instruments of powerful personalities.[117] It goes without saying that this was the situation under Stalin.

Policy is made on a case-by-case basis, often on the spot, by officials claiming to be personal representatives of the supreme patron, proximate to him, rather than according to any consistent laws.[118] The system is little characterized by adherence to, or limits imposed by law and is rather based on political expediency, and authority has little to do with formal office holding. Russian leadership cults are therefore a manifestation of a larger cultural understanding of political power as personal and patrimonial rather than based on formal, institutional, or state ideas.

When Stalin discussed implementing or enforcing a policy, he spoke of persons, not institutions. Policy changes were a matter of finding the right mix of cadres, and he promiscuously created apparently superfluous and overlapping agencies because the main thing was who worked in them, not what they were chartered to do. These agencies were not so much institutions as places to house important Stalin plenipotentiaries and tools for their use. Theoretically, the RSFSR Commissariat of Agriculture could have carried out collectivization at the end of the 1920s, but it was full of "alien" people. A USSR Commissariat of Agriculture was formed and staffed with "our people." The RSFSR version continued to exist, but was ignored. Enforcement was a matter of sending "our people" somewhere to rectify things. "Writing a paper will not do any good. We will have to send some of our people there to straighten it out."[119] Ultimately, Bolshevik leadership was about sending "our people" more than about the rule-bound procedures of a bureaucracy.

That political power flows from proximity to important persons has a long history in Russia. As far back as ninth-century Kievan Rus, the prince's closest retainers were members of his *druzhina,* a Russian word with the same root as that for "friends." The prince's soldiers were "his people" (*svoi liudi*). Power radiated from these retainers and professional soldiers because they were proximate to the prince.

In the Muscovite period, "power and administrative position were not necessarily associated with one another, and indeed for centuries they were specifically distinct."[120] It was proximity to the prince, usually cemented by blood and marriage ties, that produced political power. One key political event was the prince's (later tsar's) marriage. His bride's father, uncles, brothers, and male cousins took over the government and occupied the key positions. The bride, if the prince or tsar had reached majority, was herself generally out of power but she was a proximity link for the male members of her clan, which functioned as a patronage network with political meaning.

Although Soviet clan networks were more about political connections than kinship, some of the association of kinship with political power survived into the Soviet period. Above we heard Stalin speak about destroying an enemy's "kin, his family," and it was often the case during the terror of the 1930s that relatives of an arrested Bolshevik also faced arrest or at least permanent stigma. The modern blurring of kinship and politics also explains Stalin's reaction to Beria's son Sergo's proposed marriage to Maksim Gor'kii's granddaughter. In medieval Muscovy, marriages were alliances that affected the political life of the entire clan and heads of kinship clans arranged, approved or disapproved marriages of important clan members. Stalin could have been a boyar clan head when he told Sergo that because of the dubious non-party types surrounding Gor'kii's family, "I see your marriage as a move to establish links with the oppositionist Russian intelligentsia," and queried Sergo as to whether or not his father had instigated the engagement.[121]

The clearest manifestation of proximity as a marker of political power is clientelism, and there is little doubt that patron-client networks governed Muscovite Russia. Students of medieval and early modern Russia have shown that membership in a client group, whether based on clan connections or sworn loyalty, was much more important than formal status or function or position.[122] They have shown how "proximity—physical access guaranteed by blood or marriage relationships, in most cases—was both the warrant and the objective of political activity."[123] Conversely, "exile from the presence of the sovereign was the symbolic expression of such disgrace, which also included more tangible punishment, such as incarceration and confiscation of wealth. Unfortunates were said to have been deprived of the sight of the tsar's 'bright eyes.'"[124]

Little changed in the imperial period. Proximity to persons and clientelism continued to govern the Russian political system, famously called a "government of men, not laws."[125] Peter the Great's replacement of the old *mestnichestvo* appointment system with a "modern" Table of Ranks meritocracy did little to change the importance of clientelism and personal precedence. Indeed, from the beginning of Peter's reign to the end of the eighteenth century, virtually all significant appointments to high position can be traced to two clan networks, the Naryshkins and the Saltykovs.[126]

Despite Catherine the Great's love for Enlightenment rational law, "No one seemed to grasp clearly that good laws in themselves would do little to improve justice and governmental efficiency so long as people continued to organize themselves in patronage groups and to make these groups the prime focus of their activity."

In the imperial period, proximity and patronage continued to dominate the political system, with closeness to the autocrat, "monarchical proximity," being the measure.[127] At the beginning of the reign of Catherine the Great in the eighteenth century, Nikita Panin observed, "government business was determined by the influence of individuals rather than by the power of state institutions."[128]

The nineteenth century saw several moments when rationalizing and modernizing reforms were in the air. In the early part of the century, Mikhail Speranskii had the ear of Tsar Alexander I and developed an administrative reform aimed at producing a rule-bound constitutional system. Conservative resistance, however, doomed his plans. Later in the nineteenth century, there were numerous attempts to create a *Rechtsstaat,* an autonomous legal order governed by rules rather than persons. These too failed, or in some cases produced only insignificant reforms because, as under state-as-abstraction Peter I who nevertheless willed the state as his patrimony, in the nineteenth century the anti-institutional principle of personal authority trumped all other concepts. Catherine the Great understood this, and her heirs learned it when they played with reforms and then allowed conservatives to crush them.[129]

There is little doubt that in modern Russia in general, and in the Stalin period in particular, power and authority were a function of one's proximity and connection to even more powerful persons, rather than of formal office holding. Politburo members were authoritative figures because it was known that Stalin had selected them to work with him. Conversely, being banned from his presence, from his famous after-hours dinners and his "bright eyes," meant disgrace and loss of power.

Their proximity was visually and symbolically confirmed on formal occasions when they were photographed standing next to the dictator. Returning for a moment to Lenin's mausoleum, the image of Politburo members standing on the mausoleum reviewing military parades on important days is a familiar one. Kremlinologists used to study the places Soviet leaders stood in order to divine who was moving up or down in the hierarchy. Perhaps less obvious to us, however, was the semiotic message the entire scene carried, an ancient message that almost surely resonated in Russian cultural consciousness: as the Politburo members stood and watched the parades of the most modern, technologically sophisticated missiles, these members and descendants of Lenin's clan were literally standing on the semimythical progenitor's sacred body mediated by the cold marble of Shchusev's modern structure.

A better symbol of power as personal and proximate is hard to imagine. Stalin stood on Lenin. Politburo members did the same but also reinforced their authority by standing next to Stalin. The bodies and ashes of Soviet heroes were only a few meters behind, adding their aura to the scene, and thus completing a symbolic spatial ensemble of power as a function of both apostolic and physical proximity. When Stalin died, he joined Lenin in the mausoleum for a few years, and even when he was evicted, he was not far away and his successors created a new symbolic apostolic chain by standing on Lenin. In both cases, the permanence of the "state" was on display, being performed, as a constellation of personalities and personal relationships.

Aside from symbolism, it was often the case that certain authoritative politicians became members of higher bodies like the Politburo, Orgburo, Secretariat, and Central Committee as a sign, a recognition, of personal power they had already accrued through proximity to Stalin. Many of the younger politicians who frequented Stalin's office and functioned at the decision-making level of Politburo members did not formally actually become Politburo members until the next party congress, as confirmation of authority they already deployed because of their closeness to Stalin. A. A. Zhdanov, N. I. Ezhov, and G. M. Malenkov are examples from the 1930s. Ezhov was already effectively functioning as an Orgburo member before 1934, when that status was made official for him. Malyshev, Patolichev, Pervukhin, Saburov, and Zverev also achieved power before Politburo membership in the 1940s.

In a similar understanding of power, ranking politicians changed the status of organizations they came to head. Power and authority ran from the person to the institution, not vice versa. Everyone understood that the NKVD had been "demoted" when its leadership changed from Beria, a Politburo member, to Kruglov, who was not. Similarly, in 1949, the Ministry of Foreign Affairs lost status when Molotov, a Politburo member, was replaced by Vyshinskii, who was not.

At lower levels, politicians made judgments about each other based on perceptions of whether a person was "close to" (*blizkii*) or "connected with" (*sviazan*) a higher-up, and these words appear frequently in official and unofficial documents. When Alexander Radzivilovskii arrived in Ivanovo as the new NKVD chief, his new appointment was in itself not enough to establish his authority. But the existing staff established that Radzivilovskii was a *blizkii* of Kaganovich, who in turn was close to Stalin. Therefore he must be obeyed. Even when a new appointee was obviously unqualified, proximity gave him power and forced obedience. In 1937 a physical education instructor was sent to Ivanovo to head the provincial NKVD Secret Political Department. The fact that N. I. Ezhov knew him was enough to establish his authority.[130]

When in 1937 Stalin decided to remove powerful regional party bosses, he did so not only by ordering the police to arrest them. Proximity to the provincial clan leader was the daily measure of power for rank-and-file party members. His local cult provided a cultural symbol of that power. His removal therefore had to be explained in understandable cultural terms and perceptions of power had to be reestablished. Certainly arrest by the NKVD upon charges of treason was an important explanation. But with arrests flying in all directions, there was always a bit of doubt about actual guilt. That the previous leadership of the NKVD had recently been removed wholesale and itself charged with treason did little to cement the absolute credibility of police arrest.

There was also doubt about whom should be obeyed after the local leader's fall. So in each case Stalin sent one of his close Politburo associates from the party apparatus (never the police or military) to preside over a local party meeting that discussed the removal. Stalin intimates Kaganovich, Andreev, Malenkov, Molotov, and Zhdanov were particularly active emissaries. As we shall see later, this purge by visitations of members of the prince's *druzhina* served several functions. It allowed a representative from the center, one unencumbered by local ties or loyalties, to sort out friend from enemy, enemy clan member from outsider.

Symbolically, however, it also performed a display of personal power and hierarchical proximity. The arriving grandee made a speech explaining and ratifying the arrests of local dignitaries, and participated in the discussion of their "crimes." But the most important thing was that the emissary was known to be close to Stalin and to have been sent by him. That authority, based as always on proximity to person rather than institution or constitution, demonstrably trumped and replaced that of the former chief and was therefore the ultimate ratification of the removal. The chain of proximity, the very understanding of power, which could have been ruptured by the sudden removal of the heretofore all-powerful local grandee, was now repaired and restored: personalized power now ran through the emissary to Stalin.

Leadership cults at all levels of Soviet society and the manifestations of leader cults after Stalin suggest that something more is at work here than an individual's personality needs; something more than local leaders copying Stalin who had consciously modeled himself on Lenin, or had simply selected a method of rule based on the clan heritage of his native Georgia. It simply will not do to imagine Stalin and his associates rationally choosing rule-by-cult among a menu of available options, or even consciously choosing patrimonial rule. Stalin did not just copy Lenin (or Ivan the Terrible), and regional party secretaries did not just copy Stalin. Because we find this understanding of politics and government from Riurik to Putin, at all levels of the hierarchies at all times and places, it was inescapable. This was the deep structure by which Russia had always been governed. There were no alternative models to contemplate.

For many centuries, patrimony had been as much a part of Russia as speaking the Russian language. Metaphorically, patrimonialism and the cults that reflected it were indeed the language of politics, and there was no choice but to speak it. In their political practice, Stalin's successors from Khrushchev to Brezhnev would speak dialects of it, but they were intelligible to the elite and the population. When Gorbachev tried to change the understanding of the state and the nature or political practice, he might as well have been speaking Swahili. Nobody understood him, and he failed. Putin returned to the familiar language, and he endures.

3 The Party Personnel System
Upstairs at the Central Committee

It is understood that no policy can be conducted except as the expression of appointments and transfers.

—*Lenin, 1920*

WHEN WE TAKE a detailed look at patrimonialism and personalization in the Stalin period, and at the related questions of the structure of top party institutions, party personnel allocation, and the Bolshevik elite's self-representation as leaders, we will see that personnel appointment was the heart of Bolshevik power and administration and was so understood at the time.

We will also see that the leading bodies of the party were always ephemeral collections of personalities that never developed a rule-bound institutionalization that would allow institutions to project their rules, procedures, and authority onto senior political actors or determine their behavior. "Upstairs" at the TsK, institutional vagueness was to the liking of senior leaders from the beginning. In fact, important bodies like the Politburo and Orgburo existed informally before their "official" organization, and continued to exist even when they no longer met. These bodies were in fact not so much institutions as they were markers or identifiers for clusters of grandees whose power was personal, proximate, and arbitrary.

"Downstairs" at the TsK, (the subject of the next chapter) the staff pressed for a Weberian rationalization and depersonalized bureaucratization, in which the behavior would be structured by impersonal procedures and rules. But we will see how patrimonialism and personalized power consistently won out over "modern" functioning, quite aside from the considerable influence of Stalin's personality.

☆

After 1917, the Bolshevik party had to adapt itself from making revolution to governing a huge territory in which the previous administration had either fled, been destroyed by civil war, or was hostile to its new communist masters. They had little to work with in terms of resources, tools, or experience.

Although the party had grown tremendously during the revolution and civil war (from about 24,000 members at the beginning of 1917 to more than 700,000 in 1921 when the Civil War ended) many of the recruits were undependable and uncommitted people who had simply joined the winning side. Even counting everybody in the party, however, the total was a drop in the bucket of the vast Russian population. The peasant bulk of the population had won its centuries-long battle for the land and could be counted on to take a dim view of any nationalization schemes the socialist Bolsheviks might propose. Similarly, the mass of urban and rural traders were not likely allies.

The party's weak presence in the countryside was only part of the problem. Russia's new masters had never run anything and they hated bureaucracies; on the contrary, as professional revolutionaries they had dedicated themselves to destroying bureaucracies. The Bolshevik leaders constantly complained that what remained of the tsarist bureaucracy was staffed by officials hostile to the party.

Before the 1917 Revolutions, the organization of the Bolshevik party was more a wish than a reality. There was no party apparatus at all. Party committees with amorphous and changing memberships were scattered across the Russian Empire in tenuous communication with one another. In theory, they were subordinated to various superior committees, including a Central Committee, a Russian Buro, and other mobile bodies with no physical locations or constitutional authority. There was therefore no coherent and generally accepted party leadership structure or hierarchy, no clearly defined network of committees, no stable local or national party membership rolls, not even a collection of previous party decrees or resolutions.

There were no written party rules or membership cards; individual membership was by personal self-attestation and declaration. It would take decades to develop anything resembling an accurate file system of party membership records. For many years, absent such records (and even later with them) personal references were at least as important as qualifications in getting a job. "Here is where I worked. These comrades know me there" were important parts of all job applications. In another example of the persistence of the personal, up through the end of the USSR party membership applications always required producing personal references.

BOYARS AND SECRETARIES

We don't know much about how routine matters were handled in a Muscovite prince's palace, and procedure varied from century to century.[1] But from what we do know, something like this probably happened: a request for adjudication on some matter came to the palace. If the question was routine, *d'iaki,* who were clerical staff in chanceries (*prikazy*) with specialized knowledge could decide the matter. More important matters were decided by a senior grandee (a boyar) collegially in consultation with the staff of the relevant *prikaz,* who issued a decision in the name of the boyar "with colleagues" (*s tovarishchami*). If the question was controversial or otherwise difficult to decide at this level, it was bumped "upstairs" for a discussion by assembled boyars. If they could not decide, it went to the tsar.

If the matter was weightier from the start (geopolitics, military, economic or legal reform, etc.) it was decided by discussions in various constellations of boyar meetings and the tsar. At this level, there were no fixed procedures or rules governing the process but there was a rough pecking order of boyars, with proximity to the tsar as measure of rank (his relatives or close friends being most senior). From the time a question or proposal entered the palace to its resolution, its fate was determined not by formal rules and regulations of committee competence, but by personal, even arbitrary decisions made by groups of noble boyars in informal groups of various sizes in the rooms and corridors of the palace.

The *d'iaki* could have considerable influence in a matter's routing and resolution. They became professional, permanent clerks whose work was made easier by documented precedents, files, rules, and paperwork. Even on very important matters, senior boyars often consulted them.

Their skill at keeping and moving paperwork (*deloproizvodstvo*) also made them indispensable to the nobles. But this was a hierarchical system, and the boyars were keen on protecting their monopoly on decision making, foreign and domestic policy, and appointment to office. Noble was noble, and the boyars kept their corporate prerogatives intact and their arbitrary fingers in every pie. Nothing important could be finally decided without the presence of at least one boyar grandee who obligatorily blessed or rejected every proposal personally, fixing his seal on the result. There could be no important decision without the imprint of a boyar's seal. Clerks and staff had no seals. Even if our guess about the details of Muscovite palace practices is not perfect, it is highly likely that the *d'iaki* and the boyars had different modes of work, specialized knowledge, and, perhaps, different interests.

Without equating boyars with commissars, we can see remarkable similarities between old Muscovite and Bolshevik practices. As the following chapters show, in the case of Bolshevik personnel selection, minor matters could be decided by the specialized staff (*d'iaki* in a *prikaz*) of the TsK personnel department, Orgraspred, also known at various times as Uchraspred, Raspredotdel, Orgotdel, or Orgraspred. Somewhat weightier or controversial matters went to a staff conference, consisting of a single TsK secretary (boyar) presiding over Orgraspred staff (*d'iaki*) and producing a decision in the name of the boyar-secretary "s tovarishchi." Serious questions of national importance went directly to senior noble councils (Secretariat/Orgburo) or to the Politburo (the "tsar's in-laws") who met with the tsar (general secretary—Stalin) on the most important questions. But as in ancient times, the particular grouping/committee of Bolshevik grandees that would hear and decide a question was often unclear; they knew it when they saw it. At every level, there were understandings (but no written rules, at least none that were consistently followed) that disputed or difficult matters at any level went up the chain for judgment and dispute resolution: Staff conference → Secretariat → Orgburo → Politburo → Stalin.

UPSTAIRS AT THE CENTRAL COMMITTEE

The Old Bolsheviks, who had worked for years to overthrow the tsarist system, were mistrustful and hostile to that part of the bureaucracy they inherited. But more than that, they were hostile to bureaucracy in general. Like nineteenth-century tsars, they felt that bureaucracies—even their own—tied their hands and tended to make policy rather than carry it out.

Nevertheless, after the revolution, it was obvious to everyone in the party leadership that the party needed some kind of structure to cope with the new tasks of governing. Formally, the three top party bodies—Politburo, Orgburo, and Secretariat—were formed in March 1919, at the 8th Party Congress.

Actually, the 8th Congress only codified an existing arrangement; these three committees had existed informally for some time. Back in 1917, the 6th Party Congress established several ad hoc subcommittees of the Central Committee to act on important questions when the TsK was not in session; one of these was called a Political Buro.

Since the February 1917 Revolution that overthrew the tsar, Iakov Sverdlov, his wife Klavdia Novgorodtseva, and Elena Stasova had worked together to begin to keep track of party members' locations and work. They were referred to as the party's "secretaries" or "secretariat," with Lenin's colleague Sverdlov understood to be a kind of executive "secretary" and Novgorodtseva and Stasova as his assistants.

Until his death in 1919, Sverdlov made personnel allocations based on his personal connections and knowledge of a vast number of the party faithful. Absent an institutional mechanism, his personal prestige and authority were the reasons party members accepted assignments he offered them. He worked largely according to personal contacts, sometimes receiving and assigning twenty-five party workers per day. As V. V. Ossinskii told the 8th Party Congress, "Sverdlov kept in his head information on all party workers in Russia and where to find them. At any moment he could tell you where each one was, and he could move them around. Now he is dead and nobody knows where any of the party workers are."[2]

Sverdlov may have had a great deal in his head, but he put little down on paper. The records of his secretarial meetings are messy, disordered scraps which often fail to record who was present, what was proposed, and what was decided. Generally the party's records at this time were truly disorganized. The few Sverdlov papers preserved in the archives seem almost plaintive attempts to order a messy situation that he was tracking in his head day to day. Lists with many blanks tried to record such basic information as who were the senior party workers in each province. At one point, Sverdlov tried to sketch a large flow chart categorizing party organizations in various "groups": by size of party organization, by size of town, by military front, by party *stazh* of the leaders.[3]

In January 1919, Sverdlov and Novgorodtseva were joined by N. Krestinskii and M. Vladimirskii in what the Central Committee now called an "Organizational Buro," which in practice was an expanded Secretariat, and which actually was nothing more than giving Sverdlov's primitive recordkeeping operation two helpers and a new name. This informal pre-Orgburo "Organizational Buro" met fifteen times.[4]

In March 1919, the 8th Congress decreed that "the Central Committee forms a Political buro for political work, an Organizational buro for organizational work, and a Secretariat headed by a secretary who is a member of the Orgburo."[5] This decision coincided with Sverdlov's death and consequent calls to systematize top party organization. After Sverdlov's death, Novgorodtseva attended several meetings of the newly formed official Orgburo, presumably for continuity and perhaps to translate Sverdlov's chaotic notes and practices. Stasova stayed on a few months longer to help out.[6]

On paper, these bodies looked like stable institutions. They had specified functions (Politburo for political and policy questions, Orgburo for personnel). They had a known membership elected by the Central Committee. They had prescribed meeting times and formal agendas. They discussed the items on their agendas in order, took votes, recorded their decisions, and promulgated them in written form. Staff kept track of the committees' work by keeping various sets of protocols, each numbered and subnumbered to identify decisions resulting from agenda items.

A Politburo meeting typically consisted of around fifteen Politburo members and candidates (a remarkably consistent number over the decades) plus others interested in or reporting on the matters on the agenda.[7] The Politburo was to meet on Thursdays at 11 A.M. and adjourn no later than 2 P.M.. If some matters had to be held over, an additional meeting could be held on Friday or Monday. Before Politburo meetings, the Secretariat was to clean the Politburo's agenda of inessential questions, those not requiring immediate decision, and those that could be settled at lower levels of administration "in soviet or party order."[8] TsK members had the right to attend Politburo meetings, and although they typically did not do so unless the agenda touched on their work, as many as a dozen might show up. A dozen or more chiefs and deputy chiefs of the TsK departments and representatives from the Control Commission, the Komsomol, and the political arm of the Red Army, as well as lower-ranking specialists by invitation according to agenda topic, rounded out a room full of several dozen attendees.[9]

As might be expected, Politburo agendas contained large strategic and political questions of agricultural and industrial policy, military affairs, and especially foreign policy. But as we will see, they also contained many items of personnel appointment and minor technical matters that we would expect to be handled by the other top committees or by bodies far below these.

The Orgburo, where personnel appointments were supposed to take place, was to meet on Mondays and Thursdays at 9 P.M.. The TsK Secretaries took turns chairing Orgburo meetings. As with the Politburo, potential agenda items for the Orgburo were sifted by the Secretariat (which could mean a single secretary), which was also empowered to make decisions in the name of the Orgburo. "All questions decided by the Secretariat and receiving no objection from an Orgburo member become confirmed decisions of the Orgburo."[10]

Like Politburo meetings, Orgburo sessions were attended by the committee's members and candidates.[11] All secretaries of the TsK were Orgburo members, as was the chief of Orgraspred (typically the only TsK department head with this rank). The remaining membership was drawn from senior Bolshevik grandees specializing in various areas, such as unions, the military, transport, and culture. Basically, therefore, the Orgburo was an expanded version of the Secretariat with broader expertise.[12] As with Politburo meetings, Orgburo meetings included a large number of invited "guests" who were interested in or reporting on agenda matters, including TsK members and various specialists.

TsK department heads may or may not have attended, but heads, deputy heads, and assistants of Orgraspred were always there. These personnel office departments specialized in the workings and personnel needs of various bureaucracies and therefore advised the Orgburo on appointments.

Before the end of 1921, the Secretariat did not meet as a formal body, but after the end of the Civil War, the Orgburo was so swamped with agenda items that the leadership looked for ways to screen questions that might be decided elsewhere. So the Secretariat began meeting as a committee after the 10th Party Congress in 1921 because "the practical work on the Orgburo required . . . a special meeting of the Secretariat of the TsK that would meet before the Orgburo to examine the less important questions." Early agendas of Secretariat meetings reflected the fact that it was never intended to be a committee. They were informal lists of tasks without reference to who was present or what was decided except for an occasional checkmark and handwritten "decided" or "postponed" in the margin. For example, "Request from the Kostroma province committee to leave Comrade Khronin to work in Kostroma, despite his transfer to VSNKH in Moscow. Postponed until Rykov arrives. Comrade Miliutin to acquaint himself with the matter" was an agenda item. It was "postponed."[13]

Meetings of the Secretariat were scaled-down Orgburo meetings. One or two secretaries of the TsK presided over a group consisting (sometimes) of a couple of TsK members, representatives from the Komsomol, army political administration, and trade unions, plus several TsK instructors (traveling representatives specializing in various provinces), and most chiefs of TsK departments or their deputies (but not chiefs of Orgraspred's sections, who attended Orgburo meetings instead.) Because of their streamlined size and the generally noncontroversial nature of their agendas, meetings of the Secretariat briskly covered and decided many more questions than either Orgburo or Politburo meetings. For example, in 1925 a typical Orgburo meeting might decide between fifteen and twenty questions at the meeting and another five to fifteen later by telephone-polling the members. But in the same time, the Secretariat plowed its way through fifty to seventy-five questions at the meeting and another seventy to a hundred later by polling.

In the summer of 1922, another screening layer was added: the Conference of TsK Department Heads, which was "to not only more carefully prepare questions for the meetings of the Secretariat, but to a significant extent unburden its agenda of petty questions of a current routine character."[14] This staff conference was to screen agenda items for the Secretariat, which then screened for the Orgburo and Politburo. In 1925, the Conference of Department Heads was replaced by an internal Orgraspred Staff Conference.[15] Instead of TsK department heads, the staff conference now consisted of heads and assistants of Orgraspred's specialized groups and subdepartments, chaired by a single TsK secretary.[16]

In addition to the TsK secretary and a couple of his own clerical secretaries, the room could be crowded. Those present typically included heads of TsK departments (Agitprop, Women, Rural Affairs, Personnel, and so forth) and their deputies (about a dozen people), a Komsomol representative, two or three TsK instructors, and several assistants to the chief of Orgraspred who specialized in various types of personnel appointment, for a total of around twenty people.[17]

Many of the items presented by the department heads in conference seem to have had a random character having little to do with their departments; they were just things that drifted across their desks. This body charged with recommending personnel appointments also concerned itself with "offering aid to the children of Karl Liebknecht," a brochure on *Our Industry!* or "*Izvestiia*'s contest for the best agricultural collective," alongside cadre decisions.[18]

Certainly, most of their personnel decisions do seem to have been about relatively minor postings. Examples include picking county (*volost'*) organizers for the Komsomol, a visit by a TsK instructor to the Chuvash territory, a suggestion that Comrade Dobzhinskii travel to Minsk for a conference, appointment of a secretary for the Union of Communist Students, Comrade Shul'man's request for a vacation (declined), and dispatching Comrade Ittin for instructional work in physical education in the Caucasus.[19]

INDETERMINACY OF COMPETENCE

Theoretically, an institutional hierarchy of committees had taken shape by the early 1920s, with the Politburo on top, followed by the Orgburo, then the Secretariat, and finally the Conference of Department Heads, with the ostensible ranking depending on the importance of the personnel appointment or question involved. A given question could be finally decided by a single TsK secretary (as a decision of the staff conference), two or three secretaries (as a meeting of the Secretariat), all TsK Secretaries plus several high-ranking Old Bolsheviks (as a meeting of the Orgburo), or all top grandees (as a meeting of the Politburo).

From the bottom, each committee, beginning with staff at the conference, was supposed to triage questions, either deciding them on the spot or routing them to the appropriate body above. The goal was to unblock the Politburo's and Orgburo's (and ultimately the Secretariat's) clogged agendas and to rationally decide questions at an appropriate level. TsK members could protest committee decisions to the next higher committee, for example from the Orgburo to the Politburo.[20] Lower committees were formally subordinate to higher ones. As Stalin said, "Isn't it the case that the Secretariat and the Orgburo are subordinate to the Politburo?"[21]

But in reality, things were not so clear.

First, we see an indeterminacy in the agendas and competences of the committees. Although there was a rough rank order in triaging questions to the various top committees (foreign and internal security questions always went to the Politburo, for example) it does not look as if the importance of a question always correlated with the rank of the committee deciding it. In a single week in 1928, the importance of agenda questions seemed exactly the *opposite* of the purported rank of the committee studying them. Starting at the bottom, the Secretariat debated important orders from the political administration of the Red Army on party conferences among troops and officers. Three days later, the Orgburo took up the national question of rural credit—a vital issue during NEP and on the eve of dekulakization, and heard a report on the situation in the Krasno-Presnensk district party organization in Moscow—a hotbed of anti-Stalin "rightists." Meanwhile, the Politburo was spending time discussing the need for an all-Union center of cotton-weaving cooperatives.[22]

Why was acquiring the library of former Baron Ginzberg a matter for the Orgburo and not some lower body?[23] It is equally unclear why buying the library of former revolutionary Evalenko was a matter for the Conference of Department Heads (with Bubnov reporting), while the same week, getting hold of former revolutionary Rubakin's library was a matter for the Politburo (with Kamenev reporting).[24] The answer probably had more to do with Kamenev being an old friend of Rubakin's than with the intrinsic worth of the libraries, or the rank of the committees.

The Secretariat took important decisions on key party organizations, on political work in the Red Army, and other matters that would appear to have been at least in the province of the Orgburo if not the Politburo.[25] Throughout the 1920s, the Orgburo also frequently took decisions above what would appear to be its station. For example, it approved I. N. Smirnov's assignment of one Comrade Iakovlev to Siberia. Technically, this was in the province of the Politburo, but Orgburo (and Politburo) member Molotov told the Orgburo to go ahead and vote, and that he would make sure it would be all right with the Politburo.[26]

We might expect this to be simple confusion of committees linked to birthing pains in the early years, but it continued. After the 17th Party Congress in 1934 had abolished cadre departments in city party committees, the Orgburo took it upon itself to reestablish them, a matter that the Politburo might well have taken up.[27] Three years later, in 1938, the Orgburo appointed V. E. Volkhov USSR deputy commissar of agriculture, a posting clearly on the Politburo's nomination list.[28] There are many such examples.

The idea that the lowly staff conference dealt only with petty questions is not completely accurate either. The conference also considered a number of issues that would appear to have been far above its competence, approving appointments that would seem to have required Orgburo and even Politburo approval. Tax policy, nationality issues, the party's presence in the countryside, party composition, the role of women in the party, banditism, connections with the masses are examples.[29] Without referring the matter to a higher body, the staff conference approved the appointment of Comrade Petrov as judge of the Supreme Court, and appointed party secretaries in Penza and Voronezh and in the touchy national areas of Groznyi and Tataria.[30] On the other hand, the same day as the latter decisions, the Politburo handled far less important matters that should have fallen to the staff conference: approving a conference of transport workers and an agricultural exhibit, and appointing the rector of a Moscow technical school.[31]

From the beginning, the agendas of all the committees were crowded with minor matters. In October 1919, in the midst of a military crisis and food shortages, the Orgburo took up the matter of providing books for workers.[32] In October 1920, during the struggle with the White armies of Wrangel and Denikin, the Orgburo became embroiled in an argument—and analyzed a lengthy correspondence—about the cafeteria in a government building. At the same meeting, the Orgburo spent time on Comrade Chudnovskii's refusal to pay his party dues (he should be told that it is impermissible not to pay them) and on Comrade Miachin's expulsion for not showing up for volunteer work and meetings (he should show up).[33] In April 1921, one of the highest political bodies in the USSR took up the questions of dormitories and summer vacations for university students.[34] That summer, a meeting of the Secretariat chaired by TsK secretaries Molotov and Mikhailov specified the sizes of teapots and the number of pillows and towels for TsK instructors on business trips on trains, and made sure they were to be provided with three changes of linen and "not fewer than 4 teacups."[35]

It never stopped. Nearly fifteen years later, in 1935, at the same time as it was creating party cadre departments in city party committees and considering the results of a huge party purge (the "Verification of Party Documents"), the Orgburo worried about nonpolitical but "impermissible inaccuracies" in Professor Ushakov's *Short Dictionary of the Russian Language* and the proper distribution of theater tickets. The Orgburo discussed dental education and decided to ask the Secretariat to draft a statement on it and forward it to the Politburo![36] At a single meeting that same month, in addition to commissioning an upcoming national census, discussing Procurator Vyshinskii's recommendations on sentencing a "Trotskyist Group" to death, worrying about the London Naval Conference, and appraising Japanese designs on Mongolia, the Politburo fretted about a fifteenth anniversary celebration for Udmurtia, a budget for rest homes in Orenburg, and the use of old school buildings.[37]

Similarly, lower bodies actually overturned the decisions of higher ones. The Secretariat often reversed the Orgburo's appointment of officials.[38] Sometimes even the staff conference reversed higher body decisions. On 28 April 1923, the department heads' conference decided "to repeal (*otmenit'*) the order of the Orgburo from 22 March and to leave Comrades Bondarev and Rudakov at the disposal of the Southeast Buro of the TsK." At another meeting at about the same time, the staff conference repealed five more Orgburo decisions.[39]

INDETERMINACY OF MEMBERSHIP

In addition to the indeterminacy of competence, from the very beginning these committees had an amorphous, ad hoc, and overlapping character that they never lost and that suited the needs and temperament of top party grandees. The Orgburo and Politburo constantly drafted "plans of work" and just as constantly ignored them.[40]

Before 1939, the Politburo, Orgburo, and Secretariat were the exclusive preserves of the Old Bolsheviks. The two dozen or so top members of the TsK who sat on the Politburo, Orgburo, and Secretariat had only a loose idea about the prerogatives or even the membership of these committees. Although at first glance the Bolsheviks seemed careful and precise about committee membership—for example carefully delineating between full and candidate members of the Politburo, Orgburo, and Secretariat—in reality they were quite informal about it.

In the beginning, when so many top Bolsheviks were in and out of Moscow on various Civil War military assignments, the composition of these committees was informal, changing, and based on who was in town at the time. One 1920 Orgburo meeting was attended by Orgburo members Stalin, Rykov, Preobrazhenskii, Krestinskii, and Serebriakov. But Trotsky, Kamenev, Zinoviev, Smirnov, and Kalinin, who happened to be present but were not Orgburo members, voted anyway. The resulting five-to-five tie vote was then referred to the larger TsK for polling.[41]

TsK secretaries Molotov and Mikhailov worked as a team in the early 1920s holding Secretariat meetings and briskly moving through agendas. On several occasions others wandered in and the protocols had to be rewritten to reflect a different "committee's" decision. Once when the two of them were working their way through a Secretariat agenda, they were suddenly joined by Zalutskii, Iaroslavskii, and Kalinin who happened to be members of the Orgburo. Molotov and Mikhailov were Orgburo members too, and the meeting proceeded without missing a beat, but was now renamed a meeting of the Orgburo.[42]

As with the other indeterminacies discussed above, this membership vagueness did not wear off. By 1935, the Secretariat had reverted to its pre-1921 pattern: it largely stopped meeting as a formal committee, and one or more secretaries took decisions informally. In April 1935 the Politburo had referred a question to the Orgburo on preparing translators for Asian languages, but the Orgburo was not scheduled to meet for a while. So the Secretariat took up the question at its 7 April meeting (the only Secretariat meeting of 1935 and the last time the Secretariat would meet as a committee until World War II) and approved it. In the middle of the meeting, several TsK members who were also Orgburo members wandered in. The room now had a majority of the Orgburo present so the protocol of the Secretariat meeting recorded approval of the translator question, with approval by the Orgburo by polling![43]

On 26 July 1938, "the Central Committee orders" that Comrade A. B. Nikolaev be removed as a department manager at the State Committee on Reserves under the Council of Ministers for incompetence. The typed paper was circulated and signed by Andreev, Kaganovich, Malenkov, Ezhov, and Zhdanov. An appropriate number of nobles having made the decision to fire poor Nikolaev, almost as an after-thought someone wrote in by hand "Orgburo," and despite the fact that Andreev and Malenkov were not Orgburo members, it was recorded as an Orgburo decision on a day the Orgburo never met.[44]

The power of these Bolshevik grandees was based on proximity to leading personalities, not on titles or membership. On several occasions in the summer of 1923, L. M. Kaganovich, chief of the Orginstrukt (party cadre assignment) department, and therefore nongrandee staff, chaired the meetings of the Conference of Department Heads, even though he was not a secretary of the TsK. In fact, at one of the meetings Kaganovich chaired, with no Secretariat or TsK member present, the staff conference reversed several Orgburo appointment decisions.[45]

On the surface, this seems to have been not only a violation of the rules, but a matter of staff making decisions. But here we have an example of a person's actual rank and power having nothing to do with his institutional position. Kaganovich was already an insider in Stalin's circle and was known to be close to the general secretary. (That was how he had become head of Orginstrukt in the first place) Therefore in the understanding of the time, he could fulfill the role technically reserved for a TsK secretary because of his personal proximity to Stalin, regardless of his actual job. In patrimonial systems, rules and formal ranks do not matter so much as persons, power, and proximities. Kaganovich had become a noble and nobody much cared if he was in the right room or on the right committee.

How can we explain why the rules were broken, why there was little rhyme or reason to routing a question to one committee and not another, why committees decided questions clearly outside their competence and reversed the decisions of higher bodies without even referring the matter upward for discussion? And, at the level of the department heads' conference, how can we understand why staff, who were not members of the TsK elite, were allowed to influence decisions and appointments far above their rank? The answer has to do with Old Bolshevik noble grandees trying to retain corporate control through a loose system of personal power.

The presence of a grandee at the staff conference, (by the rules, a secretary of the TsK), is one key to these apparent institutional anomalies and violations of rules. On a given question, if he judged the matter to be minor or uncontroversial, or if he had enough expertise to judge it, or if the matter had to be decided quickly, the secretary present would approve it regardless of its importance, "petty" or otherwise, and regardless of the committee it "should" be routed to. The presence of a TsK secretary (himself a Politburo member) in the chair of the conference meant that a high-ranking party noble could "bless" any staff recommendation outside any committee, and it only took one member of the noble caste to do so. From the beginning, if a TsK secretary signed off on an appointment proposed at the department heads' conference, it automatically became a decision of the Secretariat and, if not protested by an Orgburo member, automatically became a recorded decision of the Orgburo, even if the Secretariat or Orgburo never actually met on the subject.[46] Which grandee made the decision sometimes depended on who was in the building at the time that a decision was required, and the form in which the decision (Orgburo, Secretariat, or Politburo) was written up depended on who happened to be in the room when it was decided.

A single secretary could therefore speak for the entire upper nobility. The secretary sitting in the departmental conference was also a member of the Orgburo and Politburo, and therefore a member of the insiders' circle of top nobles in the party. Because of *his* rank and quality, the departmental conference had status beyond its apparent institutional charge. His fellow grandees trusted him to make sound decisions in the interests of the party as they and their generation understood them.[47]

Table 3.1 shows the decreasing meeting frequency for the Politburo, Orgburo, and Secretariat during the 1920s and 1930s. By 1934, the Politburo and Orgburo were meeting about once a month and the Secretariat virtually stopped meeting altogether. Whether an actual committee met and provided a scene in a room for that to happen did not matter so much as the presence or the signature of that grandee. It was his rank and prestige, not an institution or committee, that mattered. By 1937, a single TsK secretary routinely wrote "za" ("in favor") and signed "summary digests" of proposed appointments which were the result of staff recommendations and subsequent conversations between and among grandees and staff. By his signature, these appointments

Table 3.1 Orgburo and Secretariat Meeting Frequency, 1920–40

	Politburo	Orgburo	Secretariat
1920	1–2 per week, about 6 per month	Every 3 days	Every 3 days
1921	1–2 per week, about 6 per month (first *oprosom* decisions)	2 per week	2 per week
1922	1–2 per week, about 6 per month	1–2 per week	1–2 per week, sometimes daily (first *oprosom* decisions)
1923	1–2 per week, about 6 per month	1 per week or per 10 days (first *oprosom* decisions)	1 per week
1924	1–2 per week, about 6 per month	1 per week	1 per week
1925	1–2 per week, about 6 per month	1 per week through Nov., then only *oprosom*	1 per week to 14 Dec. then no meetings to 22 Jan.
1926	1–2 per week, about 6 per month	1 per week	1 per week
1927	1–2 per week, about 6 per month	1 per week, to 14 Nov., then *oprosom* to 3 Jan.	1 per week to 18 Nov., then *oprosom* to 23 Jan.
1928	1–2 per week, about 6 per month	1 per week	1 per week
1929	1–2 per week, about 6 per month	1 per week to Nov., then 1 per 10 days	1 per week to Oct., then 1 per 10 days
1930	6–8 per month	1 per 10 days	1 per 10 days
1931	2 per week	1 per 10 days to March, then 1 per 2 weeks; no meetings Oct.–Nov.	1 per 10 days to Nov., then 1 per 2 weeks
1932	2 per week	1 per 2 weeks. No meetings June–July, Aug.–Nov.	1 per 10 days
1933	1 per 10 days	1 per 3 weeks to July, then 1 per month	No meetings to 19 Jan., then 1 per month

(*continued*)

Table 3.1 (*continued*)

	Politburo	Orgburo	Secretariat
1934	1–2 per month	12 per year	No meetings in 1934
1935	1–2 per month	12 per year	1 meeting in Apr.
1936	0–1 per month	12 per year, but no meetings in Apr., July, Aug, Nov.	No meetings in 1936
1937	7 per year	6 per year. No meetings May–Sept.	No meetings in 1937
1938	6 per year	11 per year. No meetings in Apr.–May, Sept.–Nov.	No meetings in 1938
1939	2 per year	12 per year	No meetings in 1939
1940	1 per year	12 per year	No meetings in 1940

Source: Author's calculation from RGASPI, f. 17, op. 112 and 113.

were recorded as decisions of the Secretariat or Orgburo, which had not met.[48] The committees never functioned as rational rule-bound institutions. They had never been or done that.[49] By the end of the 1930s, therefore, the grandees had returned to the system of the early 1920s, when a single TsK secretary (almost never Stalin) advised by staff, could on many matters speak for the Politburo, Orgburo, and Secretariat. This was a working and arbitrary personalized nobility of the elect.

This vagueness of competence, agenda, and committee membership was intentional; it maximized the flexibility of the Bolshevik oligarchs to do what they pleased the way they pleased. It also reflected a very old patrimonial personal arbitrariness that resisted institutionalization. It didn't matter if the actual committees met as such.

Stalin, as general secretary of the party, had a major role in preparing agendas for the Politburo, Orgburo, and Secretariat, and he rarely missed a Politburo meeting. But he attended meetings of the Orgburo and Secretariat only intermittently in the 1920s, usually when a nationalities question was on the agenda. By 1928, he attended only nine (of more than seventy-five) Orgburo meetings and only four (of more than eighty) meetings of the Secretariat. He attended the first Secretariat meeting (4 January) of 1929 and no others during the year. He attended Orgburo meetings on 30 December 1929 and 6 January 1930, but no others in either year. For the rest of his career, he attended one or two Orgburo and Secretariat meetings a year, usually at the beginning of the year when economic plans or committee plans of work were discussed or when a major party reorganization issue was on the agenda.[50]

Stalin's absence in no way meant that he was not involved in personnel decisions, many of which were made outside committee meetings. But we can note here that the personal, noninstitutional Old Bolshevik noble system predated Stalin's rise to power by several years, and that the patrimonial understanding it reflected predated him and his cronies by centuries. Russia had always been ruled this way. Stalin therefore did not create or choose the system, but rather inherited it. But he did use it more skillfully than his rivals.

Occasionally the casual attitude of some grandees irritated the others. The first agenda item at the Orgburo meeting of 6 September 1920, chaired by Molotov, was "To take notice of the lateness of comrades Rykov and Tomskii and of the fact that the next meeting of the Orgburo will start precisely at 9 o'clock."[51] Molotov seems to have taken punctuality more seriously than anyone, because at the Orgburo meeting he chaired on 9 May 1921, he "suggested" taking down the names of Orgburo members and candidates who were late and taking "appropriate measures" against them. Everyone voted for the proposal except Mikhail Kalinin, who had a "special opinion."[52] But at the very next Orgburo meeting three days later, Stalin was himself half an hour late, Dzerzhinskii was more than a hour and a half late, and perhaps to make his point, Kalinin dragged in precisely two hours and twelve minutes late, according to the record.[53] After a couple of months of forcing the stenographers to record everyone's arrival and departure times, Molotov gave up.

Despite the Molotovs of the world, flexibility was the rule. As Lenin had said, "The fact of the matter is that the chief actual task of the Orgburo is the distribution of party forces, and the task of the Politburo is political questions. But it is obviously understood that this difference is to a well-known extent artificial. It is understood that no policy can be conducted except as the expression of appointments and transfers."[54] When Bolsheviks outside Lenin's noble roundtable criticized this vagueness, he reacted angrily and revealingly ridiculed the very idea of a written set of rules: "Do you want us to write a constitution? It is difficult to draw a hard and fast line between the Political Buro and the Organizing Buro, to delimit their functions precisely. Any question may become a political one, even the appointment of the superintendent of a building. If anyone has any other solution to suggest, please let us have it."[55] For the Old Bolshevik elite, the main thing was to retain control, and they were dubious about rigid institutions that could limit their freedom of maneuver.[56]

TURNING IT LOOSE WHILE KEEPING CONTROL: *OPROSOM* AND *NOMENKLATURA*

The grandees tried a variety of mechanisms to reduce the agenda load of the Politburo and Orgburo. A series of Politburo and Orgburo orders in 1921–22 specified that the Secretariat was to screen everything coming to those bodies and make decisions on them if possible. A prescreening layer was added when the conference of Central Committee department heads was formed to preview agenda items even before the Secretariat.[57] The number of agenda items grew and grew over the years, and the Old Bolshevik nobility wrestled with ways to cope with their self-imposed workload while at the same time retaining control.

Why did the number of items requiring the consideration and approval of top bodies grow so rapidly? The biggest factor, of course, was the expansion of the bureaucracy. The complexity of Soviet government increased dramatically in the twenty years following 1917. The size of the apparatus grew tremendously after 1929 along with the economy, now a matter for state administration. The number of commissariats grew almost every year, and at the top members of the Politburo came more and more to be economic administrators. In 1924, only three of seven Politburo members were involved in economic management. By 1934, the proportion had risen to seven of fifteen, and the duties of the other eight involved economic administration at least tangentially. With this expansion came an increasingly heavy workload for the Politburo. In 1930, 2,857 items came before it; by 1934 the number was 3,982.[58] The last Politburo meeting of 1930 (December 25) had 100 items on its agenda. The last meeting for 1936 (December 27) had 453.[59] The Politburo, like other cabinets, had "a full agenda of issues for decision; it is to prevent overcrowding of the cabinet agenda that mechanisms for taking decisions elsewhere are established." They needed "a repertoire of formal and informal mechanisms for pro-cessing" the huge number of matters coming before it.[60]

Lenin had another assessment as to why the committees worked as they did, based on Russian national character. "It's just the usual thoughtless way the Russian intelligentsia does things . . . first you tamper with it, then you do something, and [only] then do you think about it, and when it doesn't turn out, then you run to Kamenev and complain and drag it to the Politburo. Of course all difficult state questions have to come to the Politburo . . . but think first and then act, because if you speak [at the Politburo] you better speak with documents."

Lenin had other answers as well. He confessed that he himself had personalized the administration by acting as a personal link between the commissariats, where things should be decided, and the Politburo to which everything seemed to be gravitating. "So everything gets dragged from the commissariats to the Politburo. I bear great guilt for this because the connections between commissariats and the Politburo were maintained by me personally. . . . The commissariats should be responsible for their own work, rather than things going to them and then automatically to the Politburo."[61]

But that did not happen. The very nature of the system prevented institutionalization, guaranteed personalization, and conspired to send everything upward to the Politburo.

Aside from Lenin's blaming the habits of the Russian intelligentsia, plus his own personalization of the system, there were several cultural reasons that so many decisions percolated upward. First, a kind of semimilitarized legacy of the Civil War meant that a wide variety of matters seemed sensitive and properly reserved for the top leadership, more so than in other states. Questions having to do with police and repression, and anything having to do with foreign policy and trade were, by unspoken agreement, reserved for the secret precincts of the party's general staff. Nobody at lower levels wanted to risk taking a decision that could come back to haunt them in this politicized atmosphere of the armed socialist camp. English businessman John Urquhart was shocked that no less than the Politburo interested itself in (and vetoed) his proposed trade deal, something that would never have happened in another country.[62] The thinking among Bolshevik bureaucrats was that nobody ever got fired or arrested for passing a decision upward, especially one about foreigners or big money.

Second, a huge number of the items clogging the agendas of the Politburo and Orgburo were protests, counterprotests, and requests for adjudication or refereeing. Thin-skinned Bolshevik aristocrats were easily slighted and insulted and they appealed to higher bodies to restore their honor and reputations. A series of *konflikt* committees were formed to deal only with these. Many of these protocol items were listed as *protest,* or *obrashchenie* (appeal), or *pros'ba* (request) when the matter was actually a complaint about someone. Agencies and leaders fought over valuable personnel, budgets, time spans to fulfill tasks, and all kinds of turf. From the beginning of their existence, a basic element of the Secretariat, Orgburo and Politburo charters had to do with resolution of disputes and righting of wrongs. Of twenty-five items on a 1921 Orgburo agenda, fourteen were demands to change jobs or complaints about bosses; three more were protests against one agency raiding another's workers.[63]

Politburo decisions of 1921 and 1922 specified that in a conflict, both sides were to submit seven copies of their argument, a refutation of the other's accusation, and an exact proposed text or resolution for the Politburo. If an aggrieved party was not satisfied with a Secretariat resolution or compromise, he could demand that the Orgburo take it up. In case of further disagreement, the Politburo judged the matter.[64] Over the years, this progressive judging and appeal formula was repeated for many types of conflict, and was embedded in resolutions of party congresses.[65]

It was therefore not difficult to escalate an unresolved matter to the top if one were not satisfied with a resolution. Of course, low-ranking protesters were encouraged to accept early resolutions, but high-ranking grandees had the understood right to have their matters judged by their grandee peers on high. So the judging function of these bodies—an ancient form of patrimonial political activity—meant that their agendas would always be full of complaints and demands for refereeing by the king or his retainers.

The problem of choking the top bodies with minor questions never disappeared. The most important reason for the crowded Orgburo and Politburo agendas was that despite their protestations, the senior Bolshevik aristocrats did not really want many less vital matters to bypass them. Despite their complaints of overwork, they *wanted* all decisions great and small to at least come across their desks for blessing. They

were reluctant to leave any decision even slightly important to someone not of the blood, some latecomer to the party and its traditions,
someone who hadn't been through the underground and the fire and
storm of the revolution.

They adopted all kinds of expedients to speed up and streamline consideration of the huge number of issues facing them. At Politburo meetings, Lenin insisted that each reporter get no more than three minutes to
speak; seven for especially complex matters. Items requiring any discussion at all were immediately referred to a working commission (*de-
lovaia komissiia*) that was to report back and present a draft resolution;
this was the birth of the "Politburo commissions," which Khrushchev
would call "octets" and "sextets" that decided most questions in practice even down to his day. As Mikoian recalled, "only this can explain
how Lenin could deal with so many varied questions in such a short
time."[66] At other times, standing or ad hoc commissions were charged
with recommending decisions on various topics.[67] Stalin may or may
not have been a member of each such group; it is highly likely (but not
certain) that he ultimately approved each decision so produced.[68]

Bolsheviks notwithstanding, it was also a structural problem. Called
"segmented" or "fragmented" decision making in social science literature, such informal personal arrangements are not at all uncommon in
many modern government systems (the U.S. government being a prime
example).[69] "Real debates occur therefore in smaller groups, either
formally constituted . . . or informally called together—typically when
two or three members see each other, one of them being, in many cases
at least, the prime minister. Thus . . . true debates of the full cabinet are
relatively rare."[70] Given what we know of Stalin's practice, the following account by a British cabinet member during the term of Margaret
Thatcher would not be far wrong if "Stalin" were substituted for "Mrs.
Thatcher":

> She would have an idea, or somebody would, and she would talk to
> them. She would bring two or three people in for the second meeting
> and we'd discuss it a bit further. . . . She . . . would then identify those
> in the cabinet who had the most concerns about that policy and then
> they were talked to . . . so they were brought in and when you have
> built that you then have something you can put to a cabinet subcom-
> mittee, get it agreed, and by the time it came to the cabinet it was a fait
> accompli. (Lord Wakeham.)[71]

Meanwhile, back at the Politburo, the onslaught of agenda items continued. At the end of 1929, the Politburo ordered that no requests or reports from lower bodies to the Politburo could exceed five to ten pages and that they must reach the Secretariat no later than six days before the Politburo meeting, complete with a predrafted Politburo resolution.[72] A year later, in November of 1931, the Politburo reduced the maximum size of submissions to four to five pages, but a few days later settled on a maximum of eight pages.[73] Stalin ordered in September 1932 that no more than fifteen items could appear on any Politburo meeting's agenda.[74] By the spring of 1931, *all* requests for Politburo decisions from localities were shunted to the Secretariat for decision, except for questions of "exceptional importance" that could come to the Politburo.[75]

But the most important expedient the Politburo and Orgburo used to get through the mountain of paper was decision making *oprosom,* "by polling" the members by telephone. Already by the spring of 1921, questions not requiring extended discussion were routed to Politburo members for their approval by telephone or voting card outside normal committee meeting times. The Secretariat and Orgburo followed suit in 1922.[76] By 1926, questions decided by polling began to outnumber those decided in meetings, and by the beginning of 1931, the number of questions decided *oprosom* exceeded those on the agenda by a wide margin. By the end of 1934, at its final meeting of the year, the Politburo took up eight questions at the meeting, but the protocol indicates that 260 questions had been decided *oprosom.*[77] By the end of the 1930s, the Politburo and Orgburo agendas each contained many hundreds of items, the vast majority of which were approved by one member or more outside a meeting and then confirmed unanimously by the others over the phone or in the corridor.

The important point here is that the Politburo, Orgburo, and Secretariat could have simply sloughed all this off completely. They didn't. While they screened and double-screened items through committees, cut down discussion time, used subcommittees of the Politburo and Orgburo, and approved things amongst themselves by polling each other outside meetings, they never let go their prerogative: in some way or another every single decision, however trivial, was looked at and blessed or rejected by a grandee.

The same thing can be said of the *nomenklatura* system, which began in the 1920s. The *nomenklatura* of a given institution was a list of the positions that institution had the right to confirm. In the 1923 system, of about five thousand party and state positions to be confirmed by the Central Committee, thirty-five hundred (*Nomenklatura* No. 1) could only be proposed and confirmed by the Politburo, Orgburo, or Secretariat. An additional fifteen hundred jobs (*Nomenklatura* No. 2) could be filled by other bodies but were subject to confirmation and approval by these top three committees.

Our sources suggest that the *nomenklatura* system was really intended as a way to systematize existing practice and to decrease the appointment burden on the Central Committee apparatus. Months before its establishment, in March 1922 V. P. Nogin told a party congress that the Orgburo and Secretariat were facing around a hundred personnel questions per day. TsK Secretary Molotov, who was becoming Stalin's right-hand man, complained that the apparatus was burdened by far too many personnel appointments. The 22,500 personnel proposals passing through the apparatus in the previous year and the average sixty walk-in applicants per day were far too many to be handled properly. He said that high-level confirmation of most of them was "unnecessary" and proposed sharply reducing the Central Committee's appointment responsibilities to the leading "responsible workers."[78] As we saw, the original *nomenklatura* lists reserved for TsK appointment or approval amounted to about five thousand positions. This corresponded with existing practice: in the year before establishing the system, the TsK had vetted 5,167 posts, and in the previous year 4,738. The 1923 *nomenklatura* system thus codified existing practice and scale for appointment of responsible workers.

The nobles' goal was to reduce the scale, but they failed over and over again because this goal conflicted with a more important one: to retain corporate control. In 1925, a revision of the Central Committee *nomenklatura* did reduce the number of posts requiring direct TsK appointment from 3,500 to 1,870. But another 1,640 slots required preapproval by a TsK secretary, and another 1,590 were to be approved by Politburo and Orgburo commissions, for a total of 5,500 positions requiring grandee approval, which was actually more than under the 1923 system.[79]

Another revision was attempted in late 1928 that seems to have reduced the number of positions requiring top grandee approval to around four thousand, but the number kept creeping up anyway. Every time a revision was attempted, the story was the same.[80] Huge lists were drawn up by staff and negotiated with the party grandees. The archives are full of rough-draft lists with excisions, cross-outs, and additions ás the process went on.[81] Endless discussions, drafts, negotiations and disagreements among staff and Bolshevik nobles made such revisions a cumbersome process.

Ultimately, the central *nomenklatura* system was designed to retain authority over "the basic commanding heights," as TsKK member Dmitri Kurskii put it.[82] Thus, in 1929 after several revisions ostensibly seeking reductions in top-level vetting, for the USSR Commissariat of Finance the Politburo reserved the right to appoint the commissar, his three deputies, and five members of the collegium. Even the two members of the national insurance board and its financial agents were reserved to the top committees (the Orgburo and the Secretariat, respectively). Another nine appointments to the Russian Republic Commissariat of Finance were reserved to the three top committees.[83] Although it is perhaps not surprising that the top bodies would control appointments to the political police (GPU) including the entire central departmental apparatus and provincial chiefs (46 slots) their coverage also included 360 members of joint stock and trading associations.[84] That year, in an average province, the posts requiring top committee appointment or approval included the top party officials, chairman of the cooperative board, newspaper editors and trade union officials, and the provincial chiefs of the secret police, the procuracy, the courts, and higher educational institutions: eighty-eight in all.[85]

Each revision of the *nomenklatura* system had as a stated purpose to shift the vetting of some positions downward, to the provincial committees. The idea was that the provincial committees would in turn shift some of their appointment prerogatives downward to the districts, so appointments could better match conditions on the ground. In practice, though, the results were quite different. Aside from the continued creeping upward of Politburo/Orgburo approvals noted above, provincial party barons were reluctant to part with their traditional appointment vettings and refused to pass approval power downward. Although provincial party committees were supposed to reduce their own *nomenklaturas* by 25 percent, in fact they increased them. In August 1926, the Vologda Provincial Party Committee had 393 positions on its appointment list; Voronezh had 364 and Stalingrad 374. The Smolensk City (not provincial) Party Committee had a whopping 946 appointments under its control. In Ukraine, practically nothing was passed down: there, city and rural district party committees had no *nomenklatura* lists at all. Moscow complained that such bloated *nomenklatura* lists precluded any kind of recordkeeping or rational planning.[86]

The reasons for this *nomenklatura* stickiness should be obvious. Despite the best of intentions, the most logical thinking, and even direct orders, nobody wanted to release whatever appointment prerogatives they had. In a patrimonial system, power was patronage and rational institutional planning always took a back seat.

Even though the grandees felt overworked, they just couldn't let go of their noble prerogatives. The oligarchs at the top of the party, Stalinist and oppositionist alike, were veterans of the prerevolutionary underground and had been Lenin's comrades in arms.[87] They felt themselves awash in the sea of new party recruits and as a generational cohort must have felt things slipping from their control. They had to delegate much decision making to staff but were unwilling to completely relinquish their elite supervision, so they had to settle for a system of vetting and approving of prepared decisions. Ten years after the revolution, the dozen or so top nobles in the country still insisted on looking at thousands of personnel appointments themselves, and passing judgment on hiring everyone from commissars to insurance agents to rectors of provincial universities. As Lenin had said, "Any question may become a political one, even the appointment of the superintendent of a building."[88]

4 The Party Personnel System
Downstairs at the Central Committee

It is the kind of work that makes you a target for anybody and everybody who is discontented about anything related to their fate.
—*Orgraspred chief L. M. Kaganovich, 1923*

DOWNSTAIRS WE FIND the TsK staff, whose work was entirely different from that of the grandees, and who had different interests. Beneath the Politburo, Orgburo, and Secretariat the main personnel work of the TsK was organized into a series of departments under the Secretariat. Over the decades of Soviet power, these departments were periodically reorganized, combined, split, abolished, and reestablished with confusing regularity, but their specializations remained more or less constant: personnel assignment, agitation and propaganda, rural/agricultural work, industry, press, culture, schools and education, international affairs, and the like. The size of the total Secretariat staff grew quickly after the Civil War and varied over the years, but was usually in the range of six to seven hundred persons.

At various times (1934–39, 1948–54) such departments assigned personnel within their areas of expertise, but most of the time personnel ("cadre" or "organizational") recommendations were centralized in a single department of the Secretariat. Founded in 1919 as two separate departments, *Uchetno-raspreditel'nyi otdel* (recordkeeping-assignment) and *Organizatsionno-instruktorskii otdel* (organizational adviser), they were fused in 1924 under the name *Organizatsionno-instruktorskii otdel*. Separated again in 1930 into state (*Raspreditel'nyi otdel*) and party assignment (*Otdel rukovodiashchikh partiinykh organov*, ORPO)

Table 4.1 Size of TsK Secretarial Staff Departments, 1919–30

1919	30 –> 80 by end of year
1920	130
1921	602
1922	705
1923	741
1924	694
1925	767
1927	657
1930	375[1]

Sources: *Deviatyi s"ezd RKP(b), mart–aprel' 1920 goda: Stenograficheskii otchet* (Moscow: Partizdat, 1960), 507, 806; *Vosmaia konferentsiia RKP(b), dekabr' 1919 goda: Protokoly* (Moscow: Partizdat, 1961), 221; *Izvestiia TsK VKP (b),* (5 March 1921): 23–24, and (March 1922): 54; *Dvenadtsatyi s"ezd RKP(b), 17–25 aprelia 1923 goda: Stenograficheskii otchet* (Moscow: Partizdat, 1960), 79; *Piatnadtsatyi s"ezd VKP(b), dekabr' 1927 goda: Stenograficheskii otchet,* vol. 2 (Moscow: Gosizdat, 1962), 123; *Trinadtsatyi s"ezd RKP(b), mai 1924 goda: Stenograficheskii otchet* (Moscow: Gosizdat, 1963), 128; *XVI s"ezd Vsesoiuznoi Kommunisticheskoi Partii (b): Stenograficheskii otchet* (Moscow: Gosizdat, 1931), 93.
1. After a 50 percent cut ("rationalization") in 1929. After 1930, party sources no longer provided information on the size of the Secretariat staff.

departments, they were reunited in 1939 as the *Upravlenie kadrov,* only to be divided again in 1948. Here, for the sake of convenience and to avoid confusion, we will use the most common generic name, Orgraspred.[1]

As its constituting documents show, Orgraspred's functions were not limited to personnel assignment:[2]

I (a) To establish and strengthen the organizational connection with party organizations in the localities, getting to know them and their activities and advising [*instruktirovanie*] them;

(b) The study and communication of experience of party building;

(c) Drafting leadership orders, circulars, and instructions in the area of organizational, assignment, and recordkeeping work of the party;

(d) Systematization and harmonization [*soglasovanie*] of party directives;

. . .

(f) Systematization of recordkeeping, selection and assignment of party workers of appropriate qualifications in the center and the provinces;

. . .

(h) Conducting the transfer, promotion, and mobilization of party workers;

. . .

(j) To fulfill the concrete tasks of the Secretariat and Orgburo of the TsK on any and all questions of organizational, assignment and recordkeeping work.

. . .

3. Assistants to the chief of Orgraspred carry out work in preparation of questions having to do with selection and assignment of party forces in various branches of the economy.

. . .

Orgraspred was authorized to conduct departmental conferences "to work out in preliminary form the questions that it will present to the Orgburo and Secretariat, preparing draft decisions on these questions." Orgraspred's "organizational subdepartment" was also authorized to "work out and draft TsK orders on all organizational questions," maintain permanent connections with all central and provincial party organizations, and "systematize party legislation."

As we shall see, these varied mandates gave Orgraspred staffers considerable power. It became common practice for guberniia, and later oblast party secretaries to travel to Moscow and report periodically on their party work to the Orgburo. Some of these reports/conferences were published in the party press. But it became typical for provincial party delegations to report first to Orgraspred staff, which evaluated their reports and framed them for discussion by the Orgburo.[3]

Throughout most of the 1920s, Orgraspred carried out all this work with a staff of seventy to seventy-five people in its central apparatus. With the increased tasks of industrialization and collectivization, the staff grew to ninety-five in 1929–35. The central Orgraspred staff of "responsible workers" consisted of a chief of department (Ivan Moskvin for much of the 1920s), nine deputy chiefs, nine assistants (*pomoshchiki*), eighteen instructors, and technical personnel including archivists, secretaries, and so forth.[4]

According to statute and apparent practice, each of the deputies and assistants was in charge of several issues or branches of production. For example, in 1929 Deputy N. I. Ezhov was in charge of studying and making cadre recommendations for agricultural plan fulfillment, the seven-hour working day, and promotions of rural cadres. His colleague Zh. Meerzon covered certain local party organizations, criticism campaigns, nationality questions, and mass work among party recruits. Assistant P. Gorbunov specialized in distribution of cadres for credit and finance, soviet administration, and banking.[5] Internal paperwork and departmental conference proceedings suggest that these staff members took their work seriously and that each became expert in his area and the personnel needs therein.[6]

In the best case, personnel slots were filled in the following way. A request would come in to the TsK from a party or state organization. Orgraspred would refer the request to the assistant (*pomoshchnik*) or the deputy who specialized in the area.[7] That staffer would then study the request, and if he found it valid and appropriate (not always the case), he would try to match the needed skills with known qualifications and recommend a candidate.

The first paper in the file was a Secretariat worksheet, filled in by TsK staff to describe the action. It contained spaces for the candidate's name, age, length of time in the party, education, and nationality, previous position and evaluation of his work there. Then,

    10. Proposed new position
    11. Agreement of current organization to release him
    12. Agreement of proposed organization to receive him
    13. Agreement of the comrade to the transfer[8]

Orgraspred staff thus had to secure the agreement of the candidate's old boss, his new boss, as well as of the candidate himself to the transfer. The recommendation would then go to his superior (chief or deputy chief of Orgraspred) for approval.

If these bases had been covered (and sometimes if they had not) the proposed appointment now went to the staff conference, either of Orgraspred or of TsK department heads. This conference triaged the appointment, according to a variety of factors discussed above, and sent it to the Politburo, the Orgburo, or Secretariat meeting. If the matter was truly minor or uncontroversial (not always the same thing), it would be approved by the TsK secretary chairing the staff conference.

If, on the other hand, the staff conference sent the appointment upstairs for a decision, they wrote an "explanatory memo" (*ob"iasnitel'naia zapiska*) to accompany the recommendation. These memos consisted of several short paragraphs summarizing the candidate's experience and qualifications, the agreement or disagreement of those involved, followed by an Orgraspred recommendation. Examples include:

> To the Secretariat . . . Orgraspred TsK considers the transfer of Comrade Agrov and his replacement by Comrade Shiron advisable and asks for confirmation.

And . . .

> In view of the situation in Leningrad Oblast, Orgraspred TsK does not oppose replacing Comrade Krastin with Comrade Kondrat'ev.

And . . .

> In view of the above, Orgraspred asks that the Siberian Territory's request be denied.[9]

In the mid-1920s, 90–95 percent of Orgburo assignments were settled by Orgraspred proposal blessed by a TsK grandee.[10] Although we do not have good archival sources on this for the 1930s, anecdotal evidence suggests an analogous acceptance rate.[11] Many positions Orgraspred considered were so minor that they did not require sending upstairs for confirmation. It seems that at least two-thirds of Orgraspred placements were not on the TsK *nomenklatura,* and thus did not require approval by one or more grandees.[12] It should be remembered, however, that the very top positions in party and state—around fifteen hundred by the late 1920s—were on *Nomenklatura* No. 1 and therefore appointed directly by the Politburo, Orgburo, or Secretariat, and another roughly thirty-five hundred required their personal confirmation. Certainly many of these at the lower end were proposed by Orgraspred, but it seems that top positions (provincial party staffs, people's commissars, their deputies and collegia, and Soviet executive committees, and so forth) were exclusively in the preserve of the top nobility. Still, looking at the entire range of positions, Orgraspred was a very powerful force in deciding personnel assignment.

DOWNSTAIRS VS. UPSTAIRS

The lack of structure preferred upstairs irritated the staff far more than it did such grandee sticklers like Molotov. As we will see, staff wanted predictability, procedure, rules, and order; all things that could only reduce the arbitrary field of maneuver of the Old Bolsheviks, and the grandees resisted systematization at every turn.

The grandees' personal "interference" in the staff's attempts at a rational bureaucratic system irritated them, although there was nothing they could do about it; the matter was too indelicate, if not dangerous, to bring up. Aside from the fact that those upstairs were very powerful bosses, it was considered inappropriate for a Bolshevik to complain about his work, salary, or workload. A Bolshevik was supposed to be a good soldier and by and large the staff followed orders. Nevertheless, we can find implicit and obliquely explicit complaints downstairs.

WORKLOAD

If we look only at their personnel assignment duties in Table 4.2, it is clear that Orgraspred's staff faced a heavy workload. Even after the massive waves of Civil War military and other mobilizations ended, Orgraspred was filling hundreds of vacancies each month. Orgraspred workers were putting in twelve-to-thirteen-hour workdays.[13] Data on the number of annual placements is episodic for the 1920s but seems to range from six to twelve thousand per year. Thousands on the *nomenklatura* had to be assigned or vetted, plus the two-thirds of Orgraspred placements that were not on the TsK *nomenklatura*.[14]

The personnel assignment staff at Orgraspred were not highly paid. In 1928, the chief (*zaveduyushchii*) of Orgraspred, the nine deputy chiefs, and the twenty-two responsible instructors all made the same salary (225 rubles per month); the nine assistant chiefs for personnel assignments made 200–210 rubles. Other "responsible workers" earned from 150 to 200 rubles. Even though, for some Orgraspred workers, the job included access to special stores, this was hardly a princely sum in the late 1920s.[15]

At the same time, the TsK grandees were constantly trying to cut costs, which meant reducing staff and resisting salary increases. As early as 1922, the first of several orders of the Secretariat was "to consider pay raises to Sec workers impossible."[16] A standing "Rationalization Commission" with a mission to cut costs operated since at least that year.[17] In October 1923 a meeting of a "Commission to Reduce Staff in the *Apparat* of the Secretariat VKP(b)" reported to the Secretariat. Via the commission, department heads reported to the Secretariat that they were prepared to reduce their staffs by an average of 10

Table 4.2 Orgrasped Personnel Assignments, 1919–30

	Total assignments	Of them, responsible workers	Assignments per year	Assignments per day
1919	21,500	2,726	21,500	
1919–20	25,000		25,000	30–70
1920–21	42,014			50
1921–22	22,500		22,500	60
1923	10,727		10,351	70
1924	6,082	4,500	6,082	
1925	12,277	9,419	8,184	
1927	8,761	7,445	4,380	
1930	~11,000		~4,400	

Sources: Vosmoi s"ezd RKP(b), mart 1919 goda: Protokoly (Moscow: Partizdat, 1959), 185; Graeme Gill, *The Origins of the Stalinist Political System* (Cambridge: Cambridge University Press, 1990), 163; *Desiatyi s"ezd RKP(b), mart 1921 goda: Stenograficheskii otchet* (Moscow: Partizdat 1963), 41–45, 56, 49, 111; *Deviatyi s"ezd RKP(b), mart–aprel' 1920 goda: Stenograficheskii otchet* (Moscow: Partizdat, 1960), 34, 503; *Dvenadtsatyi s"ezd RKP(b), 17–25 aprelia 1923 goda: Stenograficheskii otchet* (Moscow: Partizdat, 1960), 81, 804; *Odinnadtsatyi s"ezd RKP(b), mart–aprel' 1922 goda: Stenograficheskii otchet* (Moscow: Partizdat, 1961), 65; *Trinadtsatyi s"ezd RKP(b), mai 1924 goda: Stenograficheskii otchet* (Moscow: Gosizdat, 1963), 132–33, 806; *Vosmaia Konferentsiia RKP(b), dekabr' 1919 goda: Protokoly* (Moscow: Partizdat, 1961), 30, 217, 221.

percent. This represented, across all departments, a reduction from 682 to 618 workers.[18] Another "rationalization" of TsK staff in 1929 cut the size of the staff in half. But the problem never went away. Orgraspred staff managed to soften the 1929 "rationalization" ordered by the Org-buro. As instructed, they did indeed cut their staff from 97 to 90, saving 1,142 rubles a month. But the overworked Orgraspred staff tried to protect itself: the seven cut were all clericals: typists, couriers, and so forth.[19] In January 1934, the Secretariat ordered that nobody could be hired in the TsK *apparat* without the personal confirmation of either Stalin or Kaganovich, "and to oblige TsK department heads to strictly follow this order."[20]

Because of the long hours, low pay, and overwork created by the ungrateful grandees, a job in the Secretariat staff was hardly attractive.[21] Party etiquette prevented staff from openly complaining. A Bolshevik was supposed to devote himself selflessly to whatever work was assigned him without complaint. Given this tradition, Orgraspred and Secretarial staff instead voted with their feet. In 1922, Molotov reported that half of the eleven instructor positions were vacant, and others noted that they really needed twenty-one.[22] In 1925, of 767 workers in the Secretariat apparatus, 704 had changed jobs in the past eighteen months.[23] Even into the 1930s, Orgraspred and its successor ORPO always had plenty of staff vacancies.

COMPETING FOR CADRES: ORGRASPRED IN THE MIDDLE

It was a fact of life for decades after the revolution that experienced and reliable administrative talent was scarce in the party, and this colored and deformed personnel assignment in a variety of ways. First, the shortage of talent meant that personnel assignment was a seller's market. Potential appointees with good records could maneuver for good positions and refuse bad ones. Second, party committees and senior Bolshevik nobles deployed various strategies and personal influence to secure good cadres, and fought for them.

Given the shortage of competent and experienced cadres, these requests were sometimes insistent and plaintive.[24] From Kirgizia:

> Our agricultural administration has done absolutely nothing in the past year because there is not one Communist who could comprehend all the work, much less put it into order. We have left our deputy commissar of agriculture position vacant in the hope that we would receive an experienced comrade from Moscow. We are still waiting and very much beg you to send someone. Otherwise things will fall apart.[25]

From the Siberian Buro:

> We hear there are many unemployed Communists in Moscow. We need them! Please send us someone. In the last mobilization, we received only unsatisfactory people. This time, please send us no unqualified people, drunks, squabblers, troublemakers, sick people, or those with big families. Please warn them that they will be working in the deep countryside.[26]

In Kazakhstan in 1923, the Akmolinsk gubkom faked a divisive conflict and reported sharply split votes in order to justify Moscow sending them another pair of hands, a new leader to act as referee.[27]

Orgraspred frequently was forced to referee disputes about valuable cadres. In 1926, it had confirmed one Kantor as a board member of the state publishing house (GIZ) transferring him from the book union (Knigosoiuz). Knigosoiuz protested, and Orgraspred tried to mediate by suggesting Kantor work at both jobs. GIZ then protested, and the Orgburo stepped in to overrule Orgraspred and confirm the original decision for GIZ.[28]

That same year, Orgraspred tried to transfer G. Grinfeld from the Commissariat of Trade (NKVneshTorg) to Sovkino, the national film production organization, without asking NKVneshTorg. The latter exploded that "we weren't consulted. The first we heard of his transfer was the day he left! We need him. He has languages and is very useful as our representative in Paris. Besides, he has no film experience." Under pressure from Sovkino head Shvedchikov, this time the Orgburo backed up Orgraspred's recommendation.[29]

Viatsk flatly refused to return Comrade Chuzhkov to Moscow when Orgraspred requested it. "We communicate that Comrade Chuzhkov was mobilized for responsible work in the countryside and has been working here for 4 months as a district party secretary. To send him to your disposal in light of insufficient numbers of workers in this organization the gubkom considers impossible."[30]

The staff at Orgraspred thought of themselves as professionals doing important work and did not like to be ignored by the boyars or insulted by bureaucrats. Nevertheless, it happened. These uneven contests between staff and Old Bolshevik nobles could take several forms. Sometimes, it was necessary for an upstairs grandee to defend them. Sometimes, Orgraspred refereed disputes between grandees, but without comparable rank and personal prestige (or the support of someone who did have them) it was hard to make their compromises stick. Sometimes, because they were staff, Orgraspred could safely be ignored; they stayed out of the way while the titans fought it out and announced the result to the staff.

WE WANT COMRADE DEMIN

On 6 May 1921, the People's Commissariat of Agriculture (NKZem) asked for the return of Comrade Demin to them from his temporary assignment in Simbirsk. The commissariat pointed out that he had been sent to Simbirsk in 1919 for temporary work, and because he was a valued professional, NKZem had never intended to part with him permanently.

On 10 May, Uchraspred[31] staff and the Secretariat then wired Simbirsk, saying that "absent serious objections," Comrade Demin should be returned. Two days later, Simbirsk replied that they had received the telegram, but there was no deputy for Demin and his exit would cause serious harm to agriculture in Simbirsk. "So we insistently request" that you leave him here. By the way, Simbirsk wrote, he's also doing useful work in unions. This was a common tactic of local organizations that wanted to keep a valued worker: to transfer his duties to another specialty, thereby removing him from the roster of his previous employer which now had no claim on him.

Uchraspred had seen this trick before, and a week later wrote to Simbirsk demanding that "you please explain his transfer from the guberniia agricultural department to the guberniia trade unions." Simbirsk ignored the Moscow staff. Receiving no answer, Uchraspred repeated their demand two weeks later, on 8 June 1921. Still Simbirsk refused to answer, so on 6 July Uchraspred wrote again to Simbirsk, asking them to "speed up your answer to our 20 May letter." Finally, on 25 July, two months after the original Uchraspred telegram, Simbirsk appeared to give up and announced to the TsK that Demin had agreed to the transfer. Their answer was transmitted to the Orgburo.

Nearly two weeks later, Uchraspred wrote to NKZem to check that Demin had actually been transferred back to their assignment roster from Simbirsk. NKZem answered the next day that Demin was not listed as a worker on their roster, but they would ask their departments for further information. Three days later, on 9 August, NKZem wrote to the Secretariat that Demin was still attached to Simbirsk![32] Simbirsk had won, Uchraspred had lost.

During the Demin affair, Simbirsk was at various times led by three famous Old Bolshevik heroes: Ian Sten (party member since 1914), V. N. Meshcheriakov (since 1905) and A. V. Popov (since 1904). Against them as commissar of agriculture was V. V. Ossinskii, who was also an Old Bolshevik (since 1907) and a candidate member of the TsK, but at the time of the Demin affair he was a leader of the Democratic Centralists opposition group, and being thrashed by the party majority. In fact, at party congresses he went out of his way to denounce the Secretariat and its staff.[33] His current prestige, therefore, was no match for those grandees successively running Simbirsk.

In this case, Demin had refused to leave Simbirsk and Simbirsk had cooperated in not letting him go. Absent a powerful grandee personality to force the issue, Simbirsk won the battle. Although Simbirsk eventually answered the Orgburo's letters (even to defy them), it did not even bother to reply to Uchraspred's telegrams. This must have made the staff furious.

WHERE IS COMRADE PETRIAKOV?

In another case, staff were caught in the middle of a boyar battle. On 29 November 1926, A. P. Smirnov, people's commissar of agriculture, asked the Secretariat and the Ulianovsk gorkom to release and transfer one N. M. Petriakov from deputy chief of land administration in Ulianovsk to chief of land administration in Donetsk (North Caucasus Territory).[34] The next day, at its preparatory conference, Orgraspred agreed, and forwarded its recommendation to the Secretariat for approval at its meeting of 3 December.[35]

Meanwhile, Ulianovsk party secretary F. I. Verstonov protested losing Petriakov, and used a familiar tactic. He transferred Petriakov from agriculture to director of the Ulianovsk Food Trust, thus removing him from the NKZem *nomenklatura* of positions it controlled. At its meeting of 3 December, the Secretariat denied NKZem's request and Orgraspred's recommendation supporting it, and upheld Ulianovsk's refusal to part with Petriakov. As soon as he heard about this, A. P. Smirnov angrily protested the Secretariat's decision to the Orgburo. "Despite my insistent requests, Ulianovsk has protested and improperly transferred Petriakov." He demanded that the Orgburo take up the matter, reverse the Secretariat, and order Ulianovsk to comply, thus halting its "incorrect actions."[36]

Both Smirnov and Ulianovsk's Verstonov were Old Bolshevik nobles. Born in 1896, Verstonov had joined the party in 1913. Smirnov, however, was senior party aristocracy. He had been in the Social Democratic movement since 1896, before Verstonov was born, and a member of the Russian Social Democratic Labor Party (forerunner of the Bolsheviks) since 1898. Smirnov therefore had a huge advantage in terms of personal prestige and *mestnichestvo,* but just in case, he wanted the matter heard and decided in the Orgburo because he was a member of that body and could more easily use his personal influence there. Sure enough, on 3 January 1927, with Smirnov present, the Org-buro reversed the 3 December Secretariat decision, pulling Petriakov from Ulianovsk and putting him at the disposal of the TsK, and there-fore of Smirnov.[37]

Verstonov didn't give up. Ulianovsk protested the Orgburo decision *downward* to the Secretariat. At this point, on 18 January, Orgraspred suggested calling a meeting of all interested parties and sent a telegram to Ulianovsk scheduling the meeting for 21 January at which "it is neces-sary to have your representative present."[38] Sensing that he had no chance in Moscow, on 20 January 1927, the day before the meeting, Verstonov sent a telegram from Ulianovsk to the Secretariat: "Our party conference starts today. We can't send a representative. Please postpone." The Secretariat agreed to postpone the meeting to reconsider the Org-buro order for a week. On 28 January 1927, the day of the meeting, the Ulianovsk comrades did not show up. The Secretariat postponed the meeting for another week. Still no Ulianovsk comrades in sight.[39]

Ulianovsk had decided to defy the TsK and Orgraspred by ignoring them. After all, that worked sometimes in the past, as in the Demin case. They never showed up, and on 4 February 1927 the Secretariat resolved "to instruct the Ulianovsk gubkom on the impermissibility of further delaying the Petriakov transfer."[40] Ulianovsk stalled another week, but with both the Secretariat, the Orgburo, and A. P. Smirnov's grandee prestige against them, they gave up, and on 25 February 1927, the Secretariat reported that "Petriakov has arrived and taken his documents [for the transfer]"[41]

The Petriakov case showed that Orgraspred could be ignored, espe-cially when titans above them were in combat. Ulianovsk variously ig-nored, stalled and lied to Orgraspred. The case also showed the indeterminacy of bureaucratic relations and the unclear boundaries be-tween the Orgburo and the Secretariat, especially when faced with inter-ference and insistence from powerful competing Old Bolshevik nobles like Verstonov and Smirnov. Verstonov the Ulianovsk guberniia secre-tary squared off against Orgburo member Smirnov, and held his own for three months by delaying and playing the system, but finally lost. Such jousts between senior knights invariably trumped Orgraspred's efforts.

Other times, though, Orgraspred's noble overseers jumped to its de-fense when it found itself in a grandee crossfire. In November 1923, the newly appointed party first secretary in Gomel' (Belorussia) A. L.

Gilinskii, complained to Uchraspred chief Kaganovich that outgoing secretary M. M. Khataevich was raiding Gomel', taking his former cadres with him to Odessa:

> We've now received two papers from Uchraspred about transferring workers to Odessa. . . . I understand that Comrade Khataevich, knowing the workers here, knows how to request the best workers, but such a system is no good.

Poor Gilinskii found it hard to compete not only with Khataevich but with Odessa.

> It creates a mood here about wanting to go to Odessa, which with its urban size, the seaside, and Comrade Khataevich as an acquaintance is in many respects more alluring [!] than Gomel'. There are a thousand reasons why a comrade would agree to be sent to Odessa.
>
> Every day we here shake our heads and wonder how to put the cork back in the bottle after these TsK transfers, which puts us in an impossible position. . . . I categorically insist that Uchraspred stop contributing to these liquidationist sentiments here.

Kaganovich defended his Uchraspred staff:

> Respected Comrade Glinskii,
>
> 1. Your censure of Uchraspred on the subject of Comrade Khataevich allegedly encouraging the defection of Gomel' workers to Odessa is completely baseless. Requests about removing or transferring workers are not demands; Uchraspred has the right to ask a gubkom, and you don't need to be afraid not to do so. You have no examples of categorical transfers away from you.
> 2. You cannot deny Comrade Khataevich, who is himself a gubkom secretary, the right to negotiate with Uchraspred on workers.
> 3. As for the liquidationist sentiments caused by Uchraspred, you are even more wrong than in the above matters, because from the moment of your appointment in Gomel', we have sent you 12 workers, according to the attached list . . .
>
> Therefore, you were wrong to send such a stormy letter as yours to Uchraspred.
>
> With com. greetings, Kaganovich

In the 1930s, transfers continued to be sensitive issues, and Orgraspred staff were careful to touch all the bases, especially when powerful grandees were involved. In 1935, N. I. Ezhov of ORPO wrote to Stalin,

"Comrade Stalin. I summoned Pshenitsyn. He agrees to become second secretary in Sverdlovsk. I had a telephone conversation with Kabakov [Sverdlovsk first secretary]. He is very satisfied with Stroganov [the outgoing second secretary] being placed at the disposal of the TsK. He agrees with the candidacy of Pshenitsyn, and asks for quick approval."[42]

Actual disputes over transfers likewise did not die down. In January 1936, Orgraspred (now ORPO) supported the request of B. Tal', chief of TsK Press and Publications Department, to transfer Comrade Elizarov from editor of *Stalingradskaia pravda* to assistant chief of Tal''s department. Elizarov agreed, and ORPO sent the editor of *Kurskaia pravda* to Stalingrad to replace him. But Stalingrad first secretary, the powerful I. Vareikis, raised an objection. Tal' was no match for Vareikis, and the transfer was apparently killed.[43]

DREAMING DOWNSTAIRS: A REGULAR PLANNED SYSTEM

It should not be surprising that Orgraspred, which did all the legwork and heavy lifting for personnel appointments, would prefer regularized, rule-bound bureaucratic procedures to make their work more orderly and predictable and defensible from criticism. There was an endless number of internal staff meetings discussing ways to streamline and systematize their work.[44] But while the grandees upstairs did not object to system in principle, they often blocked attempts to create it.

Old Bolsheviks tended to prefer the personal touch, giving great weight to criteria like "who knows him?" or "whom did he work with?" But staff complained that "cases of personnel appointment based on nepotism and old boy networks [*kumovstva*], or home town are not rare and create an unbusinesslike atmosphere."[45] Part of this personal connection approach to appointment was relying on the obligatory personal references one had to provide for party membership. These letters of recommendation carried more weight upstairs than downstairs, where they distrusted them and thought that "People fight over them because they are about personal connections and personal unpleasantness. . . . For example, you work in some institution where there is a spat (*skloka*). Maybe you are guilty or not, but after that it's very hard for you to work normally. . . . So in [your] next job, where you used to work they write a reference that you are no good, so we can't assign you."[46]

Orgraspred staff preferred to use known facts and qualifications, rather than dubious personal opinions, to place people in jobs. But of course, letters of recommendation continued to be required.

Just as frustrating for Orgraspred's efforts to plan and rationalize (and be respected) was the tendency of party members to simply refuse an assignment, as Demin and Petriakov had done. We also saw how well-known anti-Stalin oppositionists refused to accept reassignments and complained about them, invoking the traditional Bolshevik knight's right to independence and right to refuse a task beneath their station. But it was not only senior grandees or oppositionists who recognized and used the traditional right of refusal. To take only one of hundreds of examples, in November 1919, at the height of the Civil War when party members were being mobilized for military service, "Comrade Krestin-skii reports that regardless of the repeated proposals of the TsK that Comrade Kloizner leave Tambov because he is mobilized to the front, he with the support of the Tambov gubkom has not left as of this time."[47]

A sampling of Orgraspred files only for the second half of 1926 produces many examples from these years. In July, Comrade Lisitsyn refused to be transferred to Kazakhstan. Ignoring the Orgburo for four months, he finally won and was sent to Samara instead.

In August, N. M. Shvernik had to tell the Orgburo that rather than go to Penza as ordered, "Comrade Naumov categorically refused to speak about the place and character of his work, stating that he considers the Secretariat's decision incorrect."

That same month, Comrade Zhanaia wrote to Molotov, "So that there will be no misunderstanding, I state immediately and directly that I will not go to exile in Belorussia. The question is closed. If they order me to go somewhere as party duty, then I have the right to consider it otherwise."

In September, Kh. Kantor refused to be transferred to work at *Pravda,* which had requested him and secured Orgburo approval. *Pravda* had to give up, telling the Orgburo that Kantor is "reluctant to come here, so he is not suitable."[48]

In early 1927, the Orgburo confirmed Old Bolshevik N. A. Arkhangel'skii to be head of a textile trust in Iaroslavl'. But a memo from Orgraspred's assistant head Chuzhin in September noted that "in the three months since then, Comrade Arkhangel'skii has not showed up for work, refusing to take up his position. Because of the difficult position in the trust, we are forced to nominate another candidate." Orgraspred then proposed Ia. A. Rodionov to head the trust. The Council on National Economy, the Central Committee of the Textile Union, and Iaroslavl' gorkom all agreed, and Rodionov took up the position. Arkhangel'skii had waited them out and was off the hook.

Orgraspred staff hated being targets for these complaints. As Orgraspred chief Kaganovich ruefully noted, "A party member has the right to complain about being incorrectly assigned." Work in the personnel staff was very hard and the number of complaints was "colossal." "It is the kind of work that makes you a target for anybody and everybody who is discontented about anything related to their fate."[49]

The Orgraspred staff's dream of systematic planned job placement was also disrupted by large numbers of haphazard walk-ins who showed up at their offices looking for work. The privileges of Bolshevik status included the right to simply walk off a job you did not like and demand another one. Already by late 1918, party secretary Iakov Sverdlov was receiving twenty to twenty-five comrades per day seeking new assignments. By 1919, the number showing up at the TsK looking for a new assignment grew to sixty to eighty per day, a level that would remain more or less constant in the 1920s.[50] Upon arriving at Orgraspred's "Reception," the "Guest" would fill out an autobiographical card and then be referred to an Orgraspred assistant or deputy chief.[51]

The prima donna attitude of individual Communists who did not feel themselves bound by a job assignment, and simply walked away from it if they found it illogical or uncomfortable, annoyed the staff. TsK staff complained about these walk-ins who showed up at the Secretariat demanding new jobs and, worse, per diem money to cover their unauthorized trips to Moscow! At one TsK staff conference (of Orgraspred) in 1926, Comrade Mogil'nyi lamented,

> A few days ago a comrade from Ukraine wandered into the office. Like he was a traveling star on tour. Maybe the TsK would give him a job in Moscow? But we told him, "You were only a short time in Ukraine, and you should work there." He said, "But they wouldn't give me a good job there, and I want to work in Moscow." I explained to him that he needed to apply to the TsK Ukraine and TsK Ukraine would give him work.[52]

The following year, the inflow of entitled walk-ins grew. In the second half of 1927, 2,429 party members passed through the Secretariat on some business or another. Seventeen hundred twenty-one of them (72 percent of all visitors) arrived there on their personal initiative, and without being sent by their home organizations demanded travel pay for this unauthorized trip, and by personal request (*lichnaia pros'ba*) demanded new jobs.[53]

A TsK personnel staffer complained to his section head that "many members of the party have the impression that party organs are obligated to offer any party member a position."

> There are "permanent" Orgraspred visitors who day after day sit in the Orgraspred reception and look for more responsible work, explaining the need for transfer by previous unsatisfactory position and complaining that they are being used irrationally. These "itinerant Communists" disturb the work of both Orgraspred and other organizations. . . .
>
> Orgraspred visitors can be divided into two groups: permanent and occasional. In the "permanent" group are those who always are dissatisfied with their positions . . . but who themselves don't know what they want. . . . Unfortunately, we see this most with longtime party members.[54]

A few months later, Orgraspred deputy chief Bogomolov complained at an internal staff conference that "We give thousands of assignments. Often the same guy gets 6 or 7, and keeps coming back complaining." (Voice: "It's like a labor exchange!")[55] That was not at all what Orgraspred staff had in mind with their plans or self-image.

In such cases, the senior Bolshevik overseeing Orgraspred tended to back up the staff. S. V. Kosior, for example, as TsK Secretary told Orgraspred that they were not obligated to give jobs to walk-ins, much less pay their travel expenses, which rightfully were the responsibility of their home organization, assuming that organization had actually sent them. When Orgraspred refused such walk-ins, "they burst forth from us as if from a scalding steam bath" and ran to Kosior, who turned them down and sent them back downstairs.

Other times, Kosior and others annoyed the staff. One walk-in, who apparently knew Kosior, secured his permission to remain in Moscow, even though he had walked off his job in the provinces and Orgraspred had ordered him home. He returned from Kosior "with a very serious face." The staff allowed him to remain in Moscow but told him to find work himself. It was dangerous and inappropriate for staff to complain about their upstairs betters, but they did anyway, carefully and to each other in the closed counsels of their internal staff meetings. The staff mentioned, in a disapproving way, Kosior's decision, worrying that such cases could "push toward protectionism [in other words, protection by a patron] where a comrade goes to certain comrades and pleads based on personal acquaintanceship."[56]

At the same meeting, a recent Kosior speech had appeared to question overdoing "planned assignment," the dream of Orgraspred. Discussants argued and tried to reassure themselves this was not the case.[57] Their displeasure with another senior grandee, Aaron Sol'tz of the TsKK, was more direct. One Bogorat had been expelled from the party for collaborating with the occupying Germans in World War I and even engaging in sabotage on their behalf. Four hundred witnesses were called and Bogorat was expelled. Sol'tz ordered him immediately restored to the party and to his leading position, where Bogorat promptly drove away all the existing staff, who then had to be replaced.[58]

Sometimes staff frustration could lead to quite pointed and dangerous outbursts about the actions of senior grandees. The Shakhty Affair of 1928 had led to a widespread campaign against old regime technical specialists, who now suddenly had to be replaced. This was hardly part of any kind of "planned assignment" and one Orgraspred cadre blurted out, "Sure, it's easy to kick out hundreds of specialists, but then you have to replace them with others."[59]

More often, however, when the nobles upstairs intervened the staff grumbled quietly. This was even the case when serious projects and proposals for systematization and rationalization emerged from below, only to be crushed by the nobility who feared that their personal arbitrary power would be limited.

RULES AND LEGISLATION

Those upstairs might have remembered Lenin's sarcastic outburst, "Do you want us to write a constitution?" Whether or not they did, staff got no more grandee support in their attempts to systematize party decrees in a single document. Like all good bureaucrats, the TsK staff valued consistency, and wanted a system whereby decisions from upstairs did not cause confusion by contradicting previous party rulings.

Orgraspred's charter made it responsible for systematizing party "legislation" (*zakonodatel'stvo*).[60] This turned out to be easier said than done. In December 1924, a staff Commission to Systematize Party Legislation held its first meeting and resolved to publish a multivolume collection of all party decrees since October 1917.[61] One suspects that senior Old Bolshevik grandees may have had as much interest in systematizing previous decisions as the French kings had in the seventeenth century for the analogous efforts of the Paris *Parlement*; it had provoked a civil war then. Such codification of precedent could only reduce the personal freedom of maneuver of the Old Bolshevik elite; the last thing they wanted was for officials at various levels citing precedent as part of their arguments.

At any rate, the project ran into high-level resistance from the beginning. Old Bolshevik grandees who headed party organizations whose orders would be included began to object. A letter from the Central Control Commission to the Systematization Commission complained that the proposed list of TsKK documents left huge gaps and suggested a separate TsKK chapter with the TsKK in charge of selection.[62]

At the commission's meeting of 10 January 1925, chairman Khataevich reported a decision of the TsK that rather than a complete reference collection, the commission should produce a "handbook" for party workers and would include not all decrees, but rather only the most important decisions and circulars, which selection was to be made upon recommendations by subcommissions. These subcommissions were to be based on schemas that immediately became subjects for debate. Arguments produced several contradictory plans and resulted in several complicated drafts of parts and chapters.[63]

Other problems related to debates on whether to include old documents on "obsolete" issues or documents that "contradicted one another." The Bolshevik nobles had already started down the path of deciding what was historical truth, and it is not hard to imagine vested interests and political utility becoming criteria for whether a document was "contradictory" or "useful," as would be the case even for some documents written by Engels. The top leadership had not been enthusiastic about this staff systematization effort from the beginning, and its enthusiasm waned as the staff's intended scope became clear. Sometime in mid-1925, a copy of one of the Systematization Commission's meeting protocols passed through the Politburo. It carried the suggestion that "old" and "obsolete" and "contradictory" documents would be systematically worked through by subcommissions and then by the TsK for confirmation, and it seems that an alarm bell went off. Perhaps the overall disadvantage for the grandees became obvious, or perhaps the monumental workload for the TsK in adjudicating documents seemed too formidable (or threatening), but in the margin of the protocol, next to the section on the roles of the subcommissions and the TsK, someone wrote "?!" and the Systematization Commission died a quiet death.[64] Upstairs, there was again notable lack of enthusiasm for the systematization that those downstairs dreamed of.

REGISTERING AND ASSIGNING EVERYBODY

Orgraspred staffers were impatient with appointments being "delayed" in the Secretariat because of too many questions arriving there; decisions should be made "with maximum precision and speed." Staffers proposed that more appointments should be made expeditiously by an Orgraspred department head in consultation with a TsK secretary (i.e., an abbreviated version of the staff conference): "do we really have to delay things so much?"[65]

Staffers wanted to keep more questions for decision at their level for the sake of efficiency and, we might well imagine, to enhance their power. At one point, an energetic staffer made off with Kosior's seal which he used to stamp Orgraspred proposals as if they had been approved by a TsK secretary. Much as his staff colleagues may have admired the idea, the act produced a scandal. "This must never happen again." Staffers may have gritted their teeth as they accused the light-fingered staffer of "deceit" and of turning Secretariat approval into a formality.[66]

The staff preferred rational "planned" assignment of cadres. As it turned out, their idea of "planned assignment" meant dramatically expanding the number of appointments made centrally based on an efficient system of precise recordkeeping. Here too, the grandees upstairs would rein in the dreams of the staff and quash their grandiose plans.

There were several "unplanned" ways appointments were made, and staff hated them all. Especially in the early Soviet period, mobilization of thousands of comrades at a time for military or economic work was common. Given the emergency nature of almost everything, and lacking personnel records or any mechanism to rationally assign personnel, it had to be so. Mobilization, as one TsK member called it, was appointment by "impulse" having a "shock" character.[67] Party committee leaders and personnel staff alike hated this method. Party committees had their valuable members drafted for mass work; staff had to fight them for the people, and in any case were prevented from studying personnel rationally. Secondly, an appointment could be made "by travel" (*po putevkam*) when a comrade was sent somewhere for a specific job and then managed to stay for various reasons. Thirdly, Bolsheviks had the right to simply demand a new job (*po lichnoi pros'boi*).

Orgraspred staffers constantly spoke out in favor of "planned" appointments based on studying the needs of a position and matching them with a candidate.[68] It meant "maintaining a policy of specialized workers, not throwing them from one assignment to another without reason." It meant "not appointing workers fired from one place for incompetence (*negodnost'*) and then sending them to responsible work in another place." It meant studying the "exact situation in a given organization" before assigning people there. And, in general, it meant adhering to "the correct recordkeeping and study of workers."[69]

In order to have "planned" assignments, it was necessary to have good personnel records, and the lack of these was the largest logistical obstacle to systematic and rational assignment. But some grandees upstairs, while they approved of good records in general, were dubious about filling out forms and thought that maybe the staff was outrunning itself by trying to assign too many cadres in general.

As early as 1919, Moscow started sending out questionnaires, but few of them were returned.[70] A 1920 party congress resolution called for exact recordkeeping (*uchet*) for Communists and rather minimally asked local party organizations to submit a list of only 5–10 percent of their members' experience and job qualifications.[71] In 1922 V. P. Nogin told the 11th Party Congress that despite "endless questionnaires . . . nobody knows what anyone is doing." In his own file, he reported, there was nothing but a letter from someone looking for him!

Molotov replied that provincial party leaders simply refused to send in the information.[72] Provincial party leaders did not comply for at least two reasons. First, they surely thought that informing Moscow about the qualifications of their precious workers would result in losing them to reassignment elsewhere.

Second, Old Bolsheviks in general considered filling out forms to be beneath their standing. As one senior provincial party secretary said, "What, am I some kind of poor peasant bum to you, that I should have to fill out a personnel file?"[73] Often, Old Bolsheviks were affronted and insulted by staff attempts to evaluate their qualifications and complained to the TsK. Kaganovich (himself a staffer in the early 1920s) remembered how "the TsK had to examine these local conflicts, complaints, and dissatisfaction about how we evaluated them."[74]

A 1928 Orgraspred report to the Orgburo noted that

> Complications of our work demand major management qualifications and knowledge of their business . . . the basic task is to know concretely not only how to do your job, but how to independently orient yourself to complex questions of politics and economy.
>
> Work in the past years shows that the absence of files on responsible workers and knowledge of their work doesn't allow for the possibility of matching workers with needs, kicking out useless workers, and, worse, [can prevent] elevating them up the career stairs and appointing them to high posts.
>
> The absence of a system of personnel accounting files, strict accounting of abilities and needs, is the basic reason why now people absolutely alien to us are sitting in the most important positions.[75]

Personnel recordkeeping was still a problem in the 1930s. Only by the end of the 1920s did Orgraspred even manage the beginnings of a personnel filing system, but even as late as 1935, Ezhov (who headed the TsK personnel apparatus at that time) would complain that "in the *apparat* of the Central Committee we are presently beginning only now to find out the composition of the leading party workers in the regions and districts."[76]

In the early 1920s, before he himself became a grandee, Lazar Kaganovich worked in the Orgraspred trenches. At an Orgburo conference at the end of 1923, he presented a report on Orgraspred, which he headed. He pointed out that any planned study of cadres when 120 to 130 visitors streamed through Orgraspred looking for jobs was impossible; the "current crush of people" crowded out any planned work, and precluded what he thought should be monopoly control of appointments by Orgraspred.

Nobody in the Orgburo grandee audience could disagree with good recordkeeping. But then Kaganovich went too far and pressed a grandiose staff proposal. He outlined a plan for a centralized human "party budget" of 73,000 people—more than seven times the number currently being assigned—to be assigned "scientifically" in the state and party apparatus, a number he thought necessary to run the party and state. It would not be easy to build up such a cadre, "but if every month, step by step, we in each organization and institution lay down the fundamentals of a party budget, then after some time we will have a general overall party budget and the party will know that her workers are working where the party needs them, and not where they accidentally land."[77]

Kaganovich went on to suggest, as Orgraspred workers would for years, that assignment based on personal acquaintance and preference had to be replaced by systematic and rational placement.

> For example, at the head of the Commissariat of Finance, you have Comrade Sokol'nikov who loves party members and loves to get them from us. But at the head of Foreign Trade stands Comrade Krasin, who one must say doesn't really love Communists, and regardless of the fact that there are fewer Communists at Foreign Trade than at Finance, we give our [Communist] workers to Finance and not to Foreign Trade. We should give our people to Foreign Trade to secure the commanding heights. So as you see, party workers are not being used where they are needed.[78]

Kaganovich knew that his idea to centrally appoint more, not fewer, cadres would spark controversy. As we have seen, however, Politburo and Orgburo members were more interested in reducing the number of central assignments to reduce workload. That had been the purpose of the *nomenklatura* system. Kaganovich's suggestion that Moscow staff should gather records and plan and assign over seventy thousand workers alarmed some of the top nobles who thought Orgraspred was overreaching.

M. Tomskii interjected that he agreed with Kaganovich on the need to study cadres' qualifications and build up files, but thought that the plan was overcentralized. "We need a critical and careful approach to the policy of appointment on a universal scale . . . so I am a little skeptical." Molotov agreed with Tomskii that of course we should try to find out about everybody, although as for Kaganovich's grandiose staff plan, "that does not mean we should assign that many." We should study many, appoint not so many. For Stalin, overcentralizing personnel assignment, in Orgraspred or elsewhere, would make it hard for local leaders to promote their people from below; there would be nothing left of the policy of promotion. He said Kaganovich's plan was, in any case, impractical and inadvisable because "such a firm plan as proposed by Comrade Kaganovich risks putting Kaganovich in the position of having to attain the unattainable."[79] Like the staff plans to systematize all party decisions and other ideas, the proposal for centralized, rationalized, bureaucratic appointment of everyone was quietly dropped.

By 1936, the TsK staff was typing up "summary digests" (*svodki*) of their proposed appointments, some of them quite senior. A list of proposed appointments from Malenkov, head of ORPO (which had replaced Orgraspred) to TsK Secretary Ezhov in 1936 contained several provincial party secretaries, a position far beyond the jurisdiction of staff in the 1920s.[80] Across the front of the neatly typed list (a list of appointments, not a protocol of proposals), a single TsK secretary scrawled "za" ("in favor") and his name. These were then recorded as decisions of the Orgburo which, of course, did not meet. By 1938, such *oprosom* lists were literally rubber-stamped by a TsK Secretary.[81] Kaganovich, Zhdanov, Ezhov and other TsK secretaries had rubber stamps made up. In Kaganovich's case, it said:

> Comrade Kaganovich—za. (see his original actual signature on *svodka*
> No. ___)[82]

At first glance, this 1930s procedure looks very much like giving a larger role and status to staff. When a secretary rubber-stamped a list of appointments, he must have looked it over first for names he recognized and having no objection, blessed the list. Staff produced the lists that the grandee rubber-stamped. In fact, however, nothing had really changed. More and more the grandees trusted the staff recommendations, but they always insisted on having the final say. It was noble rank and prestige, not an institution or committee that mattered.

In the 1920s, Orgraspred was headed by Ivan Moskvin. Although a member of the TsK and Orgburo, he was not a secretary of the TsK. Therefore, he carried his staff's nominations upstairs, where a TsK secretary presided over the Staff Conference and had the final say.

In the 1930s, however, the head of ORPO was a higher-ranking official. Ezhov (ORPO head 1935–36) worked downstairs running the staff, but was himself a TsK secretary at the time.[83] He didn't need to carry recommendations upstairs to be blessed. In his capacity as chief of cadres staff, he had already supervised preparation of the staff conference list, as Moskvin had done in the 1920s. Now, in his capacity as a TsK secretary grandee, he rubber-stamped his own recommendations downstairs.

Functionally, nothing had changed since the 1920s: a TsK boyar still had to approve staff nominations. Staff still prepared lists of recommendations, which were still considered in a meeting with a single TsK secretary. But with the head of personnel staff now a TsK secretary, the process took place one stage earlier. It stayed downstairs, but now the staff's boss was no longer a nonnoble, a "one of us" Moskvin. One clearly gets this sense from the texts of Orgraspred meeting stenograms of the 1920s, where Moskvin took a comradely, egalitarian tone with this staff. Ezhov's tone with staff in the 1930s was different: he gave orders and instructions.[84] The boss was now a grandee who directly controlled them.

So the change of the 1930s may actually have been the opposite of a growth in staff power. The rubber stamp of their nominations meant not that staff had sneaked up to the decision making upstairs, but rather that a representative of that lofty precinct had now figuratively invaded their territory. Their neat, blanket-approved lists of nominations belie the fact that they still had no independent power, no stamps.

The difference in view between the upstairs grandees and the downstairs staff reflects, in microcosm, the difference between rational bureaucratic authority and traditional patrimonialism. The staff wanted rational bureaucracy. The elite wanted patrimonialism, with all its arbitrary flexibility. It was their métier, the key to their power. And as we have seen, it permeated Russian and Soviet cultures in a profound way. Patrimonialism won. As the next chapter shows, however, it came with a price: conflicts and political clans.

5 Principled and Personal Conflicts

If someone gets promoted to a post, do you think it's because of his qualifications? In most cases, it's not. His only value is whose person is he, who will he support. Is that a party? No, it's a system of chieftains, not a party organization.

—*Stalin, 1931*

PATRIMONIAL POSTURING BASED on individual power, pride, and honor were not limited to the Old Bolshevik notables in the capital. This self-image and behavior permeated the entire party. On all levels, party members thought of themselves as some version of the elect, the privileged, those with special knowledge and mission. Party members, especially those who had served years in the underground and/or those who aspired to personal power, thought of themselves as natural, even entitled leaders, even if—or perhaps because—the locale for deploying personal influence was sometimes modest and limited.

Given the shortage of qualified party personnel and the scant party membership among the populace, it was natural for local Bolsheviks to band together in teams around an authoritative leader. Political power was understood to be personal and patrimonial anyway. In the absence of countervailing institutions, such groups rapidly developed into cliques and patron-client groups. And, as was often the case, if there was more than one strong personality in a locality, a struggle would soon erupt between the two prima donnas and their dependant groups. In these years, such disagreements and "spats" (*skloki*) or "frictions" (*treniia*) among local party leaders were endemic and characterized party organizations throughout the period.

The constant fighting, personal sniping, and appealing to Moscow was tiresome and inefficient; it paralyzed party work in the entire region. Personal networks were so entrenched in local party organizations that newcomers, even if they came as chiefs with Moscow mandates, were not always able to take charge. When A. I. Mikoian was sent to Nizhnyi Novgorod, the local clique isolated him, and it took him nearly a year to establish his authority and overcome local "clan" resistance.[1] In Mari, N. I. Ezhov ultimately failed to establish himself as unquestioned chief, and the archives are full of similar cases in which leaders established from Moscow were either recalled or ejected by the locals.[2]

Moscow party leaders complained about these squabbles. The archives, as well as the pages of the TsK's journal *Izvestiia TsK,* are filled with discussions of them, and Krestinskii specifically mentioned the most serious in Kazan, Saratov, Voronezh, and Briansk. At party congresses in 1921 and 1922, TsK Secretary Molotov discussed some of the reasons for these conflicts, often called *gruppirovki,* which included struggles among strong personalities with their clients, young versus older party members, urban versus rural cadres, local versus recently arrived leading cadres, arguments between returning Red Army Communists and the established leaderships, and disputes over nationality policy.[3] As Stalin told a party congress, "all these heterogeneous elements which go up to make the provincial committees bring with them different attitudes, traditions, and tastes and on this basis brawls and feuds erupt." And, as Stalin noted, real issues of principle were almost never involved.[4]

This was party life in 1921–23. In Kostroma "certain comrades who love to push 'their opinions' everywhere cannot cooperate and by their activities divide comrades into 'yours' and 'ours' groups of partisans."[5] In Rybinsk, two groups of Old Bolsheviks vied for power, with one group of former revolutionary undergrounders accusing the other of being "highly educated Marxists" who busy themselves with "unimportant things." An Orgburo staff report found that the fight was "purely personal" with no political issues involved. The same "unprincipled" two-group struggle inspired by personal frictions characterized the *skloki* in Simbirsk.[6] In Tula, according to a staff study, "the conflict between Comrade Khodorovskii on the one hand and members of the Tula gubkom on the other has no political disagreement and the conflict arose and grew thanks to tactless conduct. . . ."[7] In Arkhangelsk, Comrade Kulikov created around him "a tight group of offensive drunks" to run the party organization.[8]

In other places, entrenched groups of local Bolsheviks resisted the intrusion of new party workers assigned from outside. In Astrakhan in 1922, squabbles divided Communists into "old Astrakhaners" whose authority was based on their knowledge of "special conditions in Astra-khan," and "newcomers from everywhere," as they called them, who claimed to deserve the leading positions without any basis or qualifica-tions. The newcomers, led by Comrade Emelianov, in turn accused the "old Astrakhaners" of drunkenness, bureaucratism, favoritism, and cronyism (*kumovstvo,* a common charge in those days). The new group seized control of the guberniia party committee and started "cleaning up" by firing Comrade Liak, the responsible secretary of the gubkom! The old Astrakhaners retreated to the guberniia Control Commission and counterattacked by dissolving the guberniia party committee alto-gether. Finally the TsK sent instructors (authoritative representatives) to sort out the fight. The emissaries replaced the gubkom and guberniia control commission wholesale, but even so improvements in party life were "still far from a success" and "calming down is going very slowly" because corruption and favoritism continued. The fight paralyzed the Astrakhan party organization for a year and a half.[9]

A celebrated battle that erupted between the party's Siberian Re-gional Buro and the Omsk party organization over prerogatives to ap-point personnel involved local press battles, mutual party expulsions, and mass threats to resign from the party. The Orgburo got involved to referee the dispute and eventually had to dissolve the Omsk organiza-tion, expel many of its leading party officials, and order a "reregistra-tion" of party members in the area.[10] At one point, the entire Ukrainian party leadership was removed by Moscow when the former refused to implement central policies. In these and other places, infighting para-lyzed the party committee. But this was not the TsK's only worry. Dis-gusted by the posturing and sniping of their leaders, large numbers of rank-and-file members left the party, deserting in disgust.

It was often the case that leaders and factions seized control of vari-ous party and state organizations and used them against their oppo-nents, just as senior Bolsheviks did in Moscow.[11] As in Astrakhan, one personal faction controlled the guberniia party committee and the other the guberniia control commission in Vologda and Penza. Both sides jockeyed for position and precedence based on their length of party membership and past services (Bolshevik *mestnichestvo*).[12] Both sides used their authority to install their supporters in key positions and to harass their rivals, and even attack them by expelling them from the party. It was not uncommon for one faction to use the occasion of a regular party membership screening to find fault with members of the other group and expel them.[13] Both leaders complained to Moscow and sought support there.

In Mari, one group led by N. I. Ezhov controlled the gubkom, while his rival I. P. Petrov and his followers controlled the executive committee of the local soviet (ispolkom). The documents we have do not tell us of the personal or political issues involved, if any, although a Moscow-based party referee noted in a report that there was probably guilt on both sides.[14] Both Petrov and Ezhov wrote to Moscow complaining about each other. Almost immediately, Petrov's friends began to whisper that this was a "Ezhov group." Ezhov complained that "There is talk about the organization of two groups, a 'Ezhovist' and a 'Petrovist.' "[15] Petrov "had struggled against my [political] line since I arrived here."[16]

The party committee (doubtless with Ezhov's help) voted to fire Petrov from his ispolkom chairmanship and convinced the TsK to place him "at the disposal of the Central Committee" for another assignment. The provincial Control Commission recommended expelling him from the party, and there was talk of arresting him.[17]

Both Ezhov and Petrov went to Moscow to lobby. Those friendly to Petrov on the Orgburo formed a committee that recommended keeping him in Mari. Ezhov wrote to a friend, "I myself talked to each and every member of the committee."[18] He was ultimately successful, and the Orgburo finally approved the Mari decision to remove Petrov. It is, by the way, a sign of the shortage of administrative cadres that a character such as Petrov was eventually given a new post in Vologda. But this was an example of the TsK's "plague on both your houses" tactic, and an Orgburo decision in early November extended Ezhov's annual "vacation" for another month at full salary and he never returned to his post in Mari. By January, a new responsible secretary had taken over.[19]

A similar personal battle took place in Penza between Responsible Party Secretary Rozhnov of the gubkom, on the one hand, and Comrade Gorshkov of the guberniia Control Commission on the other.

Gorshkov denounced Rozhnov as a former Social Revolutionary and a weak leader in general. In reply, Gorshkov played the *mestnichestvo* card and praised his own longtime party membership. In turn, Rozhnov and his followers denounced Gorshkov's vanity and amour-propre (*samoliubie*), claiming that Gorshkov was motivated purely by personal ambition. In February 1922, Gorshkov and Rozhnov ran against each other for party first secretary. Incumbent Rozhnov won with an absolute majority, but the struggle continued and even escalated.

Selivanov, a department head in the local soviet, committed suicide after a run-in with regular police (*militsiia*) chief Dolgikh, an ally of Rozhnov. Martynov, head of the political police (GPU), not only did not like Dolgikh but had by now sided with the dissident Gorshkov group and used Selivanov's suicide as an issue against Secretary Rozhnov and the gubkom. Martynov launched an investigation that did not nail Dolgikh but did succeed in convicting some others.

At this point, the Moscow GPU sent an investigator to check out the Penza GPU. Each side unloaded denunciations of the other to the inspector. Rozhnov and his gubkom told the GPU investigators about Martynov's drinking on the job, as well as his purchase of vodka with state funds and other financial irregularities. At one point, Rozhnov complained about revolver shots coming from the dormitory where the Moscow inspector was staying, but Martynov claimed that they were only doors slamming. Despite the charges against Martynov and the Penza GPU, the Moscow inspector made no punitive recommendations, and the guberniia Control Commission, controlled by Gorshkov's and Martynov's friends, also did nothing.

Feeling himself strengthened, Martynov now arrested Rozhnov's man Dolgikh. This was too much for Rozhnov, who now wrote to the TsK, adding that he had now found out that Martynov had stolen flour from the GPU stores. He suggested that both he and Martynov should be recalled.[20] When that was not forthcoming, Rozhnov countered by engineering the arrest of Martynov. The Orgburo reacted:

> The arrest of Penza GPU chief Martynov was illegal and could have been avoided through normal channels with the recall of Comrade Martynov. Investigation showed that the accusation of bribe taking made against Martynov was undeserved. . . . The accusation of drunkenness can to a significant degree be applied to many other responsible workers in Penza.[21]

Soon thereafter, both Rozhnov and Martynov were recalled to Moscow and reassigned.

The Moscow party center adopted a variety of tactics to stop the frictions and *skloki;* such efforts were called "refereeing" or "mediating." Sometimes the competing nobles were summoned to Moscow to make their cases at the Orgburo. Sometimes an authoritative TsK representative was dispatched to the province to settle things, which often meant convening a party conference in his presence. Sometimes the leader of one of the factions was transferred out, with his followers dispersed to various locales. Sometimes a more drastic solution was adopted in which both competing grandees were transferred out and their entourages dispersed.

Central Committee Secretary for Personnel N. Krestinskii regularly discussed *skloki* at party congresses, and noted that the TsK was frequently obliged to transfer leading comrades from place to place ("to no less responsible positions") in order to break up cliques involved in *skloki.* Grigorii Zinoviev told the TsK that regular transfers of cadres from place to place were a good way to resolve local conflicts.[22] Krestinskii was not so sure, seeing mass transfers as a last resort, and there was an ongoing debate at the top about how to deal with them. Others also thought that constant movement of party workers was bad for stability, and meant that "outside" leaders would always be intruding into long-standing local party society. Some, like Mgeladze from Saratov, saw both sides. Constant movement, he said, "converted party workers into nomads," and people were joking that the TsK was playing with people like puppets. On the other hand, "Of course, if a person heads a group in opposition to the local party organization, it is necessary to remove him. But if the guilty comrade has strong ties with the local organization, which supports him, even mistakenly, then don't remove him."[23]

Molotov agreed with his Secretariat predecessor Krestinskii on the use of personnel reassignment as a last resort to stop *skloki*, but itemized the methods the Central Committee used before turning to reassignment: highlighting the conflict in the party press, sending secret TsK letters to the party organization, and dispatching instructors to the scene to try and make peace. Only when these failed was it appropriate to reassign leading cadres elsewhere, and even then there were several approaches: removal of a few key players and recall of one of the feuding groups, or more drastically recall of both feuding groups and their replacement by entirely new party staffs.[24] As we saw in Mari and Penza, this drastic "plague on both your houses" solution was not uncommon.

Those who picked fights and stirred up *skloki* were variously labeled *sklokist, gruppirovik, oppozitsionir*. They were denounced locally and nationally for never being satisfied, for constantly provoking arguments, and for weakening the authority of the party by dividing it, all in attempts to maneuver themselves and their clients into power. They were considered to be chronic troublemakers who rocked the boat, even in high seas.

OPPOSITION AND THE OPPOSITION: THE VIEW FROM THE PROVINCES

The history of ideological opposition movements in the Bolshevik party after the revolution is well known. The Left Communists in 1918 opposed Lenin's Brest peace with the Germans and advocated carrying revolutionary war into Europe. The Democratic Centralists (1919–20) had argued for more collegial decision making at the top of the party and against the tendency of Lenin and a few key leaders to make decisions without consultation. The Workers' Opposition (1920–21) wanted more proletarian members in the party and favored giving the trade unions a significant role in government.

Beginning in 1923, Trotsky launched a trenchant criticism of Stalin's "regime of professional secretaries," claiming that they had become ossified bureaucrats cut off from their proletarian followers. Trotsky argued that the survival of the Bolshevik regime depended on receiving support from successful workers' revolutions in Europe, and he accused Stalin and other leaders of losing interest in spreading the revolution.

Bukharin, Zinoviev, Kamenev, and Stalin closed ranks to isolate Trotsky, accusing him of trying to split the party because of his personal ambition to lead it. They argued that Trotsky was only using "party democracy" as a phony political issue: during the Civil War he had never been for anything less than iron discipline. Now, they charged, his criticism weakened party unity. Faced with the unity of the other Politburo members, the party's inclination to unity and discipline (a response to the chaos of the recent Civil War), and Stalin's influence among the party apparatus, Trotsky could not win. Although his slates and resolutions showed some strength in youth cells and in Moscow, his candidates were roundly defeated locally. In Iaroslavl', in fact, there was even a *sklok* inside the leadership between Shelekhes and Kabakov about who was too soft on the Trotskyists![25] Trotsky was stripped of his military post in 1924 and gradually marginalized in the top leadership.[26]

The following year, in 1925, Zinoviev and Kamenev split off from the party majority by launching their own New Opposition, arguing that the NEP policy of conceding constantly increasing grain prices to the peasantry was depriving the state of capital for industrialization, bankrupting industry, confronting the proletariat with high bread prices, and indefinitely postponing the march to socialism. In 1926, Trotsky joined Zinoviev and Kamenev in the United Opposition.

Stalin and Bukharin denounced the United Opposition as another attempt to split the party by challenging the existing policy and violating the centralism aspect of democratic centralism. The votes from the party secretarial apparatus, loyal to Stalin and not eager to provoke a dangerous turn in party policy, won the day and the United Opposition went down to defeat in 1927. Zinoviev and Kamenev were stripped of their most powerful positions. Trotsky was expelled from the party and exiled to Central Asia. Two years later, in 1929, he was deported from the country.

Except for Stalin, these "oppositionist" contenders for Lenin's succession are usually presented as the "conscience" of the revolution.[27] Their positions are seen as principled. The speeches in which they—often with intellectual brilliance—presented their positions to the party masses discussed agricultural and industrial options, foreign policy, and other grand strategies, and were always informed and buttressed by theoretical references to the writings of Marx and Lenin. The struggle seemed ideological, and among the top leaders in Moscow, it is hard to discount (at least completely) their adherence to principled positions. The leftist opposition sincerely believed in rapid industrialization, even at the expense of the peasantry, and the rightists just as sincerely believed that it was necessary to placate the peasants.

Stalin, by contrast, is seen as an unprincipled intriguer. His ambition is seen as the driving force as he opportunistically switched ideological positions to outmaneuver his opponents. He used control of the party personnel apparatus to plant his supporters in the provincial party committees, who in turn sent delegates to the national party meetings and who supported him and not others. There is much truth in this view, and Stalin's rise to unchallenged personal power in the party is impossible to understand outside of his control of the personnel apparatus.

Yet this understanding is incomplete and needs serious qualification. It cannot explain key aspects of Stalin's rise, including the broad consensus in the party—even among oppositionists—for strong discipline, centralization of personnel assignment, and a firm "organizational line."[28]

The Stalin-centered story also overemphasizes Stalin's personal direction of the apparatus, its efficiency, and even the centrality of the struggle for members in the rest of the country. The usual interpretation posits a "circular flow of power" in which Stalin appointed the provincial leaders and they in turn supported him in his struggle with the oppositions in return for their jobs and his backing.[29] Even without an ambitious politician aiming for dictatorship, even without an internecine struggle for Lenin's mantle, the process of defeating "opposition" would have proceeded much the same because it was a logical response to the interaction of party traditions and goals in a difficult environment. In fact, Stalin did not invent the demand for strict unity; it was inherent in the situation.[30] It came as much from experience in the provinces as from party traditions of the center.

In fact, the struggle with the opposition must have looked very different from the provinces looking toward Moscow, rather than the reverse, which is the way we usually see it. And because the vast majority of votes enabling Stalin's victory came from provincial delegates, their point of view was crucial. Looking closely at the sources, there are few reasons to imagine that these leaders thought that they owed their jobs to Stalin, and quite a few reasons to think that resisting "opposition" in principle was more important to them than supporting any particular politician, including Stalin.

It is difficult to posit massive provincial delegate support based on gratitude or loyalty to Stalin for giving them their jobs. At precisely the time Trotsky was criticizing the "regime of secretaries," it seems that most of them were not appointed or "recommended" by Stalin's office. As Kaganovich told the Orgburo, "Of 100 secretaries we have, more than 50 percent were directly elected without TsK recommendation, 33 percent were recommended by the TsK but unanimously reelected at conferences in the provinces, and only 15 percent of the secretaries we

have were recommended but not yet elected. Most of these 15 percent
are in border areas; there national conflicts required us to change the
secretaries."[31] Kaganovich's data came from an Orgraspred report the
month before; the actual data were even more favorable to his case: of
191 (rather than 100) guberniia party secretaries, 53 percent were
elected from below, 32 percent were "recommended then elected," and
15 percent appointed from the center. Actually, among first secretaries
of guberniia party organizations, *none* were merely appointed, and
only 24 percent were "recommended then elected."[32] Also mitigating
the "circular flow of power" argument according to which appointed
secretaries packed their party congress delegates with pro-Stalin members is Khrushchev's recollection that at the height of the struggle with
the Left Opposition (1925), party congress "delegates were elected
democratically then."[33]

Why, then, did provincial party barons support Stalin?

There are good reasons to believe that based on their perception and
experience, provincial party leaders saw the struggle in Moscow as nonprincipled and nonideological. They regarded the oppositionists as simply the latest wave of dangerous, troublemaking *sklokisty*, whose
actions were based purely on personal ambition. They may have seen
the leaders of the opposition less as a "conscience" and more as noble
boyars jousting for precedence, exactly as the *sklokisty* did locally.

Many of the criticisms raised by the oppositionist challengers had
little relevance to the day-to-day activities and concerns of party workers in the provinces. Trotsky's and Zinoviev's critiques of Stalin's policy
on the Chinese and German revolutions, their hairsplitting about theories of permanent revolution or "primitive socialist accumulation,"
must have seemed wholly irrelevant to the provincial parties. Indeed,
to those trying to govern with a few loyal party supporters in a sea of
hostile social and religious forces, it must have seemed bizarre to make
so much of events in far-off places when things were so dire right here
at home, where violent bandits could still ride down on Soviet settle-
ments and ambush party members.

Looking to Moscow from the provinces, it may have seemed that all
of those famous knights changed their principled positions constantly
as they jousted with each other. Stalin's flip-flops are well known. An
opponent of using bourgeois specialists in the Civil War, he defended
them in the early 1920s, then attacked them again in 1928, then de-

fended them again in the early 1930s. A staunch defender of the mixed-economy gradualism of NEP for most of the 1920s, he suddenly lurched to the left at the end of the decade and occupied a position not far from Trotsky's, which he had bitterly attacked just months before. Zinoviev and Kamenev, who had strongly supported a conciliatory policy toward peasants in 1924, attacked Stalin and Bukharin for that very thing in 1925–27. Zinoviev, who had loudly and brashly attacked Trotsky's ideas on party life and the economy, was by 1925 saying that Trotsky was right. Trotsky had been a strict disciplinarian and enemy of factions until the early 1920s when he became just as fierce an advocate of open discussion. Bukharin had been a leader of the Left Communists in 1918, but in the 1920s was the most prominent leader of the rightists.

For those party workers who followed the verbiage of the struggle for power in Moscow, it was also easy to see the oppositionist leaders as opportunists and hypocrites, especially on the question of party discipline. In their time, each of the oppositionist movements from the Democratic Centralists to the Workers' Opposition to the Trotskyists to the Zinoviev-Kamenev group had, when they were in power, called for centralization and strict punitive personnel measures against others for violating party discipline. Now, though, when they had gone over to opposition they had become champions of leniency, a soft interpretation of party discipline, the right to criticize, and the right to be immune from punitive "organizational measures" in the area of personnel. Future oppositionist Zinoviev in 1919 had argued for the TsK's right to shift personnel around as needed to break up cliques and ensure obedience, but when his control over Leningrad was subjected to the same practice, he howled.[34]

Trotsky strongly advocated firm practices unless his personal rival Stalin was employing them. In 1920, he told the 9th Party Congress that the party did not need provincial party committees elected from below, but rather provincial buros appointed in the center. He chastised his follower Preobrazhenskii for criticizing party centralization; he said the party needed a strong "organizational center" with the ability to appoint provincial party secretaries, regardless of the electoral principle. But his attack on Stalin was largely based on the TsK's "regime of appointment" that violated party democracy.[35]

As late as 1925, when Zinoviev came into open opposition to the Stalin machine, he led a dissident but handpicked Leningrad delegation to the 14th Party Congress. Local party leaders like I. P. Rumiantsev and others chided Lev Kamenev in 1925 for being in favor of iron discipline and a hard "organizational line" only when he was in the majority.[36] Martymian Riutin, who would be shot in 1937 for authoring a sharp condemnation of Stalin's rule in 1932, must have rued his statement back in 1923 that it was natural to have a stable leading group: "A party that discredits its leaders is unavoidably weakened. Parties are always led by chiefs (*vozhdy*)."[37]

It would be wrong to characterize the factional politics of the 1920s as being based entirely on either personality or policy.[38] Obviously, some Bolsheviks great and small put policy analysis first and held to their analyses. Others, however, just as obviously followed the twists and turns of their patrons' purported analyses. The point is not whether senior Bolshevik grandees were or were not sincere in their adherence to policy and ideology, but rather how the struggle was perceived in the provinces and in the party as a whole. To embattled party workers out in the wild, battling poverty, fire and flood, a sullen peasantry, nationality conflicts, hunger, bandits, remnants of the White forces, and other tribulations, it must have been difficult to understand how anyone could worry much about the proper theoretical evaluation of NEP. From outside Moscow, to the party majority, it looked like personal *skloki,* colored by ideology.

The struggle of the party titans in the 1920s probably looked even more like a struggle of personalities but each of the contenders deployed a personal political machine.[39] Moscow party members seemed to attach themselves to one or another of the top leaders permanently, following him through his ideological and policy twists and turns. There seemed to be more or less consistent factional personal loyalties. Regardless of the current left or right ideological position of one of the top leaders, party members identified themselves as "Trotskyists," "Stalinists," or "Zinovievists." They followed their boyar leader through the political spectrum; loyalty and patronage were a major part of this struggle. Everything seemed personal. Motivations for attaching oneself to a major leader were surely varied. It is easy to imagine personal ambition causing one to become one of the "-ists" in the expectation that one's career would rise with that of the patron. That's how Bolshevik *mestnichestvo* worked, after all.[40]

Seeing the opposition struggles as personal was of course consistent with the Russian view of the personal nature of political practice discussed at length above. It was also consistent with local experience: Even though sometimes it seemed to the locals that the conflict was one of knights jousting far away over the horizon in Moscow, the apparently personal nature of the fight recalled local experience of party committees with the unpleasant nonprincipled personal *skloki* that had paralyzed the party in the provinces.

That is also how the locals talked about it. In party documents discussing situations in regional party committees, "opposition" was a generic term for unprincipled splitting and factionalism long before the formation of the Trotskyist opposition. *Gruppirovka* (factionalism, cliqueism, groupism) manifested itself as *oppozitsiia,* or "opposition" long before the rise of the famous "named" oppositions. *Skloki* and *gruppirovka* were routinely referred to as "opposition" in these documents. "Oppositionist" was simply a synonym for a disgruntled, ambitious outsider.

Rybinsk's purely personal conflict between rival Old Bolsheviks was called a "sharpening of opposition" when the outsiders "went into opposition." In Tula, where there was "no political disagreement" in the conflicts, "oppositionist moods of local responsible workers entered into impermissible *skloki,* causing a breakdown of the organization." In Vologda, part of the leading workers "decided to put themselves at the head of oppositionist sentiments." Young party members, returning from the Civil War and with no ideological point to make, sought to claim leading positions by "going into opposition and quickly gaining authority." In Penza where, as we have seen, the personal fight between the party committee and dissidents allied with the GPU led to arrests and counterarrests, the dissident group "put themselves into opposition" to the party committee, and became known as the "oppositionists, motivated only by personal considerations."[41]

A TsK "Survey of Conflicts" in early 1922 talked about "violations of party discipline" in which groups "failed to subordinate" themselves to proper party authorities. "In a whole series of gubkoms, *gruppirovka* is increased by the careless conduct of the gubkom in failing to overcome conflicts and *skloki.* . . . This can lead to opposition." "Personal conflicts arose under the color of the Workers' Opposition, but the basic issue is dissatisfaction with the personnel composition of party organs. . . . In all these cases, detailed investigation of the conflict showed that *gruppirovka* was behind them all."[42]

In Astrakhan, the newcomers led by Comrade Emelianov were called "oppositionists" while the "old Astrakhaners" fought back by post facto attaching an ideology to their personal *gruppirovka*: a "syndicalism so one-sided in favor of workers that the workers themselves rejected them." In Astrakhan, as elsewhere, opposition was based on personal *skloki* and *gruppirovka*, with ideology added on later as "color."[43]

Party workers trying to hold their committees together in the face of chronic personal spats and conflicts placed a premium on unity and pulling together to do the job. Each of the oppositionist groups had been the ones to challenge a much-wanted stability by launching their various critiques of the Stalinist majority. Right or wrong, they were dissidents and were rocking the boat. The principled critiques by local oppositionists were not only implicit challenges to the unity and patronage control shaped by the local secretary, but were also disruptive sallies that weakened the local party effort by threatening to split it. Whatever the merits of the oppositionist critiques, anything that threatened to divide local party cells was unwelcome to those trying to run things in difficult conditions.

Stalin once explained to Comintern head Georgi Dmitrov, "Why did we prevail over Trotsky and the rest? Trotsky, as we know, was the most popular man in our country after Lenin. . . . We were little known. . . . But the middle cadres supported us, explained our positions to the masses. . . . the middle cadres decide the outcome of our cause."[44] Khrushchev, who was one of those middle cadres, agreed and remembered, "we had no doubts then that Stalin, and those who had gathered around Stalin and were supporting him, were correct."[45]

Kaganovich remembers that "a majority of the Politburo took a more restrained position toward Trotsky than local comrades. . . . representatives of local party organizations were particularly inclined to more severely punish Trotsky and especially his factional allies." When Kaganovich (who as head of the TsK Organizational Department was responsible for communications with local committees) told Stalin about these local moods, Stalin told him to "explain to all the comrades with such sentiments that the Politburo is concerned about unity in the TsK and the party and are trying at this stage not to conduct our arguments outside the boundaries of the TsK."[46] Stalin therefore wanted first of all to keep the matter within the Old Bolshevik nobility and second, to prevent the kind of paralyzing local political blood-baths that the fight against *skloki* produced when factions forcefully attacked each other.

Many provincial leaders drew an explicit distinction between central and local party views of Stalin's Secretariat, which they defended. Comrade Volin of Kostroma told the party congress that oppositionist critics of the Secretariat who delivered "hysterical speeches and base-less statements" were all from Moscow.

> Those comrades who work in the localities, constantly doing soviet and party work in the provinces and districts, unconditionally consider the TsK's work productive. . . . I know this well because I work in the localities, not in Moscow. I've been to a series of provinces and know what the situation is there. I think that all of us local party workers leading and closely carrying out party work, think that the organizational-political work of the TsK has really improved.[47]

From the provincial leaders' insecure position, *any* challenge to the precarious status quo must have seemed risky and dangerous. The party had swollen since the Civil War with the addition of hundreds of thou-sands of raw, untested members without revolutionary background and experience. Opening the party to full party democracy and control from below, as Trotsky argued in 1924, threatened not only their posi-tions as local leaders but also the stability of the party and its tradi-tions. What did the callow, ignorant youths and self-seeking newcomers who had recently joined the winning side know about the party or its goals? Cracking down on the economic liberties and position of peas-ants, who were the majority of the population (as Zinoviev and Kamenev suggested in 1925) seemed risky.

At the 14th Congress, Zinoviev and Kamenev led a unified opposi-tionist Leningrad delegation in an attack on Stalin and his leadership. Zinoviev broke with the traditional united Politburo report and gave what he called a "co-report" in addition to Stalin's which was sharply critical of Stalin's Politburo majority.

His attack was seconded by several well-known members of a Len-ingrad delegation that, while calling for party democracy, had rigged elections there to ensure that only oppositionists represented the city.[48] Other speakers pointed out that the oppositionists had been all for discipline when they were in the majority and now suddenly were for open criticism.⁴⁹ Not even pleading from Lenin's widow, Krupskaia, for sympathy toward the Leningraders could overcome the indignation felt by most delegates at what they regarded as Zinoviev's apparent attempt to divide and split the party for reasons of personal ambition. Whatever was left of party freedom of speech dissolved as the delegates laughed at her and at Kamenev's plea not to apply personnel sanctions against those who used their right to voice their opinions at party congresses. As another sign of the personalization of the struggle, rival groups of delegates at the congress chanted "Zinoviev, Zinoviev!" and "Stalin, Stalin!"

A majority of the party regarded the oppositionists as the most recent appearance of personally ambitious *sklokisty*, so the oppositionists were voted down, marginalized, and if they didn't give in, expelled from the party. Sometimes the battles were fierce. Kirov recalled the 1926 floor fights in Leningrad factories between the TsK majority and Zinoviev's supporters: "Here everything has come to war. And what a war! Yesterday I was at the Treugol'nik [Factory] where there is a collective of 2,200 people. The fighting (*drak*) was unbelievable. I haven't seen such a meeting since the October days and couldn't have even imagined such a meeting of party members. From time to time in certain parts of the meeting things came to a real fistfight!"⁵⁰

The battle with the oppositionist *gruppirovki* left a legacy in the party, and one the opposition would not have liked. The opposition had argued for reducing Stalin's power. But the ensuing struggle actually cemented his power and reputation; he was now regarded as the leading spokesman for party unity against a potential split in the party, which was most party members' worst nightmare.

The oppositions had called for the right to defend—even publicly— minority positions in party bodies. The result was the opposite: the bitter struggle with them only served to harden the idea that this was dangerous. Before the battle with the opposition, split votes in these bodies were recorded. When the protocols of these meetings were circulated to the broader party elite (TsK members, for example) dissenting votes were noted as "special opinions" of some Bolshevik knight or other who had the right to be heard. Thus, for example in reporting an Orgburo member's dissent to a decision of that body, "Comrade Krestinskii, in a special opinion, suggested . . ."⁵¹ We know that through the years there were always arguments in the Politburo, Orgburo, and

Secretariat. But after the battle with the opposition, only unanimous votes of the Politburo and Orgburo were reported even to the limited elite public of the TsK, much less to others outside. There were no more comradely "special opinions."

☆

There is no doubt that Stalin used his personnel power to maintain his position and to weaken his oppositionist critics. Such measures in the 1920s were nothing like the lethal force he would apply in the 1930s, and tended to be measured and incremental. Throughout most of the decade, such "organizational measures" were aimed not so much at firing or demoting oppositionists as it was at breaking up concentrations of them. As we have seen, when a struggle between two factions (whether based on personal cliques or political argument) paralyzed a party committee, the TsK stepped in and either sent an emissary or removed one or both factions. The same techniques were used to break up oppositional concentrations in party committees, whose dissident members were dispersed to new positions. Celebrated cases in the Urals and Ukraine at the beginning of the 1920s followed this pattern, as party committees that had gone wholly over to the opposition had their members dispersed to new positions. This was the case following the 14th Congress, when Zinoviev's dissident Leningraders were "exiled" from the city to new (but not necessarily lower-ranking) positions elsewhere.

When this happened, Stalin and his supporters always had plausible justifications that sounded more practical than political. How could the party tolerate oppositionists rigging elections in Ukraine in 1920 to return a favorable majority?[52] How, Molotov asked, could the TsK tolerate oppositionist control in Tula, Ukraine, and elsewhere, where party members who disagreed with the local oppositionist leadership were put in jail?[53] The hypocrisy of such rationalizations is probably more apparent to us than it was to local party activists at the time, who desperately needed reliable personnel and did not particularly want to carry on nitpicking ideological debates with local dissidents. They wanted to maintain local order and protect their own power bases, and Moscow's interventions served their interests. It was indeed sometimes the case that local party factions "chased out" ideological dissidents, demanding their recall to Moscow.[54] The fact that oppositionists had themselves demanded stern central measures against local party troublemakers earlier did not enhance their case or lend sympathy to their complaints. And, because of the shortage of talented and hardworking party administrators, transferred oppositionists were usually offered equivalent positions elsewhere, and to the average party worker, their transfers did not seem so punitive.

At the 11th Party Congress in 1922, some oppositionists complained about the Secretariat persecuting opponents by transferring them to lesser positions. But the two examples given were not convincing. Oppositionists Sergei Mrachkovskii and Timofei Sapronov were in fact transferred out of the Urals. Molotov defended these transfers as "business" rather than political.[55] Indeed, Mrachkovskii moved from commander of the West Siberian Military District to commander of the Volga Military District (a promotion, actually), and Sapronov moved from secretary of the Ural Buro of the TsK to full TsK membership and secretary of the Presidium of the TsIK. In fact, the use of central personnel measures against troublemakers and dissidents enjoyed broad support in the party and was a matter of group consensus as much as it was Stalin's personal tactic.

FORMATION OF THE REGIONAL CLANS

Beginning at the end of 1923, Trotsky had complained that most provincial secretaries were appointed rather than elected. Actually, the universal practice whereby the TsK "recommended" or appointed secretaries outright began in earnest later, *after* Trotsky's defeat. As we have seen, at the time Trotsky began his criticism, most provincial party first secretaries were nominated and elected from below, without a TsK recommendation. It had long been a tactic of the TsK to send in a new secretary in places of chronic *skloki* (Arkhangel'sk, Briansk, Viatsk, and others) or nationality conflict, and Trotskyism was considered an example of this.[56] Ironically, therefore, his critique gave major impulse to the phenomenon he criticized.

In fact, regional party family circles, or clans each headed by an authoritative party patron arose *locally* in the early 1920s, long before the opposition critiques or Stalin's rise to power. They were a response to local party factionalism and squabbling. From the second half of the 1920s Moscow tended more and more to solve *skloki* by *reinforcing* the local secretary's power to suppress other factions. It was made clear that the "responsible" or first secretary had seniority over the parallel soviet leadership, and within the party structure the first secretary not only was supreme, but alone was answerable to Moscow for "fulfillment of decisions."[57] This was the party version of industrial "one-man management."

Tight as control by a first secretary might be, it could not overcome the natural personal conflicts that characterized Russian and Soviet politics, and *skloki* continued, albeit more rarely, into later years. In 1929, a party worker in the Urals wrote a "strictly personal" letter to Molotov about a "big threat of *skloki* among the leadership cadre of regional party workers." Shvernik and Kabakov led competing factions in Sverdlovsk with mutual accusations on both sides.[58]

In 1932, Stalin had to referee a *sklok* in the Lower Volga territory. He wrote to Kaganovich, "I managed to acquaint myself with the situation inside the leadership of the lower Volga. Both Pshenitsyn and the chairman of the krai ispolkom are guilty. They both must be called to order and obligated to work with Ptukha. If not, we need to replace both and send someone else."[59]

In 1937, North Caucasus KPK representative Kakhani wrote to Stalin, Molotov, and Andreev about a conflict between part of the territorial party committee led by Pivovarov and another led by First Secretary Riabokon'. Pivovarov, an "opportunist" according to Kakhani, got the territorial party buro to pass all kinds of resolutions censuring the Kabardino-Balkarskii national party group when Riabokon' was out of town. We "need to strongly call him [Pivovarov] to order and not allow him to turn the multinational territory into an arena for fights and *skloki*."[60]

At first, Stalin had seen something good coming out of the battles with *skloki*, the creation of a "tight-knit unified core" in party committees:

> I should say that *skloki* and frictions, aside from their negative side, have a good side. The basic source for *skloki* and quarrels is the gubkom's striving to make a tight-knit unified core inside itself enabling it to work as one. This goal, this striving, is both healthy and legal, although the way it works out sometimes doesn't further that goal. . . . Nine-tenths of these spats and frictions, regardless of the unjustifiable forms they take, contribute to building a stronger core for leadership work. . . . It's not necessary to prove that if there were no such leadership groups in

gubkoms, then there would be no gubkom leadership. . . . That is the healthy side of *skloki*, which should not be overshadowed even when they take terribly unpleasant (*urodlivye*) forms.[61]

These personal "family circles" have been well described in the scholarly literature.[62] They were mutual protection networks centered around powerful patrons. Members protected each other and their chief, while advancing the interests of the group at the expense of other circles. Eventually, they came to control virtually every aspect of life in their provinces: budgets, industry, agriculture, education, police and judiciary, and the press.[63] Their leaders were indeed princes of their provinces. Provincial political power was personal power.

Scholars have also noticed the continuities in practice from imperial to Soviet times. With the fall of the tsar, "Clientelism not only continued, but also enjoyed a very significant renaissance that had enormous political implications. . . . The office of governor represents an early analogue of the later Soviet regional party secretaries who, in fact, more completely emulate the old tsarist notion of *khoziain* of the province with their relative independence, control of appointment power and enormous and highly personalized executive authority."[64]

We saw in Chapter 2 how regional party barons created their own personality cults. When they moved from province to province, powerful Bolshevik nobles also brought their entourages with them. When I. P. Rumiantsev moved from the Vladimir party organization to Smolensk in 1929, he brought with him a "Vladimir group" consisting, among others, of A. L. Shil'man (who became second secretary) and V. Vasilevskaia who filled various district secretaryships and worked in provincial party committee departments. When they arrived, they coopted leading locals Iu. Rappoport (a district party committee secretary) and V. Arkhipov (who would run the Smolensk city party organization).[65]

When A. K. Lepa was transferred from Uzbekistan to Tataria in 1933, he brought his "Tashkent tail."[66] The most famous "tail," because Stalin singled it out for national attention and criticism, was the group B. P. Sheboldaev brought with him from Saratov to the Azov–Black Sea territory in 1934. The "Saratov Brothers-in-Law" (*svoiaki*—another slang term for "tail" members) consisted of two dozen Sheboldaev loyalists, who like all such, in turn imported their own entourages.[67] As one Rostov party member said, "A majority of these were personally recommended by Comrade Sheboldaev, who knew them from previous work. Most of you have heard the current term 'Saratov *svoiaki*."[68]

Allowing the creation of strong patriarchal "family circles" was the price to be paid for order and unity in the oblast committees. By the mid-1920s, Stalin had decided to permit the formation of strong clans in the provinces, each headed by a powerful first secretary that he would support. Such clan machines would overrule (if not squash) *skloki* and permit the party to carry out major policies like collectivization and industrialization that required a strong, disciplined machine locally. Although Stalin would begin publicly to severely criticize "artels" and "tails" in the 1930s, he had accepted them as a fact of life before that.[69] He had largely refrained from public criticism of them, and his office had routinely approved regional appointments of territorial party leaders' chosen followers. In tsarist times, "In general, the State turned a blind eye to favoritism and nepotism, but when such manipulation was brought to the attention of the courts, it was inevitably presented as a transgression of the law, an unjust and intolerable utilization of connections."[70] On rare occasions, however, Stalin refused to allow a grandee to take a large "tail" with him to a new job, and instead micromanaged the transfers requested. When in 1931 his own client A. A. Andreev became commissar of means of communication (NKPS), the latter requested removing five deputy commissars, replacing them with five people from the North Caucasus where Andreev had been first secretary a year before. Stalin didn't like it:

> Evidently Andreev wants to collect in NKPS all of the North Caucasus people. That is hardly advisable. We can give him Kalashnikov. Zhukov too. As for Mezhlauk, we need to think about it. We have to specify if Blagonravov would be First or Second Deputy; in the worst case we can not take him away from OGPU. . . .[71]

Although Stalin had to permit the creation of "little Stalins" all over the country, he soon realized that their clans could be in conflict with his. He found himself in the paradoxical position of strengthening them as he criticized them privately. For example, at the November 1927 TsK plenum, he lashed out at the mutual protection networks of *krugovaia poruka*:

> Both in the center and in the localities, decisions are made, not infrequently, in a familial way, as in the home, so to speak. Ivan Ivanovich,

a member of the leadership group of such and such an organization, has made a terrible mistake and made a mess of things . . . Who doesn't make mistakes? Today, I, Ivan Fedorovich, will let him get away with it. Later, Ivan Ivanovich will let me get away with it, for there is no guarantee that at some point I will not make mistakes. Decorous and calm. Peace and goodwill. Who says that a mistake overlooked will undermine our great mission? No way! We'll find a way out somehow.[72]

On 19 October 1931, Stalin, again in secret, told the Orgburo,

I have the impression that there are no real party organizations in the Transcaucasus. There are chiefs and gangs (*atamanshchina*). If someone gets promoted to a post, do you think it's because of his qualifications? In most cases, it's not. His only value is whose person is he, who will he support. Is that a party? No, it's a system of chieftains, not a party organization. Who's person is he? Who will he support? Who will he fight? Who will he drink with? Who will he visit as a guest? . . . That's a fact. . . . If you pick people that way, then they will screw you up. It's no good. It's a chieftain system, completely without a Bolshevik approach to picking people. . . . It's a gang. . . .

If we now have chieftain regimes, then two years ago in the Ukraine we had feudalism. You can't call it anything else. . . . So everybody kept their mouth shut and begged each other's pardon, and served up fine resolutions to each other and everything was rotten. We said that was no good and broke up the chieftain system [in Ukraine]. . . . [73]

Stalin didn't like anyone's clan but his own, and he even pretended that he did not have one. Stalin, of course, was every bit as much a patrimonial chieftain as those he criticized. His group's original insiders were Molotov, Kaganovich, Voroshilov, Kirov, and Ordzhonikidze. In the second rank stood Mikoian and Kalinin. Members entering later included Zhdanov, Beria, and Khrushchev. Stalin nurtured and protected his clan followers over the years as a loyal patron.[74] He could not very well denounce clans while being chieftain of one. He got around this hypocrisy by refusing to admit, even in private correspondence with inside members, that they were a clan. He called them instead a "leading group" that had come together spontaneously. One of the very few times he even referred to his group was in a letter to Kaganovich in 1931, in which he mentioned the "leading group that historically formed itself [without a specific agent, using the reflexive *slozhivsheisia*] in the struggle with all forms of opportunism."[75]

Like a typical clan leader, Stalin spent a good bit of time refereeing and balancing his clients. Zhdanov struggled with Malenkov; Ordzhonikidze with Kuibyshev; Kuibyshev with Andreev; Ordzhonikidze with Molotov.[76] Although Kaganovich tells us that these fights were business, not personal,[77] we have evidence that they ran deeper. Aside from Mikoian's recollection that "Sergo did not love Molotov very much,"[78] we have correspondence in which Ordzhonikidze calls Molotov an "obscenity" (negodniai). Molotov and Ordzhonikidze began to ignore each other, and their mutual attempts to isolate the other threatened the government. In all these fights, but especially in this one, Stalin was at pains to moderate and act as referee.[79] Stalin also liked to set his boyars against each other as a matter of policy. As Beria told his son, "He was a master of this art. He whispered to one man something bad about another, then did the same with the latter."[80]

In 1949, Nikita Khrushchev "soon saw that my arrival in Moscow conflicted with plans made by Beria and Malenkov. I formed the impression at that time that Stalin (although he didn't say this to me) had summoned me from Ukraine because he wanted to alter the disposition of forces there in some way and reduce the roles of Beria and Malenkov. . . . My transfer to Moscow created a counterweight to Beria, as it were, and tied his hands."[81]

The functioning personal networks headed by Politburo boyars were part of unwritten and unofficial Soviet practice, and are best found in memoirs.[82] These memoirs are quite tendentious: each Politburo member remembers himself as virtuous, surrounded by evil conspirators. Memoirs by the offspring of Stalinist leaders each depict their parent as heroic and sympathetic (Beria's son even credits his father for inventing Khrushchev's reforms and Gorbachev's perestroika.) But while these self-justifying texts can tell us little of the moral qualities (not to mention negative achievements) of the person in question, they do provide an unparalleled glimpse into the atmosphere of personalized politics, struggles among courtiers and clans, and Stalin's moderating and balancing role. Thus Beria's son surely paints an unbelievable picture of his father, but is probably correct in reporting that his father told him, "There can be no question of friendship between members of the Politburo, it's a snake-pit."[83]

POLICE CLANS

Personal clans dominated the political police (GPU, OGPU, NKVD) as well as the party. Like party clans, they were led by authoritative police officials with inner circles of close collaborator-lieutenants, surrounded by larger orbits of officials.

Based on shared camaraderie in the Civil War, subsequent shared postings in troubled areas (Caucasus, Central Asia, Ukraine), or long-time common service in the central Moscow police apparatus, police clans can be identified in various ways. For example, members of a given group got medals at exactly the same time. They moved together from province to province, rose and fell together in job appointments. And in the end, they were arrested in groups at the same time.[84]

Unlike party clans, police clans struggled and battled and intrigued against one another. They engaged in constant maneuvers and intrigues designed to blacken their rivals. Veteran police operative Pavel Sudoplatov noted that for high party and police officials, "subjective motives and ambitions . . . played a far more significant role in political events than it seemed at the time. . . . They aimed to consolidate absolute power or to replace their staffs with new figures. . . . The standard rule was to collect dirt against everyone and then manipulate this evidence."[85] Goals of police clan intrigues were promotion of the interests of the clan and its members, and control of the central police apparatus and operational departments. Control of the center meant power because of proximity to Stalin. It meant dramatically increased patronage power to give out high-ranking positions. It also meant the ability, however subtle, to influence policy.

By the late 1920s and early 1930s there were four main personality-based police clans and a few smaller ones. The dominant clan centered around Genrikh Iagoda, a longtime ranking police official of the central apparatus. Iagoda had been first or second deputy chairman of the GPU and OGPU since 1918 and had headed many of its departments. Since 1929, given OGPU head V. Menzhinskii's illness, First Deputy Iagoda had been de facto head of the political police, and he and his people controlled the central OGPU apparatus. His chief lieutenants were G. Prokof'ev, I. Ostrovskii, K. Pauker, and M. Pogrebinskii.

The other large clan was that of the "North Caucasians" (*Severoka-vkaztsy*) centered around former anarchist E. G. Evdokimov. Although they occasionally held positions in the center, most of their postings were in the provinces, especially in the North Caucasus, centered on Rostov-on-Don. Evdokimov's chief assistants were M. Frinovskii, I. Dagin, N. Nikolaev-Zhurid, P. Bullakh, and V. Dement'ev. Evdokimov's group had come together in the rough environment of the North Caucasus and if Iagoda's clan administered from Moscow offices, Evdokimov's had made their name fighting bandits in the countryside. They specialized in large military sweeps of the hinterland and pitched battles with armed groups. Evdokimov was the only police official ever to win the Fighting Order of the Red Banner four times.[86] He liked to compare the OGPU with a military unit "in the narrow sense of the word 'militarization,' that is, the most possible resemblance of our organization to the Red Army."[87] Evdokimov was partial to "mass operations" and the ascendance of his clan in 1937 would coincide with the bloodiest of these.[88]

A clan of "Ukrainians" around V. Balitskii (K. Karslon, Z. Katsnel'son, I. Leplevskii, and others) controlled police work and cadres in Ukraine and carried out collectivization there. The Beria group led by L. Beria, V. Merkulov, S. Goglidze, and B. Kobulov dominated Georgia, Armenia, and Azerbaijan.

These police clans, like military comrades, were close-knit socially as well as professionally. As a recent account puts it, "in the process of putting together the Evdokimov clan, what counted was personal loyalty to the 'father-chieftain' (bat'ka-ataman). And in that order: first, professionalism, and second personal devotion. All remaining considerations were down the list and in essence did not count at all. By the way, Lavrentii Beria used analogous principles in the formation of a team."[89] M. Listengurt, a member of the Evdokimov clan, remembered:

> Evdokimov has his own (svoi) people, whom he raised (vospital) in the course of many years and whom he placed in the basic and decisive positions in the territory. Evdokimov's past anarchism took on the distinct character of a father (bat'kovshchina) and actual chieftain. (atamanshchina]). This expressed itself in Evdokimov not permitting his people to be insulted, nursing and protecting them when they got into trouble, promoting them, giving them awards, binding them to him, and getting them to do his will.

Listengurt remembered how Evdokimov had his people over for dinner and camaraderie. Nikolaev-Zhurid (later one of Ezhov's most vicious henchmen) played the piano and Evdokimov's brother the balalaika or guitar, and everyone sang. "More and more they resembled a family, or more precisely a kind of clan of relatives."[90] Some, like E. G. Evdokimov, even had their own cults; poems and songs were written about them.[91]

> Efim Georgievich, with you
> Went a united dreaded family
> To the heroic fight.
> Your innumerable friends . . . [92]

Before 1936, Stalin rarely tried to control the police clans. The political police was considered a specialized professional service with not only its own traditions but its particular and secret methods. Its members had special knowledge, and knew best how to conduct operations based on their tried and true methods. Many years later, Molotov remembered how NKVD chief Iagoda stayed in power, even though the party leadership didn't like him, because of his technical skill: "We had to work with reptiles like that, but there were no others. No one!"[93]

Unlike party clans, until the middle of the 1930s, the police never impinged on or threatened Stalin's power. His interventions took place only when a balance had to be struck between warring clans, or when police clan conflicts threatened to tear the institution apart. He probably had balancing police clans in mind at the 17th Party Congress in 1934, when the four rival chieftains Iagoda, Evdokimov, Beria, and Balitskii all got seats on the TsK.

Unlike high-level party personnel appointments, proposals to name officials in the police most often were rubber-stamped by the Politburo.[94] On proposed police appointments, Politburo agendas never "put off" or "declined" nominations from NKVD leaders. The assumptions were that the professionals knew best, or at least that the party was not equipped to question them on precise factual grounds. Stalin usually gave police chiefs Dzerzhinskii, Menzhinskii, Iagoda, Ezhov, and Beria free hand to name their deputies. He seems to have been interested in discipline, efficiency, and unity in the political police, and if that meant allowing leaders to build clans, so be it. When Stalin did intervene, it was to make policy or to strike a balance that preserved the unity of the service.

CLAN STRUGGLES, 1927–29: EVDOKIMOV OVER IAGODA

Late in 1927, Evdokimov claimed to have discovered widespread sabotage in the industrial enterprises of the Donbas, carried out by old regime engineers. When he took his case to Iagoda, the latter dismissed it as Evdokimov's "fakery" (*lipachestvo*). Evdokimov then took the unorthodox step of going outside the police chain of command and taking his material directly to Stalin. Stalin told him to get more evidence and come back. Evdokimov did so and Stalin took up the case, siding with Evdokimov against Iagoda. Thousands were arrested or fired, and the affair became the subject of the famous Shakhty Trial in March 1928. Iagoda was furious with Evdokimov for going to Stalin behind his back.[95]

In 1928, Iagoda and several members of his clan were implicated for "personal corruption" in a mysterious case called the "Unprincipled Center."[96] Iagoda and his people were notoriously corrupt: in a single year, Iagoda spent more than a million rubles on maintaining apartments, dachas, and rest homes that his family used.[97]

Iagoda's deputy Pogrebinskii was also involved in shady dealings. In Gor'kii, where he was stationed, he was known as the "tsar of thieves" and friend and protector of "criminal brotherhoods from the prison camps whom he reeducated and remade, and the devil knows what."[98] Knowing what was in store for him as a Iagoda client, Pogrebinskii committed suicide a week after Iagoda's arrest in 1937. Unsure that Pogrebinskii was implicated in Iagoda's "treason," Gor'kii party leader Pramnek decided on a modest funeral, but when word got out that there would be no music at the graveside, there were rumors that Pogrebinskii's criminal "brothers" would show up. "We were not certain that thousands of people might gather and cause a *shkandal'*." There were rumors that Pogrebinskii's unsavory friends might possibly exhume the body and rebury it according to their tastes. Fearing "excesses" and "disorders," the Gor'kii leadership ordered Comrades Spasov and Khaims to attend and monitor the funeral. At first, they were afraid and refused to go, only agreeing when Pramnek made fun of them: "You are not little children, go!" They went, and everything went peacefully, although they grumbled that this was really a job for the regular police (*militsiia*). First Secretary Pramnek replied, "I'm sorry, but you can't always trust the *militsiia* with everything."[99]

In response to the 1928 corruption charges against Iagoda, Stalin decided to weaken the Iagoda clan's monopoly on the central police apparatus by infiltrating it with Evdokimov people. He transferred Evdokimov from Rostov to Moscow and "suggested" to police chief Menzhinskii that Evdokimov be put on the OGPU Collegium.[100] Evdokimov became head of the central Secret Operational Department and promptly began to flood his North Caucasus clan members into the central OGPU departments and thereby undermine Iagoda as best he could.[101]

CLAN STRUGGLES, 1931: IAGODA OVER EVDOKIMOV

Just as Iagoda had done to him in 1928, Evdokimov now accused Iagoda of bungling and fabricating cases. Iagoda had been pushing a case against high-ranking military men; Evdokimov called it "baseless." Evdokimov also apparently began to gather evidence of OGPU misconduct in interrogations: use of "physical methods" (torture), sleep deprivation, false protocols, and the like. Iagoda had his own commission to investigate the same things, so Evdokimov's move was a direct challenge to him.[102]

This time, Stalin intervened to slap down Evdokimov. On 25 July 1931, the Politburo broke apart the Evdokimov clan in the center. It removed Evdokimov from his positions in the central OGPU *apparat* and transferred him to Leningrad, specifically forbidding him from taking any of his associates with him. Apparently Leningrad party boss Kirov did not want Evdokimov in his organization, so a week later, the Politburo changed its order and instead sent Evdokimov to Central Asia to fight bandits in fifty-degree centigrade desert temperatures.[103] Filip Medved, who had been OGPU chief in Leningrad and a friend of Kirov's, assumed the top position there. Iagoda relished his victory and ordered operational OGPU officers to immediately evict Evdokimov's family from their Moscow apartment.[104] Evdokimov's clan members suffered worse. B. Messing and L. Bel'skii were fired from the OGPU altogether and transferred elsewhere; Ia. Ol'skii was removed from the central apparatus and given other police work.

Although Iagoda clan member Prokof'ev took over the Special Department in Moscow, the result was hardly an unqualified Iagoda victory. It was more of a balancing of clans. Iagoda was demoted from first deputy OGPU chief to second deputy. Ivan Akulov was brought into the police from outside as first deputy. D. Bulatov was transferred from leading the party's Orginstrukt to become chief of personnel at OGPU. Neither Akulov nor Bulatov were part of Iagoda's clan; neither had worked in the police before. Ukrainian OGPU chief V. Balitskii was brought to Moscow as third deputy.[105] Finally Caucasus OGPU chief Beria got a seat on the Collegium. Iagoda's clan had successfully chased Evdokimov's out of Moscow, but at a price. These intrusions into Iagoda's Moscow apparatus were said to be aimed at "strengthening" the OGPU, but Iagoda could not have been happy about them; he still did not have a clan monopoly on Moscow center. Moreover, reflecting Iagoda's reputation as corrupt, the Politburo ordered the OGPU to report in detail to itself and the State Bank on its financial operations, especially those involving currency and gold.[106]

Subsequently the Politburo produced an explanation for party leaders, drafted by Stalin, Kaganovich, Ordzhonikidze, Andreev and Menzhinskii. It explained that Evdokimov and his associates were punished for "conducting a completely impermissible group struggle against the leadership of the OGPU." Their whispers that Iagoda's investigation of the military was "phony" (*dutyi*) "did not in any way correspond to reality." They had therefore "undermined the iron discipline among workers of the OGPU."[107]

Clearly Stalin had no love for Iagoda, but he disliked clan war more. His moves in 1931 were aimed at keeping the OGPU intact more than supporting the Iagoda clan. But Iagoda was a skilled fighter who resented this "time of Akulov and Balitskii." In short order, he froze Akulov out of the central *apparat*. Akulov lasted less than a year, later complaining of "institutional (*vedomstvennyi*) resistance" to him from inside the OGPU. After eighteen months of constant arguments, Iagoda also drove Balitskii back to Ukraine with his people in tow.[108]

The period 1933–36 was a time of "moderation" or "relaxation" of repression. In May 1933, Stalin and Molotov banned further "mass operations" against peasants and others. Arrests were to be individual, each sanctioned by a procurator. The most important institutional change came in February 1934 on Stalin's motion, when the former secret police (OGPU) folded functions into a new NKVD (USSR People's Commissariat of Internal Affairs), but without any judicial powers. According to the new regulations, the NKVD did not have the power to pass death sentences (as the OGPU had) or to inflict extralegal "administrative" punishments of more than five years' exile.[109] As Stalin's lieutenant L. M. Kaganovich put it, "the reorganization of the OGPU means that, as we are now in more normal times, we can judge through the courts and not resort to extrajudicial repression as we have until now."[110]

This new orientation was a blow to Evdokimov and his sword-wielding chekists who liked mass operations. Even worse, in 1934 Iagoda became the head of the new NKVD while Evdokimov was removed from police work altogether and made secretary of the North Caucasus Territorial Party Committee. New NKVD chief Iagoda rubbed it in when he told a secret police conference that the era of mass repression (a Evdokimov specialty) had ended, and that any calls to renew it were now an "enemy theory." "The methods and practice from the period of struggle with mass counterrevolutionaries, a habit many comrades cannot drop, must be rejected."[111] Stalin agreed. In January 1935, he wrote to Vyshinskii that policing measures should now be "gradual, without shocks" and should be carried out "without extra administrative enthusiasm."[112] Iagoda's clan was at the height of its power, and Evdokimov's at its lowest.

CLAN STRUGGLES, 1936:
EVDOKIMOV OVER IAGODA, AGAIN

Iagoda was dethroned in the fall of 1936, however, when Stalin replaced him with N. Ezhov.[113] Stalin had decided to take control of the police, subordinating it directly to the party and to himself. Ezhov retained some of Iagoda's people for a few months because they had experience he lacked, but with Iagoda's arrest in March 1937, they all fell with him. In this interim period, lacking his own clan, Ezhov replaced Iagoda's group in the center with Evdokomov's. (He would admit this later at his own trial.)[114] A large number of Evdokimov's people took positions in the central and provincial apparatus under Ezhov.[115]

There are rumors that upon being appointed head of the NKVD, Ezhov wanted Evdokimov as his deputy but Stalin refused, fearing that Evdokimov would take over the entire show.[116] Stalin did not want to replace one police clan with another, or even to balance them anymore. He understood that once the Iagoda clan was removed, inevitably North Caucasus professionals would be needed, but he kept Evdokimov himself away.[117] Stalin wanted the clan members without the clan head. He had appointed Ezhov because, among other things, he was a police outsider with no police clan. Ezhov, therefore, had to ally himself with the disgraced Iagoda clan's enemies, the North Caucasus group, and brought them into the central NKVD apparatus. M. Frinovskii became his first deputy chief of NKVD. But in the dynamics of clan politics, to the North Caucasus men, Ezhov was never "ours," and vice versa. Because clans were an integral part of a system that could not function without them, Ezhov now began to assemble his own clan. He picked junior NKVD officers and new men from the party academies. Gradually his former colleagues from the party personnel office, where he had worked for ten years (M. Litvin, S. Zhukovskii, V. Tsesarskii, I. Shapiro) became his deputies, displacing the North Caucasus men.

When Ezhov fell, his replacement Beria destroyed not only the new Ezhov clan but the remaining North Caucasus group as well. In tried and true clan politics, he completely restaffed the NKVD with his own group from the Caucasus.

Aside from these battles that required Stalin's intervention to keep the police from imploding, the clans sniped at each other on a smaller, Byzantine scale. At one point in 1936, when Iagoda felt besieged both by Evdokimov's clan and by Ezhov's meddling, he sent G. Liushkov (unaffiliated) to Rostov as NKVD chief, replacing Rud' (a Evdokimov man) who was sent to Tataria. This move got an unreliable man out of his Moscow hair, and displaced and exiled a Evdokimov clan member. As a bonus, Iagoda now had Liushkov to get dirt on Evdokimov in the latter's home territory. It took months for Evdokimov to freeze Liushkov out and secure his transfer.[118]

When the depredations of Stalin or of other clans fell upon clan members, leaders tried to protect "theirs" who had been arrested or, failing that, give them up to protect those who remained. As arrests of border guards increased, M. Frinovskii, the head of that service, tried to protect his own. In Oct. 1937, Liushkov arrested V. M. Drekov, the Far East border commander, based on testimony of the latter's deputy. Frinovskii tried to prevent disaster by ordering the testifying deputy shipped to Moscow for "reinterrogation" by his own people. Sure enough, the deputy retracted and Drekov was released.[119]

Ezhov man L. Zakovskii, NKVD chief in Leningrad, had been giving quotas to his subordinates to arrest masses of party members and leaders, apparently without TsK approval, and by April 1938, Leningrad prisons were dangerously overcrowded. On this and other matters, Ezhov tried to prevent any communications with Stalin on violations of legality by his subordinates, even going so far as to intercept complaint letters addressed to Stalin.[120] To protect the "excessive" Zakovskii, Ezhov transferred him to Moscow to remove him from the scene of the crime. The maneuver didn't work. Stalin ordered Zakovskii's removal and arrest.[121]

In late 1937 and 1938, Ezhov and Frinovskii often decided to give up some of their own to explain excesses in the mass operations of those years.[122] Zakovskii was removed on 14 April 1938 and his associates were arrested with him. In the summer of 1938, when Beria was named deputy head of NKVD, Ezhov and Frinovskii decided to quickly execute "their" already arrested Zakovskii (and S. N. Mironov and others) before Beria could question them and secure confessed "evidence" against their clan leaders.[123] And as an example of how vicious— and primitive—these clan struggles were, Beria's first arrest was Alekhin, head of the NKVD poison laboratory.[124]

THE CENTER-PERIPHERY CONTEST: STALIN VERSUS THE PARTY CLANS

Returning to the contest between Stalin and the regional party clans, we find disputes between central and territorial leaders over control of penal policy, economic plan fulfillment and allocation of budget resources, personnel appointments, powers of the Party Control Commission, punishment of oppositionists, and other issues fought out with public and private denunciations, personnel punishments and appointments, institutional and constitutional rearrangements, mandated party elections, and, finally, through violence.

For all his criticism of clans, for a very long time Stalin kept the peace and continued to approve personnel appointment proposals and most decisions of the clans' *atamany*. There were many reasons for him to hold his fire, at least publicly. He needed the senior clan leaders; there were not so many available. In the first two decades of Soviet power, there was a crying shortage of senior administrative talent; it was a seller's market. When it came time for a senior leader to be appointed, experienced high-ranking candidates were offered their choice of vacant slots, and we see secretaries frequently being moved from place to place with very few new additions joining the pool for assignment.

Senior clan leaders also had prerevolutionary party *stazh*, and many of them were themselves TsK members, so while they might not know much about industry or agriculture, this enormous personal prestige (and attendant personal connections) allowed them to be effective bosses in often fractious party committees. In every province, Stalin needed someone who could apply pressure to get things done.

Moreover, publicly undermining a provincial first secretary too strongly risked undermining the entire structure of regime control. Although Stalin and his first secretaries might have their differences, when push came to shove, they closed ranks against challenges from society and (until 1936) against the party rank and file. Stalin and the provincial secretaries were part of the same *rukovodstvo* (leadership group), and had basic common interests and apprehensions about the party staying in power. For Stalin to attack the regional leadership stratum too publicly could suggest to the public a split in the leadership, which had long been the common fear and cardinal sin. To severely discredit the provincial leaders could also send a message to the rank and file that their leaders need not be obeyed, which could imperil stability in general and the party's hold on power in particular. This was hardly in Stalin's interest, and when he did loudly denounce those leaders from above in 1937, it showed how deep and bitter the center-periphery fight had become and how dangerous it seemed to Stalin by then.

Beginning with the first Five Year Plan, our sources contain many references to regional party first secretaries not fulfilling their economic quotas (and lying about it), hiding their and their subordinates' mistakes, and ignoring Stalin's "repeated warnings" or "repeated suggestions," as when "Comrade Stalin personally warned the provincial party committee more than once about these crude mistakes and sicknesses in the leadership of the oblast party organization."[125] And until 1937, they could do so. As we will see in the next chapter, until 1937 Stalin was even willing to ignore major crimes protected by the regional lords. So he criticized them, in a comradely way and mostly behind closed party doors, but stronger action would be an undesirable last resort. Powerful as he was, he had to move carefully to reduce the power of the provincial clans.

These provincial leaders were themselves senior party leaders. They had friends and old comrades on the TsK, and even for Stalin it was dangerous to provoke a hostile majority against him there. Feeling themselves to be important party leaders, Old Bolsheviks, and Stalin's peers, they were powerful politicians with whom Stalin had to negotiate.

As James Harris has shown, beginning with collectivization and planned industrialization, the generally polite tone of central-regional discourse gave way to angry demands and threats from Stalin, who insisted on plan fulfillment. Regional leaders responded by closing ranks within their cliques, closing off information flows to Moscow, and simply lying about costs and results.[126] The imperatives of planned industrialization, which came with clear benchmark targets, brought regional performance and obedience into sharper relief, and in this period Stalin increasingly sought to hold regional oligarchs' feet to the fire.

Stalin was of course a centralizer. Regional chiefs, because of their past service as an elite corps of Bolshevik knights, wanted to be included in policymaking and the center to defer to them on matters relating to their provinces. In essence, Stalin and the regional barons both laid claim to the authority of the state.[127] The contest can also be seen as a struggle between Stalin's clan and those of the party boyars.[128]

The next three chapters describe three rounds in the match between Stalin and the regional party barons. Although Stalin eventually won the battle, to do so he had to physically annihilate the provincial Bolshevik nobles. Short of that, they showed remarkable resilience against attack and a keen sense of self-defense. For the reasons listed above, Stalin was not eager to confront the Bolshevik nobles in pitched battle. He moved slowly and delicately, and it is not at all clear that he meant to destroy them until late in the game. What is clear is that he moved in the direction of reining in their power while enhancing his own.

In one round, like an early modern French king, Stalin tried to insert his own inspectors, the "king's men" as it were, into provincial clans, but the usual pattern was for local party leaders to wine, dine, bribe, and threaten centrally appointed representatives, and coopt them into the local clans. In the second round, Stalin and the regional barons argued at length about control over lethal violence and the new 1936 Stalin Constitution. Provincial clan leaders went so far as to protest against it privately, and very nearly sabotage its implementation. This conflict came out a draw, because in 1937, the regional Bolshevik nobles had to swallow the constitution, but won back the right to deploy lethal violence in their provinces. The third round in the contest was verbal; today we would call it "jawboning." Stalin called regional party chiefs "windbags" and "feudal princes . . . who think directives were written for idiots, not for them." The period 1934–37 is full of press criticisms of "familyness," "artels," and the "tails" that leaders dragged around from job to job. This jawboning went along with specific policy and institutional changes in the early 1930s designed to centralize the press, ideology, police, and judiciary in Moscow's hands.[129] Nevertheless, verbal attacks designed to weaken the regional nobles by empowering their subordinates also failed, at least for a while.

It would take another campaign to finally dethrone the provincials. From the time of the first Moscow show trial in mid-1936, regional leaders were more and more often accused of lack of vigilance against Trotskyists and other "enemies" in their entourages. This new issue would turn out to be the one that would destroy the "feudal princes" in 1937.

6 Stalin and the Clans I
The "King's Men"

You can write to Moscow [about me] if you want, but I recommend that you don't do it. It's very lofty there and you could break your legs.
—Party secretary P. P. Postyshev, 1937

INSPECTOR FRENKEL', a Moscow-based plenipotentiary, was sent to Kuibyshev in order to ensure "fulfillment of decisions" by the regional party machine. In 1937, he reported to Moscow on First Secretary P. P. Postyshev's "bad work" and "purely one-man style of work." Postyshev, a powerful regional baron, retaliated not only by refusing to let Frenkel' speak at party meetings, but by threatening him personally in the words quoted above, even though he was a "king's man," inserted into Postyshev's fiefdom with Stalin's authority to infiltrate, criticize, and discipline. In the end, the "king's man" was sent packing. Frenkel' was removed and disciplined, not Postyshev.

As we have seen, the Old Bolshevik notables controlled their provinces with personal patrimonial authority, backed by their revolutionary prestige and well-organized patronage networks. The authority of the regional elite, combined with the locally impervious strength of their machines and their distance from Moscow, gave them considerable independence from the center and from Stalin personally.

In order to carry out collectivization and early industrialization (1929–32) Stalin had been forced to cede considerable power to these provincial barons, but in the mid-1930s he worked systematically to centralize and reclaim authority, in a campaign that can be seen both as creating and cementing his personal despotism, and as a policy of centralization that had historical precedents going back at least to the sixteenth century.

Part of the process of creating absolutism in such widely separated places as Ivan the Terrible's Russia and Louis XIV's France involved reducing and destroying the local independence of territorially based nobles ("feudal lords" as Stalin called them) and simultaneously concentrating power in a political center that was both bureaucratic and personalized. This process can be seen as a kind of centralizing bureaucratic modernization, but it was also based on a patrimonial understanding of power and authority. When Louis XIV famously said "I am the state," the "I" was at least as important as the state, and at the time, people understood power to be personal rather than conceiving it as located in an impersonal and rational bureaucratic abstraction. Analytically, therefore, it would be wrong to draw a sharp distinction between the personal and the bureaucratic components of the centralizing process. Both were present. Ivan the Terrible, Louis XIV, and Stalin all created personal despotisms with similar processes and tactics.

One such tactic was to reduce the power of regional aristocracies by inserting the "king's men" into the territorial governments. Whether Louis XIV's *intendants,* Ivan the Terrible's *namestniki,* or Stalin's commissioners, commissars, and inspectors, their purpose was always to provide the center with information that might be withheld by local powers, to investigate economic malfeasance, and to ensure fulfillment of central decisions. Their common characteristic was that they were representatives of the center, outside of and independent from the patronage of powerful regional lords. It's not a new tactic: "Charlemagne tried to make this system a regular mechanism of central government over the Holy Roman Empire, even reinforcing it with a network of *missi dominici,* or centrally selected royal envoys to the provinces. . . . From Charlemagne's *missi dominici* to Louis XIV's *intendants,* we are confronted with a seamless continuum of such agents despatched to the periphery with the mission of gathering information, reporting on abuses and helping implement central directives."[1]

At Lenin's suggestion, the party had created a Central Control Commission (Tsentral'naia Kontrol'naia Komissiia, TsKK) in the early 1920s to check on the activities of party committees.[2] Party leaders made the TsKK independent of the Central Committee and its network of party committees in order to prevent conflicts of interest and to guarantee that TsKK members could investigate members of the Central Committee itself. No one could be both a control commission and a party committee member simultaneously, and the TsKK was to have independent authority to "go after" any party member accused of bureaucratism or violation of discipline, regardless of rank. Its state counterpart, the Workers' and Peasants' Inspection (Rabkrin), was charged with parallel investigations of state and economic bodies.[3]

Although it was technically supposed to be neutral in political disputes, the Stalinist faction coopted and controlled the central TsKK quite early on: dissident activities of party members were defined as a breach of discipline. Leaders of the TsKK in the 1920s (Shkiriatov, Kuibyshev, Ordzhonikidze, Iaroslavskii, and others) were all loyal Stalin supporters.[4]

But the TsKK also busied itself with investigations of nonpolitical cases of personal corruption and nonfulfillment of economic plans. One TsKK resolution from the period listed the "main tasks" as verifying quality in heavy industry, agriculture, and light industrial production, struggling against corruption, and guaranteeing fulfillment of governmental plans. To these ends, local and regional control commissions received and processed thousands of written and oral complaints from average citizens about the work of various party leaders. In 1933, the Western Region (Smolensk) Control Commission (ZapOblKK) and the Workers' and Peasant's Inspection processed over twenty-nine thousand complaints. According to their official report, the ZapOblKK settled 55 percent of the complaints to the complainants' satisfaction. In most cases, expulsion from the party was followed by transfer of the case to police or judicial authorities.[5]

Although the original charter of the TsKK had specified independence from the regular party committees, in practice local control commissions came under the thumb of regional party clans. Members of control commissions at regional level and below were "elected" locally, meaning that the composition of the commissions that were supposed to be checking the activities of party committees, was controlled by the party committees themselves. The foxes were guarding the henhouse.[6] By the late 1920s, local branches of the TsKK across the country became little more than "institutions running errands" for party committees.[7] This was particularly apparent in the conduct of the periodic *chistki* (screenings, purges) of the party membership. Designed to remove crooks, hangers-on, and passive and noncommunist "ballast" from the party, they instead became tools of local clans to rid themselves of inconvenient or disobedient people.[8]

The future representative of the KPK (the TsKK successor body, the Commission for Party Control) in Smolensk wrote in 1933 that Control Commission purges of party committees since 1929 had been dominated by leaders of those very committees: "The basic deficiency . . . was exactly that the conduct of the purge was organized by selecting party members [for purge commissions] from their own organization. This sometimes introduced into the purge elements of *mestnichestvo*, local attitudes, and influence."[9] Already in 1922, Lenin observed:

> Further, in deciding this question, it is necessary to take into account the weight of local influence. Undoubtedly, we are living amidst an ocean of illegality, and local influence is one of the greatest, if not the greatest obstacle to the establishment of law and culture. There is scarcely anyone who has not heard that the purging of the Party revealed the prevalence, in the majority of local purging committees, of personal spite and local strife in the process of purging the Party. This fact is incontrovertible, and significant. Scarcely anyone will dare deny that it is easier for the Party to find half a score of reliable Communists . . . capable of resisting all purely local influences than to find hundreds of them.[10]

By the early 1930s, local party machines had come to dominate much in the Soviet countryside and had little fear of inspectors. Once in a while, as in the Smolensk scandal of 1928, determined representatives of the center could take control of a local clan machine. But even then, it took egregious local offences, repeated trips by inspectors, and a determined center to pull it off.[11] First secretaries of provincial, territorial and national republic, city, and even district party organizations were powerful men. Because they were often distant from Moscow, because communications (and therefore controls) were poor,[12] and because Moscow desperately needed some political presence in the countryside, local and provincial officials were practically autonomous satraps. Especially in the 1929–32 period when Moscow relied on them to carry out collectivization and industrialization, these officials became "little Stalins" in their bailiwicks. While Moscow gave the orders, it seems that local party bodies and leaders, far removed from the capital, carried out policies independently and frequently at odds with those desired by

Moscow. Campaigns—including purges—could be stalled, sped up, aborted, or implemented in ways that suited local conditions and interests.[13] Local judiciary bodies carried out trials and pronounced sentences wildly at variance with the procedures prescribed at the center but in accord with the political interests of local machines.[14]

By 1934, the domination of control commissions by party committees led to a major reorganization.[15] For Stalin, speaking at the 17th Party Congress in 1934, "The proper organization of checking the fulfillment of decisions is of decisive importance in the fight against bureaucracy and red tape. . . . We can say with certainty that nine-tenths of our defects and failures are due to the lack of a properly organized system to check up on the fulfillment of decisions" (meaning, of course, Moscow's decisions).[16] In order to guarantee such fulfillment, Stalin announced the conversion of Rabkrin and the TsKK into a Soviet Control Commission and a Party Control Commission (KPK). He justified the latter conversion by claiming that the old TsKK's main role had been preventing a split in the party. Now that the opposition had been defeated "we are urgently in need of an organization that could concentrate its attention mainly on checking the fulfillment of the decisions of the party and of its Central Committee."[17]

The new KPK was directly subordinated to the TsK. Creating a *KPK pri TsK* had less to do with bringing it under Stalin's control (he already controlled the higher levels of the old TsKK) than with taking verification out of the hands of local party leaders who had manipulated TsKK commissions. Putting the KPK under (*pri*) the Central Committee would give it more authority in dealing with local barons.

Accordingly, the 17th Party Congress decided that regional plenipotentiaries (*upolnomochennye*) of the new KPK were to be appointed by the Moscow KPK and confirmed by the Central Committee of the party; that is, by Stalin's office.[18] The new plenipotentiaries were to be completely independent of local party chieftains and were to answer only to Moscow. As newly appointed KPK head L. M. Kaganovich bluntly put it, "The party created the KPK at the congress as an operational organ of our Leninist Central Committee."[19]

Such a reorganization meant that the "king's men" of the KPK would be agents of central power inside the territorial political "family circles" to ensure the "fulfillment of decisions" locally. The reorganization fostered a new built-in hostility, a turf battle, between the local-minded party committees and the central-minded KPK inspectors. Almost immediately, the KPK began a struggle with regional party leaders over contested prerogatives of center and periphery, as well as of attitudinal and juridical differences between inspectors and party administrators. The regional party leaders would display considerable resilience and strength in resisting this new interference from the capital.

Both the regional party lords and the KPK "king's men" had their adherents and protectors at all levels of the apparatus, and there were frequent disagreements about whether or not stern measures should be taken. For example, it was widely known that party committees cut corners to achieve their economic targets.

KPK plenipotentiary Frenkel' recounted an incident that illustrates how higher up in the economic structure, the blurred line between theft and pragmatic dealings was a way of life. Once, when he had finished a speech against pilfering and illegal dealings, an official had come up to him, asking if he wanted to hear the real truth. They told him how they routinely received construction plans and orders from on high but without materials to implement them.

> We think, what to do? We went to supply organizations, showed them the plan and the documents and said, give us the materials. They just stared at us and said they had no materials and that [construction materials in] the plan were already distributed. Then the supply apparatus people said, "Ivan Ivanovich, if you give us meat, bread, and money—on a certain freight car are nails and glass; you will get everything." We thought again, what to do? If we wait, we cannot build. If we break the law, we can. We decided to break the law . . . [20]

But for Frenkel', the supply apparatus people who offered the nails and glass were criminals.

> FRENKEL': Comrade Shkiriatov does not like such things, but in Stalingrad they say, "Influence (*blat*) is a great thing."
> SHKIRIATOV: Influence . . . yes . . . (laughter in the hall)
> FRENKEL': It is not a joke. Enemies do not think to take us on openly, but rather by fouling our plan of construction. The courts are too lenient on this . . . [21]

KPK official Akulinushkin of Ukraine reported to a KPK plenum on the bartering system that characterized the work of virtually all economic agencies: "They even swap in the Vinitsa provincial party committee

cafeteria." One state farm director had sold 450 of the farm's pigs independently:

> Where did the money go? It went to the state farm. It doesn't matter
> where the money went, but rather who gave the director the right to
> sell 450 of the state's pigs? When we [the KPK] examined the case, it
> turned out that the District Party Committee, the District Soviet, and
> the district prosecutor had received pigs from the state farm, and
> everybody was happy.[22]

In Smolensk, the two poles of competing authority were Western Obkom First Secretary Ivan Petrovich Rumiantsev and KPK Plenipotentiary to the Western Oblast Leonid Andreevich Paparde. Both were
powerful officials, but their jobs, politics, and ultimately their personalities were quite different.

Rumiantsev of Smolensk was a typical provincial party noble. A distinguished Old Bolshevik of proletarian stock, he was a metalworker
who had joined the party in 1905. A knight of the revolution, he was a
longtime TsK member and had ruled the Smolensk region since 1929
with a personal touch. In the region of Smolensk, factories, enterprises,
and one entire district were named for him. Large photographs of him
and his assistants appeared frequently in the press, and his birthday
sparked a two-day celebration complete with congratulatory messages
from common folk and adulatory telegrams from his underlings. His
good-natured but efficient rule was regularly emphasized. The democratic-
minded Rumiantsev invited ordinary workers to dine at his home, where
they were allowed to use the good crystal. In the speeches of his minions,
Rumiantsev was "the best Bolshevik in the region."[23] As a privileged
member of the national party elite he received Politburo appropriations
of valuable American dollars to fund his vacations abroad.[24]

In 1935, Leonid Andreevich Paparde was appointed plenipotentiary
of the KPK to the Western Region. Before that, he had worked in Siberia as chairman of the Western Siberian TsKK (1932–34) and KPK
plenipotentiary in Sverdlovsk (1934–35). Like his predecessor in Smolensk (Ian Bauer), and like so many officials in police and other control
agencies, Paparde was not a Russian. Son of a Latvian peasant, he was
one of the early members of the Latvian Social Democratic Party,
which he joined in 1911 with party card number 124. He was a combat veteran of the Civil War, during which he received the Order of the

Red Banner on the Kolchak Front.[25] Two years before he came to Smolensk, he had written a pamphlet that explicitly blamed local party
leaders for using their influence and "familyness" to protect their own.
He was the perfect "king's man."[26]

For a Rumiantsev to show results, he needed tremendous authority;
but having that authority put him in a position of relative independence from Moscow.[27] Stalin needed the Rumiantsevs, but at the same
time feared and resented the power they deployed locally and the loose
way they did business. Local misconduct and disobedience of central
directives were endemic. They discredited the regime as a whole, but
what could be done about it? A frank discussion of local abuse might
well expose the regime's own undemocratic foundations to an undesirable public discussion.[28] Wholesale replacement or annihilation of mis-
creant local officials would destabilize an already precarious political
situation in the countryside and, in any case, would not correct the
built-in structural-geographical-political problem.

To rein in the power of the Rumiantsevs was the job of the KPK
plenipotentiaries. From 1934 to 1937, Stalin would try to maintain a
kind of dialectical tension between the Rumiantsevs and the Papardes:
first tipping the scales one way and then the other in order to have a
system that would show economic results in the countryside without
fragmenting the party's power base. This attempt by Moscow to govern a chaotic and rapidly changing system—a system of chronic tension versus control—failed in 1937, as this and other peaceful attempts
to rein in the regional clans collapsed.

On the last day of the 17th Party Congress (10 February 1934), the
newly elected sixty-one-member KPK met and elected a chairman (L.
M. Kaganovich), a deputy chairman (N. I. Ezhov), and a seven-member
buro.[29] At the session, the KPK directed its buro to draw up a statute
(*polozhenie*) for the KPK, and a special commission chaired by Ezhov
was formed to work out the KPK's structure and procedures.[30]

A few weeks later, in March, the statute appeared. The KPK was "to
organize operational control of fulfillment of decisions" of the Central
Committee. Its charter seemed to give it wide powers. The KPK had the
right to recruit party members for its work, and to control its apparatus independently from party machines in the countryside. KPK members and plenipotentiaries had the right to read the protocols of
meetings of the Politburo, Orgburo, and Secretariat, and to attend

meetings of the Central Committee and of any party organization in the country. Leaders of KPK operational groups also had the right to attend Politburo meetings.[31]

KPK plenipotentiaries were to be representatives of the center for "operational control of fulfillment," and they had the obligation to "systematically communicate" with the center on the progress of fulfillment locally. Indeed, the KPK plenipotentiaries were empowered, in cases of clear local violations of Central Committee decisions, "to give obligatory instructions to all soviet and economic organs . . . and to district party committees and primary party organizations."[32]

Of course, this early statute foresaw the possibility of conflict between KPK representatives and party secretaries. It stated that KPK plenipotentiaries "should" work and make "proposals" through the appropriate channels of regional leadership. But the statute also *required* local party committees to consider and act upon violations by their members, when such violations were reported by the KPK. If the party committees refused to take action, the KPK was required to notify the Central Committee of this fact. In case of disagreement between KPK plenipotentiaries and local party secretaries, KPK representatives "will make their proposals to the Central Committee."[33]

Three months later, the KPK had its second plenum, which took place on 26–28 June 1934, just before the June plenum of the Central Committee.[34] The most important topic discussed was the emerging conflict between local party bosses and the representatives of the KPK. Because the KPK and Central Committee plenums took place almost simultaneously in Moscow, it is reasonable to suspect that members of the Central Committee who were regional party secretaries were present in Moscow to make their views known on the KPK.

The plenipotentiaries had taken their investigatory role seriously and, not surprisingly, some of them had already run afoul of the regional party organizations they were supposed to police. In their recounting of conflicts with local party leaders, the KPK plenipotentiaries sometimes elicited knowing and ironic laughter from their colleagues.

Plenipotentiary Shadunts (from the Azov–Black Sea Territory), mentioned the powerful territorial First Secretary Boris Sheboldaev, and complained that the territorial party leadership had blocked KPK proposals to remove certain party leaders accused of malfeasance.[35] In one case, the chairman of a local rural soviet had illegally arrested citizens, imposed fines on large numbers of people and threatened collective farmers by waving his revolver at them. The local procurator had filed charges against him but had then been fired by Sheboldaev's people, who sought to protect "their own" chairman. The KPK had then intervened to restore the procurator and sack the district party leaders.[36]

Shadunts complained that the Sheboldaev leadership intentionally delayed or forbade publication of KPK decisions in the local press. "The territorial party committee wishes to put the plenipotentiaries of the KPK in the position of the former TsKK, first so that all decisions of the KPK would agree with the committee and second to make party control in its work dependent on the committee (to get resources, buildings, and so forth)."[37]

Plenipotentiary Frenkel' from Stalingrad reported that he had criticized the Stalingrad party committee. His ingenuous posing as an angelic innocent drew laughter from his KPK peers: "I tried to maintain in this maximum loyalty (laughter in the hall)." Nevertheless, the head of the territorial soviet executive committee publicly protested against Frenkel''s criticism. Plenipotentiary Akulinushkin (Ukraine) had a similar experience. When he spoke critically of the regional party clan (Provincial Party Committee), Odessa Provincial Party Committee First Secretary Veger supported him. Akulinushkin also drew sympathetic laughter from his KPK fellows when he continued, "I then went on vacation. When I returned, my speech or even presence [at the plenum] had not been recorded in the protocols (laughter)."[38]

The regional party barons were powerful figures who protected their authority and marshaled arguments in defense of that power. KPK chief Rubenov from Kiev recounted how "our provincial party committees tell us that KPK interference prevents them from competing with other provincial party committees where there is less control." He went on to pinpoint the legal crux of the matter: the KPK statute authorized plenipotentiaries to give direct orders to state and party organs, but this was "complicated" in economic areas where such orders could duplicate existing chains of command. Further, the statute mandated that all "important" decisions should be routed through the regional party leaderships. The trick, as Rubenov noted, was in deciding what were "the most important questions."[39] As Smolensk KPK plenipotentiary Paparde noted, given the prevailing political situation in the provinces a KPK representative would have to be quite brave to try and set up "a real system of control."[40]

L. M. Kaganovich wrote in the party press that "At the plenum, much was said about the independence of plenipotentiaries from the regional party organizations." Summarizing the discussion, he observed that "arguments between party committees and plenipotentiaries do and should take place" in the natural order of things. He also noted that such disputes had been "serious business" in the past three months.

Without an unseemly public discussion of the nature of all the disputes, Kaganovich was at pains to smooth over the friction by making suggestions to the plenipotentiaries. He advised them to keep the party committees apprised of their investigations: "They [provincial party committee secretaries] should not have to read about it in the press." Kaganovich wrote that KPK plenipotentiaries were forbidden from publishing the results of their investigations in the press without the approval of the party committee. He counseled the plenipotentiaries to pose "concrete practical questions" to the party committees; the two groups should avoid fighting over every issue because "they have the same goals."

Kaganovich suggested three informal "approaches" to control. First, KPK representatives should simply call people up on the telephone and point out problems. If that did not work, they should write letters to party secretaries, committees, and/or commissars. Finally, and only as a last resort, the KPK plenipotentiary could appeal to the KPK and Central Committee, where "Comrade Stalin personally" would resolve the dispute.[41]

Kaganovich's speech dampened the conflict between the two groups by reining in the activities of the plenipotentiaries. The "king's men" had been too high-handed in their conduct: hiding their investigations from party committees, publishing criticisms in the local press without clearing them with the provincial party committees, and generally "fighting it out" with local leaders. The party barons were offended and had complained. They had to be heard, and they won the round. Kaganovich was trying to quiet the situation down without destroying the independence of the KPK plenipotentiaries from the local leaders.

Regional party leaders had scored a point against the "meddling" of the KPK inspectors, and they pressed their advantage.

In his previous job in Sverdlovsk, KPK representative Paparde had run afoul of First Secretary I. Kabakov, who complained that Paparde was rude. Paparde was transferred.

From Rostov-on-Don, First Secretary B. P. Sheboldaev complained about the high-handed and secretive activities of KPK representative Brike, who according to Sheboldaev was end-running him and tattling directly to the TsK. "Sometimes we find out what he is doing only when he makes a speech to the provincial party plenum!"[42] Brike was transferred.

In Kazakhstan, First Secretary Mirzoian complained about KPK representative Sharangovich. Sharangovich too was fired.

For the next several months, a chastened KPK stayed out of the news. The plenipotentiaries seem to have spent much of their time investigating lower-level cases of corruption. In the early weeks of 1935, KPK sections in the party's organizational journal described a series of actions against criminals and various malefactors, all of whom turned out to be local leaders.

Thus the director of the Middle Volga Soviet Executive Committee had been dispensing free food to friends under the very nose of the party committees and with the connivance of two executive committee secretaries. "Systematic drunkenness" in the leadership of both soviet and party organizations had allowed him to operate freely. The local KPK plenipotentiary had broken the case and moved against the participants.[43]

In Stalingrad Region, District Party Committee Secretary Maslov managed to block investigation of large numbers of complaints directed against "his people." His assistant, Secretary Pimenov, managed to quash forty-three indictments on grounds of insufficient evidence. Under the direction of the Maslov-Pimenov group, local courts would confiscate the property of convicted persons, and then sell it to friends (including wives of the judges!). Meanwhile, Maslov, Pimenov, and their fellow secretary Leonov were running the Novoannenskii District Party Committee through a drunken haze without holding any party meetings. Inspectors from the KPK penetrated the ring and expelled all three party secretaries and the judge of the district court.[44]

Crime inside or protected by the regional clans was a problem nationally, but until 1937, Moscow preferred not to wash this dirty linen in public. For example, in the Gor'kii Automobile Factory, Director

Diakonov and four of his deputies sold 257 cars illegally at inflated prices to various individuals and organizations. They raked in three million rubles.[45] Wherever such things happened—and they seem to have been common—everyone seemed to know who was who and who was doing what. One either played along or one was frozen out. "Everybody knew what the others in a group were doing over the course of several years, defended each other at party meetings, in the control organs, and so forth." "If some old or young worker doesn't go along with these *gruppirovki,* or doesn't want to go in, then he has no prospect of promotion or support."[46]

The same things happened elsewhere. In Riazan, bandit gangs of twenty to twenty-five members included party leaders and the head of the local police (*militsiia*). They terrorized peasants in the countryside with robbery and murder. Peasants armed themselves and guarded their farms; they were afraid to report the crimes. In the rare instances when the bandits were caught, they were quickly released. It took repeated visitations from Moscow inspectors to break up the gangs.[47]

Another example highlighted the KPK's anti–local leadership attitude. Comrade Samurin, a conductor on the Kiev railroad, was expelled by his local party committee for white-collar social origins and leaving work without permission. He appealed his expulsion to the local KPK, which launched an investigation. It turned out that Samurin, a loyal railroad worker for thirty years, had been the victim of a "baseless" vendetta because he had "discredited a member of the partkom buro." The KPK reversed his expulsion and took action against the high-handed leadership of the party clan.[48]

After a year of such muted activity, the KPK became more visible and audible again in the middle of 1935 in connection with the continuing purges of the party. Unlike the screenings of the 1920s, the purges of the mid-1930s were conducted by the regular party committees, not the control commissions.[49] It became the job of the KPK plenipotentiaries to watch over the purging and to correct mistakes made by the regular party committees and secretaries.

In May, 1935, the Central Committee announced an upcoming "Verification (*proverka*) of Party Documents." The general idea was that party organizations were to purge themselves of careerists, opportunists, "enemies," drunks, bureaucrats, and those not having proper party membership documents.[50] Party chiefs were enjoined personally to supervise the process, to check the actual party cards and files assiduously. This was a huge advance for the regional party nobles. In the 1920s, the TsKK had run screenings; now, the party chiefs themselves were in charge of purging their own organizations. On May 24, Paparde made a speech in Smolensk warning party officials against "adventurers" in the party and warning them to be responsible and careful in carrying out the *proverka*.[51] They weren't. One month later, in a published resolution, the Central Committee blasted the Smolensk party for bungling the verification.[52] The Central Committee complained that in Smolensk, the operation had been entrusted to minor clerical personnel who had rushed the matter through, expelling large numbers of innocent members in batches. Western Obkom second secretary Shil'man was criticized by name (and threatened with expulsion from the party), as were several other local officials. Two days after the Central Committee decision, KPK *intendant* Paparde delivered a fiery and sharply critical speech to the assembled officials of the Smolensk city party organization. Quoting from the published decision, he noted that it was not just a matter of little mistakes but of "fundamental problems" in Smolensk. He denounced Smolensk city party secretary (and Rumiantsev client) Arkhipov personally, claiming that the latter's shoddy leadership had allowed enemies to slip through the *proverka*. His very strong speech (whose publication was delayed and truncated in the party-controlled newspaper) asserted that bureaucratism had penetrated the highest levels of city party leadership, and accused Smolensk party officials of being *chinovniki* (detested tsarist-era bureaucrats) in their baseless and hasty expulsions of rank-and-file party members.[53]

It seems likely that Paparde had instigated the Central Committee censure of Smolensk. His speech was peppered with examples of party misconduct from around the province; clearly he had researched the bungling of the *proverka* before the Central Committee censure. And, as we shall see below, similar Central Committee attacks in other regions specifically mentioned the KPK's role in uncovering problems with the screening. In the case of the verification, the KPK was acting as Moscow's informant on the bureaucratic conduct of party tasks.

Under the pressure of the KPK/Central Committee attack, Smolensk clan members hurried to cover themselves with contrite speeches, articles, and public confessions of their poor work, as etiquette required.

They quickly held a plenum and passed a formulaic resolution denouncing themselves and recognizing the Central Committee criticism as "completely justified."[54] The besieged Shil'man wrote a series of exculpatory pieces in the local press, and several district party committee secretaries did the same.[55] Both Rumiantsev and Shil'man published repentant articles in the national party organizational journal, and Rumiantsev beat his breast: "the buro as a whole, and I as first secretary in particular, made gross political mistakes."[56]

Most of these articles, while accepting the Central Committee's criticism of the province leadership, shifted blame down to lower officials in the districts outside the regional clan. One district secretary noted that the "fire" of criticism "was especially sharp against the district party committees."[57] Some of them fought back: one brave district party committee secretary, Fëdor Bolshunov, who was not a member of the Rumiantsev clan, wrote in the party press that while he and his fellow district party committee officials were guilty, so were higher-ranking members of the regional leadership: "I do not want to put all the blame on the provincial party committee. I, as secretary of the district party committee and member of the provincial party committee buro, fully recognize my blame, but the obkom of the party gets much blame too." He pointed out that a provincial party committee instructor had been present in his district when the *proverka* had become fouled up.[58]

In the following months, Paparde hardly let up. After the required repetition of the proverka in Smolensk, he made another speech to the obkom plenum in which he noted a striking lack of self-criticism on the parts of party leaders. Singling out the leaders of El'ninskii, Krasinskii, and Sukhinicheskii districts by name, he complained about continued bureaucratism. Making an example of one of them, Zimnitskii of Sukhinicheskii district, Paparde said that "Comrade Zimnitskii did not say much at the plenum. . . . Evidently the lessons of the *proverka* have not penetrated into the consciousness of Comrade Zimnitskii."[59]

The occasion of the verification uncovered the political warfare taking place between regional party clans on the one hand and the KPK *intendants* on the other. Paparde asserted himself against the Rumiantsev clan as often as he could. He frequently summoned district party committee secretaries to his office for questioning and reprimands, sometimes humiliating them by making them wait in his corridor for hours. (On one occasion, he assembled several of Rumiantsev's secretaries in his office at

1 A.M. and kept them there until daybreak.) Party clan members complained about Paparde's "nonparty methods" and long-winded lectures to them; after such a session one of them said that "never in my life have I had such a headache." Rumiantsev complained that Paparde was relying on the testimony of malcontents; that is, of people outside the ruling clan whose all-important "prestige" was thereby damaged. For his part, Paparde defended his authority and stressed his independence from the provincial party committee's (that is, from Rumiantsev's) control.[60]

At a party meeting attended by dozens of party members and officials, Rumiantsev and Paparde openly attacked each other:

RUMIANTSEV: Decisions of the TsK plenum touch on the organs of party control [i.e., the KPK]. It doesn't follow that one can portray oneself as without sin or free from mistakes.

PAPARDE: What do you mean, concretely?

RUMIANTSEV: It would have been better to respond to the essence of the criticisms made here, for example about your five-hour harangues of district party committee secretaries you summon.

PAPARDE: You don't think I responded?

RUMIANTSEV: In your place I wouldn't have tried to pull in Lenin's teaching when discussing the offenses of your inspectors who always use improper methods in their investigations, which can only be interpreted as showing a loss of confidence in the leadership. There have been several cases in which a party secretary found himself at the KPK only because he complained about me.... This is because you get your information on the work of the provincial party committee from people who don't deserve to be trusted about it.... We're talking about the prestige of the provincial party committee. Yes! Prestige is necessary.

PAPARDE: Comrade Rumiantsev accuses me of disrespectful criticism ... I think that this attitude toward criticism is wrong. Criticism must be businesslike.

RUMIANTSEV: "Businesslike." What a creative use of Stalin's word ...

PAPARDE: I think that to go down the road of unprincipled, petty criticism of any little gap, pure formalities, when the matter is about serious questions of cleansing the party of two-faced elements, is simply no good.[61]

Such an open argument "in front of the children" as it were, shows the depth of conflict between KPK inspectors and the governing regional party chiefs.

Regional KPK plenipotentiaries like Paparde were not able directly to attack powerful provincial party committee first secretaries, many of whom were Central Committee members. So the plenipotentiaries made their criticisms in two ways. First, as we have seen, they attacked the district party committee party leaders, thereby casting doubt on the work of the whole regional party organization. Second, they secretly reported on the work of the powerful regional lords to the Central Committee. Sometimes, as in Smolensk, the regional party leadership retreated and beat its breast in public.

But at other times, provincial party leaders fought against the "interference" of the KPK and even the Central Committee. In Saratov, powerful A. I. Krinitskii was first secretary. There, in the course of the 1935 *proverka,* KPK representative Iakovlev had complained to Krinitskii and his party committee about excessive expulsions. Krinitskii had ignored his complaints and the KPK plenipotentiary then reported to the Central Committee. Krinitskii was a Central Committee member and former chief of one of the Central Committee departments, so it was necessary to bring big guns to bear. The Politburo formed a commission chaired by Ezhov and dispatched Central Committee secretary A. A. Zhdanov to Saratov to sort things out.[62]

Zhdanov addressed the assembled members of the Saratov regional party committee, accusing the local leadership of "mass repression" in expelling party members.[63] He noted that Krinitskii had summarily fired twenty-six of thirty-seven district party committee secretaries without consulting the Central Committee, and had removed other party workers who were technically on the Central Committee's *nomenklatura.* Aside from these local abuses, however, in this particular case Zhdanov defended the actions and powers of the local KPK representatives. Observing that the KPK plenipotentiary Iakovlev was right to report to Moscow with "the material upon which the Central Committee decision was based," he attacked Krinitskii for running roughshod over the KPK. "The attitude of the Saratov territorial committee and of First Secretary Comrade Krinitskii to the representatives of party control in Saratov territory, who uncovered and in a timely manner put the question of the mistakes of the territorial party committee before the Central Committee, did not serve the interests of the matter."[64] Krinitskii defended the prerogatives of the territorial committee by claiming that the activities of the KPK in his region "constitute a second center" of political power which competed with the party. In his concluding remarks, Zhdanov called such complaining about the KPK "mistaken chatter" which ignored the correct suggestions of the KPK. "It is necessary to speak of the personal shortcoming of Comrade Krinitskii as a leader, to whom the Central Committee has entrusted leadership of one of the largest party organizations in the country."[65]

Krinitskii was humiliated but unrepentant. Some weeks later, in the autumn of 1935, he wrote the traditional recognition of wrongdoing which always followed national public criticism of a major figure.[66] But Krinitskii's mea culpa was hardly that. He claimed that much had been done since Zhdanov's visit to correct mistakes, and that those mistakes had existed only out in the districts. Everything was better now. Krinitskii was angry; his article did not contain the customary formulation: that the Central Committee had been "completely correct" in criticizing him. It said nothing at all about his personal mistakes, nothing about the major jurisdictional dispute between party organizations and the KPK (which was not even mentioned), and very little on the necessity for the territorial party committee to carry out the usual *kritika/samokritika*.[67]

Even though Moscow had defended its *intendant* Iakovlev against Krinitskii, the latter would continue to fight him. In April 1937, Krinitskii dug up some dirt on Iakovlev; he discovered that Iakovlev had "wavered" in the fight with Trotskyists back in 1923 and demanded his recall. In an exception to the general policy of letting the provincial party barons have their own way, Stalin backed Iakovlev, and wrote to Krinitskii that he

> acted wrongly in posing the question of political confidence in Comrade Iakovlev. The TsK knows of Iakovlev's former deviation in 1923, which was reversed in 1924, and since that time, Comrade Iakovlev has given no basis for any doubt about his Bolshevik firmness. The TsK trusts Comrade Iakovlev and suggests that the [Saratov] party consider this matter closed.[68]

Enjoying the backing of the Central Committee, KPK plenipotentiaries had led the attack on the work of regional party leaders in the 1935 *proverka*. But it would be a mistake to believe that these party secretaries, from the obsequious Rumiantsev to the truculent Krinitskii, were without considerable influence nationally. In early 1936, the regional leaders struck back, using the Third Plenum of the KPK in March of 1936 for a general dressing-down of the KPK.

The previous plenum of the KPK in July 1934 had called for a national plenum every three months, so the Third Plenum of the KPK was a year and a half overdue. And when it came, on 7–10 March 1936, it was signaled only by a brief, forty-word "communication" (*soobshchenie*). None of the speeches delivered at the plenum were published or mentioned in the press and there were none of the usual explanatory press editorials or articles accompanying the terse announcement. Clouded in secrecy, the Third Plenum of the KPK produced only two published resolutions.

One of these related to the work of the party collegia of the KPK: the sections whose work related to routine expulsions and appeals of party members.[69] Hidden amidst technical points of the resolution was highly ambiguous language restricting the rights of the KPK to investigate the work of party organizations. Apparently, in addition to their routine work processing appeals, KPK collegia had busied themselves with investigations of party leaders, and the next point read: "Party collegia are forbidden to occupy themselves with any work not having direct connection to their basic work of considering and receiving appeals in declarations on party offenses by various members of the party."

In other words, party collegia were to concern themselves with appeals, not complaints about party leaders. But if they received such complaints, they could "consider" them . . . or not. Their only obligation in such cases was to transmit the complaint to the appropriate party organization. Such a procedure, however vague, would serve the interests of party leaders by protecting them from investigation by KPK party collegia, and by ensuring that they received all complaints made against them. Another passage of the resolution, which insisted that the work of party collegia should always be "closely connected" to party committees, emphasized the apparent victory for party secretaries' authority.

Party secretaries scored even more points against the plenipotentiaries. The second resolution from the Third Plenum concerned them directly.[70] After an initial statement praising the independence of KPK plenipotentiaries and citing their good work in Saratov and elsewhere, the resolution proceeded to criticize their activity and to reiterate the statutory limitations on their powers.

The heart of this resolution was an attempt to force the plenipotentiaries of the KPK to "work with" and be "closely connected" with the territorial party committees. It is difficult to know how this could be consistent with true independence: "The Plenum of the KPK obliges all plenipotentiaries to regularly inform the first secretaries of provincial and territorial party committees and the Central Committees of national parties of their plans of work . . ." (The 1934 *polozhenie* had only suggested that plenipotentiaries should do this.) Failure to do so in a timely and satisfactory manner "is not a correct understanding of the independence of the KPK plenipotentiaries from local party organizations" and is harmful to the general effort. The resolution went on to make the somewhat hollow claim that "These measures do not in any way limit the independence (*nezavisimost'*) or autonomy (*samostoiatel'nost'*) of the plenipotentiaries." As a sop, the KPK plenipotentiaries received a promise that "Any time any question of disagreement arises concerning the suggestions [of KPK plenipotentiaries] to provincial party committees or Central Committees of national parties, it can be submitted to the KPK or the Central Committee for resolution." To add insult to injury, and no doubt at the request of the regional party barons, the resolution closed with a call for the Moscow leadership of the KPK to check the credentials of KPK plenipotentiaries to make sure that they were qualified for their jobs.

These resolutions show a strong resurgence on the part of the party clan leaders, and their success in pressing their claims. The result was a virtual chastisement of the KPK checkers; they were clearly in retreat. A contemporary press treatment noted that N. I. Ezhov (by now head of the KPK and soon to become head of the secret police) spoke at the meeting and that he stressed the "independence" of KPK plenipotentiaries, but the overall tone of the resolution was the exact opposite.[71] In fact, Ezhov berated the plenipotentiaries for worrying too much about their independence and for thinking that their job was only to criticize party organizations. "This, of course, is completely wrong." But Ezhov went much further. He put forth the proposition that it was the KPK plenipotentiaries (rather than the party or economic organizations involved) who were responsible for economic fulfillment. ". . . our plenipotentiaries and KPK groups must understand that they answer to the Central Committee and the Buro of the KPK for the correct and timely fulfillment of Central Committee decisions."[72] According to Ezhov, the job of the KPK was not to criticize or to "spend your time thinking up new questions to put before the Central Committee." They were to verify fulfillment and nothing else.[73]

Sensing the changing winds and smarting under the high-level criticism, the plenipotentiaries made contrite and apologetic speeches at the plenum. Brike, of Azov–Black Sea, now recalled how provincial party first secretary Sheboldaev had correctly chastised him for going behind the territorial party committee's back and complaining to the Central Committee. Rather than defending himself, Brike stressed the smooth relations between the KPK and the provincial party. Plenipotentiary Rubenov, who had been one of the more strident speakers at the previous plenum, now claimed that there was no friction between him and the provincial party committee. And Sharangovich of Kazakhstan crooned that "on concrete questions of our work there have not been any serious disagreements" between the KPK and the regional party organization. Plenipotentiaries Shadunts and Frenkel', who had also been fierce critics of party organizations, were directly criticized for being too "severe" in their "style of work."[74]

Back in the provinces, the KPK also retreated. In Smolensk, the KPK plenum received the obligatory publicity from party organs, but local KPK *intendants* like Paparde were silent. The texts of the resolutions were published in the province party journal with commentaries clearly showing that their gist was to prevent the KPK from stepping on the prerogatives of party secretaries, considering questions rightly belonging to party committees, and generally overstepping their bounds.[75] Because of sheepishness, anger, or fear, no article on the decisions of the Third Plenum written by a KPK official appeared in the local press of the Western Oblast. After all, the national press had noted that the decisions of the meeting were taken on Stalin's personal initiative.[76]

Party nobles in the provinces still had significant clout and influence in Moscow. Though they had taken a beating during the membership screenings of 1935, they were able in 1936 to force a limitation and censure of the KPK. Gone were the 1934 rules enabling KPK representatives to give binding instructions to district party committees; the suggestion to cooperate with local party barons had become an obligation. KPK plenipotentiaries were now obliged to tell party secretaries whom they were investigating and to reveal their future investigative plans. They themselves were now made responsible for fulfillment of decisions, but without the authority to criticize or sort out blame among various organizations.

For more than a year following the March 1936 Third Plenum, the KPK was almost invisible in the national and local press. Paparde, for his part, seems to have been chastened. At the Smolensk plenum following the Third KPK Plenum, he refrained from his usual attacks on local party leaders, preferring instead to deal with agriculture, the "safer" topic from the June TsK plenum.[77] Occasionally, a short article would announce the routine expulsion from the party of some drunks, embezzlers, and crooks, but the struggle between the party secretaries and the KPK plenipotentiaries was for a time hidden from public view.

But in the spring of 1937, there was a revival of the war between the local KPK and the party committees, culminating in a dramatic personal confrontation between Rumiantsev and Paparde. The context was the February, 1937 plenum of the Central Committee which in addition to condemning Bukharin, Rykov, and other members of the "Right Opposition," had criticized the regional party secretaries for "bureaucratism." Based on a strong keynote speech by A. A. Zhdanov, seconded by Stalin, the plenum had attacked the high-handed, authoritarian, and "undemocratic" practices that had made regional party secretaries such powerful magnates. Making a play for grassroots support against the "feudal princes," the Central Committee denounced the secretaries for a lack of self-criticism and scheduled new party elections for the spring of 1937.[78] The election proposal showed that Stalin and his leadership were becoming serious about trying to weaken the power of the territorial secretaries. The voting was to be by secret ballot, with multiple candidates nominated from below and was therefore a direct assault on the regional party barons' patronage power.[79] Both Zhdanov and Stalin called for much stronger criticism and self-criticism by the party bosses.

The revival of the attack on party bigwigs was mirrored in local KPK activity. The February 1937 TsK plenum had given encouragement and sanction to those who wanted to attack "feudal princes" locally, and for the first time powerful provincial party committee secretaries came under direct attack. For three days, a Smolensk plenum discussed the February plenum. After hearing the reports of local party leaders, Paparde interrupted Smolensk city party secretary Arkhipov's speech, demanding to know why no practical steps were being taken to reduce bureaucratism. Several speakers then counterattacked by defending Arkhipov and Rumiantsev and criticizing Paparde and his high-handed activities.

Paparde turned his fire against Rumiantsev personally by bringing up the case of one Reznikov—an official of the provincial party committee since 1934 and a member of Rumiantsev's "team." The KPK had told Rumiantsev that there was compromising evidence against Reznikov, and had got the local procurator to sanction his arrest. Rumiantsev then called NKVD headquarters in Moscow, which replied that there was nothing incriminating on Reznikov; this was confirmed by Smolensk NKVD officials. Rumiantsev refused to fire his client Reznikov and instead scheduled a meeting of the provincial party committee buro to discuss the question. In the meantime, Paparde went over Rumiantsev's head and expelled Reznikov from the party anyway. Rumiantsev protested to Paparde about this usurpation of the ruling clan's authority.[80]

In the local round of party meetings following the February 1937 plenum, Paparde lashed out at the secretaries in the local party press: "Evidently, the party activists do not recognize and understand the basic meaning of the Central Committee Plenum's decisions. . . . It is necessary to criticize directly, truly, regardless of person."[81] Although he spread his fire across several districts, the attack on the leadership of Monastyr' was the best publicized. Personally attending a party meeting there, Paparde complained that local leaders spent all their time talking about how to get themselves good apartments and ignored the suggestions of workers. "In Monastyr' district there are gross violations of party instructions and leadership," he complained. He singled out district party committee secretary Kosykh by name, denouncing him for rudeness and a haughty attitude toward subordinates.[82]

The criticism directed against provincial party secretaries was severe, but it had a limited impact. In Smolensk, Rumiantsev drew his wagons into a circle against Paparde and the KPK. He confided to his intimates that Paparde was a "petty intriguer" who was "not one of us." On another occasion, Rumiantsev dressed down one of his own district secretaries who had talked to Paparde: "Who is your boss, Paparde or the provincial party committee?" In the words of one insider, Rumiantsev began an "open struggle" against Paparde.[83]

Paparde's attack on secretary Kosykh in Monastyr' was blunted by a resurgent Rumiantsev. Although Kosykh was raked over the coals publicly for a considerable period of time, he was not removed from office.

(His assistant, second secretary Zheltov, *was* sacked.) Kosykh's clan protection was strong enough to save and indeed to promote him. Despite Paparde's attack, Kosykh was still secretary of Monastyr' in May, 1937 and was "elected" to the obkom plenum at that time. He was running the provincial land administration (Oblzemustroi) in July, and as late as January 1938 was still a member of the provincial party committee.[84]

☆

Regional party clans were able to fight off the intrusions of the "king's men" from the KPK. The party barons were capable of defending themselves against centralizing institutions and the vaunted powers and independence of the central plenipotentiaries were whittled away almost from the beginning. As in the past,

> From Charlemagne's *missi dominici* to Louis XIV's *intendants* . . . the vast majority of accounts conclude that they rarely performed as expected: central envoys need local collaboration to carry out the tasks on the basis of which the authorities evaluate their performance, and this never comes without cost. . . . Thus these alleged agents of central control end up caught in webs of local solidarities and mutual protection that they are unable and often unwilling to dissolve. . . . local power elites were forced to collaborate with the intendants, but they often proved rather successful in circumventing, neutralizing, co-opting, or corrupting them.[85]

In the end, the regional clans could only be crushed, in Stalin's unimaginative and primitive view, by the wild onslaught of terror. Stalin would show that he was capable of killing a lot of people in his quest for centralized power; indeed, he could have killed his disobedient barons much earlier and in covert ways less perilous to his state order, had this been his original plan. It obviously was not; his struggle with them was incremental, reactive, and sometimes even defensive. Perhaps because they themselves were a clan, Stalin and his followers were incapable of creating regularized, procedural mechanisms of inherent centralization and coordination that are present to some degree in all modern states.[86] Indeed, it is not certain that he wanted that at all, at least to the degree that it could limit his personal patrimonial power. It may simply have been a matter of Stalin and his clan attacking competing boyar clans. And in this round, the boyars won.

7 Stalin and the Clans II
Who Can Vote? Who Can Shoot?

> *Demands for the use of harsh forms of repression continue to come in from a number of regions.*
>
> *—Stalin, 1933*

ELECTIONS, PRO AND CON

Until 1937, Soviet elections were rigged with one candidate for each seat, preselected by the local party clan, and with open ballot voting.[1] This meant that regional party clans could easily control these elections and ensure the election of their own. The Stalin Constitution of 1936 produced a new electoral system in which elections to soviets were to be universal, equal, direct, and secret with multiple candidates for each position. The constitution, "the most democratic in the world," according to Soviet propaganda, is usually seen as a public relations gimmick, to make the USSR seem a plausible ally of the Western countries against Nazi Germany, countering sentiment there that the USSR was an unacceptable dictatorship.

But aside from public relations or the possible democratization of the system, the constitution had serious domestic political effects as well. Whatever he thought about democratization, Stalin saw the new constitution as a weapon in his struggle with the regional nobles. They saw it that way too.

For example, in his hunt for "enemies," Stalin doubted the enthusiasm of regional party leaders to unmask "Trotskyists." The February–March Plenum texts are full of complaints about this. It was a main

206

topic in Stalin's remarks, and he devoted his first speech to exposing "rotten theories" that some leaders held minimizing the threat of dangerous enemies.[2] P. P. Postyshev had been relieved from his post as Kiev first secretary the month before for ignoring "signals from below" about enemies such as the recently elected "enemy" Radkov; real elections would have kept him out:

> POSTYSHEV: I didn't verify people in a businesslike way, at work. . . . I am convinced that if there were elections now, Radkov would not be elected in any party organization.
> STALIN: That's the point.[3]

In fact, Stalin said several times that the new voting system was a tool to put pressure on local and regional leaders in general. He told Roy Howard, the owner of Scripps-Howard newspaper chain, that many Soviet institutions worked badly. Officials were ignoring "practical questions" of daily life important to ordinary citizens. He told Howard that "universal, equal, direct, and secret elections in the USSR will be a whip in the hands of the population against officials in the organs of power who work badly."[4] A few days later, *Pravda* said that "verification by the masses of Soviet citizens in the elections will also be a verification of every party organization, a verification of how closely connected this or that party organization is to the masses."[5] Suggesting that officials needed to be verified, not to mention "whipped," was convenient demagoguery designed to blame local leaders for shortages and other problems of daily life. But it was also a significant sally in the center-periphery struggle of the 1930s and it did not go unanswered by the regional barons.

Stalin took the electoral reforms seriously and publicly associated himself with them. The 7th Congress of Soviets and the party's Central Committee announced in February 1935 the need to introduce some changes into the Soviet Constitution of 1924. Equal, direct, and secret elections were mentioned, as was a general strengthening of legality.[6] Stalin was chairman of the Constitutional Commission, and he personally chaired the meetings of the commission and two of the twelve subcommissions (General and Editorial); his signature appears several times on various protocols of their meetings.[7] In mid-April 1936 a rough draft was sent to the Secretariat of the Constitutional Commission, which produced a revised third version (*novyi variant*).[8] This version was then personally studied and "corrected" by Stalin, who in early drafts demonstrably crossed out "open" elections and wrote in "secret."[9]

Even without the added threat of democratic elections in their own home party committees (which Stalin would force on them the following year), for regional nobles free voting for the soviets could mean "losing one of their two positions, the soviet one, that enabled their leadership."[10] For these leaders, the most familiar (and the easiest) way to govern had always been by force. Force and terror, which Stalin had authorized them to use during and immediately after collectivization, had cemented their power and turned the "family circles" of the 1920s into the hard political clans of the 1930s. For local leaders persecution was "a tool of rural administration."[11] Stalin's waning interest in unlimited repression, evident at least since 1933, was bad enough. Now with the new electoral system, he seemed to be threatening the very structural basis of the local barons' power. They continued to fight back with the only tool they had: silence.

In the first days of June 1936, a TsK plenum approved the text of the new constitution, and Stalin himself gave the main speech on the matter. This was the first opportunity for senior party leaders, including the barons from the regions, to consider the electoral reforms. Perhaps anticipating a cool reception from the regional leaders, Stalin circulated the draft text only on the first day of the meeting, giving TsK members no time to think, strategize, discuss, and organize around the question.

Traditionally, any speech by a major central party leader, especially one by Stalin, was immediately acclaimed by speakers who quickly registered with the meeting's presidium in order to come to the podium and "fully approve" the "absolutely correct" proposal, whatever it was. This time, however not a single regional leader rose to speak. Molotov, who chaired the meeting, had to call for speakers: "Does anyone wish to speak? I ask you to sign up." Nobody signed up and no regional leader spoke at the meeting in support of the constitutional reforms. Instead, a "voice" in the room said, "Let's take a break. It is necessary to think." A division in the leadership, or even the notion that TsK members had to "think" about how to respond to Stalin, could hardly be presented to the public or the party as a whole, so in the final edited stenogram of the minutes for broad party distribution, the "voice" was recorded to have said, "The question is clear. There is no need to discuss. Let's take a break."[12]

The question was by no means clear, and there was very much a need to discuss, but there was no way to do it in the prevailing culture. It was impossible, given party norms at the time that stressed "iron unity," to openly speak out against a leadership proposal. A real debate could be bitter and would be reminiscent of the battles with the opposition of the 1920s. One could tailor one's remarks, adjusting the level of enthusiasm with language to express anything from acclaim to lukewarm support, and this was often done. But the only way regional leaders could actually oppose a proposal was to keep silent when custom required them to speak. This was a bombshell, or as one historian called it, a "boycott."[13]

The draft constitution was published in the Soviet press on 12 June 1936 and submitted to the public for an "all-Union discussion." Throughout the summer and into the fall, the press carried a constant stream of editorials, reports, and quotations from Soviet citizens on the merits and deficiencies of the document. The evidence suggests that the Moscow leadership took the matter seriously and paid close attention to the process, but regional leaders ignored or sabotaged it. In the weeks following the June 1936 Plenum (at which Stalin and Ezhov also attacked regional leaders for excessive, incompetent, and repressive use of the recent party membership screenings, and where it was also necessary to doctor the minutes to hide the conflict)[14] regional leaders avoided writing the traditional positive press articles about the constitution. Their articles and editorials avoided approving the new document and rather distracted attention from it by writing about economic successes. Only central leaders wrote in support of the new electoral system.[15]

Central officials were angry when local leaders were also lax in organizing the national discussion of the constitution. I. A. Akulov of the TsIK issued a number of irate and threatening communications to local bodies. Detailed files were kept on local measures to organize discussion meetings and on their size and frequency. The central leadership used the occasion to criticize and browbeat local officials for their laxity and dereliction in conducting the discussion.[16] When the progress of the campaign seemed to lag, Chairman of the TsIK Mikhail Kalinin sent a telegram to all local soviets and executive committees throughout the country on 14 August 1936. Kalinin complained that

> Many soviets and executive committees are not helping, are not pro-
> moting nationwide discussion . . . are not organizing the recording and
> generalization of suggestions and amendments. . . . This situation is in-
> tolerable. Chairmen of soviets and ispolkoms are obliged to ensure a
> genuine discussion of the draft Constitution by all citizens. . . .

Local soviet officials were ordered to send reports to the Presidium
of the TsIK twice a month on the progress of the discussion, along with
summaries of the suggestions from the populace.[17] They didn't. On 23
September 1936, Akulov wrote again to local leaders, warning that
"despite the telegram of Comrade Kalinin, you are weak in reporting
the results to us." The drumbeat of central criticism of local bureaucrats continued through the fall of 1936, both in the press and in secret
communications.[18]

The information on the national discussion that the leaders did send
to Moscow reflected a dubious popular attitude toward the electoral reforms, perhaps deliberately crafted in the summaries produced by those
regional officials. In rural regions, and indeed across the USSR, around
17 percent of all suggestions represented a protest against allowing formerly disenfranchised persons (kulaks, priests, former White officers, and
so forth) to vote; it was the second most popular suggestion in Smolensk. In an internal TsIK memorandum of 15 November 1936, complaints about Article 135 (the voting system) outnumbered those on all
other points except those on the rights and benefits of citizens.[19]

The vast majority of those speaking in Pavlovskii district (Gor'kii
territory) and in Orshanskii and Borisov districts in Belorussia did not
want priests to vote. A peasant from Kalinin province thought that
maybe the children of priests and kulaks could vote but "kulaks and
priests must not be given electoral rights." Sergei Belkanov, a testy
peasant from Ognego, Cheliabinsk province, said, "We *kolkhozniki*
greet the new Constitution. But we have some questions. What about
priests? Will they or will they not be able to vote?"[20] This was music to
the ears of regional family circle leaders, who forwarded these sentiments "from the masses" to Moscow.

The next elite forum for discussing the new electoral system came in
November 1936 when Stalin spoke to the Extraordinary 8th Congress
of Soviets, called specifically to ratify the constitution. Stalin rejected
any suggestion that members of "alien classes" be denied the vote and
quoted Lenin's statement that universal suffrage would someday be

restored. He minimized the danger of allowing "white guards, kulaks, priests, etc." to vote. Rather than complaining about the new elections or using repression, they should work to convince their populations. Stalin mocked the critics:

> They say that this is dangerous, that enemy elements such as white guards, kulaks, priests and so forth can sneak into the higher organs of Soviet power. But what are they actually afraid of? "'If they are afraid of wolves, don't go into the forest.'" In the first place, not all former kulaks, white guards, or priests are dangerous to Soviet power. In the second place, if the people do elect dangerous elements, then it would be a sign that our agitation work went badly and we would fully deserve that disgrace.[21]

As they did in the aftermath of the June 1936 Plenum, regional leaders showed their hostility to the proposal. This time, they had had time to think, and rather than keep silent, they chose either to warn that the elections could give aid and comfort to "enemy elements" or to avoid the question altogether by bragging about their economic achievements.[22]

But it was the February–March 1937 Plenum of the TsK that saw an open argument over the upcoming elections and a new proposal to extend the secret ballot to party committees. This was the meeting that arraigned and condemned Bukharin and Rykov, and because historians have focused attention on these prominent and tragic victims, we have failed to notice another important agenda item for current party affairs. It was a forum for Stalin and Zhdanov to criticize the regional party leaders for their use of patronage "to secure a measure of independence from the Central Committee." A. A. Zhdanov gave the main report on the elections, noting the upcoming 1937 voting for the new Supreme Soviet and calling for the extension of the new contested, secret ballot voting to the election of party committees.[23] Indeed, the first press mention of the plenum carried Zhdanov's resolution, days before any coverage of Bukharin and Rykov, and even before publication of Stalin's speeches to the plenum.[24]

It was time, Zhdanov said, for a major turning point (*povorot*). Popular faith in us Communists, he said, was not a free gift based on previous services. It had to be earned by democratizing party organs from top to bottom. This meant free and secret elections of party committees, strict discipline and subordination of party committees at all levels to higher bodies, and ending the practice of "cooptation" whereby

Communists were appointed to leading committees not by election but by the decision of the bodies themselves.

Zhdanov decried "familyness" (*semeistvennost'*) in which everything was decided behind closed doors by small groups having common interests, among them self-protection. Stalin agreed.[25] Most clan leaders had packed their buros and inner committees by cooptation rather than election. Zhdanov concluded by calling for two major reforms. First, the party must "unconditionally liquidate" the practice of cooptation and abide by party rules requiring election to all leading bodies. Second, the party needed to forbid voting by lists, and "move from open to secret voting by individuals, with party members having an "unrestricted right" to object to any candidate." This was a major escalation of the center-periphery conflict. Extending the secret ballot and contested seats from soviet to party organizations meant an attack on the ability of clan leaders to exert patronage, and in a further escalation, it was spoken of in public.

The conclusion of Zhdanov's speech was marked by stunned silence. The "prolonged applause" that sometimes marked a senior leader's speech was absent. This manifest discontent in the grandee audience was compounded by the fact that once again, nobody signed up to speak. The disconcerted A. A. Andreev, who was chairing the meeting, said:

> ANDREEV: I don't have anyone signed up [to speak]. It is necessary to sign up.
> SHKIRIATOV: Speakers need to prepare themselves.
> ANDREEV: Comrade Eikhe, go on.
> EIKHE: I can't. I'm not ready. I will speak tomorrow.
> STALIN: We have to have at least a provisional conclusion.
> IAROSLAVSKII: I ask that you sign me up.
> STALIN: There, Iaroslavskii!
> ANDREEV: Comrade Iaroslavskii has the floor.[26]

Iaroslavskii set the tone for the following speeches: not to talk much about the *party* elections Zhdanov had announced, but rather to focus on the *soviet* elections and the dangers they posed. Iaroslavskii was followed by only fifteen speakers, far fewer than usual, and almost all of them concentrated on economic achievements (and problems), the dangerous rise of religion, the danger from "enemy elements," (particularly the problems posed by vocally anti-Soviet kulaks returning from exile) and failures in party work. None of them overtly praised the new electoral system, and most did not dwell long on Zhdanov's central points about "familyness" or the system of cooptation rather than election of party secretaries. Stalin interrupted several of the speakers to bring them back to the subject of cooptation: "How are things there with cooptation?" "Cooptation is still going on?" He had to interrupt Vareikis twice: "Comrade Vareikis, you cannot get by without cooptation?" and minutes later, when Vareikis ignored him, Stalin repeated "Nevertheless, you cannot get by without cooptation? (laughter in the hall)."[27]

From the chair, Andreev had to insist that speakers who were focusing on enemies should instead stick to the subject:

> Comrades, before giving another comrade the floor, I should warn you that several of the speakers are not speaking on the subject. We have the third point of the agenda and fourth, but on the second point on elections, the speakers are ignoring the question of democratization within the party and this is wrong.[28]

In his concluding words, Zhdanov singled out Sverdlovsk first secretary I. Kabakov's speech:

> Comrade Kabakov spoke about everything. He talked about film mechanics, about material supplies, about radio; all these are important and essential things. . . . But when Comrade Molotov put the question to Comrade Kabakov about how things stood with cooptation, he said, "I will talk about that later." Then he returned to his favorite subjects and dwelled on them but the root question that was put, evidently, did not turn about to be essential or important.[29]

Stalin himself grilled P. P. Postyshev, who had recently been fired from leading the Kiev party organization:

> STALIN: Well, did elections happen in general anywhere [in Kiev]?
> POSTYSHEV: Yes, Comrade Stalin, we had new elections almost always on the eve of a party congress.
> STALIN: Only on the eve of a party congress, so it depended on that? . . . Why did they never take place?
> POSTYSHEV: We waited for instructions from above (many interruptions in the hall). Yes, yes, we waited for something from above.
> STALIN: And the rules?
> POSTYSHEV: We forgot the rules, Comrade Stalin.

STALIN: So it happens that they say: the line of our party is right, the Central Committee is not bad, there are successes, what the hell more do you need? What elections? Never![30]

The rhetorical conflict between center and periphery at the February–March Plenum was not only characterized by avoidance and distracting tactics. Within the limits of party discipline, discourse, and decorum, and sometimes outside it, the regional leaders were practically in revolt. An unseemly argument erupted between TsIK president M. Kalinin and several regional secretaries over the technical aspects of elections. The secretaries demanded to be included in the process. Regional secretaries Eikhe, Mirzoian, Liubchenko, Postyshev, Kosior, and even Beria harangued and ridiculed Kalinin, and both sides revealed the depth of disagreement by adopting an uncomradely "we" and "you" discourse. A united leadership was supposed to be only "we."

This was radical discourse. The last time it had happened was at the December 1930 TsK Plenum, when Bukharin had characterized the leadership as "you." Molotov and Shkiriatov angrily interrupted him because such a division implied a split in the leadership. Shkiriatov asked "Why are you saying this?" and Molotov angrily interjected, "Hey, look here!" Language mattered.[31]

KALININ: Comrade Eikhe wants an electoral law. But the law refers only to the Supreme Soviet and is being worked out now.

EIKHE: *We* are asking that *we* be included in this work.

KALININ: The law doesn't give all the answers. The Constitution has all you need.

MIRZOIAN: In an electoral district can there be one candidate or is it permissible to have 2 or 3?

LIUBCHENKO: What [districts] will be included in an oblast?

KALININ: I already said that an okrug will not extend beyond an oblast. Do *you* understand this or not?

LIUBCHENKO: Can there be several [electoral districts within an oblast]?

KALININ: Each candidate will represent only one okrug and voting is in this okrug only. In other words, a French system of elections.

POSTYSHEV: Everything is clear now, there are a lot of Frenchmen here! (laughter in the room). . . .

KALININ: So, when *you* say there is no electoral law . . .

KOSIOR: *We* are not saying that.

KALININ: Comrade Eikhe said that.

KOSIOR: Why are *you* blaming us?

KALININ: I'm telling *you* that all these questions will be answered when the draft is discussed, and then *you* will speak. . . .

BUDENNYI: And if *you* circulate [the drafts] in advance?

KALININ: But how can *we* circulate an unapproved draft?

EIKHE: Only to party organizations.

KALININ: That is possible.

POSTYSHEV: That would not be bad.

KALININ: If Eikhe and Postyshev and others want to receive the draft, then they will always get one.

BERIA: It's necessary to circulate.

LIUBCHENKO: And in a timely manner. . . . [32]

KALININ: Comrade Eikhe came here and wanted to bring things down, to blame (*svalit'*): "no, there is no electoral law."

EIKHE: That is pressure, Mikhail Ivanovich.

KALININ: Of course I am pressuring *you*. I think that *you* have every possibility for full preparation.[33]

Even some central officials were dubious about secret ballot elections. N. M. Shvernik, head of the trade unions, was caught off guard:

SHVERNIK: I think that it is necessary to conduct these reelections for the trade unions.

KAGANOVICH: By secret ballot?

SHVERNIK: I don't know about secret ballot.

(Laughter. Voice: He is afraid!)

SHVERNIK: About the secret ballot *we* have introduced a proposal. But I don't know if Comrade Stalin has explained if they should apply to trade unions. I think it wouldn't be bad. *We* can maybe conduct secret ballot elections (laughter in the hall).[34]

The regional party secretaries did wrest one concession from the Stalinist central leadership: a postponement of party elections. Ukrainian party secretary S. V. Kosior said that holding the party elections in April, as proposed, would be very difficult because it would come in the middle of the spring planting and the entire party organization would be mobilized for that effort. He asked to postpone the elections to May. Zhdanov thought Kosior was just stalling: "Stanislav Vikent'evich, after spring comes summer and then fall." No, answered Kosior, May is when we have our provincial party conferences anyway. "But it is completely impossible to do it in April. In April we are in no condition to do this."[35] Party secretaries Ikramov, Khataevich, Mirzoian, and others supported Kosior's suggestion, and Zhdanov finally agreed to amend the resolution to schedule May elections.[36]

After the plenum, regional party bosses did not give up on deflecting secret ballot elections, either in party or soviet institutions. Even after the Stalin group made the position clear at the plenum, two weeks later Kosior nagged Stalin on a specific point that was already decided: "I ask for speeding up giving instructions on questions that at the moment remain unclear: Are the elections to party organizations and for delegates to party conferences and buros to be with open or secret ballots?" Stalin quickly replied, yet again, "Conduct all elections by means of secret ballot."[37] Just to pound the answer home once again, Stalin then sent a Politburo decision to all regional party secretaries: "To forbid voting by list in elections of party organizations. Voting will proceed by individual candidate, thereby extending to all members of the party an unrestricted right to object to candidates and criticize them. To establish a closed (secret) ballot in the elections of party organizations."[38] These democratic election rules were published in July 1937.[39]

The center was not sanguine about the regional officials conducting elections for the Supreme Soviet according to the new procedures. The text of the electoral law contained detailed procedures to safeguard ballots and protect against overt falsification. As Iurii Zhukov noted, "It is hard to doubt whose possible falsification of election results these measures were directed against. Only first secretaries of district, city, provincial, and territorial party committees had the possibility and unofficial rights that would permit them, if necessary, to change the number of votes for or against this or that candidate."[40]

Moscow was indeed worried about regional officials faking election results. Later, in the weeks preceding the December 1937 Supreme Soviet balloting, G. M. Malenkov, a key Ezhov aide and Central Committee operative, quietly took charge of the matter, which always had been handled by the TsIK rather than the party. In a secret telegram to all local electoral commissions, Malenkov, newly appointed head of the Central Election Commission, ordered that special procedures be followed in the elections.[41] As soon as the ballots were received and counted, local officials were to immediately telephone or wire the Central Election Commission the name of the candidate elected, the number of voters in the district, the number voting for the candidate, the number voting against, and the number of write-in votes. This information was to be communicated to Moscow *before* the official local electoral protocols were filled out, and local leaders were to tell the press nothing about the vote count (except the name of the winning candidate) until Moscow agreed. Originals of the ballots, tally sheets, and protocols were to be sent to Moscow via the NKVD courier service.[42]

Provincial officials would in fact try to subvert the electoral process anyway, without outright falsification. In party elections, local secretaries sometimes refused to reveal how many "no" votes were cast against particular candidates. The Politburo sharply condemned this practice in a special decision.[43] In some places, they illegally restricted the franchise for soviet elections by claiming that "those under investigation" (which could well include entire categories of the local population) could not vote. Voter lists were being falsified, electoral boundaries were still not fixed, and many persons were being excluded from voting lists contrary to the Constitution. The circular called on local procurators and courts to investigate these practice. To strengthen the point, Chairman Kalinin issued an order (*postanovlenie*) the next day specifying that all persons had the right to vote unless they had explicitly been deprived of electoral rights.[44] In another "urgent" telegram, Kalinin ordered immediate compliance and complained about "insufficient work" in making lists of voters, forming electoral districts, providing paper and printing facilities for ballots and lists, and preparing electoral meetings. On occasion, when local soviet officials refused to comply, or did so dishonestly, they were arrested by local procurators.[45]

The RSFSR TsIK of Soviets complained in a secret April, 1937 report to Kalinin that "Local ispolkoms and soviets in a series of places not only do not fulfill the decisions of the Presidium, but also ignore questions and reminders from the TsIK. . . ." The same report recounted a story in which the Western Oblast (Smolensk) ispolkom had not fulfilled a routine TsIK request for two years. Eleven follow-up reminders had produced no reply to Moscow, "and only after we sent an instructor to the place was it established that NOTHING HAD BEEN DONE to fulfill this order. . . . It is completely evident that such disorder cannot be tolerated."[46]

Despite what we are used to thinking, officials and citizens at all levels took elections seriously in 1937. In addition to the argument between central and regional officials about them, an argument so sharp that

Central Committee meeting transcripts had to be doctored to hide it, central officials paid close attention to electoral developments in other ways. In the regions, peasants also took things seriously. Violations went straight to the top. In Saratov province, someone burned down the meeting hall where the electoral commission was meeting.[47] In Odessa, a kolkhoz activist objected to the candidacies of two locals. They murdered him.[48] Such incidents on the ground attracted the attention of USSR Procurator Vyshinskii. At a higher level, RSFSR Commissar for Forestry Ivanov failed to provide sufficient paper for ballots. One hundred and eleven shipments of paper were lost in transit, which constituted "criminally sloppy fulfilling of this important task." Ivanov was fired and he and his deputies were "brought to criminal responsibility."[49]

At the February–March Plenum of the Central Committee, as we have seen, many speakers warned of the "reactivation" of anti-Soviet elements, including religious groups, former White Guards, and especially kulaks returning from exile. Regional chiefs were not so worried about the actual voting (which could of course be "managed" in the counting) as they were about the preelection campaign, which gave "enemies" the right to organize for the election and a forum from which they could openly speak against the party list and the leadership behind it. This would lead to a crisis that, eventually, worried Stalin too.

Beginning months before, during the 1936 national discussion of the Constitution, distinctly anti-Soviet remarks were not uncommon. Grigorii Gorbunov, a peasant from the Ukraine and a former SR, had said:

> If we have a secret ballot, we will choose whom we want. I hope that they will elect me. The new constitution says that there will be a Supreme Soviet: I think that then there will be no more Party, or that it will merge with the Supreme Soviet. The Constitution permits the organization of parties apart from the VKP(b). Accordingly, we are organizing our party, our press, and we will carry out our line.[50]

Many of Gorbunov's neighbors agreed with him. Others thought that the new constitution meant that private peasants could "live as before." Kulaks were returning from exile, spreading rumors that the elections meant that socialism would be defeated, and demanding their old property back. "Priests and evangelists" were demanding reopening of prayer houses, and peasants were asking for closed churches to reopen. Even poor peasants and *kolkhozniki* showed some signs of vacillation: *kolkhoznitsa* (collective farm woman) Kaniushina from Leningrad province said that "The kulaks never repressed us. They helped us . . . now we give most of the best quality bread to the state . . . and get a poor price."[51] Other comments at the time of the constitutional discussion were equally hostile to Soviet power. For example, *kolkhoznik* P. Kalinin (described by the recorder of his comment as a "loafer") said, "It is not for us to discuss the constitution. We did not write it." An anonymous *kolkhoznik* said that "If the Ukraine is able to secede from the USSR, it will be very rich again."[52]

Local officials were confused and sometimes intimidated by returning peasants who had been exiled during collectivization. In Kursk province, the presidium of one rural district's soviet proposed "to immediately return the house of the former kulak Zuzul to him." In another Kursk district,

> Former kulak Rogozin, returning from exile, singlehandedly occupied the house previously confiscated from him, evicting the kolkhoz nursery. The rural soviet, finding out about this, did not do anything.[53]

In January, regional police officials were asking questions. As the Tatar ASSR NKVD chief wrote to Moscow,

> For us the line to follow in our conduct is not clear in connection with the new constitution. We ask you to explain if all previous orders of the NKVD USSR on this subject [kulak exiles] remain in effect or if we should rely on the corresponding articles of the Constitution and apply them to those people as citizens of the USSR enjoying all rights as citizens.[54]

Local officials knew that their own high-handed behavior and misconduct had not won them many friends among the local electorate. An April 1937 TsIK report to Kalinin noted that "Many times misconduct (*proizvol*) and lawlessness, committed by various organs of power and various workers in the center and localities, give strength to the hands of the class enemy to discredit our state system and weaken the power of the country."[55] In Belyi district, near Smolensk, Comrade Ivanov spoke of his unit's usual rural party work: "If we act this way in the elections then we will undoubtedly suffer a defeat." Throughout the summer of 1937, local officials tried to convince Moscow of the dangers of contested elections, saying implicitly that "either we local officials get reelected or else overt anticommunists will win." In Smolensk, activists warned that "alien elements," "enemies," priests, and even "friends of Hitler" could be elected.[56]

In October 1936, deputy NKVD chief G. A. Molchanov had written to Politburo members about how kulaks and anti-Soviet elements were disrupting election meetings. He wrote that kulak and Muslim elements were spreading provocative rumors "in connection with the publication of the new Constitution" about the dissolution of the collective farms and reopening of churches. He quoted one *kolkhoznik*, "We have to wait for the congress [Supreme Soviet]. As soon as they confirm the new law, everybody will leave the kolkhozes because the new constitution says everyone can live as they please." Another said, "Soon we will get an order that we can leave the kolkhozes. It's the end of the Communists."[57]

In January 1937, a special NKVD report noted "the tendency among settlers to return to their native places and demand return from the kolkhozes of the property confiscated during collectivization. . . . Certain special settlers [deported kulaks] express terrorist sentiments in relation to rural activists who took part in their deportation." The report quoted several peasants, including one who said, "The new constitution gives us special settlers rights as citizens of the USSR. In a few days, everyone will go home. The first thing we will do is settle scores with those activists who dekulakized and deported us, and then we'll go somewhere where they can't find us."[58] In Omsk, First Secretary Bulatov spoke of the fifty thousand peasant exiles in the north:

> All of them are awaiting permission to return to their homes. Some of them are well-disposed to Soviet power, some are hostile. Some have terrorist feelings, and say for example "now with the new Soviet Constitution I will leave for home they exiled me from and there I'll settle scores with the ones who sent me away" (voice: some of them aren't waiting for permission and are just leaving).[59]

From Stalingrad, a January 1937 report said that counterrevolutionary groups were trying to take over electoral meetings. Anti-Soviet peasants, routinely described as kulaks, were conducting illegal meetings in villages. In Omsk, "counterrevolutionary elements can steal our Soviet voters from us and use them against us."[60] Sectarians were going from village to village stirring up trouble.[61] "To further their aims, counterrevolutionary enemy elements have already named preliminary candidates from their midst in order to push them through the elections to soviet organs so they will vote against the Communists."[62] The following month, Leningrad reported dangerous sentiments as well. "There is no bread and we are sitting hungry. Soviet power and Stalin are all guilty in this."

A confiscated leaflet addressed to workers and peasants declared:

> For a long time you have agreed to refrain from revolting for bread. Comrade peasants and workers, we are hungry. It's time to rebel, destroy the rural soviets, stores, and bread warehouses. As in 1905, if there is no bread, we will bravely rise up and we will win. . . . We will take Leningrad. Brothers and sisters, fathers and sons are there. The Red Army is ours, in it are our brothers and sons who will not beat their brothers and sons; they are for us. Rebel, tear down! Give us bread! Bravely, comrades, prepare yourselves for anything.[63]

Local party leaders were panic-stricken at the possibility of open electoral campaigns in the countryside. At party meetings from Smolensk to Vladivostok, party secretaries warned of the danger. To take only one example, in the Kara-Kalpak Oblast, District Party Committee Secretary Pankratov told an oblast conference:

> And now in connection with restoring voting rights to those previously disenfranchised, their agents have been unleashed across the republic. They have more agents than we have members in the party organization.[64]

Police reports about dangers in the countryside were not new. After all, the police had a vested interest in finding as many dangers as possible, and exaggerating the ones that were real, in order to justify their existence and augment their budgets and powers. Since the early 1920s, the police had produced regular compendia (*svodki*) on the mood of the population and much of that reportage had been negative. On the other hand, depending on the year, there was serious opposition and resistance and sometimes the police had an interest in minimizing it to show the good job they were doing.[65] Now, though, in mid-1937, the police texts were more urgent. The new constitution threatened to give license and voice to the background popular hostility that with returning kulaks was less and less a background. And who knew where free elections could lead?

On 17 June 1937, West Siberian NKVD chief S. N. Mironov sent his boss N. I. Ezhov a "Memorandum on the Affair of an SR-Monarchist Conspiracy in Western Siberia." Mironov wrote that his NKVD officers had uncovered a joint conspiracy of exiled princes, nobles, and former White officers who, along with exiled kulaks, had formed an insurrectionary movement that had "prepared an armed overthrow and seizure of power." He also mentioned rightists and Trotskyists. "And if one considers that on the territory of Narym and Kuzbass there are 208,400 exiled kulaks and 5,350 exiled former White officers, plus active bandits and punitive detachments, it becomes clear on what a broad base the insurrectionary work was built."[66]

Mironov asked permission for two measures. First, he wanted to send a full NKVD division "with a large operational group" to Narym. Second, he asked Moscow to send a circuit session of the Military Tribunal to convict about five hundred people whose cases "will be completed very soon," and for permission to form an extrajudicial troika to convict others "with a simplified procedure" (*v uproshchennom poriadke*) language mirrored in the upcoming Order No. 447, discussed below. He concluded by noting that West Siberian First Secretary Eikhe supported his requests, "and was prepared to ask the authorizing instances [i.e., the Politburo] to agree to formation of troikas."

Typical of its genre, Mironov's request mentioned some specific conspirators and dangerous kulaks along with catchall phraseology that could include anybody, with a request for Moscow's permission to shoot masses of people without procuratorial or judicial review. Like all successful Stalin-era bureaucrats, Mironov knew which buttons to push with Moscow. A miasma of kulak perfidy and sabotage, insurrection, class enemies, and bandits was likely to trigger a response, and the subsequent "mass operation" Order No. 447 would reflect this generalized "enemy."

The same blending of enemies happened elsewhere. In Omsk, as early as February 1937, party leaders were lumping bandits, insurrectionary elements, nobles, traders, former White Army officers, priests, and sectarians into united "nests of counterrevolutionary activists."[67] In June, Omsk NKVD chief Salyn combined bandits, fascists, White Guards, kulak exiles, SRs, Mensheviks, anarchists, Zinovievists, and Trotskyists "into a united front" of enemies.[68] At about the same time, in Voronezh district party committee secretary Kruglov said: "it's significant that 20 churchmen, sectarians, and priests activated their counterrevolutionary work, helped by former monks, traders, kulaks, and Trotskyists."[69]

Mironov was asking permission to launch a mass operation. Such operations were already under way in some provinces before Stalin ordered them. In West Siberia, 382 people had already been arrested and another 1,317 had already been identified by the investigative work of secret NKVD agents. In Omsk, NKVD chief Salyn (often mistakenly considered an opponent of mass operations) had also launched his own operation. He told an oblast party conference that "in the past year we have uncovered vast insurrectionary organizations.[70]

Ezhov forwarded Mironov's request to Stalin five days later, with his recommendation, "I consider it necessary to permit the formation of troikas for the extrajudicial examination of cases in order to liquidate the anti-Soviet insurrectionary organization."[71] Although Stalin received Ezhov's packet on June 22, it was not until nearly a week later, on 28 June, that the Politburo approved Mironov's request and authorized a troika for West Siberia.[72]

Beginning at this point and lasting to nearly the end of 1938, the Soviet secret police carried out a mass terror against ordinary citizens.[73] This mass operation accounted for about half of all executions during the Great Purges of 1937–38. By the time it ended in November 1938, 767,397 persons had been sentenced by summary troikas; 386,798 of them to death and the remainder to terms in GULAG camps.[74] The process saw systematic physical tortures (approved personally by Stalin) of a savage nature and scale, fabricated conspiracies, false charges, and mass executions. As such, the operation of 1937–38 must be counted among the major massacres of the bloody twentieth century.[75] It seems clear that Stalin's decision to approve a mass operation flowed from local fears about opposition in the countryside, unleashed and legitimized by the new constitution that was so unpopular with local barons.

In approving Mironov's request and extending it to other provinces, Stalin was making a sharp reversal in a policy he had laid down since 1933, when he had banned this kind of lethal mass operation. Both before and after 1933 there had been mass operations conducted by the nonpolitical, regular police (*militsiia*). These were mostly aimed at clearing the cities of recidivist criminals, those without residence permits and passports, and other categories of common criminals.[76]

Punishment was typically exile or a short sentence to a camp. These sweeps were therefore nonlethal and more than anything reflected the inability of the regular police to maintain order short of periodic clumsy sweeps.

The kind of operation Mironov had in mind, and that Stalin approved was different. Although it did contain a few of the same targets, it was to be conducted by the political police, with punishments of either summary shooting or long sentences to hard regime camps. This was the kind of mass operation that had been banned since 1933, and compared to the regular *militiia* sweeps, had an entirely different history and lineage. To understand this, we have to go back a few years and examine another aspect of Stalin's struggle with the provincial clans: the history of the contest about executions and who could decide on them.

Regional party barons were used to ruling their territories with force, not elections. Now Stalin was forcing them to use elections. He had been trying to limit their prerogatives on the use of force for years.

Since the early 1920s, Stalin had tried to capture a monopoly on death sentences, depriving the local clans of that power. During the Civil War and shortly thereafter, summary executions of enemies were common. But as far back as the mid-1920s, Stalin and the center had attempted to take the power to decide death sentences out of the hands of local party and police officials who wanted to keep it and use it. An April 1924 Politburo order (which had to be reaffirmed in March 1926 and repeatedly thereafter) established a long-standing policy whereby local courts could not impose death sentences in political cases without the preliminary approval of the TsK.[77]

Later, in 1926, the Politburo established a Commission on Political-Judicial Affairs and ordered that local soviet and party organizations were to forward all indictments with "social-political" significance, including death sentences, to the commission. Moreover, local party organizations were forbidden from giving "any directives" to judicial or investigatory organs on these matters without preliminary examination by the Politburo.[78]

But as V. P. Danilov noted, once forced grain collections began in 1927–28, "completely independently (with the agreement of the corresponding party and state leaderships) local organs of the OGPU carried out arrests, confiscations of property, and pronounced sentences of prison term or exile and so forth."[79] Nineteen twenty-nine and 1930 saw a veritable civil war in the countryside, a cycle of official mass repressions and peasant resistance. Kulaks were arrested and shot or deported according to category. At this point, Stalin certainly did not forbid the use of lethal violence in the countryside, but he insisted on the right to approve and control it.

In May 1928, the Stalingrad gubkom wrote to the TsK that "the situation demands application of Article 107 to kulaks engaged in food speculation.[80] The article would be applied in very limited scale [only] in relation to kulaks. We ask TsK approval." Stalin agreed.[81] In September, 1929, the Politburo approved a request from B. P. Sheboldaev, first secretary of the Lower Volga territory, to shoot "up to 50 leaders" of a purported SR-kulak insurrectionary organization. The Politburo's answer noted, however, that with the exceptions of violent crimes against soviet and party officials, such "anti-Soviet actions" were better examined in the courts, "in judicial order." The following month, in response to another Sheboldaev telegram, the Politburo "permitted" the Lower Volga territorial party committee "on its own responsibility" to carry out punishments on persons accused of kulak terror. But Sheboldaev was obliged to pass the information along to the Politburo's Commission on Political-Judicial Affairs.[82]

During dekulakization and collectivization, telegrams poured in from the provinces asking for the right to conduct extrajudicial repression by troika. In October 1929, the Politburo agreed with the need for "decisive and quick repressive measures, up to shooting, against kulaks organizing terrorist attacks on soviet and party workers." The same Politburo directive, however, insisted that "conduct of corresponding measures, as a rule, is through judicial organs and in specific cases, [but] when special speed is required, to punish through the GPU . . . with the agreement of the oblast party committee of the VKP(b) and in more important cases with the agreement of the Central Committee of the VKP(b)."[83] Six days later, the OGPU Collegium in Moscow issued an explanation of the Politburo directive, stipulating that troikas could apply sentences only after receiving telegraphed approval of Moscow OGPU headquarters, and adding a three-month limit on troika powers to repress.[84]

In December 1929, the central Commission on Political-Judicial Affairs became even more involved in controlling local procedures on death sentences. A Politburo directive ordered courts to send copies of their sentences to the commission even before the appeals process. The commission would provide its "orders" to the appeals court. After the court's decision, the commission insisted on final review of the case.[85]

The Politburo's "special folders" show that the pattern established in the 1920s was confirmed in the 1930s: the initiative and requests for mass lethal operations came from the provinces. Local party or police officials asked for permission to carry out death sentences, and the TsK might or might not approve, and that approval often carried limitations. Stalin insisted on the right to control repression, and although he was willing to sanction mass shootings, his preference was to handle such things "in judicial order." His policy was therefore not based on moral or humanitarian grounds but on the twin bases of concentrating power in his own office and expediency.

In February 1930, the OGPU was given the right "during the time of the campaign to liquidate the kulaks as a class" to allow their plenipotentiaries in the provinces extrajudicial review of cases. The order stipulated, however, that such review must involve the participation of a procurator and the local soviet executive committee.[86]

That judicial supervision did not always take place, however, for in March 1930, a directive letter of the RSFSR Supreme Court complained: "Examination of appeals has shown that the courts in examining KR [counterrevolutionary] cases have generally committed gross deviations from the correct line of criminal-judicial policy . . . convicting a significant number of middle peasants and even poor peasants. . . . Furthermore, in a series of KR cases, which demand verification of the essence of the case's facts and circumstances, a judicial investigation did not in fact take place even when the final sentence was death."[87]

In April 1931, the Politburo had to once again "categorically confirm previous TsK decisions that death sentences for political cases must not be pronounced without the sanction of the TsK and orders the Supreme Court and Procuracy on their responsibility to enforce this order."[88] Three months later, the Politburo had to repeat the order yet again: all death sentences, even those of the OGPU Collegium, had to be confirmed by the Central Committee. Nor could citizens arrested for political crimes be held without interrogation longer than two weeks, or under detention for more than three months.[89] That the Politburo found it necessary to repeat this stricture is a sign that it was not being obeyed by the provincial clans.

As we have seen, all death sentences for political crimes had to be approved by the Politburo's Commission on Judicial Affairs (variously renamed Commission on Political Affairs and Commission on Highest Measures of Social Defense). Unfortunately, Politburo commission archives are still closed, but by chance we have scattered decisions of the commission on seventy-nine regional and republic death sentences for the period March–August 1932 in the files of the Politburo, which routinely approved the commission's decisions. Of those cases, the central Commission found the local death sentences in half (thirty-nine) to be excessive and reduced those to ten years in prison.[90] The provincials were harsher than the center.

In 1932 and 1933, local and regional party officials continued to request the right to impose death sentences. Faced with the crisis of famine and crop failures, the Politburo usually approved in cases of food hoarding and insurrection, but with restrictions. On 22 November 1932, in response to a telegram from Ukrainian leaders, the Politburo "granted" (predostavit') to a special commission in Ukraine (Kosior, Redens, Kiselev) in the period of grain gathering the right of final decision of death sentences only during the harvest. The Central Committee of the Ukrainian Communist Party was obligated to report the exact results to Moscow every ten days. The right was extended on 10 and 20 March 1933.[91]

On 9 February 1933, the Politburo "complied with the request" (udovletvorit' pros'bu) of the Belorussian Central Committee to extend to an OGPU troika the right to apply death sentences in cases of counterrevolutionary organizations, groups of kulaks and White Guard elements.[92] In April, the Politburo similarly "extended" the right to examine cases of uprisings and counterrevolution (with application of death sentence) to troikas in Central Asia and Leningrad, the latter troika composed of Kirov, Medved, and Kodatskii.[93]

The language of these documents elucidates the center-periphery relationship. Regional clan leaders sought the right to apply mass lethal violence, a right they did not have on their own. In the grain collection crisis of 1930–33, Stalin then "granted" or "satisfied the request" of local leaders. It is of course true that Stalin authorized and advocated severe repression against opponents of collectivization. But the documents show that in nearly every case, it was regional barons who first raised the question. The right to shoot was something locals had to seek and something Stalin sought to control and protect.

By mid-1933, however, the grain crisis seemed to be abating and Stalin reined in the power to execute. On 2 May 1933 he met with OGPU leaders, and his notes from the meeting show that he was interested in limiting the number of people authorized to make arrests, to "free up the prisons legally," and specify the dispositions and release of large numbers of those arrested.[94] Five days later, the Politburo revoked the right of all troikas (except those in the Far East) to apply any death sentences.[95]

The following day, Stalin and Molotov circulated a decree ordering a halt to mass arrests in the regions. The directive stated that

> The moment has come . . . when we are no longer in need of mass repression. . . . demands for mass expulsions from the countryside and for the use of harsh forms of repression continue to come in from a number of provinces, while petitions by others for the expulsions of one hundred thousand families from their provinces and territories are presently in the possession of the Central Committee and the Council of People's Commissars. Information has been received by the Central Committee and the Council of People's Commissars that makes it evident that disorderly arrests on a massive scale are still being carried out by our officials in the countryside. Anyone who feels like arresting does so, including those who have, properly speaking, no right whatsoever to make arrests.

Stalin and Molotov's circular complained about "mass, disorderly arrests," "an orgy of arrests," in which locals "have lost all sense of proportion." Mass arrests had become not only inefficient, but a liability in that they could stir up opposition to the regime. "Comrades . . . do not understand that the method of mass, disorderly arrests—if this can be considered a method at all—represents only liabilities which diminish the authority of Soviet power. . . . Making arrests ought to be limited and carried out under the strict control of the appropriate organs." He ordered that all arrests must have preliminary approval of a procurator, and ordered a reduction in the prison population from 800,000 to 400,000.[96]

After the May 1933 decisions, the Politburo continued to approve local requests for the right to apply death sentences, but much more rarely and always with restrictions. In July 1933, the Politburo "extended" that right to a troika of the West Siberian OGPU for bandits terrorizing the local population, but made the head of the territorial OGPU personally responsible. In August 1933, the Politburo decided to "temporarily" permit (*razreshit'*) troikas in Ukraine, North Caucasus, Middle Volga, Belorussia, Urals, West Siberia, and Kazakhstan to apply death sentences, also to active bandits.[97] It was not until more than a year later, in September 1934, that the Politburo approved a proposal to extend to Western Siberian territory first secretary Eikhe the right to approve death sentences for two months. In this case, the decision came at the initiative of Politburo member V. M. Molotov.[98]

In the meantime, as we saw above, in the spring of 1934, the OGPU was abolished and its police functions incorporated into an all-Union People's Commissariat of Internal Affairs (NKVD). Unlike the OGPU and its predecessors, the NKVD did not have the power to pass death sentences, even on those already in its custody in camps and prisons.[99]

Shortly thereafter, the Politburo established a Supervising-Judicial Collegium of the Supreme Court. Nevertheless, the Politburo found it necessary to repeat its strictures: all death sentences, even those coming before the new collegium, were subject to confirmation by the Political Commission of the Politburo.[100]

Three months later, L. M. Kaganovich sent a telegram to Stalin from Cheliabinsk: "I would consider it possible to confer the right to confirm death sentences for one month on a troika composed of Comrades Ryndin, Chernov, and Shokhin. I ask you to communicate your decision." Stalin replied, "I don't understand what this is about. If you can, it is better to get by without a troika and confirm the sentences in the usual [judicial] procedure. Stalin."[101]

For the next three years, lethal troikas and the mass operations they conducted were in bad repute in Moscow. Thus in October 1935, Acting Procurator of the USSR Roginskii protested to Kaganovich and Molotov against the actions of a troika in the North Caucasus that had sentenced two people to death for taking and receiving bribes under articles of the criminal code that envisioned five-to-ten-year sentences. Before the sentences could be reviewed, the accused were summarily shot by locals.[102] From what we know of police clans in the North Caucasus, this is not a surprise.

In this period, therefore, the pattern was one in which local party chieftains were more inclined to lethal mass repression than Moscow. Stalin said that such operations were inefficient and alienated the population, and insisted on giving permission in each individual case.

Yet in 1937, in response to Mironov's July telegram from West Siberia asking for a new mass operation, Stalin approved NKVD Order No. 447 which framed and authorized the largest one ever. This was a sudden reversal of the trend against lethal operations. Ezhov had very recently denounced such operations in a speech to the Central Committee, noting that "the practice of mass arrests . . . is now harmful." He noted that the Central Committee had criticized them since 1933 because such mass sweeps were ineffective at identifying real enemies.[103] At an even more recent conference of senior NKVD chiefs as late as 19 March 1937, he again recalled the decree of 8 May 1933 ("You all know about it") in which there was "sharp criticism" of mass arrests."[104] Yet now, that is exactly what the NKVD was being ordered to do. After listening to their chief Ezhov denounce mass operations twice in the same month, NKVD men may have been perplexed, but maybe not unhappy to hear Stalin reviving them.

We will never know why Stalin chose this moment to change his mind. He seems to have finally accepted the regional barons' warnings about danger in the countryside. During the five days following, he decided to extend the troikas to the entire USSR. His telegram to all regions of 3 July targeted "a large number of former kulaks and criminals" who had returned to their home territories upon expiration of their sentences and had become "the chief instigators of all sorts of anti-Soviet crimes." The "most hostile" were to be executed; the "less active but nevertheless hostile" were to be exiled to distant regions. Within five days, regions were to nominate troika members and propose numbers for both categories.[105]

Between Stalin's 3 July telegram and NKVD Operational Order No. 447 that actually initiated the mass operations, a number of changes took place that reflected yet more regional input. Ezhov organized a series of operational conferences of regional police officials that took place in Moscow on 16–18 July. Significant differences between Stalin's telegram and Order No. 447 show the input and interests of locals.

Stalin's telegram had only identified kulaks and criminals who had "returned home at the completion of their sentences." But after the conferences with local leaders, Order No. 447 expanded the list to include priests and sectarians, members of "anti-Soviet" political parties, fascists, former White Army officers, tsarist-era bureaucrats (*chinovniki*) and policemen, spies, terrorists, bandits, criminal recidivists, and even horse thieves. This was far broader than those returning home after their sentences, as Stalin had specified. Order No. 447 also targeted escapees, criminal elements still in exile and camp, and "those previously avoiding punishment." Although Stalin's telegram had suggested exile for "less dangerous elements," Order No. 447 called for them to be sent to hard regime labor camps.

In July 1937 many regional officials proposed repression targets *higher* than those the Politburo was ultimately willing to accept, and it reduced more than half of them. At the beginning of July, 40 of 64 provinces and national republics had submitted target arrest numbers in response to Stalin's telegram. Altogether, these local suggestions had totaled 207,345 proposed arrests. At the end of July, and after the conferences with local representatives, Order No. 447 reduced this 40-province total by about 20,000 arrests, to 187,450. Of the reductions, 95 percent (18,770) were in the category slated for execution. Of the 40 provinces proposing targets in response to Stalin's telegram, Order No. 447 reduced the number to be shot in 19 provinces, raised it for 17 and left it the same for 4. It reduced the number to be sent to camp for 22 provinces and raised it for 18. Some of the reductions of local requests for execution were dramatic: Belorussia from 3,000 to 1,000, Azov–Black Sea from 6,600 to 5,000, West Siberia from 11,000 to 5,000, and Moscow from 8,500 to 5,000.[106]

We saw previously how Evdokimov's North Caucasus police clan had experience with and favored mass operations. At the July meetings, every police official we can identify as a North Caucasus group member proposed high mass operation targets that were reduced at the meeting.[107]

Molotov recalls how Khrushchev, in his capacity as first secretary of the Moscow region, "brought his lists of enemies of the people to Stalin." Stalin doubted the numbers reported—"They can't be so many!" "They are—in fact, many more, Comrade Stalin. You can't imagine how many they are!"[108]

Order No. 447 established limits (*limity*) rather than quotas; maximums, not minimums. As we have seen, the setting of limits to restrain local conduct of mass operations had a long history and Order No. 447 was perfectly consistent with Stalin's longtime worry about losing control of wild local repression. Ezhov's order warned local officials that they "do not have the right independently to raise them [the limits]. . . . In such cases, they are obligated to present me with an appropriate justification." It is possible, as some have argued, that Stalin and Ezhov wanted and expected the locals to ask for increases, that Stalin fully expected excesses.[109] There are no documents supporting this view, and it is contradicted by the language used, by what we know of how Stalin's words were law, and by the history of the center-periphery relationship. As we have seen, for years Stalin had been putting limits on mass executions by provincial leaders. In light of that history, if Stalin had at this moment expected or wanted an open-ended terror, there would be no reason to mention "limits" at all. Language mattered to Stalin, and such statements would have been counterproductive if he had wanted the larger scale of terror that many local grandees preferred. Instead, Stalin and Ezhov felt it necessary to issue warnings to the contrary and insist again on their right to control terror. Reflecting Stalin's concern that locals might get out of control (or out of *his* control), Order No. 447 twice warned that "excesses" in local implementation of the operation were not permitted. This again mirrored his complaints and warnings in his May 1933 memo that outlawed mass operations. Stalin wanted to have his cake and eat it too: to have a centrally managed campaign and avoid paying the price that campaigns carried.

Clearly, the process involved something quite different from the simple imposition of a long-prepared Stalin plan. Sometime in the ten days 2–12 July, Stalin reversed himself on mass operations generally, and then approved greatly *expanded* categories for repression and increased punishments, while at the same time *reducing* the proposed number of arrests and placing limits on them. Based on the evidence we now have, it seems logical to consider that it was local representatives who pressed for expanding the categories and punishments. Stalin now agreed. This was a negotiation. In return for a broader list of targets, Stalin insisted on reducing many of the locally proposed limits and on his right to approve, for each province, the size of the operation. He had done precisely this in his interplay with the regional power centers since the early 1920s.

Order No. 447 was therefore consistent with the long-standing center-periphery dynamic of the 1920s and 1930s which formed the precedents for the mass operations of 1937. In the 1920s and in 1937, it was local party and police authorities who asked for mass operations. Stalin approved them as exceptions, with limits, and demanded reports and accountability to Moscow. As we saw, in that period Stalin had sought to control, restrict, limit, and finally outlaw mass operations. Except in dangerous, insurrectionary situations, they were messy and uncontrolled and ended up discrediting the regime as much as they helped it. In fact, virtually all the elements in Order No. 447 had precedents in the 1930–33 period. Local request and instigation, categories of arrest, vague targets locally chosen, specified limits of arrests, and fixed time periods had all been parts of the center-periphery contest over repression in previous years.

The 1937 mass operations also resembled the repressions ordered by Stalin during collectivization. In 1929, as in 1937, repressive measures were to be applied outside the usual judicial channels.[110] During collectivization, the center had also mandated limits for two categories of victims (shooting and exile), prescribed time limits, left victim selection in the hands of local authorities, and established troikas to carry out the violence. In 1929 as in 1937, target groups were only vaguely defined. Who was a kulak? Local party and police officials could and did decide.

Terror and violence had been among the regional party chieftains' main tools. As V. P. Danilov noted, "Among local workers in both party and state administrative systems, there were more than a few hotheads, internally disposed to command-repressive actions."[111] Iurii Zhukov put it this way: "Broad-scale repression directed against tens and hundreds of thousands of peasants was useful first of all to first secretaries of provincial and territorial party committees."[112] As Stalin had complained in May 1933, "demands for the use of harsh forms of repression continue to come in from a number of regions," where "comrades are willing to replace and are already replacing the political work conducted among the masses and designed to isolate the kulaks . . . by administrative-chekist 'operations.'" As Postyshev said of this period, "It is necessary to say directly and precisely that repression was in those breakthrough years the decisive method of 'leadership' of many party organizations."[113]

And in the event, local party and police officials committed the "excesses" that Stalin and Ezhov had warned against. Order No. 447 plus subsequent known limit increases gave permission to shoot about 236,000 victims. Locals shot many more. We are fairly certain that some 386,798 persons were actually shot, leaving 151,716 people shot without currently documented central sanction from either the NKVD or the Politburo.[114] In Turkmenistan, for example, where we happen to have full data on all approvals, we know that the Politburo approved 3,225 executions but local authorities shot 4,037, an excess of 25 percent over approved limits.[115] In Smolensk, Moscow gave an approved limit of 4,000, but local authorities shot 4,500 and continued shooting victims even after a November 1938 decision firmly ordering them to stop. They simply backdated the paperwork and continued shooting.[116]

Some regional chiefs were enthusiastic about the mass operations. Among party leaders there are numerous cases of real ferocity. In Turkmenistan, First Secretary Chubin was so involved with the mass killings that in 1938 he tried to secure the recall of a new NKVD chief sent to stop them.[117] First Secretary Simochkin in Ivanovo liked to watch the shootings and was curious about why some of his subordinates chose not to.[118] Among the police, there is no evidence that any NKVD leaders protested against the mass operations, and some of them were fierce purgers.[119] In several Siberian regions, those arrested were often tortured and shot without any paperwork at all. When it was too cold to dig graves, their bodies were dumped into rivers where in the spring they floated past people enjoying the riverbank. Sometimes local chekists strangled their victims or beat them to death.[120] So much for Stalin's warning against "excesses."

There seems little doubt that the precipitants of this bloody decision were the unexpected dangers perceived in the new constitution combined with dissident regional party leaderships who felt their hands were being tied. At the time, almost everybody made the connection between the mass operations and the new constitution.[121]

We have documents from peasants to oppositionists to Central Committee members that make the link. Aside from the obvious panic in the elite caused by insurrectionary sentiments of returning kulaks discussed above, the link was clearly perceived by contemporaries. Arrested prisoners in Tataria thought that the Bolsheviks were afraid of the elections and had launched a preemptive strike from concern that enemies would seize control of the voting in the districts.[122] In Orenburg, the son of a kulak said, "But the Communists should not think that they have struck a blow. Soon we will settle with them. In the elections to the Supreme Soviet, we will show them *kto kogo*."[123]

In Ordzhonikidzevskii territory, peasants knew what it was all about. One peasant said, "mass arrests are taking place exactly at the same time as the elections in order to isolate our brothers. They [the Bolsheviks] are afraid so they are keeping us from getting into the soviets. They know already that the Communists will collapse in the elections." According to another, "They are arresting people who in the past were active White Guards, local Cossack leaders, and kulaks. These are being taken in connection with the upcoming elections to the [Supreme] Soviet, in order not to let them into the elections." A third said, "now they are arresting kulaks because soon there will be elections. They will put them away because of the new constitution."[124]

In Ukraine, Mensheviks (often perceptive observers of Bolshevik thinking) agreed. One said, "If there wasn't this terror, then the elections would not run at all smoothly." Another said, "There is terror in the country now. They are arresting and shooting innocent people. It is a preelection fever. They think terror will dull the initiative of the masses, that they will blindly vote for the candidates of the Communists."[125] Nikolai Bukharin wrote in his last letter to Stalin that a general purge was in part connected with "the transition to democracy."[126]

Finally, First Secretary Kontorin, party baron of Arkhangel'sk, openly told the Central Committee in October 1937 that "We asked and will continue to ask the Central Committee to increase our limits for the first category [executions] in connection with preparations for the elections."[127]

Perhaps it is only coincidence that the very day of publication of the electoral law on open contested voting that the provincial barons so opposed, the Politburo approved the launching of a mass operation against those the regional chiefs feared. Hours later Stalin sent his telegram to provincial party leaders ordering the kulak operation and allowing them to shoot the same elements they had complained about as dangers in the election.[128] Stalin insisted that the regional grandees conduct contested elections, but at the same time gave them (literally) the ammunition to defend themselves. Even without this coincidence, if it was one, there is ample evidence that the Supreme Soviet elections of 1937 played a crucial role in impelling Order No. 447, and that the context had to do with Stalin's struggle with the provincial barons and their clans.

Regional party and police leaders' steady drumbeat of warnings about returning kulaks and anti-Soviet elements had made the situation seem increasingly frustrating and dangerous. Finally, in June 1937 Stalin reversed himself on mass violence and made the decision for a lethal nationwide mass operation. He did not change the new secret ballot electoral system; that was too useful a tool for holding bureaucrats' feet to the fire. But by July 1937 he had become convinced that the dangers posed by vocal plebeian opposition were in fact serious enough to reverse his stand against mass killing.

The regional barons won the battle for mass operations, and they ended up winning the electoral dispute when months later Stalin quietly dropped the dangerous idea of contested elections and returned to single candidates.[129]

But, as the next chapter shows, the regional barons would lose the war. Stalin granted them and the regional police the right to repress at precisely the time that an entirely separate campaign was pressing them on another front. For Stalin, there was no contradiction between appointing a regional secretary to a troika, giving him arbitrary right to decide life and death for thousands one day, and arresting him the next. The point was that in these particular circumstances, the mass operations would defend and protect the indispensable institution of regional party clan fiefdoms—which he perceived as unfortunately necessary for the regime—rather than the leaders of the regions themselves, whom he had come to distrust.

8 Stalin and the Clans III
The Last Stand of the Clans

Both in the center and in the localities, decisions are made, not infrequently, in a familial way, as in the home, so to speak. . . . Today, I, Ivan Fedorovich, will let him get away with it. Later, Ivan Ivanovich will let me get away with it. Decorous and calm. Peace and goodwill.

—*Stalin, 1931*

AS HAD BEEN the case since the early 1920s, a newly arrived leader appointed by the center nearly always found himself in the midst of an existing party organization. The local Communists were mostly natives of the locale with webs of preexisting friendships, clans, and loyalties, and were naturally suspicious and resentful of the new leader. Until and unless the new boss could either win the trust of the locals and build his own working client group from them, or import his own friends and supporters, he would be an outsider. Since the early 1920s, when faced with a new boss from outside, locals had complained that they had been passed over. "Here come the Varangians to teach us lessons"[1] and similar complaints were common among locals, and passive resistance, bickering, and *skloki* had been more the rule than the exception since the end of the Civil War. Despite the imprimatur of the TsK, any newcomer could be frozen out, as happened to even so ranking an official as A. I. Mikoian, a personal friend of Lenin's and Stalin's, in Nizhnyi Novgorod.[2]

Stalin needed some configuration of local leadership that would work with reasonable unity to fulfill the economic and political demands of the TsK. But given the traditions of local *skloki* (and the related opposition movements) that was easier said than done. Oftentimes, none of the local home-grown Bolsheviks had the stature or experience to lead a province. Stalin's experiments with such promotion from below in the 1920s had shown that elevating a local clan favorite son to provincial leadership led to even more intense localism, and because it supported existing local networks of favoritism, it could lead to widespread criminality.

The Smolensk scandal of 1928 was the classic example. Local Communist Pavliuchenko had been given command of the province as first secretary, and within a short time his friends and relatives established a self-contained provincewide corrupt mafia, complete with extravagant private banquets, bribery, embezzlement, outright theft, and orgies at state-owned country houses. Stalin realized his "localism" mistake and broke up the Smolensk family. Among senior province officials, nine of the worst offenders were arrested, and ten others, including Pavliuchenko, were fired and "returned to production."[3] Some thought that more should be punished, but this was weighed against the chronic shortage of reliable cadres to fill vacant slots.[4]

Later, in order to prevent localism and the accompanying corruption, the new practice (especially in economically important provinces) was to bring in a high-ranking leader, and back him to the hilt. To avoid the Mikoian mistake, in which the new appointee had been left to twist in the wind on his own, this meant giving the new boss free rein to staff his province as he saw fit, to control the soviet and punitive apparatuses, to override any local *skloki* or resistance, and to leave him in place as long as he produced results. Of course, as we have seen, *skloki* were a way of life in the Bolshevik party and local factionalism and resistance to provincial bosses and their teams continued.

Although Stalin and his personnel assignment colleagues in Moscow resolutely backed their appointee, sometimes the local situation became so conflict-ridden as to be untenable. Sometimes, first secretaries had to be transferred, exchanged, and shifted around to fill particular needs. When things got hot in an oblast and both sides complained to the TsK, Stalin would summon both of them for a conference in Moscow, where he or another high-ranking member of his clan mediated.[5] He nearly always sided with his appointed first secretary, but when he wished to undermine one of the provincial leaders, as we shall see, he could always tap into this suppressed but still potent local factionalism and mobilize it against the regional boss.

☆

In March 1936, the Central Committee divided Ivanovo Industrial Oblast into two parts: Ivanovo Oblast and a new Iaroslavl' Oblast. A new head had to be found for the spin-off Iaroslavl' area, and Anton Romanovich Vainov became head of the "Organizational Buro of the Central Committee for Iaroslavl' Oblast."[6] After a year's preparation working in Iaroslavl', Vainov was appointed first secretary of the newly created Iaroslavl' Oblast Committee of the VKP(b).

The thirty-nine-year-old Vainov came from Donetsk via Moscow. Four years younger than Nikita Khrushchev, Vainov also joined the party in 1918. In the early 1930s, he had been second secretary of the Donetsk Oblast Party Committee responsible for metallurgy, and had been a member of the TsK of the Ukrainian party since 1934. By 1936, at the time of his appointment to Iaroslavl', he was deputy chief of the Industrial Department of the TsK in Moscow, working under A. A. Andreev. The three major cities of the new oblast, Iaroslavl', Kostroma, and Rybinsk, along with its thirty-six districts, were undergoing major industrial expansion in the first two Five Year Plans, and these three cities were also major transshipment centers on the Volga and the new network of canals and lakes that made up the northern river transport routes. Industrial expert Vainov seemed perfect for the job.

So Comrade Vainov had his work cut out for him when he moved to Iaroslavl' in 1936. He knew nothing of the province and its Communists, and faced an existing party organization that had until recently been part of I. P. Nosov's Ivanovo machine. Now part of the new Iaroslavl' Oblast, these "Ivanovtsy" gravitated around I. A. Nefedov, who had worked in the area since at least 1932. For Vainov, as in tsarist times, "Once he arrived in 'his' province, a governor had to work through officials who were clients of his predecessor, and who needed to be either purged or transformed into a new network loyal to the new governor. Hence the intense distrust and animosity at the first encounter of a new governor with local officialdom. He also needed to manage the complicated relationship with the rival network represented by local nobles and headed by their marshal of the nobility."[7]

Probably in an attempt to head off local resentment of the incoming "Varangian" Vainov, he made the local "marshal of the nobility" Nefedov second secretary of the new Iaroslavl' Oblast party organization. He thus coopted Nefedov and made him an ally rather than an opponent. In the beginning, Nefedov was wary and resentful of Vainov. One party official recalled Nefedov's reaction to Vainov's arrival: "Here in Iaroslavl', before the organization of the oblast, there was a feudal principality that thought the TsK was far away. . . . They [Nefedov] lived in clover, getting warm applause when they went to activist meetings, warm applause when they came to party meetings, and suddenly the peaceful life of the feudal princedom was messed up by the organization of Iaroslavl' Oblast." Early on, Nefedov was truculent and sarcastic about Vainov's arrival. "Here comes a secretary from the Donbas, let's let him try to turn things around here, let him show what he can do here working in Iaroslavl' Oblast."[8] But Vainov won him over. He took Nefedov into the provincial party committee buro's inner circle and gave him a position of trust with major responsibilities that included supervision of ideology. Later, when Nefedov would come under fire both from local party members and the TsK itself, as a loyal patron, Vainov would try to protect him.

Nefedov's possible resistance to Vainov was completely defused. He became a loyal client who had a reputation for refusing to decide anything without asking his boss. District Secretary Repkin recounted a conversation he had had with Nefedov: "[I asked] Isn't it necessary to have a party meeting to orient the Communists? Instead of an answer, Nefedov said 'How do you see it? How do you think we should answer? What should we do?' What kind of system of leadership is this?"[9] Clan members who avoided decisions so as not to challenge the ruling grandee were a common feature in provincial clans. In Dagestan, for example, a party member characterized the head of the Dagestan Sovnarkom:

> We asked Mamedbek, the chairman of the Dagestan Sovnarkom, what measures he had taken, and he answered, "I reported to the territorial party secretary, the territorial party took everything into account, and I calmed down." Mamedbek signals, informs, and then calms down. Over there they have one mute (laughter), the chairman who never speaks and doesn't even signal. At least Mamedbek, as you see, signals and informs (laughter in the hall).[10]

Vainov also did what all senior leaders did when they moved to a new province: he imported friends and people he had trusted and worked with in his previous posts.[11] His "artel" or "tail" included twenty-three senior leaders, including nine from the Donbas where he had worked until 1936. Although this does not seem so many in a large party organization, it is important to remember that each member of Vainov's artel had his own "tail" to bring along. As one factory party organizer said, "Comrade Vainov brought the oblast activists here, and they, following his example, began to bring in party workers. Even in our factory, the director brought five or six guys, skilled workers, who had worked with him before."[12] In Gor'kii, a minor district party committee secretary "managed to drag along with him from Kologriv a whole group of people. . . . And you ask, why did he drag them along? In order to form a support group around him consisting of his people who, in a difficult moment would not give him up."[13] Also in Gor'kii territory "Comrade Dodonov, chairman of the Stalinsk Raisoviet, says that he didn't give jobs to 30 people in the raisoviet and gave none to his relatives. Comrades, it is possible that this is the case, as Comrade Dodonov says, and I in no way want to fight with him more than he deserves. But it is a fact that there is a big family of relatives there. I noted this just to be fair (laughter)."[14]

Back in Iaroslavl', Vainov had wasted no time taking over and forming an operational clan. Nefedov was successfully coopted, thus blunting the power of the "Ivanovtsy." He placed his people in the provincial party committee buro, provincial party committee departments, and the leadership of the most important districts.

The clan ruled the oblast party with an iron hand and tolerated no criticism. Clan members' rudeness to subordinates, as well as the reactions to it, recalled workers' complaints against management going as far back as 1917. Comrade Naumov later said at a party meeting, "Who among us doesn't remember the unpleasant names we district party committee workers got from leaders, ranging to the most obscene words . . . they called us 'hooligans' and 'lazy sluggards.' "[15] As one Federov, a district party committee secretary outside Vainov's clan put it,

I cannot but remember the unflattering epithets from the provincial party committee elite about district workers as "saboteurs," "gossips," "opportunists." . . . And when I tried once to protest against abuse and swearing at the district party committee secretaries and in particular at me, they really gave it to me at the district party committee secretaries' conference. Zarzhitskii with the silent agreement of Vainov, characterized my statement that one shouldn't constantly swear, as slander against the party leadership.[16]

This was happening everywhere. In Gor'kii territory, a primary party organization in Ardatsk district complained about party organizer Kolesov: "From him instead of help we get swearing, he yells that he is the master and brags a lot." Comrade Valukhin "has more than one deficiency, but there's one I want to talk about. He is rude. Surprisingly rude. . . . If a party organizer permits such rudeness in himself, then he no doubt knows that he thus educates people to be rude. And really this happens quickly." Also in Gor'kii, "people are always complaining that Secretary Pushkov of Rabotkinskii District Party Committee is rude, unbelievably rude, improbably rude. Pushkov himself says that he is not rude to everybody, but rather has a differentiated approach (laughter in the hall).[17]

From Smolensk: "a guy from the provinces came and asked Comrade Makarenko where the ORPO department was. He just waved in the general direction and said 'there' and rolled his eyes."[18] In several regions, party workers also complained about such arrogant and high-handed party leaders. From Rostov: "When I went to Sharikian, you know, he struck a Napoleonic pose and began to orate about how audaciously we took decisions, and about how he would teach us how to work and so forth."[19] From Krasnodarsk: Comrade Uvatsan told a meeting that "When Berezin became secretary of Krasnodarsk gorkom, he openly said there was no personnel file on him. Workers asked him to help create a personnel file, but he said 'What, I'm some kind of poor peasant bum to you, that I should have to fill out a personnel file?' "[20]

Arrogance was naturally accompanied by measures to suppress any criticism (*kritika/samokritika*) from below. According to Iaroslavl' Comrade Repkin, "Comrade Vainov's . . . comrades arrived in the new oblast and thought they had come to save the situation with imported people . . . with naked administrative methods toward the local people . . . and absence of any collegiality. The situation so terrorized workers that it was impossible for them to come forward and speak of deficiencies of the oblast party organization."[21]

In Dagestan, one party member said that "they are afraid of daggers in Dagestan, but they are afraid of self-criticism more than daggers."[22] In Stalingrad, "Communist criticism was called factionalism [*grupirovsh-china*] and scheming intrigue."[23] In Rostov-on-Don one activist remembered, "We tried to do this [criticize] now and then but we were harshly silenced, and, in certain specific cases, we found ourselves crushed as if in a vise."[24] "When I criticized, they called me a schismatic [*sklochnik*]. I suffered a lot from this criticism and it brought a lot on me."[25]

Vainov's clan was so strong that, like many others around the country, it thought it was safe to ignore political signals from Moscow, as Stalin put it, "to secure a certain independence from the Central Committee."[26] As late as the end of January 1937, when Moscow had already clearly called for identifying Trotskyist enemies, expanding criticism from below, and increased politicization of party meetings, Vainov's report to the First Iaroslavl' Oblast Party Conference contained only the traditional headings, such as "leading the Stakhanov movement," and "Soviet trade: our patriotic Bolshevik business." In "electing" the provincial party committee leadership, Vainov ignored Moscow's calls for democracy and real discussion of candidates. When it came time to elect the new provincial party committee in January 1937, he ran the procedure briskly. For each candidate, all of whom had been nominated by the leading group, Vainov said,

> "Next."
> "Any objections? Questions or comments? No. Let's vote. Whoever is for Comrade _____, please raise your cards."
> "Next."

One of Vainov's candidates, Comrade Khlybov, was harshly criticized by some brave comrades for his dubious relatives and for defending suspicious people in the past. Vainov and his clan closed ranks and spoke to protect him. Khlybov received fewer than 50 percent of the votes, the lowest of any candidate, but as Vainov's nominee he was still elected.[27]

The same thing was happening all over the country. In Rostov-on-Don, Comrade Ivnitskii recalled how First Secretary Sheboldaev put pressure on a district party committee to elect his candidate. As a secretary from the committee remembered,

> we made this decision, and when Boris Petrovich Sheboldaev found out about it, he summoned me and Gurevich, former Secretary of the Provincial Committee, and declared: "What kind of leaders are you to have allowed Ovchinnikov to be voted down?" I told him that perhaps it wasn't good to elect him, but I didn't say it strongly enough, forcefully enough. After this, the delegation was hurriedly transported in cars because the conference was supposed to take place very soon. Boris

Petrovich Sheboldaev personally appeared at the meeting of our delegation and defended Ovchinnikov for well over an hour.[28]

Sheboldaev was a famous protector of his clan. At a party meeting in June 1937 where his clients were attacked for their suspicious pasts, Sheboldaev said, "Let's not attack each other for what our fathers and grandfathers did. Comrades, we can't do this. We have to discuss the basic questions."[29]

In Rostov-on-Don, "when a party member speaks up at this or that party meeting with criticism, or to expose this or that enemy of the party, then the next day [the leadership] gives that enemy a positive recommendation so that he can defend himself at higher party instances."[30] "Primary party organs expel people and the gorkom lets them back in and denounces us for expelling them."[31]

In Voronezh, the powerful I. M. Vareikis also forcefully protected his own. When Comrade Chernikov of the Ostrogozhskii District Party Committee

> told Comrade Vareikis that Alferov was unsuitable for work there because he had antistate tendencies when he had been politotdel chief and there had been a provincial party committee decision about that, Comrade Vareikis answered, "Who the hell are you, Chernikov? You evidently are starting to busy yourself with personal squabbles. He worked in a workers' school (*rabfak*), in an institute, and we sufficiently studied him and trust him to lead the party organization.[32]

Later, in his new position as first secretary of the Far Eastern territory, Vareikis again protected his clients. Comrade Kuznetsov, a factory director, came under fire for not fulfilling the plan and being unpleasant ("separated from the masses"). Vareikis pled with the territory party conference, "Without a doubt, Kuznetsov gives the impression of a major, capable economic worker, one of the best in the territory." Despite Vareikis's intercession, Kuznetsov was only elected to the territorial party committee by the thin margin of 222 for and 217 against.[33]

Shortly after the January 1937 electoral meeting in Iaroslavl', a *Pravda* editorial publicly criticized Vainov and his clan's suppression of criticism, "toadying," and lack of self-criticism. Vainov and his clique made a nearly fatal political mistake when they blocked discussion of the article in party meetings, refused to pass the usual repentant resolution on it, and prevented the customary republication of *Pravda's* editorial in oblast newspapers. They thought their hold on power was that secure, but their decision would come back to haunt them. Perhaps they should have followed the advice of Shebolaev's "Saratov Brothers-in-Law" (*svoiaki*): "they told the instructors, 'do things so you don't get into the newspapers.'"[34]

☆

In the last days of 1936 and the first of 1937, Stalin moved against the clans with "musical chairs" personnel transfers designed to separate senior party chiefs from their followers. I. M. Vareikis was transferred from Stalingrad to the Far East. B. A. Semënov took his place in Stalingrad, moving from Crimea. L. I. Kartvelishvili filled the Crimea slot, sent there from the Far East when Vareikis arrived. S. A. Kudriavtsev was moved from Kharkov to Ukraine and was replaced in Kharkov by N. F. Gikalo who was transferred from Belorussia. In these and other cases, the clan leaders were now explicitly forbidden to take anyone from their "tails" with them.

The most celebrated transfers, which Stalin publicized as a lesson, were those of B. P. Sheboldaev from Azov–Black Sea to Kursk, and of P. P. Postyshev from Kiev to Kuibyshev. In Kursk I. U. Ivanov traded provinces with Sheboldaev, moving to Azov–Black Sea as second secretary and replacing the arrested Sheboldaev client M. M. Malinov. When Postyshev moved to Kuibyshev, he replaced V. P. Shubrikov, who was sent to Western Siberia. These and the other reassignments were not always explicitly about breaking up "artels": Sheboldaev's and Postyshev's sins were that they had carelessly staffed their entourages with Trotskyists who were now unmasked as enemies. But it took little imagination to see these transfers (and the way they were done without "tails") as a major Stalin sally against clans in general: he was detaching them from their leaders.

One of the problems of our sources is that we generally have only half the conversations between the centralizers and the regional party leaders. We have no shortage of statements by Stalin and other Moscow centralizers criticizing the feudal princes, but if we leave aside the fabricated testimonies after their arrests, with few exceptions the regional nobles' voices are silent. One obvious reason is that in the end, Stalin destroyed the regional leaders, and the winners always write the history.

But a more significant reason has to do with the traditions and culture of party discipline. Since the battles with the Left and Right Oppositions in the 1920s, public (meaning the rank-and-file party public) criticism of the TsK (and of Stalin) were tantamount to disloyalty. After all, this had been the Left Opposition's sin, and nationally the Stalin coalition—which included the regional party leaders—had been formed by closing ranks around the TsK against that Left. We do know, however, that in their private moments with close supporters, the regional chiefs did criticize the Moscow center. For example, the hot-tempered I. P. Rumiantsev, first secretary of the Smolensk Provincial Party Committee, was heard to deliver "un-party utterances and slogans" that were understood as "attacks on the line of the TsK." And even in 1937 when his deputy Shil'man was arrested, Rumiantsev took an "antiparty attitude to Shil'man's arrest" in an attempt to "prove the baseless nature of the charges."[35] Such revelations can be found in the transcripts of local and regional party meetings, and it is to them that we now turn for the detailed account of Comrade Vainov's fall in Iaroslavl' in 1937.

Immediately following the well-scripted Iaroslavl' party conference discussed above, with Vainov's banal and apolitical speech themes and his tightly controlled elections, *Pravda* published a sharp criticism of Vainov's cultic and patrimonial regime. Noting that the sycophantic discussion of Vainov's main speech contained wording like "in his brilliant report," "achievements of the oblast," "under Comrade Vainov's leadership there have been special successes," and "under Comrade Vainov's leadership we will reach even greater successes," *Pravda* regretted the lack of self-criticism at the conference and pointed out that the speakers had criticized neither the toadying of provincial party committee defenders nor the bad work of the provincial party committee and its departments. "The whole thing was about Vainov." True, at the end of his speech, Vainov had said that there had been weak criticism of him and none of the provincial party committee buro. But *Pravda* said that "it is a pity that this correct point was made at the end of the discussion and not at the beginning."[36]

Vainov's inner circle, the buro of the oblast party committee, immediately met and did nothing. Party etiquette and practice required the buro to discuss the *Pravda* article, pronounce it "absolutely correct," republish it and the buro's confession in the region's newspapers, and organize critical discussions of it in all the party committees of the region. Instead, the buro discussed it privately and kept it quiet. At three meetings in February, it promulgated decisions on its draft plan of work, the unsatisfactory state of the bread trade, how to handle complaints from kolkhoz members, International Women's Day, appeals from wrongly expelled party members, and other routine problems, but nothing on *Pravda*'s broadside.[37] This was an arrogant and foolish decision. *Pravda* was circulated anyway in the major towns of the oblast, so members could read its criticism in any case. They could easily note the provincial party committee's silence and infer from it not only arrogance, but more than a hint of the Vainov clan's resistance to the TsK. And *Pravda* wasn't through with Iaroslavl'.[38]

Soon there was another more general attack from the TsK. On 6 March 1937, *Pravda* published A. A. Zhdanov's speech to the February Plenum, the first speech from that meeting to be published (even before Stalin's).[39] The speech had been given on 26 February, and the two-week delay is best explained by the embarrassing fight it provoked between the territorial committee chiefs and the center. As we saw above, Zhdanov called for the "democratization" of party organizations in the regions. This meant secret ballot reelection of all party organs from top to bottom, periodic reporting of party organs to their organizations, strict party discipline and subordination of the minority to the majority, and the unconditional obligation on all party members to comply with decisions of higher bodies.[40]

The day after publication of Zhdanov's speech, *Pravda* again criticized Iaroslavl'. In an article entitled "Don't Infringe the Rights of a Party Member!" the newspaper took Vainov personally to task:

> Take, for example, secretary of the Iaroslavl' Provincial Party Committee Comrade Vainov, who as soon as he arrived in a new oblast began to gather together his acquaintances and friends from all parts of the country. The chiefs of many provincial party committee departments, the secretary of the Iaroslavl' gorkom, and many district party committee secretaries were his people, who did not know the party organization and were appointed and promoted purely on the basis of friendship and old connections.[41]

Now faced with mounting criticism from Moscow, Vainov's Iaroslavl' clan could no longer ignore the situation. The day after the second *Pravda* article, it ordered a meeting of city party activists and district party committee secretaries in one week's time to "discuss the

February Plenum of the TsK." It finally passed a belated resolution on the *Pravda* assault:

> To consider *Pravda* of 7 March absolutely correct about the danger of the un-Bolshevik practice of choosing and promoting party cadres which stimulates toadying, rank-worshiping (*chinopochitanie*), holding back the growth of local cadres, creating a gap between leaders and masses and facilitates violations of party rules. The buro recognizes that it incorrectly and belatedly oriented itself to *Pravda's* report of 5 February with the result that the party organizations of the oblast did not have criticism and self-criticism when they discussed the work on the party conference.
>
> To receive as information Comrade Vainov's statement that he recognizes his mistakes in violating Bolshevik principles of choosing cadres, especially in the area of rearing local workers, and that he was late in reacting to appearances of toadying.[42]

Three weeks later, Stalin's speech from the February Plenum was published, in which he also took the provincial party committee secretaries to task for "familial" choice of personnel. It must have given Vainov no comfort that he (along with L. I. Mirzoian) was singled out:

> Vainov took with him people from other oblasts . . . 23 people. There are a lot of them because many of them are from the soviet apparatus. 9 from the Donbas: Zhuravlëv, Vaisberg, Krimer, Ivanov, Kats, Konukalov, Iurlov, Aleksandrov and Isaev. . . . He just couldn't do without them. And these people occupy important posts. Why did Vainov have to do that? What must be the attitude of local cadres to these people arriving from outside? Of course, it is guarded. What does it mean to take people to yourself, a group of personally loyal people, from outside? It means expressing a lack of faith in local cadres. What basis do Mirzoian or Vainov have to express this lack of confidence in local cadres? Let them tell us.[43]

Pravda followed up three days later with yet another article about *artelnost'* and bad selection of cadres in Iaroslavl', this time quoting ordinary workers speaking about it.[44]

Licensed by *Pravda* and the Stalin and Zhdanov speeches, outsiders in Iaroslavl' now had their chance to attack the clan without fear of retaliation. When Vainov was forced to call a meeting of the entire Iaroslavl' Provincial Party Committee Plenum, a torrent of pent-up anger at Vainov's crew came out against the leaders, who tried to defend themselves using various tactics. This criticism from below and outside came from issues that went back twenty years or more: imposition of outsiders on locals, favoritism, haughtiness and rudeness of leaders. Stalin unleashed and authorized the party members' critical words, but he did not invent them or put words in their mouths. To this degree, the criticism from below was an autonomous political process manipulated but not created by Stalin.

When the criticism started, the embattled clan tried to defend itself with various tactics. One of these was for leaders to now try to put themselves in the forefront of criticism of the leadership. Comrade Zhuravlëv, head of the oblast transport department (and one of those mentioned by Stalin as being part of Vainov's "tail") sanctimoniously criticized "eulogizing (*voskhvalenie*) and toadying (*podkhalimstvo*) at the previous conference"—even though he had been one of the main sycophants then. Non–clan members didn't let him get away with it. Zhuravlëv was rudely interrupted:

> VOICE: "You also spoke there [at the last conference]. Why did you speak the way you did?"[45]

Comrade Shekhanov said, "Zhuravlëv from Comrade Vainov's tail is always maintaining a certain tone, for him toadying and servility are his flesh and blood: 'Comrade Vainov said this, Comrade Vainov ordered that, Comrade Vainov specified' and so forth. . . . this is leader-worship (*vozhdizm*)."[46]

The accusation of "toadying" was also aimed at the personality cults that local leaders or their underlings had created. The regional press was of course in the hands of the ruling clan. As one party said sarcastically, "the *Dagestanskaia pravda* reported that Comrade Samurskii went to Khunzakhskii where he gave a speech on the mess there, and that peasants arrived to hear the speech with indescribable joy. I asked the editor how it was possible for them to arrive already joyous if there was such a mess there."[47]

A second defense tactic was for clan members to appear to break ranks and deflect criticism against other members. As the criticism became heated, clan members turned on one another, and the Ivanovtsy-Donetsk clan split reappeared. Zhuravlëv rounded on Nefedov: "Nefedov did nothing about problems in the districts. Like an ostrich, he tucked his head under his wing . . . it's defective leadership. . . . I told Nefedov that there's information that Siper (a factory director) is a Trotskyist. But he said, 'what's wrong with you, are you crazy? He's a candidate member of the Ivanov Provincial Party Committee, the best Bolshevik in our organization.'" Speakers didn't let Zhuravlëv get away with this either. He was interrupted from the floor:

> VOICE: Why didn't you say this at the party conference?
> VOICE: It's late now.
> ZHURAVLËV: True, but better late than never.
> VOICE: Better late than never is an old excuse.[48]

And Comrade Telegina, secretary of a factory party committee, agreed: "I must say that Comrade Zhuravlëv made a clever maneuver in his speech. He directed attention to Nefedov's mistakes to divert criticism away from Comrade Vainov and the provincial party committee."[49]

A host of speakers denounced Vainov and his minions for trying to bury the first *Pravda* article in February. Repkin, a raikom secretary outside the Vainov clan, said "the *Pravda* article was 5 February, but it took the provincial party committee until 8–10 March to respond with a decision and nothing was published in the local party press. This was an attempt to hide *Pravda's* materials from the oblast party organization."[50]

Guliaev, head of the trade department of the Provincial Party Committee and another member of the clan, remembered, "Why didn't we in the buro call a meeting? We incorrectly reacted to *Pravda*." He too was rudely interrupted:

> VOICE: You are talking like you were 100 km. from the buro.
> ANOTHER VOICE: An innocent little lamb![51]

One district party committee secretary chimed in, "the provincial party committee party organization didn't even discuss the *Pravda* article." Pavlov, secretary of the provincial Komsomol, and a member of the buro that suppressed the *Pravda* piece, said, "In the provincial party committee buro we discussed the *Pravda* article and there was disagreement, we papered over our mistakes." Busiankov, first secretary of the Rybinsk gorkom, said:

> BUSIANKOV: First of all, I consider that the biggest mistake of the provincial party committee was that the decision of the buro disagreeing with the *Pravda* article was hidden [by the buro] from the members of the provincial party committee plenum and, unfortu-

nately, Comrade Vainov did not consider it necessary to reveal it at the plenum.

VAINOV: There was no decision of the buro.

BUSIANKOV: And this was done deliberately with the specific goal of disagreeing with *Pravda's* criticism.[52]

The real issue, of course, was Vainov's closed clique, his clan, and the iron hand with which he had ruled the oblast; fear had made criticism impossible. Now, licensed and protected by Moscow, speakers attacked Vainov and his people personally. Diakov, a district party committee secretary outside the clan, said, "I think that the main problem here is that in the oblast leadership and mainly in Comrade Vainov, there was a suppression of criticism."[53]

Senior clan leaders were being personally blamed for not promoting, and therefore insulting, local cadres. Federov, another nonclan outsider, spoke for the Ivanovtsy: "Is it an accident that we don't have more local cadres [in leading positions]? No. Some support the theory that our cadres haven't been through the same tough school as cadres from the south. I'm talking about Comrade Vainov's speech at one of the district party committee secretaries' conferences."[54] In Rostov-on-Don,

> Workers were elected to the territorial party committee, from production, the best part of industrial workers in our primary party organizations. And what happened with them? Their only contact with the territorial committee was to be summoned, sometimes but not always, to big meetings. Nothing more: no tasks, no responsibilities, no attempt to use them. . . . They didn't bring up, grow new people, didn't cultivate local people.

> VOICE: Why didn't they grow them?
> VOICE: Or more accurately they didn't incubate them (*vyrashchivat'sia*). Why? Because of the policy of the territorial party, consciously or unconsciously on the part of Comrade Sheboldaev.[55]

Leaders continued to complain that local talent was scarce, and were taken to task for not looking hard enough. In Gor'kii, District Party Committee Secretary Ostrovskii had to admit that there were local choices:

> OSTROVSKII: These days we don't have a reserve of possible chairmen of district soviet executive committees. It wasn't the case that we

had a group of experienced people to appoint to such work. . . . We looked but didn't find anyone so we called Moscow, which sent a person. We talked to this guy, looked him over, and to our surprise found out that we weren't so lucky with him. Fortunately, he went back to Moscow and refused to return here. So we appointed our guy (*nash chelovek*). Not in the sense that he was "our guy" (*svoi paren'*) but in the sense that he was from Gor'kii.

VOICE: Comrade Ostrovskii, so it turned out that there wasn't an absence of cadres and that there are some.[56]

In the Far East, a Moscow emissary went to far as to quote Aesop in chastising district party committee secretaries:

BUKAU: I think that Comrade Shkiriatov will help us fill out the *apparat*.

SHKIRIATOV: What helpless people you are, waiting for everything from Moscow. What, you can't appoint local people?

BUKAU: Of course we can pick people here, but we asked the territorial committee to give us 5 people and received only 1. We need the support of the territorial committees and then we can do it without crying. I think that Comrade Vareikis will help us and we'll escape this situation.

SHKIRIATOV: the old religious saying works in a nonreligious way: "God helps those who help themselves." Comrade Vareikis, sure, Comrade Vareikis but if you yourselves don't do anything nothing will come of it."[57]

Party leaders' refusal to appoint local members to leading positions was part of a more generalized resentment among the rank and file at party leaders who were distant and out of touch, or "separated from the masses" in party language. In Azov Black–Sea, Comrade Ostrovskii said:

We have party secretaries who are connected with the masses only by telephone. . . . The Komsomol strongly requested that District Party Committee Secretary Comrade Ovsiannikov speak at their conference. Comrade Ovsiannikov found an original means to do that: in his office he wrote a speech of greeting and had it delivered by telegram to the conference, which took place next door.

KAGANOVICH: just a few steps away.[58]

TsK emissary G. M. Malenkov told the Azov–Black Sea party organization that

Many secretaries of district committees found it impossible to talk to their superiors for a full 3 or 4 years. Is this the way a Bolshevik *apparat* works? I shall permit myself to ask Comrade Sheboldaev how he would feel as the chief representative of the party in the region, if upon arriving at the Central Committee he could not talk to someone, could not resolve his problems. And here there are people who have been trying hard to talk to somebody for 3 or 4 years and they can't.

VOICE: 5 or 6 years![59]

In Gor'kii, First Secretary Pramnek defended his travel to the localities:

Many comrades spoke about leaders' travels and their visits to factories, districts and so forth. . . . Many of us go to the districts and spend a lot of time in the localities. I cannot reproach myself for this. Maybe others are not so modest, but I can say openly that I personally think that they travel a lot and use all means of communication in order to be in the districts and factories. We don't think of ourselves as office people. . . . Moreover, I think that leaders cannot be everywhere. . . . What would become of the provincial committee of the party? At the next conference, you would say that the leaders are always traveling, spending too much time out of the office, are never in the provincial party committee, so there are waiting lines there and bureaucratism. That's what would happen.[60]

In Dagestan, some speakers blamed the system as well as First Secretary Samurskii:

Obkom departments are an empty place. People sit there living out their days who never see the people at all. . . . I'm not saying that Comrade Samurskii doesn't know how to work or doesn't want to. He works sincerely, strongly, but there is such a paper cobweb braided around him that he sees things through paper rather than through a clear window.[61]

Back in Iaroslavl', Nefedov had become a lightning rod for criticism, partly as a result of Zhuravlëv's efforts. One non-clique secretary said that Nefedov "actively enabled the glossing over of every political mistake in connection with this counterrevolutionary nest which was uncovered in Iaroslavl'. . . . He was an active defender of Siper and Leonov and others. Comrade Vainov knew about this but didn't say one word about it to anybody."[62]

Anticipating criticism of Nefedov, perhaps even from his own Donbas "artel," Vainov had allowed Nefedov to leave town, ostensibly for medical treatment, and thus avoid attending the meeting as he was expected to do. Vainov was nothing if not loyal. When attacked for that, Vainov replied, "I think that there is a bit of demagoguery here about Nefedov's absence. . . . He's had a heart attack in the past. I am not glossing over his mistakes, but we are sufficiently serious people that we can avoid demagogic statements." Polumordvinov, secretary of the Kostroma gubkom and a member of Vainov's entourage, lashed back at Busiankov: "Comrade Busiankov, who was at the party conference and spoke there calling the work of the buro satisfactory, now after a month suddenly finds things out and wants to remove secretaries. . . . you want to have democracy but you yourself violate it, wanting to remove a secretary in his absence." Trying to keep decisions about clan members within the clan, Vainov said, "I don't agree with the comrades who think that we can move against Nefedov on the basis of the facts presented in his absence. The provincial party committee buro should check it out and report back."[63] This is not the last time we will hear of the beleaguered Nefedov.

Vainov also dealt with the question of his clan. Since Stalin had personally highlighted it, he had no choice but to agree in principle. He said that he had made a serious mistake in the selection of cadres in that "I brought here with me a so-called tail of several workers from the Donbas where I worked a long time (and not lower workers) and who were installed at my suggestion in leading party positions." As Stalin said, he went on, leaders who do this want to be independent from the TsK and from the broad party mass. "I am saying that workers arriving from Ivanovo, Moscow, Donbas, and other regions of the Soviet Union suffered from one bad disease: they imagined themselves to be saviors. Arriving from other regions, 'here we are to save you' (Voice: 'Right')." He also took responsibility for Zhuravlëv's rudeness and toadying to him: "Why is Zhuravlëv such a toady? Only because he worked with me several years in the Donbas. Rudely or not, he's part of my tail. If another person worked in his position, one I did not bring and who was not part of my tail, there would be no toadying."[64]

Vainov fell on his sword when it came to the draft resolution of the meeting. That draft had blamed the provincial party committee in general, rather than specific leaders. As Organov, a district party committee secretary outside the Vainov clan, said, "We need to be specific. *Pravda* criticized Comrade Vainov. The newspaper *Severnyi rabochii* criticized Comrade Zhuravlëv, but the plenum proposed a draft resolution in which these were [only] mistakes of the provincial party committee. . . . if this isn't toadying then in any case it is not the sharp criticism the situation calls for." Vainov agreed, and moved to change the wording of the resolution to include "The plenum of the provincial party committee considers *Pravda*'s criticism of Provincial Party Committee Secretary Comrade Vainov completely correct . . ."[65]

But he also defended himself and disclaimed a certain responsibility for the problem, suggesting that he couldn't keep track of everybody: "You know that *Pravda* spoke of a whole series of workers [from my "tail"]. Just from simple arithmetic, that's only 7–9 people. But that's not the point. Yaroslavl' is a new oblast. Dozens of people come here from every corner of the Soviet Union. . . . so am I responsible for the work of [them all] including those whom the TsK sent here? What gets me off the hook? Nothing."[66]

Other provincial clan leaders and members defended themselves in other ways. Some, when faced with criticism that their entourages contained enemies, urged caution. As E. K. Pramnek said in Gor'kii, "Comrade Luchinin expressed it that 'the provincial party committee should better help clean out the ranks of the party of enemies. That's right. . . . But don't forget Comrade Stalin's warning: don't consider everyone who shook hands with a Trotskyists or a rightist to be an enemy. . . . That is why the more attentively, carefully, and selectively we approach this question, the better off we will be."[67]

Others, like Tataria first secretary Lepa, were, like Vainov, generally contrite, and tried to put the matter to rest with promises of future improvement: "About my so-called Tashkent tail. I told the oblast plenum, the activists of Kazan' party organization about the political mistakes. I admitted my mistakes. There's no need to go over that ground again here. We are waging a struggle against artels and familyness. Led by the instructions of the TsK plenum, we have started on the path of a decisive, brave promotion of workers."[68]

Other clan leaders used an "I didn't know" defense. Malinov, one of Sheboldaev's lieutenants in Rostov, said, "Comrades, who doesn't know about the Saratov *svoiaki*? Everybody in the organization is talking about it. . . . Really I didn't know that our *apparat* was so closed and exclusive and that party members and non–party members couldn't approach territorial committee secretaries, and when I took a look at this, as a Bolshevik should, I didn't do anything."[69]

In Voronezh, Comrade Temnikov of the clan's revision commission turned out also to have a bad memory, but his listeners didn't let him get away with it:

> TEMNIKOV: And it's not accidental that they were among those who were always in Anchikov's apartment which became a sort of club where a whole group of Anchikov's close friends gather for "amusement."
> (VOICE: Name their names.)
> Evgenii Ivanovich yesterday said in his report that at Anchikov's place a whole group of responsible workers gathered. . . .
> (Noise in the hall. VOICE: Name them all.)
> I said that Anchikov gathered people from the provincial party committee in his apartment.
> (VOICE: Who?)
> I don't remember the list.
> (VOICE: What are you talking about? You have to remember.)
> It's a long list.
> (Noise in the hall. VOICE: Name their names!)
> Comrades, I already said that Anchikov gathered a group of leading workers.
> (VOICE: Who?)
> I said that several leading provincial party committee workers were at Anchikov's place.
> (VOICE: Names!)[70]

Some denied that they had a "tail" at all, or declared that if they did, it was no longer functioning. Riabokon of the North Caucasus said: "I should say that I had no tail, and I never selected cadres according to an artel approach. Although comrades have adduced no actual facts, so that people will know in the future, during the time of my work here in the North Caucasus I brought absolutely nobody to the territory from Rostov or from anywhere else I previously worked."[71] In Tataria, Lepa said, "Comrade Zaitsev asked what had changed after the plenum. Baskin, Anderson and Kurnikov are still in their jobs. Why does he conclude that I in particular did not fulfill the decisions of the TsK? Does it say anywhere in the TsK materials that we have to remove these people? No. Be consistent. Show us some materials about an artel existing now, or that I behaved with them more mildly than others, that I didn't make demands on them."[72]

Others tried to minimize the size of their "tails" as Vainov had done: "from simple arithmetic, that's only 7–9 people." But the locals knew who was who and refused to go along. When Sheboldaev tried to minimize the numbers of the "Saratov Brothers-in-Law," Comrade Brike said, "Last evening Comrade Sheboldaev said that with difficulty he could remember 8–10 people. That's not true, Comrade Sheboldaev. I have a list of 22 people and it's incomplete. Even second-level people were imported and settled in various posts . . . showing a bureaucratic lack of faith, kicking out the best local cadres (voice: 'That's right!')."[73] Some clan leaders used the tried and true method of lashing back at their critics. Comrades Aivasov and Gafurov, noninsiders in Tataria, criticized the provincial party committee but were taken to task by one of its members:

> AIVASOV: Thus we have not fulfilled the task set us by Com. Stalin. I must say directly that the agitprop department of the provincial party committee and the provincial party committee in general has unfortunately done nothing in this regard.
> BEILIN: Why didn't you do anything? Why are you always slandering the provincial party committee?
> AIVASOV: I already talked about myself.
> BEILIN: Why in that case do you need to talk all the time about the provincial party committee? You need to work yourself . . .
> BEILIN: Listen, Gafurov, you criticize the provincial party committee and Comrade Lepa very well and thereby said nothing about yourself in the way of self-criticism.
> GAFUROV: Today I have only 10 minutes for self-criticism. I'll leave it for next time.
> (Laughter in the hall.)[74]

In the North Caucasus, Riabokon became indignant when one speaker criticized his artel, which he had denied existed:

> Just after Comrade Pivovarov's speech . . . justifiable doubts arise about what motivated Comrade Pivovarov. We have to figure it out, and figure it out politically. And I think that to figure it out politically, we will have to say that it was his attempt to avoid the blows of *samokritika*. It won't work, Pivovarov! It won't work! Why did Pivovarov have to attempt this? What were the political causes? The political

causes were based on his need not to talk about his own past serious political mistakes. . . . We are obligated to criticize Comrade Pivovarov and we will criticize him further in order to help him correct his mistakes, if he is able to do so. As for the useless conversations about who likes whom, in party affairs we can quietly push them aside as useless garbage. (Voices: Right! Right!) We will criticize your mistakes, Comrade Pivovarov, as long as you don't admit to them as a Bolshevik leader should. (Voices: Right! Right!)[75]

Vainov recognized the "artel" problem and its effect on the locals and now claimed to have secretly fought it all along: "I never talked about it, but I must tell you that I expended so much energy neutralizing the mood [resentment of his "tail"] which started from the beginning when workers arrived, about my tail's and others' incorrect relations with the so-called Ivanovists. . . . Ivanovists showed up and complained about non-Ivanovists. Kamenskii, Rudnev, and Zhuravlëv complain about the Ivanovists. I spent a lot of time neutralizing this."

Vainov's clan escaped this March provincial party committee plenum meeting bruised but intact. Vainov successfully saved Nefedov by suggesting that the buro gather more information and make a decision. More than three weeks later on 19 April, the buro met again. It resolved "to charge Comrade Vainov with preparing a memo to the TsK on the impossibility of Comrade Nefedov remaining second secretary of the Iaroslavl' Provincial Party Committee VKP(b) in connection with his mistakes."[76] Nefedov was accused of avoiding inconvenient questions and being a layabout, protecting exposed enemies, toadying, rank-worship, and "continuing to round off sharp corners" by refusing to self-criticize. Gruzel, the KPK representative, said that "when the Orgburo installed Nefedov, he was experienced here and they thought he could help. He didn't live up to it." Gruzel said it was impossible for Nefedov to remain second secretary because now he lacked any authority. Rudnev, a district party committee secretary, reminded the buro that "this question of Comrade Nefedov's mistakes comes before us not by our own initiative but rather from below and only after that did we start to discuss it."

Vainov resisted the trend and continued to protect Nefedov: "I don't want to say that everything you have said is right." Many comrades asked what he was doing about Nefedov, but "I postponed the question and thought it necessary to first of all give every comrade time to think it over." He also defended giving Nefedov permission to skip the provincial party committee plenum meeting: "I never thought that Nefedov would be so strongly criticized both by the activists and the plenum, or I would never have permitted him to leave." Because of Vainov's loyalty, we find Nefedov still in place at subsequent buro meetings of 20 April and 8 May.[77]

Most provincial barons doggedly protected their retainers even when they came under fierce attack. Rumiantsev of Smolensk even defended his man Shil'man after the latter had been arrested. Why? First of all, good clan practice required that a lord show himself to be a loyal protector, a safe bet for those who in the future might seek to join his clan. Second, if one of his retainers should turn out to be a bad apple or, worse, an "enemy," he as patron would be implicated in dubious or criminal activity for having given the enemy a job. Third, if the subordinate were to be expelled and arrested, he could be forced to give testimony against his patron. Finally, even though this was a serious political situation in which the players played for keeps, one cannot exclude the possibility that simple decency, a sense of justice, and personal loyalty played a role in a patron's defense of his clients.

Over the next few weeks, the Iaroslavl' party organization held the new party elections by secret ballot mandated by Zhdanov in his speech to the February Plenum, and the returns were mixed for the Vainov clan. In 726 of 1272 primary party organizations of the oblast (57 percent), the election meetings had found party work "unsatisfactory," and in Iaroslavl' the proportion was higher (67 percent). Across the oblast, there were objections to 26 percent of the proffered candidates (32 percent in Iaroslavl'). Nevertheless, the Vainov clan retained its hold on top positions. Although 36 percent of the new party secretaries in major party organizations were new cadres elected for the first time, "in the large party organizations, the old cadre partkom secretaries were preserved."[78] Vainov would later admit that only six secretaries of leading party organizations had been changed.[79]

Vainov's final party conference came in early June 1937. He had been under sustained attack since the beginning of the year but had held power through thick and thin. This time, though, the meeting was attended by two high-ranking guests from Moscow: L. M. Kaganovich and G. M. Malenkov. Vainov began the meeting with a self-critical recitation of his mistakes in choosing cadres and how this principle of selection by personal connections had aided Trotskyists. "It is not an accident that there are so few local Iaroslavl' cadres promoted into regional and city leading soviet organs." And "Take Comrade Nefedov who turned out to be a rotten liberal who was always passive in struggling with enemies of the people. . . . Why didn't we concern ourselves with these facts earlier?"[80]

Naumov, a party secretary outside the clan, said that Vainov's clan was a "rotten artel" that pushed around the local cadres from the beginning, and put pressure on district party committee secretaries they didn't appoint. Voice: "That's right!"[81]

Since the last meeting, the hapless Nefedov had been directly accused of sheltering enemies. Despite a resolution three months earlier to remove him, he was still in his job under Vainov's protection. He then took the podium and admitted to "crude political mistakes" since he had started working in Ivanovo in 1933.[82] It didn't help. The next day, Vainov announced that Nefedov had been arrested by the NKVD.[83]

Speaker after speaker attacked Vainov's "artel" and how it had displaced local workers. Krylov, a lowly factory party worker, continued the drumbeat of criticism:

> KRYLOV: In our factory we couldn't elect a chairman of the factory committee. Why? Because they sent us somebody we didn't know, we didn't know how he would work. Really, comrades, was it impossible to raise up people to the work of factory committee chairman in a big factory with such a large group of young people? We didn't trouble ourselves with this.
>
> KAGANOVICH: from where did they send you a chairman?
>
> KRYLOV: From the TsK of the union.
>
> KAGANOVICH: and was it impossible to find a chairman among yourselves?
>
> KRYLOV: Of course we could have.[84]

Many first secretaries were also accused of ignoring and not promoting local people. As we saw, in an early 1937 "musical chairs" rotation of several leading provincial nobles, they were forbidden from taking their "tails" with them. When Sheboldaev reached his new post at Kursk, rather than promoting local people he immediately demanded thirty new secretaries from the TsK. This was regarded as an attempt by him to "blacken and smear Kursk Oblast."[85]

Back at Vainov's last Iaroslavl' plenum, the gallant Kaganovich particularly encouraged women to speak. When Comrade Valeva took the floor, she began, "Comrades, I'm speaking for the first time, so take that into consideration." Kaganovich interjected, "Women speak better and more sharply than men."[86]

The plenum's resolution was hard on Vainov. It noted his "crude political mistakes," and "impermissible family selection" of cadres. It noted that after the February Plenum "Comrade Vainov did not re-build his work in accordance with the decisions of the TsK plenum and instead of Bolshevik mobilizing, permitted petty-bourgeois con-fusion in the party organizations and led to new failures in party work."[87]

Even then, Vainov did not go down without a fight. He asked for the floor to challenge the resolution's wording as it had been suggested by the drafting commission: "I ask to make one correction . . . where it says 'to recognize the entire political and practical activity and leader-ship of the provincial party committee as completely unsatisfactory' I suggest taking out the word 'completely' and to say 'to recognize the leadership and work of the provincial party committee to be unsatis-factory.'" It didn't work:

> COM. ZIMIN: The commission didn't change anything. That is the exact formulation that was proposed.
>
> COM. PAVLOV: Who is for accepting the suggestion of the commission, raise your cards. Who is for the proposal of Comrade Vainov, I ask you to raise your cards.—two members. To accept the proposal of the commission.[88]

On the last day of the plenum, 8 June 1937, the meeting removed Vainov from the position of first secretary and from the Iaroslavl' Pro-vincial Party Committee membership.

☆

Disciplining party clan leaders was difficult, even for a dictator like Stalin. Before 1937, Stalin tried a number of separate tactics: private, then public criticism, rotating barons to new posts, infiltrating their groups with "king's men," and holding their feet to the fire with elec-toral campaigns and party committee elections that (as they would in Khrushchev's time) threatened their patronage. The penultimate tactic was encouraging and protecting open criticism from below (as Mao would do in the 1960s). This was particularly dangerous—and Stalin deployed it as a last resort short of violence—because it could lead to discourses criticizing not only the noble leaders in particular, but leadership in general and threaten the very stability of the regime (as happened under Mao).

But the clan leaders held on. They were powerful in their bailiwicks, powerful enough to exercise tight control over their organizations and powerful enough to withstand considerable pressure from above and below. To finally break them required personal visitations and intervention from even higher persons and, eventually, violence.

Theirs was a personalized, patrimonial leadership where personal prestige was more important than rules or ostensible rank. Such a powerful prince as Vainov could of course simply be arrested. But in patrimonial terms, he had to be removed (in the eyes of his followers in the province and his peers on the TsK) only in the presence of an even more powerful personage: a member of Stalin's dominant clan. A feudal prince's persona could be demoted and displaced only by a bigger man, a "king's man" like Kaganovich, in person. In addition to appearing in Iaroslavl', Kaganovich went to Smolensk to preside over the removal of Rumiantsev.[89] Malenkov went to Kursk to depose Sheboldaev. A. A. Andreev rode a circuit from Tashkent (removing Ikramov) to Saratov (overthrowing Krinitskii), and on to Cheliabinsk, Sverdlovsk, and Voronezh.[90]

Beheading a tight clan that had commanded unquestioned local authority was a messy business. In the wake of a clan leader's removal, provincial party meetings erupted into chaos and mutual recriminations, as clan members tried to protect themselves by turning on their former boss and each other, and as non–clan members smelled blood in the water and sought to destroy anyone even tenuously connected with the defeated faction. Another of the powerful Moscow visitor's jobs was to restrain this process.

In Kursk, where A. A. Andreev traveled to oversee the dethronement of Sheboldaev, we can see the emissary's attempt to restrain the lynch mob:

> ANDREEV: It seems to me that some of you comrades are hurrying too much. Some of those denounced are known and trusted in the TsK but now some suggest listing them as enemies. Is there any basis for this?
>
> VOICE: No.
>
> ANDREEV: Are there any facts?
>
> VOICE: No.

ANDREEV: If not, then what basis do you have for doing this? It's impossible. . . . If you have any facts, then give them to me and I am sure we will investigate them no less thoroughly than you have at this conference . . . [91]

Malenkov did the same thing in Rostov:

KAMENSKII: Comrade Brike [of the KPK] has failed to secure things, that he must also be relieved of his duties . . .

MALENKOV: Comrades, the draft resolution includes an assessment of the activities of the Plenipotentiary of the KPK. The Central Committee shall concern itself with this matter, and this matter shall henceforth become the Central Committee's concern.

VOICES: But may we ask about it? (Laughter)[92]

We do not know why Stalin chose the summer of 1937 to destroy the regional princes. Perhaps he feared a conspiracy against him. In general, the Old Bolsheviks felt bypassed and underused as Stalin promoted younger officials. Some TsK members "could not keep their mouths shut about this" and wondered if Stalin was the only possible leader.[93] Of those we have met, Vainov, Sheboldaev, Riabokon, and Rumiantsev received public visitations from Politburo members and were ceremonially removed between 6 and 23 June 1937. Lepa and Samurskii followed in September and October, Postyshev and Pramnek in early 1938. Arrest followed removal in short order. Vainov was shot on 10 September 1937; Sheboldaev and Rumiantsev both on 30 October 1937; Riabokon, Lepa, Pramnek, Samurskii, and Postyshev on various dates in 1938. Between mid-1937 and early 1938, all of the seventy-one regional party clan heads were deposed and arrested save two: Khrushchev and Beria, who were functionally members of Stalin's own clan.

Stalin and his associates seem to have believed that a large-scale conspiracy was about to overthrow them. Years later, in the 1970s and 1980s, both Kaganovich and Molotov admitted their responsibility in the terror against the elite. But while not evading blame, they both claimed that the terror was necessary to preempt a coup. As Kaganovich recalled,

You see, in the situation of capitalist encirclement, so many [shadow] governments were at liberty; really they all were members of governments. There was a Trotskyist government, a Zinovievist government, a Rykov government. This was very dangerous, just impossible. Three governments could pop up from Stalin's opponents. . . . They created an organization . . . they met together—they were organizing an uprising against Soviet power and would lead it.

They had their people in the Army, they had their people everywhere. They circulated through a network of organizations. They informed each other and organized communications. . . . how could one leave that at liberty? . . . They regarded themselves as a government, an underground illegal government.

We knew that they organized a strong group. . . . such opponents who could carry out terror, murder . . . anything. Today we see various coups in all kinds of countries.

The Stalinists' suspicions were strengthened by their shared conspiratorial heritage with the presumed plotters. Old Bolsheviks were just that way.

Who could believe that these old, experienced conspirators, using the whole experience of Bolshevik secrecy and Bolshevik cooperation and underground organization, did not maintain connections among themselves and put together an organization? . . . They were old experienced Bolsheviks.[94]

Molotov agreed: "But really, let someone prove to me that we shouldn't have done this. Only someone could say this who was never a Bolshevik before the revolution."[95]

The Great Terror consisted of a number of discrete repressions of various groups, including show trials of the Old Bolshevik elite, arrests of military, economic, police, and other officials, and mass operations against ordinary citizens. All of these except the last were aimed at the elite,[96] while as we have seen, the mass operations were in some measure promoted by that elite. Space (and the subject of this book) do not permit a thorough account of the origins and process of terror against the elite, a subject which has been well treated in the literature.[97] And although we cannot know Stalin's plans with any certainty, arrests in the elite strongly suggest that at least one motivation was the destruction of clans.

Just as Kaganovich and Molotov could not believe that their fellow Old Bolshevik nobles, because of who they were, were not plotting something, they could not believe that the conspiracy did not include the main plotters' underlings. The pattern of arrests followed trails of personal connections. The arrest of an official coincided with arrests of his subordinates downward, and of his chiefs upward. Sometimes a subordinate was arrested and forced to give testimony against his boss, as with the arrests of Rumiantsev's deputy Shil'man in Smolensk and Sheboldaev's deputy Malinov in Rostov.[98] Other times, the boss was the first to go, followed by his subordinates.

We have a list of senior leaders arrested in Eastern Siberia in the first round of terror in 1937. Separate lists for party, soviet, economic, railroad, military, and police workers arrested clearly show that the decapitation of a given institution was accompanied by the arrests of those working for its chief. The arrest of a provincial party committee party secretary meant the arrest of his second and third secretaries, of chiefs of the provincial party committee departments (industry, agriculture, agitprop, and so forth), of provincial party committee instructors, and of most secretaries of the district party committees underneath the provincial party committee. Arrest of an economic official meant the arrest of his assistants and clients all the way down to bookkeepers.[99] In another example of *krugovaia poruka,* traditional Russian collective responsibility, "his people" were considered just as guilty and answerable as the arrested official.[100]

Although Moscow had information about who was who in the provincial party clans, another purpose of the visiting Politburo emissary was to listen to party plenum discussions in order to learn who was and was not a member of the targeted clan.[101] For example, as Andreev went from place to place in 1937, he regularly reported to Stalin about how the plenum discussions had added new information about local clan membership. Stalin either ordered arrests, asked for further information, or left it to Andreev or the locals to decide.[102] For example, Stalin telegraphed Andreev:

> If the plenum demands the arrest of Ikramov, you can arrest him. If not, you can limit yourself to removing him from office as secretary and send him to the TsK. His further fate will be decided in Moscow after your return there. How do the local party workers feel about the candidacy of Segizbaev? Who is this Tiurabekov? Who remains the representative of SNK? [Sovnarkom, the government apparatus.] Who will be temporary first secretary of Uzbekistan? Do you think you should go to Tadzhikistan? When?[103]

The transcripts of interrogation of arrested officials also reveal how arrests followed personal connections. It is clear from reading these texts that the interrogators had two basic instructions: to get the accused to confess to various acts of treason or espionage, and to name names. Sometimes the interrogator already had a list of connections ("accomplices"), other times he demanded that the accused list the names of his circle or clan. In either case, the task was to fill out the tree of personal connections. The interrogations are peppered with questions like,

> When did you meet ["were recruited for terrorist activity by"] _____?
> When did you hire ["recruit for terrorist activity"] _____?
> When did you meet with ["give terrorist instructions to"] _____?

M. Frinovskii, Ezhov's deputy at NKVD, knew how things worked.[104] When his time came to be arrested and interrogated, rather than waste time denying the accusations and refusing to confess (and enduring torture), Frinovskii began his own interrogation session by taking the initiative. Instead of the usual question-answer format, his interrogation consists of a long statement he proposed and composed naming all his personal connections.[105]

In all these transcripts, every family name appears in all capitals, to make it easy to scan later for this most important information. These interrogations were sent to Stalin, who read and sometimes annotated them, limiting his comments almost always to orders to arrest (or not to arrest) the capitalized persons. For example, Stalin's marginalia on Frinovskii's statement consist of: "Need to arrest Roshal'," and several repetitions of: "Who are they?" "Where are they?" "Who is there?"

Stalin had revealed his root-and-branch, clan approach to removing officials years before. Speaking in a much earlier, nonlethal context of firing or transferring clan leaders (rather than arresting them), Stalin told the Orgburo in 1931: "In order to destroy the gangs, you have to remove dozens of people; otherwise you don't destroy them. We will smash it to the bones if the chieftain regimes don't end, if they don't renounce chieftainship. . . . we will break bones in order to drive chieftainship out because you can't implant partyness without smashing the ribs that hold it together."[106] As chieftain of his own clan-gang, Stalin hated and distrusted the other clans, and in 1937, he decided to literally smash ribs in order to destroy them.

Stalin could kill a lot of people, but he could not change the system. He could destroy the clan leaders and their followers, but he could not destroy the clan culture and system, and it is by no means clear that he wished to do so.

Our detailed story ends here, with Stalin's destruction of the clans. But a glance ahead suggests that even after World War II, little had changed. As one postwar interviewee said, "the obkom [provincial party committee] plays an important and to some extent independent role in the oblast. It has a wide margin of executive initiative and may be said to be, on a small scale, God and Tsar in the oblast."[107] Another said, "Patronage was always resorted to by some people and in some cases; now, it is universal in the Soviet Union."[108] Local cliques continued to form family circles and think of themselves as a breed apart. As another recalled from the 1940s, "If you walk into a theatre in some raion town, you will see that the top Party people (*verkhushka*) keeps itself apart, all to one side. They have their own circle or clique."[109] Even in the late 1940s, when the Soviet economic bureaucracy became considerably more professionalized, its parts were always headed by members of Stalin's clan.[110]

Brezhnev would delegate power to first secretaries in the provinces. In his time, the elite was divided "into cliques, each with its own boss and its own clients . . . . Even when he became old and ill, Brezhnev remained essential as a mediator among them. . . . This was the kind of tacit understanding which had given the tsars apparently absolute power in the sixteenth century."[111]

As the epilogue will show, many of these practices continue to the present day, having outlived the Soviet Union. They are embedded in Russian history as a "deep structure." There had never been any other way to govern Russia, and upon reflection it would have been surprising indeed if Stalin could have replaced a thousand years of governing practice just by killing the current incumbents. "Stalin's terror was aimed in large measure at breaking down these intermediate networks for they obstructed the transmission of commands down the line. Yet the system depended on them, and therefore he was bound in the end to fail—which he did, like Ivan IV, though having first caused enormous suffering, and having destroyed many individuals, as distinct from the system."[112]

For ten centuries in Russia, princes, tsars, general secretaries, and presidents have each surrounded themselves with an inner circle, a clan, a *druzhina* to help them govern. In the case of Kievan princes, they were the prince's *liudi*, his fellow fighting men. In Muscovite times, they were the prince's relatives or the relatives of his wife. In

Soviet and post-Soviet times, they were the leader's comrades with whom he had worked in previous positions. The similarities jump across eras. Stalin, Khrushchev, and Brezhnev had their wartime comrades, Putin his former service mates in the KGB and Leningrad. But in all these cases, a royal or leading clan presided over a network of subordinate clans that together ruled a country based on personal connections and loyalty rather than law.

Stalin and his successors would govern the same way after the Terror as before it, with some changes. Khrushchev's and Brezhnev's attempts to build personality cults around themselves failed; Brezhnev's mass-printed and unread memoirs, along with his bemedaled portrait, became the butt of jokes. The time for naïve belief in benevolent patriarchs had passed but patrimonial mores and clans remained. These two leaders would surround themselves with those with whom they had fought or worked; each of whom, of course, had his own subordinate clan.[113] Gorbachev didn't even try for a cult, but by 1988–89 he had replaced far more boyars and lower-level clan leaders than Stalin had done. Some of these were transferred, some went into business. But they invariably took their "tails" with them. Like a Muscovite prince, Yeltsin actually surrounded himself with his kin and in-laws. That was how Russia had always been governed.

Epilogue
The New and the Old

Government business was determined by the influence of individuals rather than by the power of state institutions.
            —Nikolai Panin, on the eighteenth century

The weakness of the formal institutions designed to structure political life meant that the most important channels of political intercourse were personal.
            —Graeme Gill, on the Stalin period

The political process is still highly personalistic and feebly institutionalized, and its primary mode of operation is clientelistic and patrimonial rather than rational-bureaucratic.
            —Ottorino Capelli, on the Putin years

THIS BOOK HAS CONCENTRATED on the persistence of Russian political practices across the divide of the 1917 Revolutions that brought the Bolsheviks to power. But there is another, later twentieth-century watershed: that of the 1991 fall of the USSR. At first glance, the 1917 and 1991 divides could not be more different. Seventy years of modernization separated them, and although the USSR in 1991 was in crisis, it was nevertheless a modern state that seemed much different from the one that existed before 1917. It had a bureaucratic political culture and an industrial economic base. Modern technology had allowed it to put people in space and to build a powerful defense establishment. It had eliminated illiteracy and established universal secondary education based on a science that would appear to allow little room for ancient myths and practices. But many traditional elements of Russian political culture and practice remain to this day.

READING THE FALL: A NEW BEGINNING
OR MORE TRIBAL POLITICS?

No one will deny that the fall of the Soviet Union was a major historical, even revolutionary watershed.[1] Much has changed in a brief period of time: the Communist Party collapsed, much of the economy is privatized into market relations, governments are elected, civil and human rights are state policy, freedom of speech and thought is the norm.

When the Soviet Union collapsed, explicitly or implicitly, most observers thought that this event would at last push Russia along the evolutionary path toward a participatory democracy and/or a rational-bureaucratic polity. This line of analysis is not new. Whether the subject be the beginning of the Soviet period, the "thaw" following Stalin's death, or the fall of the USSR, in analyzing the major purported watershed events of the twentieth century, scholars repeatedly contrasted an assumed (and hoped-for) evolution toward rational bureaucratic government with an unfortunately persistent, vestigial patrimonialism/clientelism that was its opposite, and that retarded the expected institutional evolution.

This time around, the expectation of a Weberian watershed ushering in an era of "real" institutions was and is stronger than ever. After all, although many countries had transitioned to socialism, none had gone the other way. Because of this apparent uniqueness and because of the strength of democratic forces among the "reformers," most experts expected to see the appearance of a free market, democratic institutions, an orderly state and private sector, and a "civil society."

Those expectations and hopes soon needed qualification. Without minimizing the amazing positive revolutionary changes since the fall of the USSR, it now seems clear that after an initial dramatic flush of victory under Yeltsin, some of these changes seem less dramatic or enduring than we might have thought. Major industries are either government controlled or subject to state policy. Private industrialists can be destroyed and their property confiscated if the government doesn't like them. Civil rights seem to be at least partly a function of which prosecutor or court is in charge of a case, and an independent judiciary free from political pressure is still a dream. Public and private organizations still deploy groups of "official" or simply unknown armed men in ski masks to arrest or intimidate. At this writing, thousands of demonstrators are protesting rigged and stolen elections to the Duma in a system where other parties are denied any real possibility to participate. Russia is still ruled by one man, a patron who keeps himself in power by manipulating the Constitution, switching jobs with his client in dubious elections. And, of course, corruption is endemic and penetrates the system to the very top.[2]

Even in the early stages after the fall, however, something more familiar seemed to be happening: "During the privatization process, personal connections were more important than ever before, since the potential rewards were so much greater. . . . This was easiest for people who had worked in the *nomenklatura* elite in Soviet times, and simply kept in touch with their former colleagues. The Soviet Communist Party disappeared, but the *nomenklatura* survived."[3]

The transfer of power from Yeltsin to Putin "was handled in characteristically patrimonial fashion; Putin took office like "a new tribal chieftain anxious to demonstrate his authority."[4] While it was generally thought that the predicted rational bureaucratic state was in the cards for Russia, post-Soviet reality turned out to be quite different from the institutionalized legal-rational model. Instead of a democratic pluralist state, under Yeltsin and Putin authority was concentrated in the hands of a single leader. Instead of a distinct private sector, we saw the fusion of private and public sectors. "In the Russian case, there is a clear tendency for the elite networks to identify themselves with the state, which makes it very difficult to distinguish between the two."[5] On some level, that had always been true in Russian history.

Some began to criticize the lack of historical perspective in many analyses, the "false assumption" that there were only two possibilities (democratic versus authoritarian), or that there was a single possible trajectory that could be applied to all states.[6] Social scientists then posed a number of alternative models. In the literature, this period was labeled as a form of "'Third World patrimonialism with Bonapartist tendencies," feudalism, or competitive authoritarianism.[7]

Applying Bourdieu's concept of "social capital" to Russia today, Michael Urban counterposed the "Civil Society II" in Russia today to the civil society predominant in the West. The Western version, "Civil Society I," is characterized by strong civic associations, economic forms of social capital, weak interpersonal ties, the rule of law, and impersonal procedures. "Civil Society II," on the other hand, involves informal networks rather than civic associations, personal cultural capital instead of economic capital, strong instead of weak interpersonal ties, and the personalized appropriation of public offices and weak rule of law.[8]

Nevertheless, rational institutionalization and patrimonialism are often still thought to be in inverse proportion to one another, with the latter (despite its persistence) being doomed to wither away (later rather than sooner, it is now said) in the face of markets, prosperity, a middle class, and/or elections.

There had always been a contrasting view. From Merle Fainsod to Joseph Berliner to Alena Ledeneva, some were agnostic about the external, retarding, or doomed nature of patrimonialism and clientelism. Some argued that it was the necessary grease that made the system function, or at least made it tolerable. Social science research in other fields has posited no necessary contradiction between the two; they can live together quite nicely in the modern world.[9] Nevertheless, the view that patrimonialism and clientelism are institutionalization's antimatter and are therefore doomed remains an influential current in analyses today.

Although virtually all specialists agree that personal clan networks continue to be a major factor in Putin-era politics, they have different views on their dominance and future. T. H. Rigby writes that while "personal links remain a major factor in national-level politics" their stability is less clear than it once was. He argues that because of the influence of the market, "the transition from an authoritarian to a democratic polity," and "the beginnings of a constitutional order," today's clans have less power and changing memberships as individuals seek various opportunities. Their future is therefore questionable. Orlando Capelli agrees that today's clans descended from the Soviet past but have changed their nature in the post-Soviet period: "*Demokratizatsiya,* however, did not defeat *mestnichestvo,* although it altered the balance of power among its actors and modified its internal modes of operation."[10]

Aside from the debatable notion that Putin's system represents the beginnings of a democratic polity or constitutional order, others are not so sure about the withering or changing nature of clan clientelism and stress its persistent power and importance. For Vladimir Shlapentokh, "the role of informal, personal relations in post-Soviet Russia is difficult to overestimate." He has called the Putin system feudalism because of its patrimonial, nonbureaucratic character based on suzerain-vassal relations in the form of clientelism, and the privatization of state wealth and protection. For him, 'people's place in society is "determined not so much by their objective characteristics, including their political and economic position, but by the clan that protected them." For Alena Ledeneva, "It must be acknowledged that signs of change are as yet only tenuous." She is dubious about the withering away of clan clientelism in the face of marketization: "Informal networks, particularly those based on interaction between public administration and business, or the banking services, are essential for the operation of both the formal and informal economy."[11] For Geoffrey Hosking, the post-Soviet "result is a society held together largely by personal ties of a patron-clientelistic type, and by the authority of a president who holds an overriding position."[12] One study has identified twenty clans of officials and businessmen that virtually control the wealth of the country.[13]

It is certainly true, as Rigby and others noted, that clan clientelism is different today than it was in Soviet times. No longer embedded in the party *nomenklatura*, clans exist in and overlap with finance and banking, industrial management, and a host of other endeavors apparently outside the state. Their membership does indeed seem to be more porous and changing, as clan members can enter and leave networks more freely.

At the same time, though, it would be incautious to overemphasize the differences. Even in Soviet times, party clans had nonparty citizens in their orbits. Artists, nonparty members of the technical intelligentsia, and others very often had party patrons, as well as people below them who depended on them. There seems little analytical reason to limit clientelism in Soviet times to the party *nomenklatura*. In practice, surely a minister or TsK member was in the official sector, but his network may well have extended far outside it. The same is true today if, for example, we substitute "official" in today's gigantic Administration of the President, for "TsK member" in Soviet times.

Today there is a private sector with its own networks, some of which overlap with the state. But again, this may be a distinction without much difference. As many have noted, the line between the official and the private sectors today is blurry, if it exists at all. In Soviet times, with everyone employed by the state, we find a blurry line between state and society. Was a collective farm chairman an official, a boss, or a worker? A factory foreman? A part-time propagandist? Was he a state giver of orders, or a society taker of orders? Actually, everyone was both; everyone in Soviet times had a boss as well as underlings, so the public/private or state/society distinctions were not very useful then, nor are they now.

Much remains the same today in a Russian clientelism that just won't go away. Consider, for example, how clans are joined or recruited. Whereas "'modern'" networks are relatively open and are supposed to recruit independent agents on the basis of professional expertise, in Russia kin and social networks function in a "premodern" way, on the basis of loyalty and compliance. The "'selection of cadres'" (*podbor kadrov*), then and now, tests character, compatibility, and team-player qualities. Viktor Ilyukhin of the State Duma anticorruption committee explained that the formation of cadres, especially at the top level of managers in presidential and federal administrative structures, is based not on the principles of professionalism but on those of acquaintance, personal loyalty, compliance with unwritten rules, and nepotism (*kumovstvo*). Personal loyalty is the essential operating principle in public administration. According to Michael Urban, "senior officials avoid legal requirements for filling vacancies on a competitive basis, thus extending patron-client relations in their organizations," just as in the Soviet period.[14] Stalin was famous for valuing loyalty and obedience more than competence. For him, competence often resolved itself into loyally carrying out orders; competence *was* loyalty. Much the same thing might be said of Russian clans long before 1917.

CLAN STRUGGLES TODAY

The clannish nature of Russian high politics is alive and well today in Russia, and commentators today constantly discuss this and that "clan" under Putin. The Russian government today is divided into two large political groupings. The *siloviki* ("strong ones") are, like Putin, mostly veterans of the former Soviet security services. As their name implies, they tend to favor strong vertical central controls (*vertikal'naia vlast'*), semimonopolistic concentrations in the economy, to harbor a security specialist's suspicion of foreigners, and to be only modestly concerned about corruption and civil and human rights. The other tendency, the "reformers," are the remnants of the Yeltsin-era democrats of the 1990s who favor free markets, individual rights, and a more pluralistic and democratic political system. Unlike their conservative and semixenophobic rivals, the liberal reformers stress cooperation with the outside world. The same month that Putin warned against the West and sang welcoming songs with Russian spies caught in the United States, Medvedev was in Silicon Valley ostentatiously playing with an iPad.

In a very broad sense, these two tendencies have historical ancestors in modern Russian history. They recall the differences between Left and Right Communists, Stalinists and reformers, and are personified by the conflicts between Stalin and Bukharin, Khrushchev and Molotov, the contrasts between Brezhnev and Gorbachev, Yeltsin and Putin. Even before that, in a broad sense the conflict recalls Peter the Great versus the old Moscow boyars, and between Slavophiles and Westernizers that dominated Russian intellectual life in the nineteenth century.

Russian leaders handled the tension in various ways. Tsars tended to balance clans and factions. Ivan the Terrible and Stalin simply destroyed the groups that weren't their own. Modern leaders sometimes embodied both trends in their persons, or seemed to. Andropov was the KGB chief who liked Western jazz. Putin is the spy who likes free markets.

The most powerful of the *siloviki* gravitated around Vice Premier Igor Sechin, the major liberals (or rather those inside the elite) around President Dmitrii Medvedev. Although Putin's KGB background makes him the natural leader of the *siloviki,* he had also been a reformer in his St. Petersburg days under Mayor Anatolii Sobchak. He therefore stands above the fray, and referees among the tendencies and clans to keep the peace. Muscovite grand princes did the same with boyar clans, as did tsars with court factions, and Communist general secretaries with party "family circles" in the constant Darwinian clan struggle that is and always was Russian politics. It is entirely likely that Putin appointed Medvedev as his temporary successor as president as a counterweight to the powerful *siloviki.* According to one recent work, "Vladimir Putin, the so-called head of government, is in reality a tsar, a monarch (*gosudar'*), the tsar-father. He is not a personal autocrat, not an absolute monarch, and his power is not constitutional. His power is somewhat limited not by the constitution or laws, but by corporate-class custom, by secret agreements with shadowy influential groups, relatives, friends and administrative connections."[15]

At the top, the clan structure of the Russian government today bears a remarkable resemblance to those of the past. Top clan leaders are given broad areas of responsibility. To do their jobs they are given considerable freedom to staff the agencies under them with their "own people." Moreover, as we have seen, power in Russia from time immemorial has been about proximity to a powerful person and had little to do with one's official title.

At the time of this writing, according to a common understanding of the hierarchy of offices in the Russian government, one might conclude that they roughly ranked as follows, from top down: president of the Russian Federation (Medvedev), prime minister (Putin), chief of staff of the president (Sergei Naryshkin), first deputy prime ministers, then deputy prime ministers, then ministers of the cabinet. In fact, however, there is virtually total agreement among analysts both in Russia and the West that the actual rank order is entirely different and that the actual responsibilities and powers of elite members have little to do with their job titles.

Everyone knows that Putin as prime minister does not work for Medvedev as president; the opposite is the case, despite the Constitution. Most agree that after Putin, probably the most powerful figure is actually Igor Sechin, who holds the modest title of deputy prime minister (and not even first deputy). Naryshkin, who supposedly works as Medvedev's assistant, actually is a Putin aide (and his classmate from the KGB Higher School). Viktor Ivanov, ostensibly head of the Federal Narcotics Police, is actually Putin's chief adviser on personnel appointments.

In Soviet times, the major party oligarchs under Stalin each had informal areas of responsibility regardless of their job titles. For example, in 1935 each secretary of the Central Committee was "curator" of several parts of economic, party, and state activity. Andreev and Ezhov were to prepare Orgburo agendas. Andreev headed the Industrial and Transportation departments and supervised office staffs of the Central Committee. Kaganovich supervised administration of the city of Moscow, as well as serving as commissar of railroads. Stalin looked after the Culture and Propaganda Department.[16]

There is also an informal division of responsibilities among senior nobles in Russia today. Putin himself is overall coordinator and is directly in charge of foreign policy, with the minister of foreign affairs (Sergei Lavrov) as a mere adviser and spokesman. Viktor Ivanov supervises personnel appointments. Medvedev supervises questions of the judiciary and personnel, subject to Ivanov's agreement. Sechin is in charge of most of the economy (except finance) as well as the organs of state security. Vladislav Surkov, ostensibly first deputy chief of staff to the president, actually controls questions of ideology and supervision of youth groups and political parties. All of these, and others, get their power not from their offices, which can change like musical chairs, but from their proximity to Putin. Virtually every important leader at the top of Russia's government today was connected to Putin either in the KGB or during his days in St. Petersburg.[17]

Sometimes intrigues and struggles between clans sometimes come into public view. In 2003, Putin formed a new Federal Narcotics Control Service (FSKN), to provide a base for another FSB clan, that of his old St. Petersburg KGB colleague and former federal regional plenipotentiary Viktor Cherkesov, who went to Moscow to run the new service. The main FSB remained under the control of Sechin's ally Nikolai Patrushev. It was clear from the beginning that the new FSKN was really to be an FSB-2, a place to house Cherkesov and his people. It absorbed the forty thousand employees and the equipment of the former Tax Police, which gave it an entrée to investigate virtually any business in the country, as well as a role in the lucrative border control trade. Control of tax investigations through his client Cherkesov also gave Putin a direct institutional weapon that he would use against Mikhail Khodorkovskii. Essentially, a new institution was created to house a clan. Here we again see the prominence of clan politics over institutions, with institutions being ephemeral tools at the disposal of clans.

With Putin as arbiter between his two police friends Sechin and Cherkesov, the two clans maneuvered and competed peacefully with each other for a few years. The Sechin clan included Patrushev of the FSB, and head of the National Investigative Committee Alexander Bastrykin, as well as former prosecutor General Vladimir Ustinov (whose son married Sechin's daughter). Cherkesov's clan, the weaker of the two, included head of the Presidential Security Service Viktor Zolotov, then-current procurator general Iurii Chaika, and a host of former KGB officers from St. Petersburg.

Then, in 2007, the two clans went to war with each other. It is likely that the catalyst was Putin's statement that he would not run again for president. As one analyst put it, "the entire political system of Russia today is a struggle of various clans and groups fighting to see that Putin stays in power according to their scenario and not according to the scenario of their competitors."[18] So with Putin not running, according to the ancient rules of Russian clan oligarchy, there would be no tsar-arbitrator to keep the peace and balance the spoils. Since the fifteenth century, anarchic clan civil war had always broken out in Russia when a possible political vacuum replaced the arbitrating monarch, as factions and clans turned to open and violent struggle to protect and enhance their positions in the anarchy that would soon begin.

Sniping began in August 2007, when police in St. Petersburg arrested Vladimir Barsukov, a shady businessmen with suspected ties to the Russian mafia Tambov Gang. Barsukov was reputed to have ties to Cherkesov and Zolotov, and the media reported that prosecutors were investigating those connections.[19]

Open warfare erupted in October. Lieutenant General Alexander Bulbov, a senior Cherkesov aide at FKSN, and several other FKSN officers were arrested at Moscow's Domodedovo Airport on 2 October by Patrushev's FSB agents working for what was by now Sechin's investigative committee. Bulbov was protected by armed FKSN bodyguards, and according to one witness, a gunfight between the two police groups nearly broke out. Bulbov was taken into custody and charged with illegal business activities, bribery, and illegal wiretapping. Pro-Cherkesov Prosecutor General Chaika protested the arrest and ordered Bulbov's release, but the Moscow City Court humiliated the prosecutor general, accepted the protests of Sechin's investigative committee, and sustained Bulbov's arrest.

"The wars between the elites have come to the surface."[20] In the ensuing battles, Procurator Chaika arrested a senior FSB officer and charged him in the sensational murder of Anna Politkovskaia. Sechin's powerful investigative committee forced his release. Five of Cherkesov's FSKN officers were arrested by the FSB, and two others were rumored to have been poisoned. In an open letter, the last Soviet KGB chief, Vladimir Kriuchkov, along with a group of other retired security officers, urged both sides to stop fighting: "Trust us from our experience. . . . There will be major troubles and this is unacceptable."[21] Kriuchkov was vague about the players, so the matter resembled what Churchill said about mysterious, opaque Soviet power struggles: they are like bulldogs fighting under a carpet.

Sechin's clan seemed to have come out on top. Procurator General Chaika was stripped of most of his power and forced to resign, with most of his powers assigned to the pro-Sechin investigative committee. Cherkesov was not appointed head of the powerful committee, a position he apparently wanted. But Putin was not prepared to see Cherkesov defeated; he would thus lose an important counterweight to the Sechin group. At the end of October, he appointed Cherkesov chief of a blue-ribbon National Narcotics Committee, which would be on a par with Patrushev's National Anti-Terrorism Committee.

In the midst of the clan war, Cherkesov broke the first rule of oligar-chic anarchy—that all these actions must remain secret from the population—and went public in the wide-circulation newspaper *Kom-mersant*.[22] He named names and described the struggle. He defended his FSKN agency and its distinguished former KGB officers and com-plained that they were being falsely accused and persecuted in this "infighting among the special services." He warned that "there can be no winners in this war. There is too much at stake." Darkly and vaguely referring to illegal commercial connections of his FSB rivals, he titled his article, "It Is Impermissible for Warriors to Turn into Merchants." It was one thing for has-been outsiders like Kriuchkov and his old bud-dies to note the clan war; it was quite another for one of the current players to do so and to provide details. Cherkesov had violated one of the ancient rules of Russian oligarchy: secrecy.

As long ago as the Middle Ages, there was an understanding that powerful clan groupings would naturally compete with one another, but that for the sake of preserving the system, they must hide it from the populace. To prevent chaos they must do everything behind closed doors. Decisions were to be unanimous and secret. Speaking of medi-eval Russia, Edward Keenan wrote: "government . . . was conspiratorial: clans conspired against one another to expand their power. . . . One does not reveal to non-participants authentic information concerning politics, political groupings, or points of discord." The Russian proverb *iz izby soru ne vynesi* fully applies: "Don't carry rubbish out of the hut" or as we would say today, "Don't wash dirty linen in public."[23]

For his part, Putin had maneuvered in secret, not taking any public position on the struggle, which was the traditionally correct thing to do. But Cherkesov's outburst angered him. On October 19, as he was walking from one meeting to another, he was cornered by reporters who asked him about the infighting in the special services. Following the ancient rules, he refrained from providing any details or criticizing either side. Indeed he did not even admit that there was a conflict. In the reporter's words, "I asked if nevertheless there was a war in the special services or not, in his opinion." Putin gave an evasive answer; instead he spoke of the real problem: going public. His only comment was, "If I were in the place of the people defending the honor of their uniform, I would not accuse everybody around me, especially in the media." The reporter continued, "He still hadn't gone into the elevator.

He wanted to add something else: 'I consider taking that kind of problem to the press incorrect' he said."[24]

THE CULT

The cult of Vladimir Putin shows that cults of leadership and the personalization of power they represent ended neither with Stalin nor with the Soviet regime. Putin's cult consists of media branding as an authoritative masculine athlete, a strong leader, and an outspoken and salty defender of Russia and Russians against suspect outsiders. He saves people from tigers, publicly embraces children and dogs, dives deep into Lake Baikal, skis the most challenging slopes, and at the same time paints and makes pottery. Children's books like "Fairytales about Putin" have appeared.

Putin's images and iconography are both manifestations of his cult and the latest in a longtime association of the person (and his image) with the state. By 2007, one Moscow bookstore featured twenty-eight different likenesses of Putin for sale.[25] A calendar marking "The Twelve Moods of Putin," depicting various facial expressions, was produced by leading artists, one of whom said, "while drawing, we literally fell in love with him."[26]

In Nizhnyi Novgorod region, since 2005 a sect has worshiped an icon of Putin, which recently began to glow and drip holy oil (*zamiro-tochila*) because, in the words of sect leader Mother Fotina, "He has the soul of the king" and "Putin is the way to a different Russia!"[27] For his part, Putin is a bit more restrained about being personally worshiped. When a priest tried to kiss his hand during a visit to the fourteenth-century Valaam Monastery, Putin recoiled, "appeared ruffled," and quickly drew his hand back.[28]

Using more modern technology, Putin holds televised audiences during which he receives petitions for redress of grievances from supplicants and short-circuits the bureaucracy, as did Stalin and other leaders throughout history, by bestowing personal attention and favor to right wrongs. In so doing, he keeps his tsar-like image clean; he blames (his own) bureaucracy for mistakes and injustice, and encourages a naïve monarchism that was an integral part of the folklore surrounding such widely separate figures as Ivan the Terrible and Stalin.[29] During his visit to Valaam, he accepted petitions and letters from local residents standing in line awaiting his arrival. The tsar (Ivan, Stalin, Putin) is good, the nobles (boyars, bureaucrats) are bad; "if the tsar only knew what was happening . . ."

In promoting traditional Russian naïve monarchism, Putin makes frequent use of a set piece of traditional photographic iconography in which he sits in his office, ramrod-straight with a report, frowning across his desk at an empty-handed, sad-faced, slightly slumped-over official who is graphically taking the blame for some shortcoming. The lesson is clear: Vladimir Vladimirovich is on your side, looking out for your interests, overriding and replacing a state whose bureaucracy is worse than useless. Conversely, if Putin is praising his subordinate, the official himself sits ramrod-straight, and nobody at the table frowns.

Putin's cult, unlike Stalin's or Lenin's, is not based on mystical transcendent qualities, Mother Fotina notwithstanding. Unlike those of post-Stalin Soviet leaders, it is not based on apostolic succession from an authoritative ancestor (Lenin). After Stalin, the charismatic-transcendental nature of the leader cult withered away. As much as they tried to be, Khrushchev and Brezhnev were in no sense heroic. They had no apostolic connection to the sainted Lenin or to the revolution, and their reference to "the party" as a source of transcendental authority fell flat. People knew what "the party" was on a daily basis, and it was in no way mystical. Indeed, the attraction of the mystical-transcendental in general waned as the Soviet population became more urban, more educated, more sophisticated.[30]

But for all the loss of the magical, this is no less a cult. Putin is identified with the state and the state with him. A scan of today's Russian press suggests that the understanding of political authority as personal is reflected in the worship accorded today's Russian leaders:

> "I thank God for Putin!"
>
> "Vladimir Vladimirovich [Putin]! How wonderful that you were born!"
>
> "With such attention, such respect, we listen to the advice of Vladimir Vladimirovich Putin!"

The understanding of politics as personal and patrimonial endures in the practice of royal patronage. As far back as the thirteenth century, the personal patronage of a grand prince, tsar, or other grandee was crucial to the growth and prosperity of monasteries, churches, and other sites. Frequently, this benevolence was sealed and symbolized by a royal visit accompanied by a bequest and promise of continued support and favor. The connection of the royal person with the favored place was publicized, and prominence and wealth for the institution inevitably followed such visitations. The symbolism, ceremony, and economy of this personalized connection continues today. In cases where bureaucratic procedures fail, royal patronage still makes things work.

President Putin's presence, patronage and favor are instrumental in determining priorities and allocation of resources. For five years, the site of the demolished Hotel Rossiia near Red Square had remained an abandoned construction site, while various bureaucratic and commercial entities fought over what would be built there and by whom. Former mayor Luzhkov favored a hotel/business center complex with underground parking. Others had floated the idea of relocating the two houses of the Russian parliament to the site. But in January 2012, while visiting the site, Putin suggested to the new mayor, Sergei Sobianin: "You know what I was thinking? Practically all parkland in the heart of Moscow has been built over in the past decades. . . . I have the following proposal . . . maybe create a park zone here." Sobianin dutifully replied that "That would be great!" Within a few hours, years of stalemate were broken and Moscow authorities announced a competition and requested bids to develop the park.[31]

Those revisiting renovated Russian museums are often given to understand the reasons for a facelift. Recent visitors to Moscow's State Museum of Contemporary History (formerly the Museum of the Revolution, and before that, the English Club) have noticed a major improvement after years of official neglect. Rooms and corridors have been renovated and painted, exhibit space has expanded, floors have been redone. In the very first exhibition hall, numerous photographs of the visit of the smiling, then-President Dmitrii Medvedev, along with appropriate quotes, identify the museum with his favor, and renovation work began shortly after that occasion.

Medvedev also graced the New Jerusalem Monastery with his patronage. Amidst considerable publicity, he attended and spoke at a meeting of the monastery's reconstruction fund in October 2008. Immediately thereafter, rebuilding of the monastery (which had proceeded at a glacial pace for half a century since the Germans destroyed it in World War II) took off. A massive archaeological dig was begun, and the monastery cathedral was covered in a gigantic structure for systematic rebuilding.[32]

Probably the example most analogous to ancient royal visits was Putin's visit to Novodevichii Convent. In May 2012, Putin visited the convent and, just as a Muscovite prince would have done, presented the miracle-working Iverskii Icon of the Mother of God to the nuns. After declaring that "the Orthodox Church is the guardian of our moral values. It is with a feeling of joy that I transfer the icon to the church. Let it serve and help people," Putin was then informed about the former Church of the Beheading of John the Baptist just outside the walls of the convent, which had been destroyed by Napoleon's troops. As *Ekho Moskvy* reported, "and then suddenly, shortly after Putin's visit to Novodevichii Convent, the city authorities took a quick decision to re-create the church."[33]

Orthodox Patriarch Aleksei II spoke as Russian patriarchs always did in support of the supreme secular authority of the tsar: "Speaking to you I am constantly convinced that you sincerely care about making a dignified life for the Russian people and the multifaceted rebirth of the Motherland," and "You have traveled much across the Russian regions and sacrificially taken upon yourself labors on behalf of the Russian people."[34]

For his part, Presidential Chief of Staff Sergei Ivanov praised the unique experience of cooperation between the Russian Orthodox Church and the state. He promised that "the state will continue to employ the full force of the law in order to protect the religious feelings of the Russian people against any attempts at sacrilege or blasphemy. After all, it is the erosion of the spiritual foundations that has been the source of all the tragedies experienced by our country."[35]

REGIONAL BARONS AND THE "KING'S MEN"

Like Stalin and Russian leaders before and after him, Putin has had a center-periphery conflict with elite grandees who ran the provinces. Since the fall of the USSR in 1991, provincial governors were elected by popular vote. But with the rapid concentration of wealth into fewer and fewer hands that marked the Yeltsin years, powerful regional and central economic "structures" (as they were called then) were able to influence and eventually control local and regional elections. Candidates who opposed them found themselves denied access to media and meeting halls, harassed, and sometimes beaten or killed. Many—if not most—of the supposedly democratically elected provincial governors were therefore in the pockets of legal or illegal "mafias."

Even those who were not at first directly controlled by powerful economic interests realized the same thing that Old Bolshevik regional party secretaries realized under Stalin. To quote the Russian proverb, "God is in his heaven and the tsar is far away." They built their own independent political machines upon regional interests and orientations and staffed them with their own clients. With time, these governors too came under the sway of or partnered with oligarchic "structures."

Like Stalin, Putin launched an offensive against this centrifugal regionalism. In 2000, he created seven "federal districts," superimposed on the eighty-nine provinces and republics of the Russian Federation, and he dispatched his "king's men" as plenipotentiaries to the districts. Five of the original seven plenipotentiaries were Putin friends from the FSB or the military, and they were given access to records in the Treasury, Tax Inspectorate, Procuracy, and police with authority to investigate regional leaders.

But Putin's "king's men" were no more successful than Stalin's had been. Provincial governors were powerful enough to ignore the plenipotentiaries, and Putin's "plenipotentiary representatives in the seven federal districts inspire no fear. . . . The pro-Kremlin newspaper *Argumenty i Fakty* wrote that President Mintimer Shaimiev of Tatarstan treated him politely, as he might a waiter: 'First he listens attentively, then he orders his favorite dish.' "[36] Even an additional law in 2000 allowing Putin to suspend an elected governor who was under investigation by a procurator (not difficult to bring about) did not bring the regional barons to heel.

Finally, Putin used the 2004 Beslan massacre to promulgate a new decree transforming regional governors from elected officials to appointed ones, with Putin's office having the power of appointment. During a televised question-and-answer session, he justified the move "to exclude criminals from power." Putin said: "Almost every candidate always had some criminals behind his back, who using their unaccounted black money tried, and sometimes quite efficiently, to impact the election campaign process and its outcomes." Now that governor candidates were nominated by the president, according to Putin, "this more or less protects the public from criminal infiltration in at least this high regional level of governance."[37]

Like Stalin's massacre of regional leaders in 1937 and 1938, this effectively ended independent regional authority, although obviously in much less drastic ways. And like Stalin's coup, Putin's did not completely end local clan power or center-periphery tensions and conflicts, which seem somehow to be endemic in Russian politics. In a faint echo of these clan struggles, on the day this was written, Putin suggested limiting jury trials of defendants in murders and other serious crimes to courts at an interregional level instead of local venues, "to prevent acquittals based on clan loyalties."[38]

ROYAL RIVALRIES

Putin's struggle with Mikhail Khodorkovskii also has analogies in the past, bearing as it does a striking similarity to Stalin's struggle with Trotsky and any number of struggles between Muscovite princes. In both modern cases, there was a new leader who was not yet a dictator, a powerful challenger, and a particular understanding of the rules of oligarchy.

At the time of Lenin's death in 1924, Stalin was a new leader. Trotsky was head of the Red Army and had a seat on the Politburo. He had followers and a visible personality, and before 1924 there are no signs that his position was threatened as long as he played by the rules of oligarchy. At the time Putin won his first election as president in 2000, he was also a new leader. Mikhail Khodorkovskii was head of the powerful Menatep Bank and Yukos oil empire, and his position also seemed unassailable as long as he played by the rules of oligarchy.

Among the most important of those rules, in 1924 or 2000, was adherence to the collective decisions of the top ruling group and working out difficulties in secret. Indeed, these informal rules have a centuries-long pedigree in Russia. No matter what one's views, as long as one played by the rules, including that of secrecy, one could keep one's prestige and sites of power and influence. But in 1924–26, Trotsky launched a public attack on the Stalin party leadership "regime" and called for increased party democracy and participation. This was widely seen as breaking the rules. Party discipline and etiquette suggested that instead, he should have tried to work things out quietly inside the Politburo. Going public with his strident demands was seen as a serious threat to party unity that threatened the Bolsheviks' worst nightmare: a split in the party.

In 2000, Putin and his aristocrats worked under similar understandings: things should remain secret so as not to endanger the fragile regime. But Putin also made a new rule or rather updated an old one: he told the oligarch boyars that they could keep their (possibly ill-gotten) gains and positions, but they must not be public players in politics. Most oligarchs accepted the rule, but some did not. Vladimir Gusinskii, who controlled a press and television empire, used his media to attack Putin. Gusinskii was quickly crushed; he fled abroad and his press assets were confiscated. Mikhail Khodorkovskii was a different matter. He also went public, using his power to publicly criticize Putin, to fund opposing candidates for office, and to publicly ruminate that he himself might run for president against Putin.

Both Trotsky and Khodorkovskii had large networks of friends and clients; their threat was therefore not just individual. Opposing them, both Stalin and Putin headed networks and clans who would lose everything in case of defeat by the challenger. Unlike Western bureaucratic systems, where losers in political struggles simply lose their jobs, the personalized politics of Russia demand a sterner measure of defeat. The loser must not only be vilified and humiliated as an example; he has to be removed from any levers of power and, because of personalized clan politics, physically isolated from his networks and neutralized. His followers must be purged as well.

In 1925 Trotsky lost his institutional bases of operations: his Red Army leadership and his Politburo seat. But he was still present in Moscow, amidst his followers. So in 1927 he was exiled from Moscow to Central Asia. That was still too close for comfort (and communication with his people) so in 1929 he was expelled from the Soviet Union to finally cut him off from his networks. He was killed in 1940. Khodorkovskii also first lost his institutional base. He was accused of tax fraud and other crimes. His Yukos company was confiscated and sold off. But this was not enough; he had to be physically removed and isolated from his followers. So he was isolated in a prison camp in Siberia.

In both cases, in order to preserve the customary practice of secrecy about how the system actually worked, the conflicts were carefully presented to the public. Although the struggles were intensely personal, involving personal rivalries and claims to power, they had to be presented as principled or legal matters to avoid a public admission about the actual personal and oligarchic nature of the system. Khodorkovskii's destruction was simply presented as a "tax matter," although nobody in the elite believed that. Analogously, when Peter I was victorious over Regent Sofia, the victory of one aristocrat over the other, each with their clans, was presented not as a personal struggle, but as dynastically proper and legal and God's will.

Stalin was interested in how the struggle was presented and covered, and was eager that his fight with Trotsky *not* be understood as a personal or clan battle, which, of course, it was. Stalin's control of *Pravda* was not a "smoothly working control mechanism."[39] He was often surprised and angered by what he read there. In 1936, after reading *Pravda*'s coverage of such an important event as the first show trial, he wrote to Kaganovich and Molotov:

> *Pravda* . . . reduced everything to the personal element, to the notion that there are evil people who want to seize power and there are good people who hold power and fed this paltry mash to the public. The articles should have said that the struggle against Stalin, Voroshilov, Molotov, Zhdanov, Kosior, and others is a struggle against the Soviets, against collectivization, against industrialization, a struggle, consequently, to restore capitalism in the towns and villages of the USSR. Because Stalin and the other leaders are not isolated individuals but the personification of all the victories of socialism in the USSR . . ."[40]

He also wrote to Comintern leader Georgii Dimitrov: "workers think that everything is happening because of a fight between me and Trotsky, from the bad character of Stalin. It is necessary to point out that these people fought against . . . the party."[41] It was thus necessary to make the personal struggle for the throne seem principled.

Although Putin has called for Khodorkovskii to be found guilty, both Putin and Medvedev answered questions about the Khodorkovskii verdicts from a strictly judicial point of view. Just as Stalin converted the personal and clan struggle against Trotsky into a matter of Trotsky breaking the laws, Putin and his supporters have tried to make the personal struggle against Khodorskovkii a matter of simple criminal tax evasion. It would be interesting to know what percentage of the population in each case actually believed the official story.

There is another similarity. Deprived of institutional levers of control, isolated from their clan followers, and dragged through the mud of the official press, both Trotsky and Khodorkovskii reinvented themselves as democratic folk heroes who had always resisted the big dictatorial government that was crushing them. Trotsky had been one of the founders of the rigid dictatorship, an advocate of persecuting political heretics, a spokesman for a nondemocratic and highly centralized party personnel system, and a strong partisan of exploiting the peasantry to fund industrialization. Out of power, he was now in favor of party democracy, a kind of ideological pluralism in the party, and he sharply criticized Stalin's collectivization and rapid industrialization. Khodorkovskii had used every possible trick and deceit to build his financial empire and buy his way into Yeltsin's government. In prison, he became an implacable foe of corruption and a spokesman for the fair, democratic process of human rights. Trotsky's and Khodorkovskii's reinventions, which involved radical shifts in their previously professed beliefs, serve to highlight the personal nature of Russian politics. It is not clear whether or not Sofia, the loser in a personal struggle with Peter the Great, had the opportunity or need to reinvent herself in her nun's cell at the Novodevichii Convent.

THE PERSISTENCE OF PRACTICE

In this book, I have emphasized the special nature of Russian political culture. From the angle of practice, it is possible to see Russia as an example not of modernity, but of its opposite: an example of the persistence of apparently archaic practices existing in a particular, ongoing relationship to modern institutions.

We have also seen that archaic political practices seem to be more common in modern Russia than in other modern state settings. Without giving undue credit to "national character" arguments, it seems inescapable that there is something specifically Russian, something culturally embedded, going on here. It is hard to imagine glowing and dripping religious icons of the head of state appearing in other modern countries today. Continuities with past practices seem less ephemeral and more direct here than elsewhere, and they seem to exist in profound subterranean cultural places that are nevertheless not far from the surface. Among developed industrial societies, patrimonialism, clientelism, and a host of other traditional practices are more common and more enduring in Russia than anywhere else, and have played a dominant role over a much longer span of time.

Institutions have always been weak in Russian politics, persons have always been strong. But the question about the weak institutions argument is "why?" If we leave aside arguments about Russian national character, the obvious place to look is society. Stephen White has argued that the Russian commercial bourgeoisie was also not a candidate for institution-building; it was small and undeveloped and tied to the throne. The peasantry was generally disinterested in institutions and in any case lived in a personal patrimonial society. As for the Russian nobility, it was neither powerful nor autonomous and thus was in no position to challenge the throne, as it had done in western Europe.[42] To this we might add that the Russian nobility had no reason to do so. Muscovite boyars liked the idea of a strong throne to prevent civil war among themselves.[43] Later, by the seventeenth century, the monarch bound peasant labor to noble estates, and after the revolts of Stenka Razin and Pugachev, used the military power of the state to address the horrible threat of peasant uprisings.

After their establishment at the beginning of the Muscovite period, aside from the functional self-interest of the ruling strata, traditional and patrimonial political arrangements became a habit embedded in political culture and practice. As of the late twentieth century, patterns of social-political practice did not change much, at least in grand terms, and the extent of change today is unclear and debatable.

The informal elite practices discussed in this book can be found in many places and times. Clientelism, patrimonialism, and a fusion of ancient and modern practices are not unique to Russia. We see them most often in so-called developing or traditional societies. The social science literature on them often focuses on Africa or parts of Asia but they are present to some degree everywhere. Since the time of Andrew Jackson, a newly elected U.S. president uses the spoils system to remove much of the previous bureaucracy and restaff it with his own followers.

But it is clear that patrimonial practices are more prevalent in Russia than in other "modern" states, where although they still exist, they have been eroded and constitutional institutions have been strengthened. Why? Or, to ask the standard question, why didn't Russia develop modern rational institutions?"

In fact, authoritative modern constitutions are rare in the world. Rather than measure societies by this standard, or expect them to evolve or live up to them, we might better reflect on their rarity. Political clans, weak institutions, and personalized politics dominate almost everywhere. Even today, most of the world lacks strong, independent institutions. Most societies are still ruled by persons and patrons more than laws. Indeed, what we take for modernized society, with its representative governments and powerful institutions, began within a few hundred miles either side of the English Channel and exists in the world today mainly there or as transplants from there. It might make more sense, therefore, to stand our usual Russian backwardness question on its head: Why did northwest Europe modernize?

Our reflexive Weberianism would suggest that some of what we call modernization has to do with capitalism, or the lack of it. Market capitalism of the type common in northwest Europe did not penetrate Russia until very late, if at all. In early modern western Europe, large-scale long-distance trade led to a money economy, with market gardening and putting-out industries that eventually involved people outside the traditional elite. Money and market relations permeated society, including the countryside. Markets provided economic participation for much of the population through the circulation of money, and brought the accompanying possibility for advancement outside traditional class structures. Money and trade brought independence from traditional nobles for towns and commercial social groups, and led to legal institutions and protections for nonnoble individuals, as well as to abstract notions of depersonalized institutions and a state that served as goal and rallying point for the struggle against traditional kings and nobles. It was in these places that patrimonialism was weakened and constitutional institutions were strengthened.

This powerful and pervasive money capitalism was absent in Russia, which sat not only on the Eurasian plain invasion route, but on a Wallersteinian periphery of the capitalist world system.[44] Agriculture remained stunted, market networks and commercialization remained primitive and regional, and power remained patrimonial and personal, unchallenged by new groups and new wealth. Just as individualism was a response to developments in western Europe, patrimonialism was a response to different conditions in the east.

On the other hand, capitalism in itself is no guarantee of modernized bureaucratic or democratic practices. China is becoming a thoroughly capitalist system but it seems that the more capitalism takes hold, the stronger patronage, venality, and political clans become. Perhaps China's deep structures are as important as her economy?

Maybe we should avoid simple developmental models and study each country on its own, remaining sensitive to deep cultural structures as factors in their own right and giving them equal weight with, or not inconsistent with "modernization." After all, in Russia the deep structures of patrimonialism have withstood two world wars, multiple revolutions, dramatic economic change, and the fall of tsars and commissars. At this writing, the spread of capitalism in Russia is producing a middle class, and it is they who took to the streets at the beginning of 2012 to protest the autocratic Putin regime with its corrupt boyar partners. But a national poll two months later showed that a majority—59 percent—of the respondents still preferred to have a "father of the nation" to an "efficient manager" as head of state. "Efficient manager" was more popular among well-to-do respondents, while "father of the nation" led among the poor and the elderly, so it is possible that patrimonialism will die out as money spreads across the population and the older generation leaves the scene.[45] Will Russia's continued evolution toward a marketized money economy eventually erode traditional Russian political practices of clan and client? Or was my friend Nikolai right to believe that regardless of the spread of a capitalist market economy, Russian traditions and political practices would never change? So far, the question is open.

Most political commentators in Russia still believe that this is an either/or situation. As a recent editorial in a major newspaper put it, "two systems of institutions exist. The first ensures loyalty through behind-the-scenes agreements and corruption, the second through a high level of legitimacy acquired through fair elections. The development of either of these systems is impossible without dismantling the alternative."[46] But it is also not impossible to imagine the new middle class achieving fair elections while Russia continues to be ruled by political cultures and practices of person and clan for a long time. Theorists of neotraditionalism argue that archaic and modern elements can coexist in the same system. Stephen Smith wrote that the Soviet period, "the primary elements of Marxism could fuse with elements that were quite alien to it."[47]

Some argue that patrimonial, clientelist networks are not just a continuing integral part of the Russian political and social system, but in fact keep the state alive for their own purposes. They are not merely warts on the body of the state, or problematic to it; they rather use a state to govern. Or, in another sense, they *are* the state: "For the most part, the network-based governance defines what the current Russian state is, in effect, all about."[48] For the clan networks, the state can be seen as a tool to mobilize the population and to provide a façade of legitimacy. Indeed, states in general may be seen "as organizations of supply for the cliques they contain, rather than the other way round."[49] Personal power undergoes "statization;" the state apparently exists but is actually the embodiment of a personalized politics.[50]

The observation that state institutions are ephemeral is not new, nor is it specific to Russia. Timothy Mitchell argued that state structures are really "effects" of practices that lie behind them. In his view, a state institution should be viewed "not as an actual structure, but the powerful, metaphysical effect of practices that make such structures appear to exist. . . . an entity comes to seem something much more than the sum of the everyday activities that constitute it."[51] For Oleg Kharkhordin, the state does not exist "in empirical reality," but is rather a label to describe certain actions of individuals.[52] Foucault argued much the same thing; the state for him is "nothing more than a composite reality and mythicized abstraction" of polyvalent and diverse relations of force. For Pierre Bourdieu, "The notion of 'the state' makes sense only as a convenient stenographic label . . . that can take the form of more or less stable networks (of alliance, cooperation, clientelism, mutual service, etc.) and which manifest themselves in phenomenally diverse interactions ranging from open conflict to more or less hidden collusion."[53]

It would be far too simple to argue that Putin's Russia (or Stalin's, for that matter) was nothing more than a continuation of old Russia. It is not. Russia under either Stalin or Putin has had completely different ideologies, social structures, and economies than before. Over the twentieth century it became a literate and educated society, more or less integrated into world culture. These changes are dramatic. Seen in these terms, modern Russia or the USSR could not be more different from old Muscovy.

On the other hand, to focus on the important sphere of *practices* illuminates things from a different angle. There are watersheds aplenty in Russian history. It is perhaps all the more surprising when we find the persistence of practices across all these divides. But it seems that through the comings and goings of ideological, social, and economic trends, certain political practices persisted and spanned apparent watersheds. Maybe we are dealing here with "deep structures" of Russian history, as Keenan suggested. Maybe it's a matter of the ingrained "habits of thought and action" that E. P. Thompson described in another context.

It is still hard not to agree on some level with Kizevetter, whose observation began this book: "You cannot rid yourself of the impression that European Russia is growing from the debris of the devastated past. . . . [But] from the half-faded pages of these documents, through the outer shell of the jargon, old Muscovite Russia gazes upon you, having successfully stepped over the threshold . . . and settled comfortably with the new framework."

Notes

The following archive abbreviations are used in the notes.

AP RF   Archive of the President of the Russian Federation (Arkhiv prezidenta rossiiskoi federatsii)

GARF   State Archive of the Russian Federation (Gosudarstvennyi arkhiv rossiiskoi federatsii), Moscow

RGANI   Russian State Archive of Contemporary History (Rossiiskii gosudarstvennii arkhiv noveishei istorii), Moscow

RGASPI   Russian State Archive of Socio-Political History (Rossiiskii gosudarstvennyi arkhiv sotsial'no-politicheskoi istorii), Moscow

Smolensk Archive   Records of the All-Union Communist Party, Smolensk District, 1917–41.

TsA FSB   Central Archive of the Federal Security Service (Tsentral'nyi arkhiv Federal'noi sluzhby bezopasnosti), Moscow

Introduction

Epigraph: A. A. Kizevetter, quoted in Iurii M. Lotman and Boris A. Uspenskii, "Binary Models in the Dynamics of Russian Culture," in *The Semiotics of Russian Cultural History*, ed. Alexander D. Nakhimovsky and Alice Stone Nakhimovsky (Ithaca, N.Y.: Cornell University Press, 1985), 61.

1. Here and elsewhere in this work, "charismatic" is used in the Weberian sense: a type of authority drawing power from connection to something transcendent or supernatural not available to other persons.

2. I take the term "deep structures" from Edward Keenan, "Muscovite Political Folkways," *Russian Review* 45, no. 2 (1986): 115–81. See also Lotman and Uspenskii, "Binary Models."

3. Based on parameters suggested by Ken Jowitt in "Neotraditionalism," in *New World Disorder: the Leninist Extinction* (Berkeley, University of California Press, 1992).

4. One always stands on the shoulders of giants. I first began to reflect on personalized power reading Graeme Gill, *The Origins of the Stalinist Political System* (Cambridge: Cambridge University Press, 1990). Based only on the published sources available at the time, Gill argued that personalized power reflected a low level of institutionalization that was therefore separate from and in contradiction with the institutional system. The argument of this book is different in that it stresses persistence of patrimonial power from Russian history and suggests that it was itself an "institution" at the center of the system.

5. T. H. Rigby, "Russia's Clientelism, Cliques, Connections and 'Clans': The Same Old Story?" *Soviet and Post-Soviet Review* 25, no. 2 (1998): 119. Rigby believes that today, although "personal links remain a major factor in national-level politics," clientelism is weakening and perhaps fading away. This study suggests that it might be too early to tell.

6. "Kings, princes, and lesser rulers in patrimonial politics invoked the vision of patrilineage—a line extending back into the past and forward to the future, and composed of their ancestors and desired descendants—to appeal for allegiance." Julia Adams, "The Rule of the Father: Patriarchy and Patrimonialism in Early Modern Europe," in *Max Weber's Economy and Society: A Critical Companion,* ed. Charles Camic, Philip S. Gorski, and David M. Trubek (Stanford, Calif.: Stanford University Press, 2005), 242–43.

7. Max Weber, *Economy and Society: An Outline of Interpretive Sociology* (New York: Bedminster Press, 1968), 1005–59.

8. Kenneth Jowitt, *Revolutionary Breakthroughs and National Development: The Case of Romania, 1944–1965* (Berkeley: University of California Press, 1971), 69.

9. For an exploration of patriarchy and masculinity that adapts Saussure's "signs" to Weber, see Adams, "The Rule of the Father."

10. Gerald Easter, *Reconstructing the State: Personal Networks and Elite Identity in Soviet Russia* (Cambridge: Cambridge University Press, 2000); Gill, *Origins of the Stalinist Political System;* J. Hughes, "Patrimonialism and the Stalinist System—the Case of Syrtsov, S. I.," *Europe-Asia Studies* 48, no. 4 (1996): 551–68; O. Khlevniuk, *Master of the House: Stalin and His Inner Circle* (New Haven Conn.: Yale University Press, 2008); Y. Gorlizki, "Ordinary Stalinism: The Council of Ministers and the Soviet Neopatrimonial State, 1946–1953," *Journal of Modern History* 74, no. 4 (2002): 699–736.

11. Max Weber, *Max Weber on Law in Economy and Society* (Cambridge, Mass.: Harvard University Press, 1954), 351.

12. Max Weber, *The Theory of Social and Economic Organizations* (New York: Oxford University Press, 1947), 328.

13. Ibid., 328; Max Weber, *From Max Weber: Essays in Sociology* (New York: Oxford University Press, 1947), 253; Weber, *Weber on Law,* 336–37, 351.

14. Christopher Clapham, "Clientelism and the State," in *Private Patronage and Public Power,* ed. Christopher Clapham (New York: St. Martin's Press, 1982), 26.

15. Jean-Francois Medard, "The Underdeveloped State in Tropical Africa: Political Clientelism or Neo-Patrimonialism?," in Clapham, *Private Patronage and Public Power,* 162. See also Clapham, "Clientelism and the State," 19.

16. Medard, "Underdeveloped State," 181. See also S. N. Eisenstadt and L. Roniger, *Patrons, Clients, and Friends: Interpersonal Relations and the Structure of Trust in Society* (Cambridge: Cambridge University Press, 1984); René Lemarchand, "Comparative Political Clientelism: Structure, Process and Optic," in S. N. Eisenstadt and René Lemarchand, *Political Clientelism, Patronage and Development,* vol. 3: *Contemporary Political Sociology* (London: Sage, 1981), 7–34.

17. Carl Lande, "The Dyadic Basis of Clientelism," in *Friends, Followers, and Factions: A Reader in Political Clientelism,* ed. Steffen W. Schmidt et al. (Berkeley: University of California Press, 1977), xviii.

18. Alex Weingrod, "Patrons, Patronage, and Political Parties," in Schmidt et al., *Friends, Followers, and Factions,* 326; Medard, "Political Clientelism in France," 126–27. See also James C. Scott and Benedict J. Kerkvliet, "How Traditional Rural Patrons Lose Legitimacy: A Theory with Special Reference to Southeast Asia," in Schmidt et al., *Friends, Followers, and Factions,* 439–58.

19. Eric R. Wolf, "Kinship, Friendship, and Patron-Client Relations in Complex Societies," in Schmidt et al., *Friends, Followers, and Factions,* 168.

20. Eisenstadt and Roniger, *Patrons, Clients, and Friends,* 28. See also Jean-Francois Medard, "Political Clientelism in France: The Center-Periphery Nexus Reexamined," in Eisenstadt and Lemarchand, *Political Clientelism, Patronage and Development,* 3:126–27; Lande, "The Dyadic Basis of Clientelism," xviii; Weingrod, "Patrons, Patronage, and Political Parties," 326; Eric R. Wolf, "Kinship, Friendship, and Patron-Client Relations in Complex Societies," ibid., 168. For the Soviet period, Stephen White has argued for decoupling economic modernization from political arrangements: Stephen White, *Political Culture and Soviet Politics* (London: Macmillan, 1979).

21. "The Soviet Russian case was an early model of a process in which personalistic patterns of political authority and organization were adapted to new formal-legalistic structures within the institutional framework of hastily constructed post-colonial states." Gerald Easter, *Reconstructing the State: Personal Networks and Elite Identity in Soviet Russia* (Cambridge: Cambridge University Press, 2000), 173–74. The argument of this book is the converse: that institutions were adapted to personalistic patterns.

22. Gill, *Origins of the Stalinist Political System,* 198; Easter, *Reconstructing the State;* White, *Political Culture.*

23. Joseph Berliner, *Factory and Manager in the USSR* (Cambridge, Mass.: Harvard University Press, 1957); Merle Fainsod, *Smolensk Under Soviet Rule* (Cambridge, Mass.: Harvard University Press, 1958).

24. White, *Political Culture,* esp. chap. 8.

25. Kenneth Jowitt, "Neotraditionalism: The Political Corruption of a Leninist Regime," *Soviet Studies* 35, no. 3 (1983): 275–97. Jowitt argued for the persistence of charismatic authority in the Soviet period, believing that the party "substituted"

for a charismatic person. See also T. Martin, "Modernization or Neo-Traditionalism? Ascribed Nationality and Soviet Primordialism," in *Stalinism: New Directions,* ed. Sheila Fitzpatrick (New York: Routledge, 2000), 348–67.

26. For examples, see Carl J. Friedrich, and Zbigniew K. Brzezinski, *Totalitarian Dictatorship and Autocracy,* 2d rev. ed., ed. Carl J. Friedrich (New York: Praeger, 1966), xvi, 439; Hannah Arendt, *The Origins of Totalitarianism,* new ed. (New York: Harcourt Brace Jovanovich, 1973), xliii, 527; Merle Fainsod, *How Russia is Ruled,* Russian Research Center Studies, 11, rev. ed. (Cambridge, Mass.: Harvard University Press, 1967), ix, 698.

27. Gabor Rittersporn, "The State Against Itself: Social Tensions and Political Conflicts in the USSR, 1936–1938," *Telos* 41 (1979): 87–104; J. Arch Getty, *Origins of the Great Purges: The Soviet Communist Party Reconsidered, 1933–1938* (Cambridge: Cambridge University Press, 1985), viii, 276; Lynne Viola, "The 25,000ers: A Study in a Soviet Recruitment Campaign During the First Five Year Plan," *Russian History* 10 (1983): 1–30; Moshe Lewin, *The Making of the Soviet System: Essays in the Social History of Interwar Russia* (New York: New Press, 1994), xi, 354; Sheila Fitzpatrick, *Education and Social Mobility in the Soviet Union, 1921–1934,* Soviet and East European Studies, No. 27 (Cambridge: Cambridge University Press, 1979), x, 355; Sheila Fitzpatrick, "New Perspectives on Stalinism," *Russian Review* 45 (1986): 357–413.

28. See, for example, David L. Hoffmann and Yanni Kotsonis, eds., *Russian Modernity: Politics, Knowledge, Practices* (New York: St. Martin's Press, 2000); Peter Holquist, "'Information Is the Alpha and Omega of Our Work': Bolshevik Surveillance in Its Pan-European Context," *Journal of Modern History* 69, no. 3 (1997): 415–50; Stephen Kotkin, "Modern Times: The Soviet Union and the Interwar Conjuncture," *Kritika* 2, no. 1 (2001): 111–64; Amir Weiner, *Making Sense of War: The Second World War and the Fate of the Bolshevik Revolution* (Princeton, N.J.: Princeton University Press, 2001); Igal Halfin, *From Darkness To Light: Class, Consciousness, and Salvation in Revolutionary Russia* (Pittsburgh, Pa.: University of Pittsburgh Press, 2000).

29. Lewin, *The Making of the Soviet System.*

30. Richard Wortman, *Scenarios of Power: Myth and Ceremony in Russian Monarchy from Peter the Great to the Abdication of Nicholas II* (Princeton, N.J.: Princeton University Press, 2006), 4.

31. Lotman and Uspenskii, "Binary Models," 31–36. Emphasis in the original.

32. The work of Boris Groys, stressing continuities in art, led to this revision.

33. Boris Souvarine, *Stalin, a Critical Survey of Bolshevism* (New York: Longmans, 1939), 510.

34. R. C. Tucker, *Stalin in Power: The Revolution from Above, 1928–1941* (New York: Norton, 1990).

35. For a concise statement of Hellie's thesis, see Richard Hellie, "The Structure of Imperial Russian History," *History and Theory* 44 (December 2005): 88–112.

36. Robert V. Daniels, "Russian Political Culture and the Post-Revolutionary Impasse," *Russian Review* 46, no. 2 (1987): 174.

37. V. A. Kozlov, "Sheila Fitzpatrick: Russian Context," in *Writing the Stalin Era: Sheila Fitzpatrick and Soviet Historiography,* ed. Golfo Alexopoulos, Julie Hessler, and Kiril Tomoff (New York: Palgrave Macmillan, 2011), 222.

38. Richard Pipes, *Russia under the Bolshevik Regime,* 1st ed. (New York: Knopf, 1993), 503.

39. Keenan, "Muscovite Political Folkways," 171.

40. Classical "feudalism" in the West was different in ways that need not detain us here. Russia's system resembled it insofar as it involved pledges of service in return for protection and favor.

41. Any male descended from the legendary Viking founder Riurik was a prince. Any male descended from one of his retainers, or princes and boyar serving men from annexed territories, or those with special merits became a boyar.

42. Geoffrey Hosking, *Russia and the Russians: A History* (Cambridge, Mass.: Harvard University Press, 2001), 92–93.

43. Nancy Shields Kollmann, "Muscovite Patrimonialism," in *Major Problems in the History of Imperial Russia,* rd. James Cracraft (Lexington, Mass.: D. C. Heath, 1994), 41–42.

44. Trotsky argued that the Bolshevik bureaucracy created Stalin's power for their own purposes. For his analysis of the Stalin regime see Robert H. McNeal, "Trotskyist Interpretations of Stalinism," in *Stalinism: Essays in Historical Interpretation,* ed. Robert C. Tucker (New Brunswick, N.J.: Transaction Publishers, 1999), 30–52.

45. J. A. Getty, "Afraid of Their Shadows: The Bolshevik Recourse to Terror, 1932–1938," in *Stalinismus vor dem Zweiten Weltkrieg: Neue Wege der Forschung,* ed. Manfred Hildermeier and Elisabeth Mueller-Luckner (Munich: Historisches Kolleg, 1998), 169–92.

46. See, for example, Easter, *Reconstructing the State*; Getty, *Origins of the Great Purges;* James R. Harris, *The Great Urals: Regionalism and the Evolution of the Soviet System* (Ithaca, N.Y.: Cornell University Press, 1999).

47. Reinhard Bendix, *Max Weber: An Intellectual Portrait* (Garden City, N.Y.: Doubleday, 1960), 347–51.

48. Pierre Bourdieu, *Outline of a Theory of Practice* (Cambridge: Cambridge University Press, 1977), 79. It is possible, but in my view unlikely, that the Bolsheviks' Muscovite forebears were equally unconscious of the functional purposes of their practices.

49. Souvarine, *Stalin,* 510.

50. There is a substantial anthropological literature on practices, much of which separates practices from modernization, class, or economic development. The purpose of this book is not to apply or test any particular theory, although we will have occasional reference to Bourdieu's observations. To sample the literature, see Bourdieu, *Outline of a Theory of Practice*; T. M. S. Evens and Don Handelman, eds., *The Manchester School: Practice and Ethnographic Praxis in Anthropology* (Oxford: Berghahn, 2006); Theodore Schatzki, Karin Knorr Cetina, and Eike Von Savigny, eds., *The Practice Turn in Contemporary Theory* (London: Routledge, 2001); Victor Turner, *The Forest of Symbols* (Ithaca, N.Y.: Cornell University Press, 1967); Marshall Sahlins, *Historical Metaphors and Mythical Realities: Structure in the Early History of the Sandwich Islands Kingdom* (Ann Arbor: University of Michigan Press, 1981); Talcott Parsons and Edward Shils, eds., *Toward a General Theory of Action* (New York: Harper and Row, 1962; Jürgen Habermas, *Theory and Practice,* trans. John Viertel (Boston: Beacon Press, 1973); Anthony

Giddens, *Central Problems in Social Theory: Action, Structure and Contradiction in Social Analysis* (Cambridge: Cambridge University Press, 1979); Michel Foucault, *Discipline and Punish: The Birth of the Prison* (New York: Random House, 1979). A very useful survey is Sherry Ortner, "Theory in Anthropology since the Sixties," *Comparative Studies in Society and History* 26, no. 1 (1984): 126–66. Many of these studies are highly theoretical; for a critique by a historian, see E. P. Thompson. *The Poverty of Theory and Other Essays* (New York: Vintage, 1978).

51. For excellent examples see Zygmunt Bauman, *Modernity and the Holocaust* (Cambridge: Polity Press, 1989); David Hoffman, *Stalinist Values: The Cultural Norms of Soviet Modernity, 1917–1941* (Ithaca, N.Y.: Cornell University Press, 2003), and *Cultivating the Masses: Soviet Social Intervention in Its International Context, 1914–1939* (Ithaca, N.Y.: Cornell University Press, 2011); Hoffman and Kotsonis, *Russian Modernity*'; Holquist, "'Information Is the Alpha and Omega of Our Work,'" 415–50; Kotkin, "Modern Times"; Weiner, *Making Sense of War*.

52. See, for example, Molotov's account of theoretical arguments with Stalin: Feliks Ivanovich Chuev, *Sto sorok besed s Molotovym: Iz dnevnika F. Chueva* (Moscow: Terra, 1991), 491–92.

53. "Korea, North," in *The World Factbook 2011,* www.cia.gov/library/publications/the-world-factbook/geos/kn.html.

54. On heresy and the opposition see Igal Halfin, *Intimate Enemies: Demonizing the Bolshevik Opposition, 1918–1928* (Pittsburgh, Pa.: University of Pittsburgh Press, 2007).

55. Tim McDaniel, *The Agony of the Russian Idea* (Princeton, N.J.: Princeton University Press, 1996), 90–99.

56. Daniel T. Orlovsky, "Political Clientelism in Russia: the Historical Perspective," in *Leadership Selection and Patron-Client Relations in the USSR and Yugoslavia,* ed. T. H. Rigby and Bogdan Harasymiw (London: Allen & Unwn, 1983), 197.

57. Jowitt, "Neotraditionalism," 279.

58. Graeme Gill, *Origins of the Stalinist Political System,* 104.

59. Merle Fainsod, *Smolensk Under Soviet Rule* (Cambridge, Mass.: Harvard University Press, 1958).

60. See the detailed treatment of contemporary usage of "clan" in Michael Urban, "Forms of Civil Society: Politics and Social Relations in Russia," *International Political Anthropology* 1, no. 1 (2008): 102–8.

61. On pre-Soviet elite continuities, see Keenan, "Muscovite Political Folkways"; Daniels, "Russian Political Culture and the Post-Revolutionary Impasse," 169; Geoffrey Hosking, "Patronage and the Russian State," *Slavonic and East European Review* 78, no. 2 (2000): 301–20; Jowitt, *New World Disorder*; David Ransel, "Character and Style of Patron-Client Relations in Russia," in *Klientelsysteme im Europa der frühen Neuzeit,* ed. Antoni Maczak and Elisabeth Mueller-Luckner (Munich: Oldenbourg, 1988), 211–31.

62. I. V. Stalin, *Sochineniia,* vol. 10 (Moscow: Gosizdat, 1953), 329–33. My thanks to James Harris for pointing this out to me.

63. "Materialy fevral'skogo-martovskogo plenuma TsK VKP(b) 1937 goda," *Voprosy Istorii,* no. 5 (1993): 12. *Sgovor* can also mean "betrothal."

CHAPTER 1. THE OLD AND THE NEW

Epigraph: Iurii M. Lotman and Boris A. Uspenskii, "Binary Models in the Dynamics of Russian Culture," in *The Semiotics of Russian Cultural History,* ed. Alexander D. Nakhimovsky and Alice Stone Nakhimovsky (Ithaca, N.Y.: Cornell University Press, 1985), 65–66.

1. Richard Pipes, *Russia under the Old Regime* (New York: Scribner, 1974), 111.
2. I have discussed the structure, uses and abuses of more official texts in J. Arch Getty and Oleg V. Naumov, *The Road to Terror: Stalin and the Self-Destruction of the Bolsheviks, 1932–1939,* trans. Benjamin Sher (New Haven, Conn.: Yale University Press, 1999).
3. These letters' effects, or lack of them, have been debated. See G. Alexopoulos, *Stalin's Outcasts: Aliens, Citizens, and the Soviet State, 1926–1936* (Ithaca, N.Y.: Cornell University Press, 2003); G. Alexopoulos, "Exposing Illegality and One-self: Complaint and Risk in Stalin's Russia," in *Reforming Justice in Russia, 1864–1996,* ed. Peter Solomon (Armonk, N.Y.: M. E. Sharpe, 1997), 168–89; G. Alexopoulos, "The Ritual Lament: A Narrative of Appeal in the 1920s and 1930s," *Russian History–Histoire Russe* 24, no. 1–2 (1997): 117–29; S. Davies, "The 'Cult' of the Vozhd: Representations in Letters, 1934–1941," ibid., 131–47; Sheila Fitzpatrick, "Readers' Letters to *Krest'ianskaia Gazeta,* 1938," ibid., 149–70; Sheila Fitzpatrick, "Signals from Below: Soviet Letters of Denunciation of the 1930s," *Journal of Modern History* 68, no. 4 (1996): 831–67; Sheila Fitzpatrick, "The Letter as a Work of Art: A Housing Claim in the Style of an *Anketa,*" *Russian History–Histoire Russe* 24, no. 1–2 (1997): 189–202; Sheila Fitzpatrick, "Suppli-cants and Citizens: Public Letter-Writing in Soviet Russia in the 1930s," *Slavic Review,* 55, no. 1 (1996): 78–105; L. Siegelbaum, "Introduction," in *Stalinism as a Way of Life: A Narrative in Documents* (New Haven, Conn.: Yale University Press, 2000), 1–27.
4. David Ransel, "Character and Style of Patron-Client Relations in Russia," in *Klientelsysteme im Europa der frühen Neuzeit,* ed. Antoni Maczak and Elisabeth Mueller-Luckner (Munich: Oldenbourg, 1988), 225–31.
5. See Horace Dewey, "Russia's Debt to the Mongols in Suretyship and Collective Responsibility," *Comparative Studies in Society and History* 30, no. 2 (1988): 268. For an analysis of ancient *chelobitnye,* see Horace Dewey and A. M. Kleimola, "The Petition (*čelobitnaja*) as an Old Russian Literary Genre," *Slavic and East European Journal* 14, no. 3 (1970): 284–301. See also Horace Dewey and A. M. Kleimola, eds., *Russian Private Law, XIV–XVII Centuries: An Anthology of Documents* (Ann Arbor: University of Michigan Press, 1973), 1–27.
6. L. V. Danilova, E. I. Indova, N. V. Gorbushina, eds., *Krest'ianskie chelobitnye XVII v.: Iz sobranii Gosudarstvennogo Istoricheskogo Muzeia* (Moscow: Nauka, 1994), 220.
7. Alexopoulos, "Ritual Lament," 119, 121.
8. Stephen White, *Political Culture and Soviet Politics* (London: Macmillan, 1979), 108. Jeffrey Brooks, *"Thank You, Comrade Stalin!": Soviet Public Culture from Revolution to Cold War* (Princeton, N.J.: Princeton University Press, 2000) contains an excellent discussion of the patrimonial view of Stalin.

9. Alena V. Ledeneva, *Russia's Economy of Favors: Blat, Networking, and Informal Exchange* (Cambridge: Cambridge University Press, 1998), 85.

10. H. A. Lytkin to Stalin, 15 December 1943. RGASPI, f. 558, op. 11, d. 884, l. 102.

11. Sh. Zhienkulova to Stalin, 19 January 1943. RGASPI, f. 558, op. 11, d. 884, l. 46.

12. Academician L. A. Orbeli to Stalin, 21 June 1942. RGASPI, f. 558, op. 11, d. 883, l. 65.

13. Antonova to Molotov, 11 May 1953. RGASPI, f. 82, op. 2, d. 1440, l. 78.

14. D. Vinogradova to Molotov, 2 October 1937. RGASPI, f. 82, op. 2, d. 1443, l. 60.

15. Brat'ev to Stalin, n.d. RGASPI, f. 558, op. 11, d. 883, ll. 7–8.

16. Siegelbaum and Sokolov, *Stalinism as a Way of Life*, 130.

17. Dewey and Kleimola, "Petition," 286.

18. Natalie Zemon Davis, *Fiction in the Archives: Pardon Tales and Their Tellers in Sixteenth-Century France* (Stanford, Calif.: Stanford University Press, 1987), 3.

19. Siegelbaum and Sokolov, *Stalinism as a Way of Life.* 176–77.

20. "Mother of Iosif Rodionovich Ananasenko" to Stalin, 25 September 1943. RGASPI, f. 558, op. 11, d. 884, l. 7.

21. V. A. Kozlov, "Denunciation and Its Functions in Soviet Governance: From the Archive of the Ministry of Internal Affairs, 1944–53," in *Stalinism: New Directions,* ed. Sheila Fitzpatrick (London: Routledge, 2000), 130.

22. Dewey and Kleimola, "Petition," 288, 291.

23. Antonova to Molotov, 11 May 1953. RGASPI, f. 82, op. 2, d. 1440, l. 78.

24. Dewey and Kleimola, "Petition," 285.

25. Sh. Zhienkulova to Stalin, 19 January 1943. RGASPI, f. 558, op. 11, d. 884, l. 49.

26. Siegelbaum and Sokolov, *Stalinism as a Way of Life,* 132.

27. Brooks, *"Thank You, Comrade Stalin!"* xx, 319. Nancy Shields Kollman has shown that the reality of politics was that individuals sought favors "not from representative bodies, but from the personal source of all power and benefits." Nancy Shields Kollmann. "Muscovite Patrimonialism," in *Major Problems in the History of Imperial Russia,* ed. James Cracraft (Lexington, Mass.: D. C. Heath, 1994), 45.

28. Frank J. Miller, *Folklore for Stalin: Russian Folklore and Pseudofolklore of the Stalin Era* (Armonk, N.Y.: M. E. Sharpe, 1990), 41–42.

29. Vladimir Slepak, "Davai vpered, Vladimir Putin!" [Onward, Vladimir Putin!] (Song and video, January 2012). Translation by Kevin M. F. Platt.

30. The following song examples are taken from Y. M. Sokolov. *Russian Folklore* (New York: Macmillan, 1950), 635, 671–73.

31. See Miller, *Folklore for Stalin.*

32. See, for examples, S. N. Azbelev, ed., *Narodnaia proza* (Moscow: Akademiia Nauk, 1992); B. N. Putilov, *Petr velikii v predaniiakh, legendakh, anekdotakh, skazkakh i pesniakh* (Moscow: Akademiia Nauk, 2000).

33. In the *mestnichestvo* ("place order") ranking system, which was a written document, one's precedence and therefore power were calculated according to

genealogy, 'previous positions, and relative standing within a clan. For an example of *mestnichestvo* in practice, see A. M. Kleimola, "Boris Godunov and the Politics of Mestnichestvo," *Slavonic and East European Review* 53, no. 132 (July 1975): 355–69.

34. Membership in a soviet, including the national or Supreme Soviet brought no political power, insofar as these were not decision-making bodies and rarely met. Nevertheless, members of soviets at all levels had power to use their status and the influence it brought to get things done for constituents: repairing streets and schools, providing better community services, etc.

35. Stalin to Kaganovich, 4 September 1931. RGASPI, f. 81, op. 3, d. 99, ll. 16–19. Stalin's double underlining.

36. Stalin to Kaganovich and Molotov, 26 October 1935. RGASPI, f. 558, op. 11, d. 92, l. 72. Emphasis Stalin's.

37. Stalin to Kaganovich and Molotov, 26 September 1934. RGASPI, f. 558, op. 11, d. 58, l. 83.

38. "Ukaz Prezidenta Rossiiskoi Federatsii ot 7 sentiabria 2010g. N1099, O merakh po sovershenstvovaniiu gosudarstvennoi nagradnoi sistemy Rossiiskoi Federatsii," *Rossiiskaia gazeta, Federal'nyi vypusk*, no. 5286 (207).

39. Vladimir Shlapentokh, *Contemporary Russia as a Feudal Society: A New Perspective on the Post-Soviet Era* (New York: Palgrave Macmillan, 2007), 130.

40. See, for example, Zygmunt Bauman, *Modernity and the Holocaust* (Cambridge: Polity Press, 1989), xiv, 224; and David Hoffman, *Stalinist Values: The Cultural Norms of Soviet Modernity, 1917–1941* (Ithaca, N.Y.: Cornell University Press, 2003).

41. *Pravda,* 9 June 1934.

42. Ivo Banac, ed., *The Diary of Georgi Dimitrov, 1933–1949* (New Haven, Conn.: Yale University Press, 2003). Entry for 7 November 1937.

43. Dewey, "Russia's Debt," 251.

44. For a discussion of confession and the communist "soul," see Igal Halfin, *Terror in My Soul : Communist Autobiographies on Trial* (Cambridge, Mass.: Harvard University Press, 2003), xi, 344.

45. RGASPI, f. 671, op. 1, d. 273, ll. 1–65.

46. Kotolynov's testimony in RGASPI, f. 671, op. 1, d. 128, ll. 62–72.

47. See Zinoviev's interrogation. RGASPI, f. 671, op. 1, d. 134, ll. 164–65.

48. RGASPI, f. 17, op. 2, d. 575, ll. 69–74, 82–86.

49. *Voprosy istorii,* no. 2 (1993): 17, 20–21, 26; ibid., nos. 6–7 (1992): 4, 16–17.

50. "Zasluzhennyi prigovor," 4 August 1936. RGASPI, f. 671, op. 1, d. 172, ll. 497, 525.

51. Rykov's speech to the December 1936 TsK Plenum. RGASPI, f. 17, op. 2, d. 575, ll. 94–97, 100–104.

52. *Istochnik,* no. 0 [*sic*] (1993): 23–25.

53. Robert Service, *Stalin: A Biography* (Cambridge, Mass.: Harvard University Press, 2005), 340–41.

54. Dewey, "Russia's Debt," 256–58.

55. Horace Dewey, "Political *Poruka* in Muscovite Rus,'" *Russian Review,* 46 no. 2 (1987): 118, 128–29.

56. Dewey, "Political *Poruka*," 118, 121.

57. Ibid., 124.

58. Horace Dewey, "Suretyship and Collective Responsibility in pre-Petrine Russia," *Jahrbücher für Geschichte Osteuropas* 18, no. 3 (1970): 348.

59. "Where the interests of the monarch were concerned, no distinction was drawn between the intention to commit a crime and the deed itself." Richard Pipes, *Russia under the Bolshevik Regime,* 1st ed. (New York: Knopf, 1993), 109.

60. For a history of *krugovaia poruka,* see Alena V. Ledeneva, "The Genealogy of *Krugovaia Poruka:* Forced Trust as a Feature of Russian Political Culture," in *Trust and Democratic Transition in Post-Communist Europe,* ed. Ivana Markova (New York: Oxford University Press, 2004), 85–108.

61. Ransel, "Character and Style of Patron-Client Relations in Russia," 216, 221.

62. Ledeneva, "The Genealogy of *Krugovaia Poruka,*" 107.

63. Pipes, *Russia under the Old Regime,* 109.

64. See Hiroaki Kuromiya, "*Edinonachalie* and the Soviet Industrial Manager, 1928–1937," *Soviet Studies* 36, no. 2 (1984): 185–204, and his *Stalin's Industrial Revolution: Politics and Workers, 1928–1932* (Cambridge: Cambridge University Press, 1988).

65. See V. A. Kozlov, "Denunciation and Its Functions in Soviet Governance: A Study of Denunciations and Their Bureaucratic Handling from Soviet Police Archives," in *Accusatory Practices: Denunciation in Modern European History, 1789–1989,* ed. S. Fitzpatrick and R. Gellately (Chicago: University of Chicago Press, 1997), 121–52.

66. Ledeneva, "Genealogy of *Krugovaia Poruka,*" 104–7.

67. "It is not that the Bolsheviks wanted to copy tsarist practices: on the contrary, they wanted to have nothing in common with them, to do the very opposite. They emulated them by force of circumstances." Pipes, *Russia under the Bolshevik Regime,* 506.

68. Feliks Ivanovich Chuev, *Sto sorok besed s Molotovym: Iz dnevnika F. Chueva* (Moscow: Terra, 1991), 315.

69. Don K. Rowney, *Transition to Technocracy: the Structural Origins of the Soviet Administrative State* (Ithaca, N.Y.: Cornell University Press, 1989).

70. Marx was the first to call the communists "midwives of history," but the phrase was used often by Lenin and Trotsky.

71. Trotsky was the exception in the 1920s when he took Politburo disputes public; although one of the elite, he broke ranks. More than support for Stalin, this explains the exceptionally sharp reaction against him by other Old Bolsheviks. For this elite solidarity, see J. Getty and Naumov, *The Road to Terror.*

72. The periodical *Proletarskaia revoliutsiia* and the *Granat* encyclopedia were examples of collected Old Bolshevik hagiography.

73. Graeme Gill called them "the chosen ones." Graeme Gill, *The Origins of the Stalinist Political System* (Cambridge: Cambridge University Press, 1990), 104.

74. TsKK Protocol, 19 March 1921. RGASPI, f. 613, op. 1, d. 2, l. 6. This distinction between the Bolshevik nobility and the party masses was a subject not to be broached, and when the Opposition did it, they were accused of setting the rank and file against the leadership in order to split the party. This was the accusation against

Trotsky when he publicly criticized and organized street demonstrations against the Stalinist leadership. The same sin was committed by the authors of the 1932 Riutin Platform when they called for the party rank and file to rise up against the *nomenklatura*. See Getty and Naumov, *The Road to Terror*, 53–62. Later, in 1937, Stalin would himself use the same dangerous tactic when he mobilized the rank and file against party bureaucrats with a *kritika/samokritika* campaign. See Wendy Z. Goldman, *Terror and Democracy in the Age of Stalin: The Social Dynamics of Repression* (Cambridge: Cambridge University Press, 2007), and J. Arch Getty, *Origins of the Great Purges: The Soviet Communist Party Reconsidered, 1933–1938* (Cambridge: Cambridge University Press, 1985), for this "party democracy movement."

75. "O dachakh otvetstvennykh rabotnikov," Politburo resolution, drafted by Stalin, of 9 February 1938. RGASPI, f. 17, op. 3, d. 995, l. 21. The resolution established a limit of "7–8 average-sized rooms" for personal dachas. Dachas larger than that were to be confiscated. Even before this resolution, Nikita Khrushchev remembered that although he was first secretary of the Moscow party committee in the 1930s, he had no dacha of his own. He shared a single rest home building, dividing up rooms and floors with Bulganin and several Moscow party district secretaries. N. Khrushchev, *Memoirs of Nikita Khrushchev*, vol. 1: *Commissar (1918–1945)* (University Park: Pennsylvania State University Press, 2004), 105–6. Presumably the modest Stalin liked this.

76. See, for example, "Spisok tt. proshudshikh cherez Uchraspred TsK," RGASPI, f. 17, op. 34, d. 216, ll. 47–64; "Spisok sekretarei, zavorgov, zavagitpropov, pred. GIK i pred. GSPS," RGASPI, f. 17, op. 34, d. 69, ll. 21–43.

77. Thus in December 1921, a party conference decided to require secretaries of provinces (gubkom secretaries) to have been party members before February 1917. But a shortage of personnel complicated the idea. By March 1922, only 73 percent of gorkom secretaries had been pre-February members, and at that time there was discussion about softening the requirement from membership before the February 1917 Revolution to before October 1917. April 1923 saw another call to enforce the February qualification, but by May 1924, the proportion had fallen to 68 percent. See *Dvenadtsatyi s"ezd RKP(b), 17–25 aprelia 1923 goda: Stenograficheskii otchet* (Moscow: Partizdat, 1960), 705, 790, 802; *Odinnadtsatyi s"ezd RKP(b), mart–aprel' 1922 goda: Stenograficheskii otchet* (Moscow: Partizdat, 1961), 49–50, 555, 659; *Trinadtsatyi s"ezd RKP(b), mai 1924 goda: Stenograficheskii otchet* (Moscow: Gosizdat, 1963), 118.

78. Pipes, *Russia under the Bolshevik Regime*, 97, 504–5.

79. Gill calls the Politburo and Orgburo "councils of organizational notables." Gill, *Origins of the Stalinist Political System*, 158.

80. T. H. Rigby, *Communist Party Membership in the USSR, 1917–1967* (Princeton, N.J.: Princeton University Press, 1968), 52.

81. Gill, *Origins of the Stalinist Political System*, 114–19.

82. V. I. Lenin, *Collected Works*, vol. 33 (Moscow: Gosizdat, 1965), 254–56.

83. Getty, *Origins of the Great Purges*, chaps. 2 and 3.

84. Lenin, *Collected Works*, 33:256.

85. Telegrams from Stalin to Mikoian, 23 February, 4 March, 17 March 1925. RGASPI, f. 558, op. 11, d. 33, ll. 43, 48, 56.

86. Stalin to Iagoda, 26 September 1936. RGASPI, f. 558, op. 11, d. 94, l. 131.

87. Pipes, *Russia under the Old Regime*, 91.

88. L. M. Kaganovich, *Pamiatnye zapiski rabochego, kommunista-bol'shevika, profsoiuznogo, partiinogo i sovetsko-gosudarstvennogo rabotnika* (Moscow: Vagrius, 1996), 312.

89. *Dvenadtsatyi s"ezd RKP(b)*, 198–99. Gosplan was the state planning administration charged with drawing up industrial targets.

90. Nadezhda Mandelshtam, *Hope Against Hope: A Memoir*, trans. Max Hayward (New York: Atheneum, 1970), 346, and *Vospominaniia* (Paris: YMCA Press, 1970), 366.

91. See, for example, a TsK report on the situation in Tula in RGASPI, f. 17, op. 11, d. 548, l. 184. A 1922 internal TsK report also used the word *mestnichestvo* to describe personal conflicts in Riazan, Simbirsk, Saratov, Astrakhan and elsewhere. RGASPI, f. 17, op. 11, d. 548, l. 24.

92. Nancy Shields Kollmann, *By Honor Bound: State and Society in Early Modern Russia* (Ithaca, N.Y.: Cornell University Press, 1999); Nancy Shields Kollmann, *Kinship and Politics: the Making of the Muscovite Political System, 1345–1547* (Stanford, Calif.: Stanford University Press, 1987); Paul Bushkovitch, *Peter the Great: the Struggle for Power, 1671–1725* (Cambridge: Cambridge University Press, 2001), xii, 485; Valerie A. Kivelson, *Autocracy in the Provinces: the Muscovite Gentry and Political Culture in the Seventeenth Century* (Stanford, Calif.: Stanford University Press, 176); R. O. Crummey, *Aristocrats and Servitors: the Boyar Elite in Russia, 1613–1689* (Princeton, N.J.: Princeton University Press, 1983).

93. Keenan, "Folkways," 156.

94. Rigby is surely right that cliques and clans were not invented by Stalin, but were rather a product of circumstances (and we might add, of history). T. H. Rigby, "Early Provincial Cliques and the Rise of Stalin," *Soviet Studies* 33 (1981): 25.

95. For the Malenkov-Zhdanov rivalry, see Jonathan Harris, *The Split in Stalin's Secretariat, 1939–1948* (New York: Lexington Books, 2008).

96. Harvard Project on the Soviet Social System, Schedule B, vol. 13, case 359, p. 3. Widener Library, Harvard University.

97. Stalin to the 17th Party Congress, *XVII s"ezd Vsesoiuznoi Kommunisticheskoi Partii (b), Stenograficheskii otchet* (Moscow: Partizdat, 1934), 33, 34–35.

98. See the discussion of refereeing in J. Arch Getty and Oleg V. Naumov, *Yezhov: The Rise of Stalin's "Iron Fist"* (New Haven, Conn.: Yale University Press, 2008).

99. Max Weber, *Max Weber on Law in Economy and Society* (Cambridge, Mass.: Harvard University Press, 1954), 43–44, 264, 266.

100. See Chapter 3 below.

101. For an example, see RGASPI, f. 17, op. 113, d. 236, l. 72.

102. Boris Bazhanov, *Vospominaniia byvshego sekretaria Stalina* (Saint Petersburg: Vsemirnoe slovo, 1992), 73.

103. Orgburo protocol of 7 October 1921. RGASPI, f. 17, op. 112, d. 177, ll. 2–3, 57–58.

104. *Dvenadtsatyi s"ezd*, 198–99.

105. TsK staffer E. I. Kviring's speech to the Saratov Guberniia Party Conference, 21 November 1927. RGASPI, f. 17, op. 21, d. 3749, ll. 20–21.

106. *Dvenadtsatyi s"ezd,* 198.

107. Orgburo protocol, 24 January 1919. RGASPI, f. 17, op. 112, d. 1, l. 5.

108. Orgburo protocol, 24 April 1919. RGASPI, f. 17, op. 112, d. 3, l. 43.

109. Orgburo protocol, 6 January 1921. RGASPI, f. 17, op. 112, d. 110, l. 4.

110. Orgburo protocol, 15 October 1920. RGASPI, f. 17, op. 112, d. 78, l. 4.

111. Orgburo protocol, 8 February 1921. RGASPI, f. 17, op. 112, d. 127, l. 4.

112. See RGASPI, f. 613, op. 1, dd. 1–10.

113. TsKK Presidium protocol, 29 April 1921. RGASPI, f. 613, op. 1, d. 2, ll. 58, 84.

114. TsKK Presidium protocols. RGASPI, f. 613, op. 1, d. 14, l. 145.

115. TsKK Partkollegia protocol, 5 July 1924. RGASPI, f. 613, op. 1, d. 30, l. 92. TsKK Parttroika protocol, 21 July 1925. RGASPI, d. 37, l. 68.

116. *Izvestiia TsK VKP(b),* no. 1 (January 1923): 75.

117. Orgburo protocol, 11 October 1920. RGASPI, f. 17, op. 112, d. 76, l. 429.

118. TsKK Presidium protocol, 19 July 1921. RGASPI, f. 613, op. 1, d. 2. l. 137.

119. Secretariat protocol, 4 April 1921. RGASPI, f. 17, op. 112, d. 146, l. 20b.

120. TsKK Presidium protocol, 27 December 1923. RGASPI, f. 613, op. 1, d. 13. l. 77.

121. TsKK decision, 31 October 1923. RGASPI, f. 613, op, 1, d. 13, l. 16.

122. Orgburo protocol, 31 May 1919. RGASPI, f. 17, op. 112, d. 4, l. 108.

123. Orgburo protocol, 6 January 1921. RGASPI, f. 17, op. 112, d. 110, ll. 2–3.

124. It was not uncommon for senior grandees to try to hide their mutual affronts and duels from the lower ranks. See Kaganovich's report and the Orgburo resolution in RGASPI, f. 82, op. 2, d. 149, ll. 105–9, and f. 17, op. 112, d. 640, l. 4.

125. Orgburo protocol, 27 September 1920. RGASPI, f. 17, op. 112, d. 72, ll. 3, 14–15, 30–32. 26 December 1920 and 1 January 1921. RGASPI, f. 17, d. 108, ll. 6–7. 3 March 1921. RGASPI, f. 17, d. 132, l. 6. Beloborodov was finally rescued from Rostov in October 1921. Orgburo protocol, 10 October 1921. RGASPI, f. 17, op. 112, d. 224, l. 4.

126. Secretariat protocol, 16 February 1924. RGASPI, f. 17, op. 112, d. 520, ll. 214–2140b.

127. Orgburo order of 24 June 1925. RGASPI, f. 17, op. 112, d. 681, l. 15.

128. Orgburo files, after November 1919. RGASPI, f. 17, op. 112, d. 35, l. 700b.

129. Marc Jansen and Nikita Petrov, *Stalin's Loyal Executioner: People's Commissar Nikolai Ezhov, 1895–1940* (Stanford, Calif.: Hoover Institution Press, 2002), 196.

130. Dvinskii to Stalin, 26 August 1934. RGASPI, f. 558, op. 11, d. 84, l. 14.

131. Politburo resolution of 27 June 1936. RGASPI, f. 17, op. 3, d. 978, l. 75.

132. Politburo decision of 29 June 1936. RGASPI, f. 17, op. 162, d. 20, l. 1.

133. Gill, *Origins of the Stalinist Political System.* 84.

134. RGASPI, f. 17, op. 11, d. 505, l. 31.

135. RGASPI, f. 613, op. 1, d. 2, l. 12; f. 17, op. 112, d. 138, l. 20b.

136. RGASPI, f. 17, op. 11, d. 502, ll. 101–1100b.

137. For example see RGASPI, f. 17, op. 11, d. 505, l. 31.

138. TsKK protocol, 24 October 1921. RGASPI, f. 17, op. 1, d. 3, l. 166.

139. TsKK protocol, 3 November 1920. RGASPI, f. 613, op. 1, d. 1, l. 17.

140. TsKK protocol, 22 March 1921. RGASPI, f. 613, op. 1, d. 2, l. 12.

141. Orgburo protocols, 6 and 13 January 1922. RGASPI, f. 17, op. 112, d. 273, ll. 2, 6–7, 13–140b.

142. Nikolai Berdyaev, *The Origin of Russian Communism* (Ann Arbor: University of Michigan Press, 1966), 169–70. See also Ernst Troeltsch, *Making of the Soviet System* (New York: Pantheon, 1985).

143. See Igal Halfin, *From Darkness to Light: Class, Consciousness, and Salvation in Revolutionary Russia* (Pittsburgh: University of Pittsburgh Press, 2000), xii, 474; Halfin, *Terror in My Soul*.

144. White, *Political Culture and Soviet Politics*, 65.

145. Yves Cohen, "The Cult of Number One in an Age of Leaders," *Kritika* 8, no. 3 (2007): 619.

146. Pierre Bourdieu, *Outline of a Theory of Practice* (Cambridge: Cambridge University Press, 1977), 179. Emphasis in original.

CHAPTER 2. CULTS AND PERSONALITIES, POLITICS AND BODIES

Epigraph: Protocol of the Lenin Funeral Commission. RGASPI, f. 16, op, 1, d. 491, l. 12 (Enukidze); Simon Sebag Montefiore, *Stalin: The Court of the Red Tsar* (London: Vintage, 2003), 4 (Stalin).

1. Jan Plamper, "Introduction: Modern Personality Cults," in *Personality Cults in Stalinism—Personenkulte im Stalinismus,* ed. Klaus Heller and Jan Plamper (Göttingen: V&R Unipress, 2004), 5, 35.

2. Cited in Catherine Merridale, *Night of Stone: Death and Memory in Russia* (London: Granta, 2000), 47.

3. Richard Stites, *Revolutionary Dreams: Utopian Vision and Experimental Life in the Russian Revolution* (New York: Oxford University Press, 1989), 114.

4. Putin also noted that much of the communist idea was taken from religion. "The code of the builders of communism, it's all in the Bible. Look, do not kill, do not steal, do not covet your friend's wife, it's all written there." This provoked an immediate hostile reaction from nationalists and religious believers. "Putin: Mavzolei Lenina sootvetstvuet traditsiiam," BBC *Russkaia Sluzhba*, 10 December 2012, http://www.bbc.co.uk/russian/russia/2012/12/121210_putin_trustees_heroes.shtml.

5. Nina Tumarkin, *Lenin Lives! The Lenin Cult in Soviet Russia* (Cambridge, Mass.: Harvard University Press, 1983), 198–99.

6. "Relics . . . have one compelling feature that marks them out from other kinds of material object, and that is their capacity to operate as a locus and conduit of power. This power can take various forms. It can be supernatural, salvific, apotropaic, and magical." Alexandra Walsham, "Relics and Remains," *Past and Present* 206 (2010), suppl. 5: 13.

7. On the overall development of the Lenin cult, see Benno Ennker, *Formirovanie kul'ta Lenina v Sovetskom Soiuza* (translated from the 1997 German edition) (Moscow: Rosspen, 2011); Tumarkin, *Lenin Lives*.

8. What is surprising is how many historians credit such tales, which first surfaced in notoriously unreliable memoirs of oppositionists decades later. Although there is no documentary basis for the assertion that Stalin played the leading role,

it is often mentioned. See, for example, Christopher Read, *Lenin: A Revolutionary Life* (London: Routledge, 2005), 284; Tumarkin, *Lenin Lives*. 174–75; Robert Service, *Lenin, a Political Life* (Bloomington: Indiana University Press, 1985), 319–22; Robert Service, *Lenin, a Biography* (London: Macmillan, 2000), 481–82; Roy A. Medvedev, *Let History Judge: The Origins and Consequences of Stalinism*, rev. ed. (New York: Columbia University Press, 1989), xxi, 903. Other historians are more careful: Ennker, *Formirovanie kul'ta Lenina*; Dmitri Volkogonov, *Lenin: A New biography* (New York: Free Press, 1994).

9. Protocols of the Lenin Funeral Commission. RGASPI, f. 16, op. 2, d. 48, l. 105.

10. Protocols of the Lenin Funeral Commission. RGASPI, f. 16, op. 1, d. 11.

11. Tumarkin, *Lenin Lives,* 161–62, 176; Olga Velikanova, *Making of an Idol: On Uses of Lenin* (Göttingen: Muster-Schmidt Verlag, 1996), 54–55.

12. Protocols of the Lenin Funeral Commission. RGASPI, f. 16, op. 2, d. 48, l. 105.

13. Protocols of the Lenin Funeral Commission. RGASPI, f. 16, op. 1, d. 522, l. 48.

14. The documents show that the Politburo entrusted decision making about Lenin's body entirely to the Dzerzhinskii Commission. Dzerzhinskii was the middleman between the two organizations, reporting to the Politburo from the commission and relaying the Politburo's agreement to the commission's recommendations. See, for example, Politburo documents in RGASPI, f. 17, op. 3, d. 1505, l. 1 and f. 17, op. 163, d. 396, ll. 55, 57, 59, in which the Politburo receives and approves the commission's reports.

15. Protocols of the Lenin Funeral Commission, now renamed the Commission for Immortalizing the Memory of V. I. Lenin. RGASPI, f. 16, op. 1, d. 51, l. 1.

16. This is the procedure still in use today. Protocols of the Commission for Immortalizing the Memory of V. I. Lenin. RGASPI, f. 16, op. 1, d. 51, l. 1.

17. Protocols of the commission. RGASPI, f. 16, op. 1, d. 492, ll. 1–3.

18. T. Sapronov report to the commission. RGASPI, f. 16, op. 1, d. 109. l. 1.

19. Enukidze speech to the commission. RGASPI, f. 16, op. 1, d. 522, l. 53.

20. A reference to the Socialist Revolutionaries, who believed in the importance of individual persons in history and who before the revolution sought to effect change by assassinating key individuals. Lenin, on the other hand, had sharply argued that social forces, not individuals, were decisive.

21. Voroshilov speech to the commission. RGASPI, f. 16, op. 2, d. 49, ll. 1–5.

22. Dzerzhinskii speech to the commission. RGASPI, f. 16, op. 2, d. 49, ll. 1–5.

23. Dzerzhinskii speech to the commission. RGASPI, f. 16, op. 2, d. 49, ll. 1–5.

24. This is the only place in the documentation of either the commission or the Politburo where the question of political utility was mentioned. Voroshilov's speech to the commission. RGASPI, f. 16, op. 2, d. 49, ll. 1–5.

25. Protocol of the commission. RGASPI, f. 16, op, 1, d. 491, l. 12. Emphases mine.

26. A. V. Lunacharskii and L. B. Krasin, "Draft Report on the Commission to Build an Eternal Mausoleum to V. I. Lenin." RGASPI, f. 16, op. 1, d. 129, ll. 11–12.

27. See some of the projects and their evaluations in RGASPI, f. 16, op. 1, dd. 146–56.

28. See "Vsevolodovich" letter to the commission, 15 November 1925. RGASPI, f. 16, op. 1, d. 134, ll. 4–5.

29. RGASPI, f. 16, op. 1, d. 134, l. 15.

30. *Pravda*, 30 January 1924, p. 1.

31. Lunacharskii and Krasin, "Draft Report." RGASPI, f. 16, op. 1, d. 129, ll. 1–4.

32. Pierre Bourdieu, *Outline of a Theory of Practice* (Cambridge: Cambridge University Press, 1977), 167, 79. Sherry Ortner is surely right that "the degree to which actors really do simply enact norms because 'that is the way of our ancestors' may be unduly undervalued." See her "Theory in Anthropology since the Sixties," *Comparative Studies in Society and History* 26, no. 1 (1984): 126–66. This may be true even with modern-minded communists. See also S. A. Smith, "Bones of Contention: Bolsheviks and the Struggle against Relics 1918–1930," *Past and Present*, 204, no. 1 (2009): 155–94.

33. These fill nearly a hundred archival folders. See RGASPI, f. 16, op. 1, dd. 157–251.

34. Explicitly noted not only in the press but in the secret "materials" of the Politburo. Politburo resolution of 25 January 1924. RGASPI, f. 17, op. 163, d. 396, l. 57.

35. See RGASPI, f. 16, op. 1, dd. 529–32, 561–72, 720–24; f. 16, op. 2, d. 51. For example, f. 16, op. 1, d. 756 contains a large number of sketches and proposals, only from Tula.

36. RGASPI, f. 16, op. 1, d. 156, ll. 38–46.

37. RGASPI, f. 16, op. 1, d. 720. See some of the outlandish mausoleum proposals in f. 16, op. 1, dd. 145–50.

38. Velikanova, *Making of an Idol,* 32–34.

39. V. D. Bonch-Bruevich, *Vospominaniia o Lenine* (Moscow: Nauka, 1969), 459.

40. Ibid., 59. On the religious connotations of Lenin's body, see Claudio Sergio Ingerflom and Tamara Kondratieva, "Pourquoi la Russia s'agite-t-elle autour du corps de Lénine?" in *La mort du roi: Autour de François Mitterand. Essai d'ethnographic politique comparée,* ed. Jacques Julliard (Paris: Gallimard, 1999).

41. Edward Shils, *The Constitution of Society* (Chicago: University of Chicago Press, 1982), 111.

42. Max Weber, *Max Weber on Law in Economy and Society* (Cambridge, Mass.: Harvard University Press, 1954), 336–37, and *From Max Weber: Essays in Sociology* (New York: Oxford University Press, 1947), 253.

43. Shils, *The Constitution of Society,* 129–32.

44. Speaking of the lying in state ritual that Peter the Great introduced to Russia, Nina Tumarkin wrote "This was a moment of greatest intimacy between tsar and people; the lowliest peasant could gaze upon the little father." Tumarkin, *Lenin Lives.* 139. See esp. chap. 1, "Russian Roots of the Lenin Cult." See also Velikanova, *Making of an Idol,* 13–22.

45. "The cult of a leader is consciously stimulated and controlled by the state (or party) functionaries. However, it is clear that its attempts can succeed only while they are based on pre-existing values and psychological dispositions." Velikanova, *Making of an Idol,* 20.

46. See Boris A. Uspenskii, "Tsar and Pretender: *Samozvancestvo* or Royal Imposture in Russia as a Cultural-Historical Phenomenon," in *The Semiotics of*

Russian Culture, ed. Iu. M. Lotman and Boris Uspenskii (Ann Arbor: University of Michigan, 1984); Maureen Perrie, "'Royal Marks': Reading the Bodies of Russian Pretenders, 17th–19th Centuries," *Kritika* 11, no. 3 (2010): 535–61.

47. Ernst H. Kantorowicz, *The King's Two Bodies: A Study in Medieval Political Theology* (Princeton, N.J.: Princeton University Press, 1957).

48. Richard Wortman, *Scenarios of Power: Myth and Ceremony in Russian Monarchy from Peter the Great to the Abdication of Nicholas II* (Princeton, N.J.: Princeton University Press, 2006), 415.

49. Kharkhordin, "What Is the State? The Russian Concept of *Gosudarstvo* in the European Context," *History and Theory* 40 (2001):" 214–19; Simon Dixon, *The Modernisation of Russia, 1676–1825* (Cambridge: Cambridge University Press, 1999), 191.

50. Kharkhordin, "What Is the State?," 214–19.

51. Claudio Sergio Ingerflom, "'Loyalty to the State' under Peter the Great? Return to the Sources and the Historicity of Concepts," in *Loyalties and Solidarities in Russian Society, History and Culture,* ed. Geoffrey Hosking, Claudio Sergio Ingerflom, and Catriona Kelly (London: School of Slavonic and East European Studies, forthcoming), 15. See also Claudio Sergio Ingerflom, "Novoevropeiskaia paradigma 'Gosudarstvennost'': Teoreticheskie predlosylki i kognitivnye nesootvetstviia," *Rossiia* 21, no. 2 (2011): 110–27.

52. The connection between country and father exists in many languages: *Vater/Vaterland* (German), *père/patrie* (French). But in Russia, the connection is more immediately functional.

53. Kaganovich to Ordzhonikidze, 30 September 1936. RGASPI, f. 85, op. 27, d. 93, ll. 12–13. For Stalin's father image, see also Jeffrey Brooks, *"Thank You, Comrade Stalin!": Soviet Public Culture from Revolution to Cold War* (Princeton, N.J.: Princeton University Press, 2000), 70. We note here in passing that Putin has been called "the father of the nation."

54. Michael Urban has noted that even today, "'clan' is the pivotal category; for one's own team relations are rendered according to the template of the nuclear family and its gendered roles." Michael Urban, "Forms of Civil Society: Politics and Social Relations in Russia," *International Political Anthropology* 1, no. 1 (2008): 108.

55. Tumarkin, *Lenin Lives.* 109.

56. Boris Mironov, quoting A. L. Leopoldov, who wrote in 1851. B. N. Mironov, "Peasant Popular Culture and the Origins of Soviet Authoritarianism," in *Cultures in Flux: Lower-Class Values, Practices, and Resistance in Late Imperial Russia,* ed. Stephen P. Frank and Mark D. Steinberg (Princeton, N.J.: Princeton University Press, 1994), 69.

57. Brooks, *"Thank You, Comrade Stalin!"*

58. Later, as Jan Plamper argues, modern post-Enlightenment cults derived their legitimacy from "the people" rather than from God, whose death is a "precondition for the deification of man." Plamper, "Introduction: Modern Personality Cults," 19.

59. Clifford Geertz, *Local Knowledge: Further Essays in Interpretive Anthropology* (New York: Basic Books, 1983), 123–24.

60. Michael Cherniavsky, *Tsar and People: Studies in Russian Myths* (New York: Random House, 1969); Wortman, *Scenarios of Power,* 415.

61. Dixon, *The Modernisation of Russia,* 194.

62. Krasin complained to Dzerzhinskii, who ordered their release. Krasin to the commission. RGASPI, f. 16, op. 1, d. 156, l. 6.

63. "Moskvichi moliatsia na Stalina," *Moskovskii Komsomolets,* No. 25481, 21 October 2010; Nina Achmatova, "Controversy in Moscow: Stalin Icon Revered," *AsiaNews.it,* 22 October 2010. The author has seen small Stalin icons in two Moscow churches in the past five years.

64. Jan Plamper, *The Stalin Cult: A Study in the Alchemy of Power* (New Haven, Conn.: Yale University Press, 2012), xvii. Despite the similarities in prescribed gaze, Plamper nevertheless refuses to equate icons with Stalin portraits because of the supposed "realist tradition" in the latter and because the modern way Stalin portraits were produced "bore scant resemblance to the crafting of icons." It is not clear, however, that the technical mechanisms of production in themselves change the archaic iconic essence of Stalin's images.

65. "Ikona Vladimira Putina zamirotochila pered vyborami," *Kommersant,* 21 January 2012.

66. *New York Times,* 18 December 1910.

67. *RIA Novosti,* 10 January 2012.

68. Cherniavsky, *Tsar and People,* 31–33.

69. The selection of Mikhail Romanov by the Assembly of the Land in 1613 does not imply the filling of a vacant state position by a representative state body looking for the best candidate. The assembly, a self-appointed elite conclave, first offered the throne to distant Riurikid members of the extinct dynastic line, who refused. Mikhail Romanov, a sixteen-year-old boy, was selected primarily because his family was related to the extinct line of Ivan IV: Anastasiia Romanovna Zakharyna-Iur'eva had been married to Ivan, and Mikhail Romanov was Ivan IV's son Fëdor's nephew. The principle of legitimate dynasty, based on kinship and patrimonial rule, was therefore maintained and not replaced by a state abstraction.

70. I owe this suggestion to Robert V. Daniels, "Russian Political Culture and the Post-Revolutionary Impasse," *Russian Review* 46, no. 2 (1987): 169. The two instances when the Soviet leaders announced "collective leadership," following the deaths of Lenin and Stalin, are the exceptions that prove the rule. Both times the arrangement proved unstable and unworkable, and lasted only a few months until a new top leader emerged. Both times, the lack of a designated successor created a vacuum in which the "state" could not continue without a single leader.

71. Gyula Szvak, *False Tsars* (Boulder, Colo.: Social Science Monographs, 2000), 41.

72. Daniel Field, *Rebels in the Name of the Tsar* (Boston: Unwin Hyman, 1976).

73. Paul Avrich, *Russian Rebels, 1600–1800* (London: Allen Lane, 1973), 309.

74. Cherniavsky, *Tsar and People,* 75.

75. Dixon, *The Modernisation of Russia,* 190–91.

76. On pretendership in Russia, see Maureen Perrie, *The Image of Ivan the Terrible in Russian Folklore* (Cambridge: Cambridge University Press, 1987), and *Pretenders and Popular Monarchism in Early Modern Russia* (Cambridge: Cambridge University Press, 1995). See also Claudio Sergio Ingerflom, "Les représentations collectives du pouvoir et l'imposture' " en Russie, XVIIIe–XXe siècles," in *La royauté sacrée dans le monde chrétien*, ed. Alain Boureau and Claudio Sergio Ingerflom (Paris: Editions de l'E.H.E.S.S., 1992), 157–64, and "Entre le mythe et la parole: L'action. La naissance de la conception politique du pouvoir en Russie," *Annales: Histoire, Sciences Sociales*, no. 4 (1996): 733–57.

77. Robert Craig Howes, ed., *The Testaments of the Grand Princes of Moscow* (Ithaca, N.Y.: Cornell University Press, 1967).

78. Ingerflom, " 'Loyalty to the State,' " 15.

79. Donald Ostrowski, "The Facade of Legitimacy: Exchange of Power and Authority in Early Modern Russia," *Comparative Studies in Society and History* 44, no. 3 (July 2002): 544–45; Kharkhordin, "What Is the State?" 221–22. See also Paul Bushkovitch, *Peter the Great: The Struggle for Power, 1671–1725* (Cambridge: Cambridge University Press, 2001), for the importance of various groups' proximity to Peter. Vladimir Putin was similar to Peter in this: he also talked of the state and named his successor.

80. Ingerflom, " 'Loyalty to the State.' "

81. Geoffrey Hosking, "Patronage and the Russian State," *Slavonic and East European Review* 78, no. 2 (2000): 301–20; Richard Pipes, *Russia under the Old Regime* (New York: Scribners, 1974), 40–78.

82. In modern times, *khoziain* gained the additional meaning of "boss" or "chief," while retaining its ancient meanings.

83. Marshall Poe, "What Did Russians Mean When They Called Themselves " 'Slaves of the Tsar' "?" *Slavic Review* 57, no. 3 (1998): 585–608.

84. The latest work on Stalin's cult is Plamper, *The Stalin Cult*. See also Benno Ennker, " 'Struggling for Stalin's Soul': The Leader Cult and the Balance of Social Power in Stalin's Inner Circle," in Heller and Plamper, *Personality Cults in Stalinism*, 169; Brooks, *"Thank You, Comrade Stalin!,"* esp. chap. 3.

85. See Heller and Plamper, *Personality Cults;* Yves Cohen, "Des lettres comme action: Stalin au début des années 1930 vu depuis le fonds Kaganovič," *Cahiers du Monde Russe* 38 (1997): 307–45.

86. R. C. Tucker, *Stalin in Power: The Revolution from Above, 1928–1941* (New York: Norton, 1990); Robert C. Tucker, *Stalin as Revolutionary* (New York: Norton, 1973); Robert C. Tucker, "The Rise of Stalin's Personality Cult," *American Historical Review* 84 (1979): 347–66.

87. Sarah Davies, "Stalin and the Making of the Leader Cult in the 1930s," in *The Leader Cult in Communist Dictatorships: Stalin and the Eastern Bloc*, ed. Balazs Apor, Jan C. Behrends, Polly Jones, and E. A. Rees (New York: Palgrave Macmillan, 2004), 29.

88. A. Eliseev, *Pravda o 1937 gode: Kto razviazal "bol'shoi terror"?* (Moscow: Iauza, 2008), 93.

89. Montefiore, *Stalin*, 4.

90. RGASPI, f. 558, op 11, d. 4572, l. 1.

91. RGASPI, f. 558, op. 11, d. 942, l. 44.

92. Davies, "Stalin and the Making of the Leader Cult," 37, 42.

93. RGASPI, f. 558, op. 11, d. 92, l. 22.

94. RGASPI, f. 558, op. 1, d. 3226, l. 1.

95. Before the revolution, the Socialist Revolutionary Party's terrorist wing believed that assassinating individual leaders could bring down the tsarist regime. Lenin, in "The Heritage We Renounce," countered that only class-based mass revolution could do that.

96. "Pis'mo v Detizdat pri Ts.K., VLKSM," 16 February 1938. Stalin, *Sochineniia*, vol. 1 (14), ed. Robert H. McNeal (Stanford, Calif.: Hoover Institution Press, 1967), 274.

97. Tumarkin, *Lenin Lives*, 90, quoting Bonch-Bruevich.

98. Velikanova, *Making of an Idol*, 38–39.

99. Davies, "Stalin and the Making of the Leader Cult," 37.

100. Cohen, "Cult of Number One," 599. See also Plamper, "Introduction: Modern Personality Cults."

101. D. Brandenberger, "Stalin as Symbol: A Case study of the Personality Cult and its Construction," in *Stalin: A New History*, ed. Sarah Davies and James R. Harris (Cambridge: Cambridge University Press, 2005), 251; D. L. Brandenberger and A. M. Dubrovsky, "'The People Need a Tsar': The Emergence of National Bolshevism as Stalinist Ideology, 1931–1941," *Europe-Asia Studies* 50, no. 5 (1998): 873–92.

102. For this top-down functional approach, see E. A. Rees, "Leader Cults: Varieties, Preconditions and Functions," in Apor et al., *Stalin and the Making of the Leader Cult in the 1930s*, 3–28; Ennker, "'Struggling for Stalin's Soul,'" 161–95.

103. Plamper, *The Stalin Cult*, xvii.

104. Shils, *The Constitution of Society*, argues that charisma can be focused on institutions, constitutions, or ideas, all of which can be as transcendent as gods (p. 129).

105. The medium is not the message here, and the vehicle does not change or even define its contents. A modern delivery mechanism changes neither the archaic essence of the cult nor the needs it meets in society. Hitler's cultic message was delivered by a bureaucracy using the latest technologies (radio, mass printing, etc.) but it was no more modern nor less atavistic for it.

106. "Protokol i stenogramma II Stalingradskogo oblastnoi konferentsii VKP(b) s materialami." RGASPI, f. 17, op. 21, d. 4226, l. 135.

107. "Stenogramma VII Kara-Kalpakskoi oblastnoi konferentsii KP(b)UZ. 19–25 maia 1937g." RGASPI, f. 17, op. 27, d. 142, l. 367.

108. "Stenogramma VII Kara-Kalpakskoi oblastnoi konferentsii KP(b)UZ. 19–25 maia 1937g." RGASPI, f. 17, op. 27, d. 142, l. 329.

109. "Stenograficheskii otchet II-i Ordzhonikidzevskoi kraevoi partkonferentsii. 13–15 iiunia 1937g." RGASPI, f. 17, op. 21, d. 3425, ll. 48–49.

110. Mikhail Shreider, *NKVD iznutri: Zapiski chekista* (Moscow: Vozrashchenie, 1995), 109.

111. Geertz, *Local Knowledge*, 125.

112. "Stenogramma plenuma Zapobkoma VKP(b) ot 26 iiulia 1937g." RGASPI, f. 17, op. 21, d. 4093, ll. 10–11.

113. "Stenograficheskii otchet II-i Ordzhonikidzevskoi kraevoi partkonferentsii. 13–15 iiunia 1937g." RGASPI, f. 17, op. 21, d. 3425, ll. 48–49.

114. Nathan Leites, Else Bernaut, and Raymond L. Garthoff, "Politburo Images of Stalin," *World Politics* 3, no. 3 (April 1951): 317–39.

115. "What linked the monarch's own body and the series of bodies it represented, culminating in the whole body politic, was the signifier of the patrilineage, which encoded, in the repeated father-son relationship, heredity, masculinity, and the transcendent promise of immortality." Julia Adams, "The Rule of the Father," 242–43.

116. Hosking, "Patronage and the Russian State," 303–4.

117. Gill, *Origins of the Stalinist Political System,* 108, 325.

118. Reinhard Bendix, *Max Weber: An Intellectual Portrait* (Garden City, N.Y.: Doubleday, 1960), 345. For a limited reference to patrimonial power in Stalin's time, see Hughes, "Patrimonialism and the Stalinist System—the Case of Syrtsov, S. I.," *Europe-Asia Studies* 48, no. 4 (1996): 551–68; and for an approach that is entirely Stalin-centered, see O. Khlevniuk, *Master of the House: Stalin and His Inner Circle* (New Haven, Conn.: Yale University Press, 2009).

119. N. I. Ezhov, conference with peasants. RGAE, f. 7486, op. 79, d. 24, l. 9.

120. Keenan, "Muscovite Political Folkways," *Russian Review* 45, no. 2 (1986): 139.

121. Sergo Beria, *Beria, My Father: Inside Stalin's Kremlin* (London: Duckworth, 2001), 192.

122. Nancy Shields Kollmann, *By Honor Bound: State and Society in Early Modern Russia* (Ithaca, N.Y.: Cornell University Press, 1999); Nancy Shields Kollmann, *Kinship and Politics: the Making of the Muscovite Political System, 1345–1547* (Stanford, Calif.: Stanford University Press, 1987).

123. Keenan, "Muscovite Political Folkways," 140.

124. Nancy Shields Kollmann, "Muscovite Patrimonialism," in *Major Problems in the History of Imperial Russia,* ed. James Cracraft (Lexington, Mass.: D. C. Heath, 1994), 39.

125. John P. LeDonne, *Absolutism and Ruling Class: The Formation of the Russian Political Order, 1700–1825* (New York, Oxford: Oxford University Press, 1991), 21. See also David Ransel, "Character and Style of Patron-Client Relations in Russia," in *Klientelsysteme im Europa der frühen Neuzeit,* ed. Antoni Maczak and Elisabeth Mueller-Luckner (Munich: Oldenbourg, 1988), 225–31; Hosking, "Patronage and the Russian State"; Dixon, *The Modernisation of Russia.*

126. Dixon, *The Modernisation of Russia,* 137.

127. David Ransel, "Character and Style of Patron-Client Relations in Russia," 216.

128. Daniel T. Orlovsky, "Political Clientelism in Russia: the Historical Perspective," in *Leadership Selection and Patron-Client Relations in the USSR and Yugoslavia,* ed. T. H. Rigby and Bogdan Harasymiw (London: Allen & Unwn, 1983), 177–79.

129. See Daniel T. Orlovsky, *The Limits of Reform: The Ministry of Internal Affairs in Imperial Russia, 1802–1881* (Cambridge, Mass.: Harvard University Press, 1981).

130. Shreider, *NKVD iznutri,* 45, 54.

CHAPTER 3. THE PARTY PERSONNEL SYSTEM: UPSTAIRS
AT THE CENTRAL COMMITTEE

Epigraph: V. I. Lenin, *Polnoe sobranie sochinenie,* 5th ed., 55 vols. (Moscow: Gosizdat, 1968–75), 30:413.

1. My thanks to Nancy Kollman for her advice on this section. Any errors or imprecision are of course mine.

2. Ossinskii's speech to the 8th Party Congress, *Vosmoi s"ezd RKP(b), mart 1919 goda: Protokoly* (Moscow: Partizdat, 1959), 165.

3. "Skhema po uchetu partiinykh sil na 1 ianvaria 1919 g.," RGASPI, f. 17, op. 11, d. 286, l. 4ff.

4. G. M. Adibekov, K. M. Anderson, and L. Rogovaia, eds., *Politbiuro TsK RKP(b)—VKP(b): Povestki dlia zasedanii,* vol. 1: *1919–1929: Katalog* (Moscow: Rosspen, 2000), 5–6; "Predislovie k opisi, no. 1," RGASPI, f. 17, op. 112, l. 1.

5. *Vosmoi s"ezd,* 424–25. In Bolshevik usage, "organizational" work means personnel appointment, and an *orgvopros* was a proposal to appoint someone to a job.

6. Orgburo protocols of 26 March–5 July 1919. RGASPI, f. 17, op. 112, d. 778, ll. 1–8.

7. Numbers of Politburo members and candidate members ranged from roughly seven and eight respectively in the 1920s to ten and five in the 1930s, and except for a temporary interlude in 1952–53, was consistently eleven and four or five until 1970.

8. Politburo decisions of 8 and 21 December 1922. RGASPI, f. 82, op. 2, d. 168, l. 11.

9. Based on a large sample of Politburo meetings in RGASPI, f. 17, op. 3, which contains the protocols of those meetings.

10. Politburo decision of 4 April 1922. RGASPI, f. 82, op. 2, d. 168, ll. 92–93.

11. Orgburo membership was a surprisingly consistent ten to eleven members and four or five candidate members from 1919 to the Orgburo's abolition in 1952.

12. This makes sense, given that Secretariat decisions automatically became Orgburo decisions absent objections from Orgburo members. The archives of the Secretariat and Orgburo are kept in the same files, in chronological order without any separation between the two: RGASPI, f. 17, opisi 112–14.

13. RGASPI, f. 17, op. 112, d. 777, l. 32.

14. "Predislovie k opisi, no. 1." RGASPI, f. 17., op. 112., l. 2, and Orgburo decision of 4 April 1922. RGASPI, f. 82, op. 2, d. 168, l. 21.

15. See "Polozhenie ob Organizatsionno-raspreditel'nom otdele TsK RKP(b)." Secretariat protocol, 13 March 1925. RGASPI, f. 17, op. 112, d. 646, ll. 19–21.

16. For examples of these conferences see Orgraspred files in RGASPI, f. 17, op. 69, dd. 137 and 138, and f. 17, op. 68, d. 70.

17. This and the following generalizations and summaries are taken from examining the protocols of meetings of the Conference of Department Heads during the 1920s in RGASPI, f. 17, op. 112, dd. 542–45.

18. "Zasedaniia Soveshchaniia Zavotdelami TsK ot 28/IV-23 g." RGASPI, f. 17, op. 112, d. 542, ll. 2–8.

19. These typical examples were at the following meetings. "Zasedaniia Soveshchaniia Zavotdelami TsK ot 10/V-23 g. RGASPI, f. 17, op. 112. d. 543. ll. 81–85. . . . ot 12/7–23 g. RGASPI, f. 17, op 112, d. 547, l. 14. . . . ot 14/VI-23 g. RGASPI, f. 17, op. 112, d. 545, l. 142.

20. *Dvenadtsatyi s"ezd RKP(b), 17–25 aprelia 1923 goda: Stenograficheskii otchet* (Moscow: Partizdat, 1960), 818.

21. *XIV s"ezd Vsesoiuznoi Kommunisticheskoi Partii (b), 18–31 dekabria 1925 g. Stenograficheskii otchet* (Moscow: Gosizdat, 1926), 505–6.

22. Secretariat protocol, 21 September 1927. RGASPI, f. 17, op. 113, d. 660, protocol, no. 66. Orgburo protocol, 24 September 1928. RGASPI, f. 17, op. 113, d. 661, protocol, no. 67. Politburo protocol, 20 September 1928. RGASPI, f. 17, op. 3, d. 705, protocol no. 43.

23. Based on recommendations from historian Mikhail Pokrovskii and Foreign Minister Chicherin, the Orgburo on 6 April 1925 authorized negotiations with Jerusalem University. RGASPI, f. 17, op. 112, d. 653, l. 3.

24. Conference of TsK Department Heads, 10 May 1923. RGASPI, f. 17, op. 112, d. 543, l. 82; Politburo protocol, 21 June 1923. RGASPI, f. 17, op. 3, d. 361, protocol no. 13.

25. See the Secretariat protocols for October 1923 in RGASPI, f. 17, op. 112, d. 485, ll. 3–5 and d. 487, ll. 3–7, 113.

26. Orgburo protocol, 7 April 1921. RGASPI, f. 17, op. 112, d. 149, l. 40b.

27. Orgburo protocol, 2 December 1935. RGASPI, f. 17, op. 114, d. 598, l. 2.

28. Orgburo protocol, 16 February 1938. RGASPI, f. 17, op. 114, d. 639, l. 1. The Orgburo did at least send its appointment to the Politburo for subsequent approval.

29. See the agendas in RGASPI, f. 17, op. 11, d. 171.

30. See "Zasedaniia Soveshchaniia Zavotdelami TsK" of 28 April and 3 May 1923. RGASPI, f. 17, op. 112, d. 542, l. 5, and d. 543, ll. 3–4.

31. Politburo meeting of 3 May 1923. RGASPI, f. 17, op. 3, d. 349, ll. 1–2.

32. Orgburo protocol, 27 October 1919. RGASPI, f. 17, op. 112, d. 9, l. 102.

33. Orgburo protocol, 11 October 1920. RGASPI, f. 17, op. 112, d. 76, ll. 2, 6, 52. On Miachin, the Orgburo carefully deliberated and resolved "without reversing the order for his expulsion, to consider it possible to readmit him to the party anew on a general basis, that is with recommendations, a party *stazh* from the moment of the new admission."

34. Orgburo protocol, 1 April 1921. RGASPI, f. 17, op. 112, d. 149, ll. 2, 4.

35. Secretariat protocol, 10 August 1921. RGASPI, f. 17, op. 112, d. 198, l. 8.

36. Orgburo protocols of 14 August and 2 December 1935. RGASPI, f. 17, op. 114, 591, l. 5, and d. 598, ll. 2–3. The Orgburo decided that 75 percent of the theater tickets were to be on open sale at box offices.

37. Politburo protocol no. 36. RGASPI, f. 17, op. 3, d. 974.

38. See, for example, the Secretariat's meeting of 6 March 1925, where Orgburo appointments were reversed and where the Secretariat rather high-handedly decided who could receive Politburo protocols. RGASPI, f. 17, op. 112, d. 643, ll. 7, 11.

39. "Zasedaniia Soveshchaniia Zavotdelami TsK" of 28 April and 14 June 1923. RGASPI, f. 17, op. 112, d. 542, l. 4, and d. 545, ll. 143, 144, 145.

40. For examples of Orgburo plans of work for 1923 and 1928, see RGASPI, f. 17, op. 11, d. 174, l. 2, and op. 113, d. 620, ll. 22–24.

41. Orgburo protocol, 10 December 1920. RGASPI, f. 17, op. 112, d. 107, l. 2.

42. Secretariat/Orgburo protocol, 10 August 1921. RGASPI, f. 17, op. 112, d. 198, l. 8.

43. Secretariat, protocol, 7 April 1935. RGASPI, f. 17, op. 114, d. 581, l. 1.

44. Orgburo protocol no. 90, 26 July 1938. RGASPI, f. 17, op. 114, d. 532, l. 58.

45. See "Zasedaniia Soveshchaniia Zavotdelami TsK" of 14 June 1923. RGASPI, f. 17, op. 112, d. 545, ll. 143, 144, 145.

46. Politburo decision of 31 December 1922. RGASPI, f. 82, op. 2, d. 168, l. 21; Orgburo decision of 18 March 1921. RGASPI, f. 82, op. 2, d. 168, l. 1.

47. This common elite trust among grandees would vanish with the struggles with opposition movements. Oppositionists put themselves outside the original brotherhood, and after that the trusted nobles were limited to those who supported the TsK majority.

48. For examples, see: Orgburo protocol, no. 65, 8 February 1937. RGASPI, f. 17, op. 114, d. 491, l. 77. Orgburo protocol, no. 90, 26 July 1938. RGASPI, f. 17, op. 114, d. 532, l. 62. Gill rightly observes that "notables" largely ratified staff proposals (Graeme Gill, *The Origins of the Stalinist Political System* [Cambridge: Cambridge University Press, 1990], 158–59), but it is important to note that the grandees insisted on having the final say.

49. For a fuller discussion of the Politburo as a dubious institution, see J. Arch Getty, "Stalin as Prime Minister: Power and the Politburo," in *Stalin: A New History,* ed. Sarah Davies and James R. Harris (Cambridge: Cambridge University Press, 2005), 63–82.

50. For example, Stalin (and in fact all Orgburo members) attended a meeting of 27 March 1935 which discussed implementing a Politburo order to reestablish party personnel departments in city party committees. RGASPI, f. 17, op. 114, d. 580, l. 1.

51. Orgburo protocol no. 51, 6 September 1920. RGASPI, f. 17, op. 112, d. 67, l. 2.

52. In the unity-obsessed Bolshevik party, a "special opinion" was the etiquette for recording a negative vote.

53. Orgburo protocols, 9 and 12 May, 1921. RGASPI, f. 17, op. 112, d. 170, l. 2, and d. 172, l. 1.

54. V. I. Lenin, *Polnoe sobranie sochinenie,* 5th ed., 55 vols. (Moscow: Gosizdat, 1968–75), 30:413.

55. Lenin's speech to the 9th Party Congress. *Deviatyi s"ezd RKP(b), mart–aprel' 1920 goda: Stenograficheskii otchet* (Moscow: Partizdat, 1960), 86. See also Kurskii's remarks about the division of labor among committees being "in princi-

ple" while "in fact" there was much overlap. *Trinadtsatyi s"ezd RKP(b), mai 1924 goda: Stenograficheskii otchet* (Moscow: Gosizdat, 1963), 130.

56. I owe this observation to Graeme Gill: "In short, leading members of the oligarchy made little attempt to work out an administrative regime which would structure the activities of the elite political organs." Gill, *Origins of the Stalinist Political System,* 102.

57. Politburo decisions, of 31 December 1922. RGASPI, f. 82, op. 2, d. 168, ll. 1, 15–16. Orgburo decisions, of 18 March 1921, 4 April 1922. RGASPI, f. 82, op. 2, d. 168, ll. 1, 20–21.

58. O. V. Khlevniuk, *Politbiuro: Mekhanizmy politicheskoi vlasti v 1930-e gody* (Moscow: Rosspen, 1996), 289.

59. Politburo protocols. RGASPI, f. 17, op. 3, d. 808 (Protocol, no. 21) and d. 982 (Protocol, no. 44).

60. Thomas T. Mackie and Brian W. Hogwood, "Decision Arenas in Executive Decision Making: Cabinet Committees in Comparative Perspective," *British Journal of Political Science* 14, no. 3 (1984): 311.

61. *Odinnadtsatyi s"ezd RKP(b), mart–aprel' 1922 goda: Stenograficheskii otchet* (Moscow: Partizdat, 1961), 35. As Graeme Gill put it, Lenin's authority was "completely at odds with the notion of regularized authority based upon stable institutional structures." His authority was "decoupled" from institutions. Gill, *Origins of the Stalinist Political System.* 108.

62. *Dvenadtsatyi s"ezd,* 26, 114, 157, 209.

63. Orgburo agenda of 6 January 1921. RGASPI, f. 17, op. 112, d. 110, ll. 2–3.

64. Politburo decisions: 31 December 1921 30 December 1922. RGASPI, f. 17, op. 3, d. 247, l. 6, and f. 82, op. 2, d. 168, ll. 15–17.)

65. For example, "TsK members can protest decisions of the Orgburo to the Politburo." *Dvenadtsatyi s"ezd,* 818.

66. A. I. Mikoian, *Tak bylo: Razmyshleniia o minuvshem* (Moscow: Vagrius, 1999), 201.

67. On Politburo commissions see Jana Howlett et al., "The CPSU's Top Bodies Under Stalin: Their Operational Records and Structure of Command," University of Toronto Stalin-Era Research and Archives Project Working Paper, no. 1 (Toronto: Centre for Russian and East European Studies, University of Toronto, 1996), 7. O. V. Khlevniuk, *Stalinskoe Politbiuro v 30-e gody: Sbornik dokumentov* (Moscow: Airo-XX, 1995), 44–73.

68. Stalin was not a member of every Politburo standing commission. Y. Gorlizki ("Stalin's Cabinet: The Politburo and Decision Making in the Post-war Years," *Europe-Asia Studies* 53, no. 2 [2001]: 294) notes that the various "-tets" sometimes met without Stalin in the 1940s.

69. Rudi Andeweg, "A Model of the Cabinet System: The Dimensions of Cabinet Decision-Making Processes," in *Governing Together: The Extent and Limits of Joint Decision-Making in Western European Cabinets,* ed. Jean Blondel and Ferdinand Müller-Rommel (London: St. Martin's Press, 1993), 29.

70. Blondel and Müller-Rommel, *Governing Together,* 12.

71. Martin J. Smith, *The Core Executive in Britain* (London: Macmillan, 1999), 89. Compare with Gorlizki's formulation: "These narrow and informal Politburo

meetings were freed from the schedules and procedures which hamstrung the official or de jure cabinet. In the company of a small circle of colleagues, all of whom were well-known to Stalin and to each other, there was all the less reason to follow the inconvenient and time-consuming protocols of formal Politburo sessions." Gorlizki, "Stalin's Cabinet," 295.

72. RGASPI, f. 17, op. 3, d. 761, ll. 11–12. Fearing attempts to inflate the reports, the decree specified that a page could consist of no more than fifteen hundred characters: thirty lines of fifty characters!

73. RGASPI, f. 17, op. 3, d. 858, l. 2, and f. 17, op. 3, d. 860, l. 2.

74. RGASPI, f. 17, op. 3, d. 898, l. 8.

75. RGASPI, f. 17, op. 3, d. 823, l. 9.

76. The first *oprosom* votes in the Politburo came in May 1921. RGASPI, f. 17, op. 3, d. 159, protocol no. 22. See also Secretariat/OB protocols for April 1922 for the first polling votes: RGASPI, f. 17, op. 112, d. 358.

77. RGASPI, f. 17, op. 3, d. 771, protocol no. 112), d. 808, protocol no. 21; d. 955, protocol no. 17.

78. See Nogin's and Molotov's reports to the 11th Party Congress, *Odinnadtsatyi s"ezd*, 81, 56 respectively. By mid-1924, the Secretariat faced three to four hundred agenda items at each meeting.

79. "O raspredel'noi rabote partii," *Izvestiia TsK*, no. 1 (January 1926): 2. Gill, *Origins of the Stalinist Political System*, 163–64 is the best discussion of the rise of the *nomenklatura* system; see also *Dvenadtsatyi s"ezd*, 804.

80. For the materials on the 1925 revision, see Orgburo and Secretariat materials in RGASPI, f. 17, op. 69, d. 137, op. 112, dd. 648, and 654, op. 113, d. 436. For 1928, the materials are voluminous. RGASPI, f. 17, op. 34, d. 106, and op. 69, dd. 141, 566 and 620.

81. For rough drafts with changes, see RGASPI, f. 17, op. 34, d. 106, ll. 151–55. For "corrections and rejections by Orgraspred," see RGASPI, f. 17, op. 69, d. 141, ll. 34–42. In December 1925, Dmitri Kurskii reported to the 14th Congress that the Orgburo discussed *nomenklatura* changes seven times before deciding: *XIV s"ezd*, 91.

82. D. Kurskii's Accounting Department report to the 13th Party Congress, *Trinadtsatyi s"ezd*, 133.

83. "Dolzhnosti po nomenklature, no. 1." RGASPI, f. 17, op. 69, d. 620, ll. 3–4.

84. "Spisok dolzhnostei uchrezhdenii proizvodiatsia postanovleniem TsK VKP(b)." RGASPI, f. 17, op. 34, d. 106, ll. 174–77.

85. T. H. Rigby, "USSR Incorporated: The Origins of the Nomenklatura System," *Soviet Studies* 40, no. 4 (1988): 533.

86. "Rabota po raspredel'eniiu rabotnikov," *Izvestiia TsK*, nos. 45–46 (November 1926): 4–6.

87. As the generation of Old Bolsheviks died off, either naturally or in purges, their domination of the top committees ended. The "Lenin's comrades in arms" qualification was gradually replaced by a computation of years in the party. Thus members of the Orgburo in 1939 had an average of twenty-five years in the party; in 1946, it was twenty-three years. Seniority replaced Old Bolshevik status as markers of nobility.

88. Lenin's speech to the 9th Party Congress. *Deviatyi s"ezd*, 86.

CHAPTER 4. THE PARTY PERSONNEL SYSTEM: DOWNSTAIRS AT THE CENTRAL COMMITTEE

Epigraph: Orgburo conference, 8 November 1923. RGASPI, f. 17, op. 112, d. 494, l. 31.

1. The functions of the various departmental incarnations can be readily understood by their titles. *Uchetno-* implies recordkeeping; *raspreditel'nyi* means assignment, *organizatsionno-* indicates party assignment and/or center/periphery party coordination, *instruktorskii* refers to the peripatetic emissaries the TsK sent to the provinces for advice and discipline. It is significant that the party referred to personnel assignment as an organizational question. For them, organization *was* personnel.

2. The following description of Orgraspred's mandate is from "Polozhenie ob Organizatsionno-raspreditel'nom otdele TsK RKP(b)." Secretariat protocol, 13 March 1925. RGASPI, f. 17, op. 112, d. 646, ll. 19–21.

3. For an example, see Orgburo protocol, 13 March 1928, in which Orgraspred made "suggestions" and produced a draft resolution on the visit of the Sverdlovsk party leadership to Moscow. Orgraspred's draft was accepted. RGASPI, f. 17, op. 113, d. 605, l. 1. For a comprehensive treatment of regional party reporting to Orgraspred, see Christopher Monty, "The Central Committee Secretariat, the Nomenklatura, and the Politics of Personnel Management in the Soviet Order, 1921–1927," forthcoming in *Soviet and Post-Soviet Review.*

4. Orgraspred's staff was seventy-one persons in 1924, seventy-four in 1928. "Nomenklatura dolzhnostei uchityvaemykh v Uchraspede TsK," 1 February 1924. RGASPI, f. 17, op. 34. d. 256, ll. 3–5. "Shtat Orgraspred TsK VKP(b) na 15 noiabria 1928g." RGASPI, f. 17, op. 69, d. 548, ll. 28–30. "Shtat Orgraspred Tsentral'nogo komiteta VKP(b) na 15-e ianvaria 1929 goda." RGASPI, f. 17, op. 69, d. 547, ll. 34–36. "Struktura i shtaty otdela rukovodiashchikh partorganov TsK VKP(b)," 26 September 1935. RGASPI, f. 17, op. 114, d. 595, ll. 59–62.

5. See RGASPI, f. 17, op. 69, d. 547, ll. 56–59. See also RGASPI, f. 17, op. 85, d. 554, l. 1 for the specialty assignments in March 1930.

6. There is here an interesting parallel with Old Bolshevik factory managers and their technical staffs. The Old Bolshevik director worked as a politically reliable watchdog but personally had little technical expertise. His subordinate specialists knew how things worked. His job was to watch and confirm and referee.

7. See, for example the referrals in "Svodka, no. 1. Postupivshikh materialov Raspredotdely TsK za 11–12 marta 1930 goda." RGASPI, f. 17, op. 85, d. 554, l. 1.

8. For an example, see RGASPI, f. 17, op. 113, d. 236, l. 72.

9. These are in the files of the Secretariat. RGASPI, f. 17, op. 113, dd. 614, 616, 625.

10. *Dvenadtsatyi s"ezd RKP(b), 17–25 aprelia 1923 goda: Stenograficheskii otchet* (Moscow: Partizdat, 1960), 81.

11. For examples, see: Orgburo protocol no. 65, 8 February 1937. RGASPI, f. 17, op. 114, d. 491, l. 77. Orgburo protocol no. 90, 26 July 1938. RGASPI, f. 17, op. 114, d. 532, l. 62.

12. *Izvestiia TsK VKP(b),* no. 9 (March 1927): 6; ibid., no. 19 (May 1927): 14.

13. *Trinadtsatyi s"ezd.* 132–33.

14. *Izvestiia TsK VKP(b)*, no. 9 (March 1927): 6; ibid., no. 19 (May 1927): 14.

15. "Shtat orgraspreda Tsentral'nogo Komiteta VKP(b) na 15 noiabria 1928 g.," RGASPI, f. 17, op. 69, d. 547, ll. 28–30.

16. Secretariat protocol, 11 January 1922. RGASPI, f. 17, op. 112, d. 272, l. 2.

17. Secretariat protocols of 11 January 1922 and 11 March 1922. RGASPI, f. 17, op. 112, d. 272, l. 2, and f. 17, op. 112, d. 299, l. 2.

18. Secretariat protocol, 12 October 1923. RGASPI, f. 17, op. 112, d. 487, ll. 3, 5, 113.

19. "Shtat utverzhden Komis. po ratsionaliz." RGASPI, f. 17, op. 69, d. 547, ll. 24–26.

20. "O prieme rabotnikov v apparat TsK." Secretariat protocol, 17 January 1934. RGASPI, f. 17, op. 114, d. 392, l. 78. Also published in O. V. Khlevniuk, *Stalinskoe Politbiuro v 30-e gody: Sbornik dokumentov* (Moscow: Airo-XX, 1995), 138.

21. For a first-hand account of the frantic work inside Orgraspred, see Boris Bazhanov, *Vospominaniia byvshego sekretaria Stalina* (Saint Petersburg: Vsemirnoe slovo, 1992).

22. *Odinnadtsatyi s"ezd RKP(b), mart–aprel' 1922 goda: Stenograficheskii otchet* (Moscow: Partizdat, 1961), 52–53, 63.

23. Gill, *Origins of the Stalinist Political System.* 160.

24. For examples of these requests, see RGASPI, f. 17, op. 69, d. 648.

25. Kirgiz Obkom to Molotov, 28 November 1922. RGASPI, f. 17, op. 34, d. 55, l. 141.

26. Sibbiuro to Kaganovich, n.d. RGASPI, f. 17, op. 34, d. 55, ll. 73–73ob.

27. Orgraspred letter to Akmolinsk gubkom, 28 December 1924. RGASPI, f. 17, op. 67, d. 87, ll. 52–53.

28. See Orgraspred recommendations in RGASPI, f. 17, op. 69, d. 137, ll. 4, 28, and Orgburo protocols in RGASPI, f. 17, op. 113, d. 210, l. 10, d. 219, l. 5, and d. 221, l. 5.

29. See Orgburo protocols in RGASPI, f. 17, op. 113, d. 235, ll. 94–96.

30. Secretariat protocols. RGASPI, f. 17, op. 113, d. 236, lo. 112.

31. Predecessor to Orgraspred.

32. Orgburo protocols of 25 July 1921 and materials. RGASPI, f. 17, op. 112, d. 193, ll. 2–21.

33. *Vosmoi s"ezd RKP(b), mart 1919 goda: Protokoly* (Moscow: Partizdat, 1959), 165–66, 303–14.

34. Orgburo protocol, 29 November 1926. RGASPI, f. 17, op. 113, d. 256, l. 85.

35. Ograspred conference, 30 November 1926. RGASPI, f. 17, op. 69, d. 137, l. 121.

36. Orgburo protocol, 29 November 1926. RGASPI, f. 17, op. 113, d. 256, ll. 83–85.

37. Orgburo protocol, 3 January 1927. RGASPI, f. 17, op. 113, d. 256, l. 4.

38. Orgraspred files. RGASPI, f. 17, op. 69, d. 137, l. 164.

39. Secretariat files. RGASPI, f. 17, op. 113, d. 264, l. 98, d. 261, l. 6, and d. 262, l. 5.

40. Secretariat protocol, 4 February 1927. RGASPI, f. 17, op. 113, d. 264, l. 6.

41. Secretariat protocol, 25 February 1927. RGASPI, f. 17, op. 113, d. 261, l. 86ob.

42. Ezhov to Stalin, March 26, 1935. RGASPI, f. 671, op. 1, d. 18, ll. 18–19.

43. Orgburo protocols. RGASPI, f. 17, op. 114, d. 455, l. 2340b.

44. RGASPI, f. 17, opisi 68 and 69 contains a huge number of these. Others can be found in op. 113.

45. Orgraspred report, n.d. (1927). RGASPI, f. 17, op. 113, d. 496, l. 15.

46. Orgraspred report, 1 November 1927. RGASPI, f. 17, op. 69, d. 377, l. 8.

47. Orgburo protocol, 25 November 1919. RGASPI, f. 17, op. 112, d. 10, l. 40.

48. Orgburo protocols of 24 July, 10, 20 and 26 August 1926. RGASPI, f. 17, op. 113, d. 214, l. 4, d. 223, ll. 3, 4, 6, d. 225, l. 4, and d. 236, ll. 96–97. Letter of Zhanaia to Molotov, 10 August 1926. RGASPI, f. 82, op. 2, d. 888, l. 62.

49. Orgburo conference, 8 November 1923. RGASPI, f. 17, op. 112, d. 494, l. 31.

50. *Vosmoi s"ezd*, 497; *Desiatyi s"ezd RKP(b), mart 1921 goda: Stenograficheskii otchet* (Moscow: Partizdat, 1963), 49; *Odinnadtsatyi s"ezd*, 56; *Vosmaia Konferentsiia*, 221; RGASPI, f. 17, op. 34, d. 216, l. 51.

51. "Obsledovanie Raspredchasti TsK," n.d. RGASPI, f. 17, op. 69, d. 136, l. 162.

52. Orgraspred conference, October 1926. RGASPI, f. 17, op. 113, d. 226, ll. 109–10.

53. "Itogi raspredeleniia rabotnikov," *Izvestiia TsK VKP(b)*, no. 3 30 (January 1928): 2–3.

54. Letter of Nikitin to Bogomolov, 31 May 1927. RGASPI, f. 17, op. 69, d. 139, ll. 7–9.

55. Orgraspred conference, 20 October 1927. RGASPI, f. 17, op. 69, d. 373, ll. 3–4.

56. Orgburo conference, n.d. (1926–28). RGASPI, f. 17, op. 69, d. 136, l. 97.

57. Orgburo conference, n.d. (sometime 1926–28). RGASPI, f. 17, op. 69, d. 136, l. 121.

58. Orgraspred conference, 14 August 1928. RGASPI, f. 17, op. 69, d. 510, l. 20.

59. Orgraspred conference, 14 August 1928. RGASPI, f. 17, op. 69, d. 510, l. 16.

60. "Polozhenie Orgraspreda," 13 March 1925. RGASPI, f. 17, op. 112, d. 646, l. 20.

61. RGASPI, f. 17, op. 68, d. 43, l. 14.

62. TsKK to Systematization Commission, 7 April 1925. RGASPI, f. 17, op. 68, l. 42, l. 36.

63. Commission meetings of 12 December 1924 and 10 January 1925. RGASPI, f. 17, op. 68, d. 42, ll. 32–34, and d. 43, l. 4. The new working title, *Spravochnik partiinogo rabotnika,* would be the name of a subsequent handbook.

64. RGASPI, f. 17, op. 68, d. 42, l. 1. Eventually, the idea resulted in two series of publications: a very selective collection only of major decisions (*KPSS v resoliutsiakh* and its descendants) and an abbreviated edited handbook for party propagandists (*Spravochnik partiinogo rabotnika*). Neither of these collections came close to fulfilling the original staff charge to systematize all party decisions, nor were they meant to.

65. Orgburo meeting of 30 December 1929. RGASPI, f. 17, op. 113, d. 809, l. 42.

66. Orgburo conference, n.d. (1926–28). RGASPI, f. 17, op. 69, d. 136, l. 140.

67. *Desiatyi s"ezd*, 56, 111; *Vosmaia Konferentsiia*, 30.

68. For one among many examples of Orgraspred conferences pressing for "planned" appointments, see RGASPI, f. 88, op. 3, d. 68, ll. 5–11.

69. "Predvaritel'nyi proekty ob uchete i raspredelenii rabotnikov." RGASPI, f. 17, op. 113, d. 496, ll. 20–21.

70. *Vosmoi s"ezd*, 185.

71. *Deviatyi s"ezd RKP(b), mart–aprel' 1920 goda: Stenograficheskii otchet* (Moscow: Partizdat, 1960), 425.

72. *Odinnadtsatyi s"ezd*, 49, 63–65, 152.

73. "Stenogramma VIII-go plenuma Azovo-Chernomorskogo kraikoma VKP(b). 14–16 marta 1937g." RGASPI, f. 17, op. 21, d. 2198, l. 241. On the general problem of personnel recordkeeping, see Valerii Nikolaevich Sepelev, "Stanovlenie i razvitie tsentralizovannogo ucheta chlenov partii i rukovodiashchikh partiinykh kadrov, 1917–1927" (diss. kand. ist. nauk, Institut Marksizma-Leninizma TsK KPSS, 1988). See also J. Arch Getty, *Origins of the Great Purges: The Soviet Communist Party Reconsidered, 1933–1938* (Cambridge: Cambridge University Press, 1985), 25–37, 58–91, for a discussion of recordkeeping chaos in the early 1930s.

74. L. M. Kaganovich, *Pamiatnye zapiski rabochego, kommunista-bol'shevika, profsoiuznogo, partiinogo i sovetsko-gosudarstvennogo rabotnika* (Moscow: Vagrius, 1996), 312.

75. "Kratkaia dokladnaia zapiska po voprosy o postanovke uchete i raspredeleniia rabotnikov v gos. i khozorganakh." RGASPI, f. 17, op. 113, d. 496, ll. 11–13.

76. Smolensk Archive, file 116/154e, 88. Ezhov wrote the same thing to Stalin in August, 1935. RGASPI, f. 558, op. 11, d. 1085, l. 12.

77. Orgburo conference, 8 November 1923. RGASPI, f. 17, op. 112, d. 494, ll. 26–27.

78. Orgburo conference, 8 November 1923. RGASPI, f. 17, op. 112, d. 494, l. 27.

79. Orgburo conference, 8 November 1923. RGASPI, f. 17, op. 112, d. 494, ll. 46, 49, 53.

80. RGASPI, f. 671, op. 1, d. 18, l. 123.

81. V. P. Nogin's report to the 12th Party Congress, *Dvenadtsatyi s"ezd*, 81. Gill observes that these "councils of organizational notables" largely ratified staff proposals: Gill, *Origins of the Stalinist Political System*, 158–59.

82. For examples, see Orgburo Protocol, no. 65, 8 February 1937. RGASPI, f. 17, op. 114, d. 491, l. 77; Orgburo Protocol, no. 90, 26 July 1938. RGASPI, f. 17, op. 114, d. 532, l. 62.

83. Ezhov's successor Malenkov (ORPO head from 1936) was not a TsK secretary until 1939, although he ran ORPO and its successor Upravlenie Kadrov until 1936. But as with Kaganovich in 1924 (who although not a TsK secretary still chaired some staff conferences), he was clearly a secretary in the making. His proximity to Stalin was his power, not his formal job description; that proximity gave him his rubber stamp.

84. See, for example. RGASPI, f. 671, op. 1, dd. 1, 9 for Ezhov's ORPO meetings.

Chapter 5. Principled and Personal Conflicts

Epigraph: RGASPI, f. 558, op. 11, d. 132, ll. 90–99.

1. See Rigby, "Early Provincial Cliques and the Rise of Stalin," *Soviet Studies*, 33, no. 1 (1981): 3–28. Rigby perhaps overestimates the ability of outsiders to win control (ibid., 10, 13).

2. J. Arch Getty and Oleg V. Naumov, *Yezhov: The Rise of Stalin's "Iron Fist"* (New Haven, Conn.: Yale University Press, 2008), chap. 3.

3. Krestinskii's reports for the Central Committee, *Vosmaia Konferentsiia*, 29–30; *Deviatyi s"ezd RKP(b), mart–aprel' 1920 goda: Stenograficheskii otchet* (Moscow: Partizdat, 1960), 43, 45–46.

4. *Dvenadtsatyi s"ezd RKP(b), 17–25 aprelia 1923 goda: Stenograficheskii otchet* (Moscow: Partizdat, 1960), 66. See Terry Martin, *The Affirmative Action Empire: Nations and Nationalism in the Soviet Union, 1923–1939* (Ithaca, N.Y.: Cornell University Press, 2001) on *skloki* centering around nationality issues.

5. Orgraspred staff report, May 1922. RGASPI, f. 17, op. 34, d. 114, l. 80.

6. Orgraspred staff report. RGASPI, f. 17, op. 11, d. 548, ll. 139, 144.

7. Orgraspred staff report. RGASPI, f. 17, op. 112, d. 91, l. 2.

8. TsK memos. RGASPI, f. 17, op. 34, d. 114, ll. 10, 12, 80.

9. Orgraspred reports, April, August, and December 1922. RGASPI, f. 17, op. 34, d. 114, ll. 10–14.

10. Rigby, "Early Provincial Cliques and the Rise of Stalin," 30; RGASPI, f. 17, op. 112, d. 312, l. 4, d. 288, ll. 2–3, and d. 317, ll. 2–5. See also *Dvenadtsatyi s"ezd*, 796.

11. "A similar process occurred in other institutional structures as their leaders picked one side or the other in the disputes and then sought to use the institution to further the interests of the side they supported." Graeme Gill, *The Origins of the Stalinist Political System* (Cambridge: Cambridge University Press, 1990), 173.

12. The word *mestnichestvo* was used on contemporary party reports. See RGASPI, f. 17, op. 11, d. 548, l. 24, for example.

13. For Astrakhan and Vologda, see RGASPI, f. 17, op. 34, d. 114, ll. 10–14, and op. 11, d. 548, ll. 46–50. See also *Odinnadtsatyi s"ezd RKP(b), mart–aprel' 1922 goda: Stenograficheskii otchet* (Moscow: Partizdat, 1961), 371.

14. "On the Petrov Affair." RGASPI, f. 82, op. 2, d. 153, ll. 3–4. Although unsigned, this seems to be an internal report of the TsKK.

15. Ezhov report to the TsK, June 1922. RGASPI, f. 17, op. 67, d. 118, l. 146.

16. Ezhov report to the TsK, August 1922. RGASPI, f. 17, op. 67, d. 118, ll. 147, 151.

17. Protocols of the Mari OblKK, 1 March and 27 April 1923. RGASPI, f. 82, op. 2, d. 153, ll. 5–7.

18. Ezhov to Pëtr Ivanov, March 9, 1923. RGASPI, f. 671, op. 1, d. 267, l. 17.

19. Orgburo protocol, 10 November 1922. RGASPI, f. 17, op. 112, d. 385, l. 146. In January 1923 a Mari report listed Comrade Lur'e as party secretary. RGASPI, f. 17, op. 67, d. 118, l. 42. Things did not improve in Mari. In the following years, Ezhov's replacement I. I. Ivanov also became involved in personal squabbles and

charges and countercharges of criminal activity. See RGASPI, f. 17, op. 67, d. 118, ll. 21–25, 49.

20. This was common etiquette at the time. Rozhnov wanted Martynov recalled, but Bolshevik modesty required that he also suggest removing himself.

21. The Penza saga is reported in TsK investigation documents from summer 1922. Orgburo protocol, 19 June 1922. RGASPI, f. 17, op. 112, d. 342, and op. 11, d. 548, ll. 131–36.

22. Zinoviev's report for the Central Committee, *Vosmoi s"ezd RKP(b), mart 1919 goda: Protokoly* (Moscow: Partizdat, 1959), 287.

23. *Vosmaia Konferentsiia*, 33.

24. Molotov's reports for the Central Committee, *Odinnadtsatyi s"ezd*, 54–55, 155, 654–56; *Dvenadtsatyi s"ezd*, 792–98. The debate on the advisability of moving comrades around continued: *Desiatyi s"ezd RKP(b), mart 1921 goda: Stenograficheskii otchet* (Moscow: Partizdat, 1963), 109–11; *Deviatyi s"ezd*, 43–44, 62–63.

25. In Moscow province, Trotskyist candidates won in about a third of the districts, with higher rates among students (up to half) and lower results in workers' constituencies (around one-fifth). The voting was broken down and analyzed by several measures, including years in the party, occupation, residence, etc. "Godovoi obzor partapparate i ego vnutripartiinoi orgrabote po Moskovskoi gubernskoi organizatsii RKP za 1923 g." RGASPI, f. 17, op. 11, d. 193, ll. 12–25. On Iaroslavl', see letter from Andreev to Molotov, 15 February 1924. RGASPI, f. 82, op. 2, d. 1440, ll. 64–66.

26. The classic work on Trotsky is still the three volumes by Isaac Deutscher, *The Prophet Armed: Trotsky, 1879–1921*, *The Prophet Outcast: Trotsky, 1929–1940*, and *The Prophet Unarmed: Trotsky, 1921–1929* (New York: Oxford University Press, 1954–63).

27. See Robert Vincent Daniels, *The Conscience of the Revolution: Communist Opposition in Soviet Russia.* (Boulder, Colo.: Westview Press, 1988).

28. See below. Indeed, much of the impetus for centralizing personnel assignment and the creation of a full-time party apparatus had originally come from anti-Stalin oppositionists.

29. For a discussion and critique of this argument that stresses the independent interests of local politicians, see J. Arch Getty, "Stalin as Prime Minister: Power and the Politburo," in *Stalin: A New History,* ed. Sarah Davies and James R. Harris (Cambridge: Cambridge University Press, 2005), 63–82.

30. See Rigby, "Early Provincial Cliques and the Rise of Stalin," 5–6, 25.

31. Orgburo conference, 8 November 1923. RGASPI, f. 17, op. 112, d. 494, ll. 18–19.

32. "Dannye o dvizhenii i sostave sekretarei." RGASPI, f. 17, op. 34, d. 69, ll. 5–60b.

33. N. Khrushchev, *Memoirs of Nikita Khrushchev*, vol. 1: *Commissar (1918–1945)* (University Park, Pa.: Penn State University Press, 2004), 11.

34. Ossinskii, Sapronov, and Zinoviev speeches to the 8th Congress, *Vosmoi s"ezd*, 165–66, 169–71, 184–85, respectively.

35. Trotsky's speech to the 9th Party Congress, *Deviatyi s"ezd*, 76–77. Preobrazhenskii would change his mind and maintain that the Central Committee

needed the authority to appoint rather than elect provincial party secretaries. See his speech to the 12th Party Congress, *Dvenadtsatyi s"ezd,* 146.

36. See Molotov's and Rumiantsev's speeches to the 14th Party Congress, *XIV s"ezd Vsesoiuznoi Kommunisticheskoi Partii (b), 18–31 dekabria 1925 g. Stenograficheskii otchet* (Moscow: Gosizdat, 1926), 484–85 and 595.

37. Riutin's speech to the 12th Party Congress, *Dvenadtsatyi s"ezd,* 181.

38. Although "policy was not merely the plaything of factional considerations, . . . at different times the approach to ideological tenets and policy issues adopted by virtually all protagonists was instrumental in nature. None was averse to taking up a policy position with an eye to the effects this would have in the ongoing elite maneuvering at the top." Gill, *Origins of the Stalinist Political System,* 184–86.

39. Ibid., 94, 173; Rigby, "Early Provincial Cliques and the Rise of Stalin," 17.

40. There were exceptions. When Stalin lurched to the left in 1929, a number of visible senior Trotskyists abandoned Trotsky, recanted, and sided with Stalin. Radek, Piatakov, and others followed their principles: Stalin now advocated what Trotsky had argued for. On the other hand, hundreds of rank-and-file Trotskyists, many of them in prison, retained their personal loyalty to Trotsky, regardless of Stalin's new policies.

41. See Orgburo and Orgraspred reports for 1922 and 1923 in RGASPI, f. 17, op. 11, d. 548, ll. 46, 131, 132, 139, 144, 183.

42. "Obzor konfliktov," January–March 1922. RGASPI, f. 17, op. 11, d. 548, ll. 24–34. For characterization of the Workers' Opposition with the hated word *gruppirovka,* see also "Postanovleniia XII-go s"ezda RKP, Trebuiushchee dal'nejshei razrabotki TsK VKP(b)," 1 January 1923. RGASPI, f. 82, op. 2, d. 156, l. 173.

43. Orgraspred reports, April, August, and December 1922. RGASPI, f. 17, op. 34, d. 114, ll. 10–14.

44. Ivo Banac, ed., *The Diary of Georgi Dimitrov, 1933–1949* (New Haven, Conn.: Yale University Press, 2003), 66–67.

45. Khrushchev, *Memoirs,* 1:22.

46. L. M. Kaganovich, *Pamiatnye zapiski rabochego, kommunista-bol'shevika, profsoiuznogo, partiinogo i sovetsko-gosudarstvennogo rabotnika* (Moscow: Vagrius, 1996), 340–41. Historians have usually explained Stalin's restraint as a maneuver within a devious long-term plan to destroy the oppositions. This is part of a counterfactual tendency to see even liberal moves by Stalin as parts of complicated repressive plans. Logically, if he had such plans in 1924 he would have taken advantage of this local backing to move forcefully against the opposition. He did not, and Kaganovich's explanation makes more sense.

47. *Deviatyi s"ezd,* 64.

48. See Molotov's scathing attack on the Leningraders' undemocratic delegate selection: *XIV s"ezd,* 482–83 and RGASPI, f. 17, op. 113, d. 362.

49. See the speeches by Molotov, Shkiriatov, and Rumiantsev, *XIV s"ezd,* 484–85, 568–71, 595.

50. Kirov to Ordzhonikidze, 16 January 1926. RGASPI, f. 85, op. 25, d. 118, ll. 2–3.

51. See Orgburo protocols of 27 May and 24 April 1919 for "special opinions" of individual members. RGASPI, f. 17, op. 112, d. 4, l. 82, and op. 112, d. 3, l. 44.

52. Robert Service, *The Bolshevik Party in Revolution: A Study in Organizational Change, 1917–1923* (London: Macmillan, 1979), 128.

53. Molotov's organizational report to the 11th Party Congress, *Odinnadtsatyi s"ezd*, 54.

54. See Gill, *Origins of the Stalinist Political System*, 132–34.

55. *Odinnadtsatyi s"ezd.* 126, 155.

56. "Dannye o dvizhenii i sostave sekretarei." RGASPI, f. 17, op. 34, d. 69, ll. 5–60b.

57. Before the mid-1920s, it was not clear whether the local party or soviet would be dominant.

58. Gorshin to Stalin, 1 March 1929. RGASPI, f. 82, op. 2, d. 1444, ll. 53–54.

59. Stalin to Kaganovich, 18 June 1932. RGASPI, f. 558, op. 11, d. 77, l. 62.

60. Kakhani to Stalin, Molotov, Andreev, 4 April 1937. RGASPI, f. 82, op. 2, d. 153, ll. 70–75.

61. *Dvenadtsatyi s"ezd.* 66.

62. See Gerald Easter, *Reconstructing the State: Personal Networks and Elite Identity in Soviet Russia* (Cambridge: Cambridge University Press, 2000); Merle Fainsod, *How Russia Is Ruled* (Cambridge, Mass.: Harvard University Press, 1967); Getty, *Origins of the Great Purges: the Soviet Communist Party Reconsidered, 1933–1938* (Cambridge: Cambridge University Press, 1985); James R. Harris, *The Great Urals: Regionalism and the Evolution of the Soviet System* (Ithaca, N.Y.: Cornell University Press, 1999).

63. It is not always easy to identify members of the leading clan in a province. The approach used here was twofold. First, to read stenograms of meetings in which party members often criticized or defended each other. Second, at the time of regional party conferences, we find lists of the elected members of the obkom or obkom bureau, along with their jobs. See, for example, Ryndin's list in Cheliabinsk, "Protokol 2-i oblastnoi partiinoi konferentsii VKP(b) Cheliabinsk oblasti," RGASPI, f. 17, op. 21, d. 5637, l. 3, or Semënov's in Stalingrad: "Stenogramma II Stalingradskoi oblastnoi konferentsii VKP(b), t. 2.," RGASPI, f. 17, op. 21, d. 4227, ll. 10–12.

64. Daniel T. Orlovsky, "Political Clientelism in Russia: the Historical Perspective," in *Leadership Selection and Patron-Client Relations in the USSR and Yugoslavia*, ed. T. H. Rigby and Bogdan Harasymiw (London: Allen & Unwn, 1983), 187, 189.

65. "Stenograficheskii otchet V oblastnoi partkonferentsii Zapadnoi oblasti. 18–26 maia 1937g." RGASPI, f. 17, op. 21, d. 4073, l. 43.

66. "Protokoly i Stenogramma XVII Tatarskoi oblastnoi konferentsii VKP(b). 10–15 iuniia 1937g." RGASPI, f. 17, op. 21, d. 4248, l. 140.

67. RGASPI, f. 17, op. 21, d. 2214, ll. 970b, 98.

68. "Plenum Azovsko-Chernomorskogo kraikoma VKP(b). 6 ianvaria 1937g." RGASPI, f. 17, op. 21, d. 2196, l. 239. For more on Sheboldaev and his "brothers-in-law," see Chapter 8.

69. Before the revolution, an *artel'* was a group of workers in a given craft, often from the same home town, who worked and lived together.

70. Valerie A. Kivelson, *Autocracy in the Provinces: The Muscovite Gentry and Political Culture in the Seventeenth Century* (Stanford, Calif.: Stanford University Press, 176), 176. T. H. Rigby noted that this passage "will strike a familiar chord

with the seasoned sovietologist." Rigby, "Russia's Clientelism, Cliques, Connections and 'Clans': The Same Old Story?" *Soviet and Post-Soviet Review* 25, no. 2 (1998): 110.

71. Stalin telegram to Kaganovich, Molotov, and Ordzhonikidze, 1 October 1931. RGASPI, f. 558, op. 11, d. 76, ll. 84–85.

72. I. V. Stalin, *Sochineniia*, vol. 10 (Moscow: Partizdat, 1954), 329–33. My thanks to James Harris for pointing this out to me. Stalin's reference to "as in the home" is significant. Boris Mironov wrote that the Stalin regime "did not frighten the masses, nor did they protest it; rather it suited them because from childhood they had grown accustomed to authoritarian relations and simply knew nothing else." B. N. Mironov, "Peasant Popular Culture and the Origins of Soviet Authoritarianism," in *Cultures in Flux: Lower-Class Values, Practices, and Resistance in Late Imperial Russia,* ed. Stephen P. Frank and Mark D. Steinberg (Princeton, N.J.: Princeton University Press, 1994), 72.

73. RGASPI, f. 558, op. 11, d. 132, ll. 90–99.

74. T. H. Rigby, "Was Stalin a Disloyal Patron?" *Soviet Studies* 38, no. 3 (1986): 311–24.

75. Stalin to Kaganovich, 17 August 1931. RGASPI, f. 81, op. 3, d. 100, l. 101. Published in O. V. Khlevniuk, R. W. Davies, A. P. Kosheleva, E. A. Rees, and A. A. Rogovaia, eds., *Stalin i Kaganovich: Perepiska. 1931–1936 gg.* (Moscow: Rosspen, 2001), 51.

76. Sheila Fitzpatrick, "Ordzhonikidze's Takeover of Vesenkha: A Case Study in Soviet Bureaucratic Politics," *Soviet Studies* 37, no. 2 (April 1985): 153–72; Jonathan Harris, "The Origins of the Conflict between Malenkov and Zhdanov, 1939–1941," *Slavic Review* 35, no. 2 (1976): 287–303; R. W. Davies, O. Khlevniuk, E. A. Rees, A. P. Kosheleva, and A. A. Rogovaia, eds., *The Stalin-Kaganovich Correspondence, 1931–1936* (New Haven, Conn.: Yale University Press, 2003), 20–21, 303; O. V. Khlevniuk, *Stalinskoe Politbiuro v 30-e gody: Sbornik dokumentov* (Moscow: AIRO-XX, 1995), 79, 85, 242–45, 59–60, 63–64.

77. Feliks Ivanovich Chuev, *Tak govoril Kaganovich: Ispoved' stalinskogo apostola* (Moscow: Olma Press, 2001), 130.

78. A. I. Mikoian, *Tak Bylo: Razmyshleniia o minuvshem* (Moscow: Vagrius, 1999), 324.

79. RGASPI, f. 558, op. 11, d. 779, ll. 23, 29–31, 33. See also Davies et al., *Stalin-Kaganovich Correspondence,* 21; Khlevniuk, *Stalinskoe Politbiuro,* 85.

80. Sergo Beria, *Beria, My Father: Inside Stalin's Kremlin* (London: Duckworth, 2001), 145.

81. N. Khrushchev, *Memoirs of Nikita Khrushchev,* vol. 2: *Reformer (1945–1964)* (University Park, Pa.: Penn State University Press, 2006), 181. On this see also Beria, *Beria My Father,* 218.

82. See Svetlana Alliluyeva, *Twenty Letters to a Friend,* trans. Priscilla Johnson McMillan (New York: Harper & Row, 1967); Beria, *Beria, My Father*; Feliks Ivanovich Chuev, *Sto sorok besed s Molotovym: Iz dnevnika F. Chueva* (Moscow: Terra, 1991) (abridged English version: V. M. Molotov, Felix Chuev, and Albert Resis, *Molotov Remembers: Inside Kremlin Politics. Conversations With Felix Chuev* (Chicago: I. R. Dee, 1993)); Chuev, *Tak govoril Kaganovich*; N. Khrushchev,

Memoirs, vols. 1 and 2; A. G. Malenkov, *O moem ottse Georgii Malenkove* (Moskva: NTTS "Tekhnoekos," 1992); Mikoian, *Tak bylo.*

83. Beria, *Beria, My Father*, 159.
84. Most of the work on identifying police clans has been done by Leonid Naumov. See Leonid Naumov, *Bor'ba v rukovodstve NKVD v 1936–38 gg.* (Moscow: Yauza, 2003); Leonid Naumov, *"Krovavyi karlik" protiv vozhdia narodov: Zagovor Ezhova* (Moscow: Yauza, Eksmo, 2009).
85. Pavel Sudoplatov and Anatoli Sudoplatov, *Special Tasks: the Memoirs of an Unwanted Witness, a Soviet Spymaster* (Boston: Little, Brown, 1994), 325.
86. Mikhail Shreider, *NKVD iznutri: Zapiski chekista* (Moscow: Vozrashchenie, 1995), 16–17.
87. Naumov, *Zagovor Ezhova.* 198–99.
88. See S. Wheatcroft, "Agency and Terror: Evdokimov and Mass Killing in Stalin's Great Terror," *Australian Journal of Politics and History* 53, no. 1 (2007): 20–43. For various interpretations of the mass operations, see J. A. Getty, "'Excesses Are Not Permitted': Mass Terror and Stalinist Governance in the Late 1930s," *Russian Review* 61, no. 1 (2002): 113–38; R. Binner and M. Junge, "How the Terror Became "Great": Mass Execution and Camp Sentences on the Basis of Order 00447," *Cahiers du Monde Russe* 42, no. 2–4 (2001): 557–613. See also below, Chapter 7.
89. M. A. Tumshis and A. Palchinskii, *1937: Bol'shaia chistka. NKVD protiv ChK* (Moscow: Yauza, Eksmo, 2009), 190.
90. Ibid., 202.
91. For poems about Ezhov, see Getty and Naumov, *Yezhov*, xviii, 214–15.
92. Suleiman Stal'skii, "The Song of Bolshevik Efim Evdokimov." Tumshis and Palchinskii, *1937: Bol'shaia chistka*, 140.
93. V. M. Molotov, Felix Chuev, and Albert Resis, *Molotov Remembers: Inside Kremlin Politics. Conversations With Felix Chuev* (Chicago: I. R. Dee, 1993), 257.
94. See, for example, Stalin's automatic, one-word agreement to Iagoda's request to appoint his man G. Prokof'ev to a high NKVD position. Telegram from Stalin to Kaganovich, 5 August 1934. RGASPI, f. 558, op. 22, d. 83, l. 20.
95. "Materialy fevral'skogo-martovskogo plenuma TsK VKP(b) 1937 goda," *Voprosy Istorii*, no. 10 (1994): 4–6. See also Tumshis and Palchinskii, *1937: Bol'shaia chistka*, 204–8; Wheatcroft, "Agency and Terror," 30.
96. Naumov, *"Krovavyi karlik,"* 203; Shreider, *NKVD iznutri*, 10.
97. V. K. Vinogradov et. al., eds., *Genrikh Iagoda: Narkom vnutrennikh del SSSR, Generalnyi komissar godsudarstvennoi bezopasnosti. Sbornik dokumentov* (Kazan: Krista, 2000), 89–93, 440–41.
98. Ibid., 89–93.
99. "Protokol piatoi Gor'kovskoi oblastnoi konferentsii VKP(b). 5–11 iiunia 1937g." RGASPI, f. 17, op. 21, d. 872, ll. 349–51.
100. Stalin to Menzhinskii, 16 September 1929. V. N. Khaustov, V. P. Naumov, and N. S. Plotnikov, eds., *Lubianka: Stalin i VChK-GPU-OGPU-NKVD, ianvar' 1922–dekabr' 1936* (Moscow: Fond "Demokratiia," 2003), 191.
101. M. A. Tumshis and A. Palchinskii, *1937: Bol'shaia chistka*, 207.
102. M. A. Tumshis and A. Palchinskii, *NKVD protiv ChK.* 211–13; Khaustov et al., *Lubianka 1922–1936*, 275–76. Given Evdokimov's later role in the Great Terror,

using the same methods, it might seem ironic to accuse Iagoda's men of such brutality. But Evdokimov was no liberal in 1931; in the police clan struggles, matters of principle were not involved. The point was to smear the other clan any way possible.

103. Ibid., 222; Khaustov et al., *Lubianka 1922–1936*, 280.

104. Tumshis and Palchinskii, *1937: Bol'shaia chistka*, 222.

105. Even though Balitskii was also forbidden from importing a "tail" of his people with him, he nevertheless managed to do it. He installed at least eight of his clan in the central apparatus and another five to head provincial OGPU offices. See ibid., 84–85.

106. Khaustov et al., *Lubianka 1922–1936*. 275–76.

107. Ibid., 280.

108. "Materialy fevral'skogo-martovskogo plenuma TsK VKP(b) 1937 goda," *Voprosy Istorii*, no. 10 (1994): 7, 21, 15. M. A. Tumshis and A. Palchinskii, *1937: Bol'shaia chistka*, 89–90.

109. "Ob organizatsii Soiuznogo narkomata vnutrennykh del," (Politburo resolution). RGASPI, f. 17, op. 3, d. 939, l. 2. Stalin participated personally in the drafting of these regulations: Politburo resolution of 1 April 1934. RGASPI, f. 17, op. 3, d. 943, l. 10. The decree was published in *Izvestiia*, 11 July 11 1934.

110. RGASPI, f. 17, op. 165, d. 47, l. 3.

111. Iagoda speech to NKVD operational officers, 1936. Vinogradov et al., *Genrikh Iagoda*, 405–23.

112. Stalin's notes on Vyshinskii memo. RGASPI, f. 558, op. 2, d. 155, l. 66.

113. See Getty and Naumov, *Yezhov*; Marc Jansen and Nikita Petrov, *Stalin's Loyal Executioner: People's Commissar Nikolai Ezhov, 1895–1940* (Stanford, Calif.: Hoover Institution Press, 2002).

114. *Moskovskie novosti*, no. 5, 30 January 1994.

115. In addition to Evdokimov's close associates M. Frinovskii, I. Dagin, N. Nikolaev-Zhhurid, P. Bullakh and V. Dementev, there were many others.

116. Tumshis and Palchinskii, *1937: Bol'shaia chistka*, 242.

117. Stephen Wheatcroft argues that Evdokimov nevertheless played a role in NKVD central politics and the subsequent Great Purges. See Wheatcroft, "Agency and Terror." But it is not clear to what extent he could do this from far away Rostov-on-Don.

118. Tumshis and Palchinskii, *1937: Bol'shaia chistka*, 92.

119. V. N. Khaustov and Lennart Samuelson, *Stalin, NKVD i repressii: 1936–1938gg.* (Moscow: Rosspen, 2009), 230.

120. Ibid., 311.

121. Tumshis and Palchinskii, *1937: Bol'shaia chistka*, 62–77; Khaustov and Samuelson, *Stalin, NKVD i repressii*, 242–43.

122. Naumov, "*Krovavyi karlik*," 216.

123. Ibid., 218; Khaustov and Samuelson, *Stalin, NKVD i repressii*, 246.

124. Naumov, "*Krovavyi karlik*," 219.

125. RGASPI, f. 17, op. 21, d. 3952, l. 2. See also: "Plenum Azovso-Chernomorskogo kraikoma VKP(b). 6 ianvaria 1937g." RGASPI, f. 17, op. 21, d. 2196, ll. 2, 5–9, 10–13, 16–17, 22–23, 32–40. "Protokol 2-go plenuma Zapobkoma VKP(b). 18–20 iiunia 1937g." RGASPI, f. 17, op. 21, d. 4092, l. 4.

126. Harris, *The Great Urals.*

127. Gerald Easter believes that the provincial leaders represented a "protocor-poratist alternative to Stalin's bureaucratic absolutism," but he admits that they "did not articulate an alternative to the command-administrative state. They never offered an alternative vision . . ." Easter, *Reconstructing the State,* 124–32.

128. Rigby, "Was Stalin a Disloyal Patron?" notes that through the years and purges, Stalin's inner circle remained remarkably stable.

129. See J. Arch Getty and Oleg V. Naumov, *The Road to Terror: Stalin and the Self-Destruction of the Bolsheviks, 1932–1939* (New Haven, Conn.: Yale University Press, 1999) for these developments.

CHAPTER 6. STALIN AND THE CLANS I

Epigraph: Frenkel' to Stalin and Ezhov, 22 May 1937. RGASPI, f. 671, op. 1, d. 89, ll. 127–30.

1. O. Cappelli, "Pre-Modern State-Building in Post-Soviet Russia," *Journal of Communist Studies and Transition Politics* 24, no. 4 (2008): 547, 561.

2. In this connection, the Russian word *kontrol'* should be translated as checking, monitoring, or verification, rather than "control."

3. On the TsKK and Workers' and Peasants' Inspection, see E. A. Rees, *State Control in Soviet Russia: The Rise and Fall of the Workers' and Peasants' Inspec-torate, 1920–34* (Basingstoke: Macmillan, 1987); and Paul Cocks, "Politics of Party Control: The Historical and Institutional Role of Party Control Organs in the CPSU" (Ph.D. diss., Harvard University, 1968). Soviet-era works include S. N. Ikonnikov, *Sozdanie i deiatel'nost' obedinennykh organov TsKK-RKI v 1923–1934gg.* (Moscow: Gosizdat, 1971); I. M. Moskalenko, *Organy partiinogo kon-trolia v period stroitel'stva sotsializma (zadachi, struktura, metody deiatel'nosti kontrolnykh komissii, 1920–1934gg.* (Moscow: Gosizdat, 1981) and *TsKK v bor'be za edinstvo i chistotu partiinykh riadov* (Moscow: Partizdat, 1973).

4. See Leonard Schapiro, *The Communist Party of the Soviet Union* (New York: Vintage, 1971), 260–62, 271–78, 323–24.

5. Ian Bauer, "Boevye zadachi kontrol'nykh komissii VKP(b): K itogam IV plenuma TsKK VKP(b)," in VKP(b) Tsentral'naia kontrol'naia komissiia, *Resheniia 4-go plenuma TsKK VKP(b) i 3-i partkonferentsii Zapadnoi oblasti* (Smolensk; Partizdat, 1932), 3–7. See also "Rezoliutsiia III oblastnoi partkonferentsii po otch-etnomu dokladu ZapoblKK VKP(b)," ibid., 25; and M. F. Shkiriatov, *O rabote KK-RKI v raione: Doklad na IV plenume TsKK, VKP(b) 9 fevr. 1932g* (Moscow: Partizdat, 1932).

6. Moskalenko, *Organy,* 143–44.

7. Rees, *State Control,* 216; see also Schapiro, *Communist Party of the Soviet Union,* 260–61.

8. See J. Arch Getty, *Origins of the Great Purges: the Soviet Communist Party Reconsidered, 1933–1938* (Cambridge: Cambridge University Press, 1985), esp. chap. 2.

9. L. Paparde, "O podgotovke k chistke partii: Doklad na plenume Zap-Sib. Kraikoma VKP(b) 22–25 Iiuniia 1933g." (Novosibirsk: Partizdat, 1933), 32–33.

10. V. I. Lenin, *Collected Works*, vol. 33 (Moscow: Gosizdat, 1965), 363–69.

11. On the Smolensk scandal, see Merle Fainsod, *Smolensk under Soviet Rule* (Cambridge, Mass.: Harvard University Press, 1958); Daniel Brower, "The Smolensk Scandal and the End of NEP," *Slavic Review* 45, no. 4 (1986): 689–706; William Rosenberg, "Smolensk in the 1920s: Party-Worker Relations and the 'Vanguard' Problem," *Russian Review* 36, no. 2 (1977): 125–50.

12. See *XVII s"ezd Vsesoiuznoi Kommunisticheskoi Partii (b) 27 ianvaria–10 fevralia 1934g: Stenograficheskii otchet* (Moscow: Partizdat, 1934), p. 103, Smolensk Archive, file WKP 362, pp. 12, 231–32.

13. See Fainsod, *Smolensk*; Getty, *Origins*, chaps. 1–4; Gabor T. Rittersporn, *Stalinist Simplifications and Soviet Complications: Social Tensions and Political Conflicts in the USSR, 1933–1953* (London: Harwood, 1991); Roberta T. Manning, *Government in the Soviet Countryside in the Stalinist Thirties: The Case of Belyi Raion in 1937*, The Carl Beck Papers in Russian and East European Studies, no. 301 (Pittsburgh, Pa.: Russian and East European Studies Program, University of Pittsburgh, 1985); Gabor T. Rittersporn, "The State Against Itself: Social Tensions Behind the Rhetorical Apotheosis," *Telos* 41 (1979): 87–104, and "Rethinking Stalinism," *Russian History* 11, no. 4 (1984): 343–61; T. H. Rigby, "Early Provincial Cliques and the Rise of Stalin," *Soviet Studies* 3, no. 1 (January 1981): 3–28. For a look at "localization" of party organizations in the 1920s, see Brower, "The Smolensk Scandal and the End of NEP."

14. Peter H. Solomon, "Local Political Power and Soviet Criminal Justice 1922–1941," *Soviet Studies* 37, no. 3 (July 1985): 305–29; and Gabor T. Rittersporn, "Soviet Officialdom and Political Evolution: Judiciary Apparatus and Penal Policy in the 1930s," *Theory and Society* 13 (1984): 211–31.

15. The first hint of the reorganization came from L. M. Kaganovich in his speech to a Moscow party conference: *IV Moskovskaia oblastnaia i III gorodskaia konferentsiia VKP(b): Stenograficheskii otchet* (Moscow: Mospart, 1934), 51–55.

16. *XVII s"ezd*, 35.

17. Ibid. Searches in the Russian National Library, INION, BAN, and Istoricheskaia Biblioteka produced no books or articles about the KPK in the 1930s.

18. V. I. Menzhulin, *Organizatsionno-partiinaia rabota KPSS v usloviiakh bor'by za pobedy i uprochnenie sotsializma (1933 iiun'–1941g)* (Moscow: Partizdat, 1975), 257–59. See also Moskalenko, *Organy,* 143–44, who suggests that the organizational tree of the new KPK differed little from that of the old TsKK. Moskalenko believes that the chief difference between the TsKK and KPK was central appointment of the latter's plenipotentiaries.

19. L. M. Kaganovich, "O zadachakh partiinogo kontrolia i kontrol'noi rabote profsoiuzov, komsomola, i pechati," *Pravda,* 4 July 1934. See also Kaganovich's remarks in *Partiinoe stroitel'stvo,* no. 13 (July 1934): 10.

20. RGANI, f. 6, op. 1. d. 5, ll. 55–56.

21. RGANI, f. 6, op. 1. d. 5, l. 58.

22. RGANI, f. 6, op. 1. d. 5, ll. 81, 88–89.

23. For biographical information on Rumiantsev see M. Nikitin and M. Ivanov, "S rabochei prostotoi," in *Soldaty partii* (Moscow: Partizdat, 1971), 201–18. See also *Rabochii put'* (Smolensk daily newspaper) 1–3 January, 8 and 13 January

1935 (coverage of his birthday); 8 January 1935 (biographies of local leaders); 16 March and 15 June 1935, and 2 September 1936 (coverage of his speeches). See also *Partiets* (Smolensk party journal), no. 12 (December 1935): 41, 72; and no. 4 (April 1937): 10. Merle Fainsod called Rumiantsev "the Great Lord of Smolensk," see *Smolensk*, chap. 2. For interesting observations on cults of personality in earlier eras of Russian history, see Claudio Sergio Ingerflom, *Le citoyen impossible: Les racines russes du Léninisme* (Paris: Gallimard, 1988), 43.

24. RGASPI, f. 17, op. 3, d. 982, l. 48.

25. RGASPI, f. 589, op. 3, d. 11746, ll. 19–20; GARF, f. 3316, op. 8, d. 110, l. 3.

26. L. A. Paparde, *O podgotovke k chistke partii* (Novosibirsk, 1933), 16, 32–33.

27. Such authority included the right to make arrests and control prosecutions. In Belorussia, for example, party provincial secretaries had sought to control railroad personnel through illegal arrests. "Tens, hundreds were arrested by anybody and sit in jail." In the Briansk Railroad Line, 75 percent of the administrative-technical personnel had been sentenced to some kind of "corrective labor." See RGANI, f. 6, op. 1, d. 5, ll. 165–66.

28. Rittersporn, "The State Against Itself," and "Rethinking Stalinism."

29. RGANI, f. 6, op. 1, d. 1, ll. 1–5; "Pervoe zasedanie KPK," *Partiinoe stroitel'stvo*, no. 7 (April 1934): 46. Because the next full meeting of the KPK, on 26–28 June 1934, was designated the *Vtoroi plenum* of the KPK, it is strange that this first session was labeled only *zasedanie*. The difference between a *zasedanie* and a *plenum* was never explained in this case.

30. *Pravda*, 12 February 1934. Bureau members were Kaganovich, Ezhov, Shkiriatov, Iaroslavskii, I. A. Akulov, D. A. Bulatov, and Ia. Kh. Peters.

31. RGASPI, f. 17, op. 3, d. 940, l. 33; RGANI, f. 6, op. 1, d. 1, ll. 7–12; "Polozhenie o Komissii Partiinogo Kontroliia pri TsK VKP(b). Priniato Komissiei Partiinogo Kontroliia i utverzhdeno TsK VKP(b)," in *Polozhenie: O komissii partiinogo kontroliia pri TsK VKP(b)* (Moscow: Partizdat, 1934), 1–3.

32. Ibid., 7.

33. Ibid., section III.

34. *Pravda*, 4 July 1934. See also "Informatsionnoe soobshenie," *Partiinoe stroitel'stvo*, no. 14 (July 1934): 44.

35. RGANI, f. 6, op. 1, d. 5, ll. 10, 12.

36. RGANI, f. 6, op. 1, d. 5, l. 27.

37. RGANI, f. 6, op. 1, d. 5, l. 30.

38. RGANI, f. 6, op. 1, d. 5, ll. 40–41, 81.

39. RGANI, f. 6, op. 1, d. 5, ll. 90, 95, 98–99.

40. RGANI, f. 6, op. 1, d. 5, l. 133.

41. L. M. Kaganovich, "O zadachakh partiinogo kontrolia i kontrol'noi rabote profsoiuzov, komsomola, i pechati," *Pravda*, 4 July 1934, and *Partiinoe stroitel'stvo*, no. 13 (1934): 3–10. There is indeed evidence that Stalin concerned himself with KPK affairs. One plenipotentiary noted that Stalin was quick to answer their questions and requests, leaving none of them unanswered. See RGANI, f. 6, op. 1, d. 5, l. 31.

42. Sheboldaev to Ezhov, 6 February 1936. RGASPI, f. 671, op. 1, d. 89, ll. 3–5. Undated Ezhov notes on conversations with Kaganovich. RGASPI, f. 671, op. 1, d. 52, ll. 14–20.

43. "V komissii partkontroliia: O rabote khoziaistvennogo otdela srednevolzhs-kogo kraiispolkoma," *Partiinoe stroitel'stvo*, no. 3 (February 1935): 47.

44. "Kalenym zhelezom vyzhech' politicheskoe i bytovoe razlozhenie," *Partiinoe stroitelstvo*, no. 14 (July 1935): 45–47.

45. Vyshinskii to Molotov, 23 October 1934. RGASPI, f. 82, op. 2, d. 886, ll. 5–8.

46. Antselovich to Antipov, n.d. (1937). GARF, f. 3893 (7541), op. 10, d. 32, l. 8, and f. 7511, op. 10, d. 31, l. 47. When these crimes were finally aired (in party documents but not publicly), they were sometimes ascribed to "Trotskyists."

47. Glinskii report to Orgburo, 14 November 1927. RGASPI, f. 17, op. 113, d. 342, ll. 41–42.

48. "Delo o neobosnovannom iskliuchenii iz partii Tov. Samurina." RGASPI, f. 17, op. 113, d. 342, l. 47.

49. On *chistki* see Getty, *Origins*, chaps. 2–3.

50. Ibid., chap. 3.

51. *Rabochii put'*, 24 May 1935, 1.

52. "O vypolnenii zakrytogo pis'ma TsK VKP(b) 13-go maia 1935 g. v partorganizatsii Zapadnoi Oblasti," *Partiinoe stroitel'stvo*, no. 13 (July 1935): 46, and *Pravda*, 7 July 1935.

53. Paparde's speech eventually received wide local publicity. See *Partiets* (Smolensk), no. 6, June 1935, 9–11, and *Rabochii put'*, July 6, 1935, 3. But the two-week delay in publishing his remarks in the obkom-controlled daily *Rabochii put'* may be the result of the obkom's attempt to protect Arkhipov from public attack. Paparde also made a pointed speech on the bungled verification to an extraordinary session of the Zapobkom plenum on 1 July, 1935: RGASPI, f. 17, op. 21, d. 4087, 278–96.

54. "Postanovleniia plenum Zapobkoma VKP(b)," *Partiets*, no. 3 (June 1935) 25; and RGASPI, f. 17, op. 21, d. 4087, ll. 181–300.

55. See M. Malkov, "Bez uchastiia partiinykh mass," ibid., no. 6 (June 1935): 22; A. Shil'man, "Ulushchit' sistemu partiinogo rukovodstva," ibid., 3–9; V. Arkhipov, "Ispravliaem dopushchennuiu oshibku v proverke partdokumentov," ibid., no. 7 (June 1935): 25.

56. See Rumiantsev's report to city party activists in Smolensk in *Rabochii put'*, 2 July 1935, 1; I. P. Rumiantsev, "Vtoraia proverka partdokumentov," *Partiinoe stroitel'stvo*, no. 17 (October 1935): 19–21; and A. Shil'man, "Tekushchie voprosy partiinoi raboty," ibid., nos. 19–20 (November 1935): 49–57.

57. F. Khlopotykhin, "Vyshe uroven' samokritiki," *Partiets*, no. 7 (July 1935): 23–26.

58. F. Bolshunov, "Proverku partdokumentov v Rudne proveli po-biurokraticheski," ibid., no. 6 (June 1935): 19–20.

59. L. Paparde, "Ustav partii—nezyblemaia osnova vsei raboty," *Partiets*, no. 13 (December 1935,): 9–11. See also Paparde's "Do kontsa izvlech' politicheskie uroki," ibid., no. 9 (September 1936): 29–38, in which he returned to the theme of the mistakes of Arkhipov and the Smolensk city party organization.

60. See RGASPI, f. 17, op. 21, d. 4091, ll. 42, 52, 71, 87, and op. 21, d. 4087, l. 278 for these and other examples.

61. "Stenograficheskii otchet II-go Zapobkoma VKP(b) ot 10–12 marta 1937 goda." RGASPI, f. 17, op. 21, d. 4091, ll. 170–74.

62. RGASPI, f. 17, op. 3, d. 965, l. 3.

63. "Uroki politicheskikh oshibok Saratovskogo krakoma," *Pravda*, 12 July 1935. Zhdanov's speech was also published in *Partiinoe stroitel'stvo* (nos. 13 and 15 [July 1935]), and as a separate pamphlet of the same name. Given later events, the application of the term "mass repression" in connection with the rather benign expulsions of 1935 seems strange.

64. *Partiinoe stroitel'stvo*, no. 13 (July 1935): 45.

65. Ibid., no. 17 (October 1935): 17–18.

66. A. Krinitskii, "Saratovskie bol'sheviki v bor'be za ispravlenie oshibok," ibid., 39–41.

67. Krinitskii ran a tight shop in Saratov. The local party journal rarely criticized the kraikom, and even in 1937 when regional party machines were falling over themselves to self-criticize, the Saratov machine preferred to boast of its successes. See, for example, "Rech' tov. A. I. Krinitskogo pri zakrytii plenuma Obkoma VKP(b), 2 ianvaria 1937 goda," *Partiinaia rabota* (Saratov), no. 1 (January 1937): 13, and no. 3 (March 1937): 45, for Krinitskii's report on the February 1937 Central Committee plenum.

68. Telegram from Stalin to Krinitskii, 3 April 1937. RGASPI, f. 558, op. 11, d. 56, l. 46. Stalin addressed the telegram to all members and candidates of the territorial party committee, just in case Krinitskii did not pass on Stalin's censure of him.

69. "O rabote partkollegii KPK i poriadke izlozheniia partiinykh vzyskanii na chlenov i kandidatov VKP(b)," *Pravda*, 17 March 1936.

70. "O rabote upolnomochennykh KPK," ibid.

71. "Tretii plenum Komissii Partkontrolia," *Partiinoe stroitel'stvo*, no. 7 (April 1936): 4, and V. Bogushevskii, "III Plenum Komissii partiinogo kontrolia," ibid., 8, 11.

72. RGANI, f. 6, op. 1, d. 14, ll. 149–51.

73. RGANI, f. 6, op. 1, d. 14, l. 155.

74. RGANI, f. 6, op. 1, d. 13, ll. 41–42, 95, 113–23, 188.

75. "O rabote upolnomochennykh KPK," *Partiets*, no. 3 (March 1936): 1–4. See also the article by obkom instructor B. Okun', "O partvzyskaniiakh," ibid., no. 4 (April 1936): 44–49.

76. V. Bogushevskii, "Vypolnenie reshenii plenuma Komissii partiinogo kontrolia," *Partiinoe stroitel'stvo*, no. 11 (June 1936): 21. Bogushevskii was a secretary of the KPK's national bureau.

77. RGASPI, f. 17, op. 21, d. 4090, ll. 87–91.

78. For a detailed examination of the February Plenum and its aftermath, see Getty, *Origins*, 137–53, and J. Arch Getty and Oleg V. Naumov, *The Road to Terror: Stalin and the Self-Destruction of the Bolsheviks, 1932–1939* (New Haven, Conn.: Yale University Press, 1999).

79. The elections were in fact so conducted. See Smolensk Archive, files WKP 110, pp. 258–79; WKP 322, pp. 52–57; WKP 105, passim. For the national election results, see *Pravda*, 23 May 1937. Nationally, about half of all party secretaries were voted out of office.

80. RGASPI, f. 17, op. 21, d. 4095, ll. 161–70. Attacking an important leader by criticizing his handling of a particular personnel case was a common tactic in the 1930s. See, for example, Kosior's attack on Postyshev at the February 1937 Plenum of the TsK over the latter's handling of one Nikolaenko. RGASPI, f. 17, op. 2, d. 612, tom 3, ll. 10–15.

81. *Rabochii put'*, 16 March 1937, 2.

82. "Nebol'shevistskii stil' rukovodstva," ibid., 17 March 1937, 2; and "Sobranie monastyrshchinskoi partorganizatsii," ibid., 29 March 1937, 2. For Paparde's original attack on Kosykh, see RGASPI, f. 17, op. 21, d. 4091, l. 114.

83. RGASPI, f. 17, op. 21, d. 4091, ll. 211, 298–99.

84. Indeed, he may have outlived Paparde. When Rumiantsev was arrested in June 1937, his KPK nemesis Paparde succeeded him temporarily as first secretary. Paparde was himself arrested in January 1938 and accused of "wrecking" back in 1930 as part of the party clan in Western Siberia. *Rabochii put'*, 20 May 1937, 1; 11 July 1937, 2; 15 September 1937, 1; 10 January 1938, 1. The last mention of Paparde in either the Smolensk Archive or the local press was in November 1937: *Rabochii put'*, 22 November 1937, 1. Paparde confessed to everything in a fifteen-minute trial and was shot on 29 August 1938. Delo Paparde. RGASPI, f. 589, op. 3, d. 11746, ll. 16–18, 98.

85. Cappelli, "Pre-Modern State-Building," 561.

86. Scholars are divided on the question of whether Stalin ever intended or wanted a regularized, legal state as opposed to the voluntarist and violent system usually attributed to him. For various views, see Moshe Lewin, *The Making of the Soviet System* (New York: New Press, 1985), 281–85; J. Arch Getty, "State and Society Under Stalin: Constitutions and Elections in the 1930s," *Slavic Review* 50, no. 1 (1991): 18–35; O. V. Khlevniuk, Politbiuro: *Mekhanizmy politicheskoi vlasti v 1930-e gody* (Moscow: Rosspen, 1996), 128–57.

CHAPTER 7. STALIN AND THE CLANS II

Epigraph: RGASPI, f. 17, op. 3, d. 922, ll. 50–55.

1. In open voting, one could cross out the proffered candidate or refuse to put one's ballot in the box, but everyone would see and take note.

2. See "Materialy fevral'skogo-martovskogo plenuma TsK VKP(b) 1937 goda," *Voprosy Istorii*, no. 3 (1995): 3–15.

3. "Materialy fevral'skogo-martovskogo plenuma TsK VKP(b) 1937 goda," *Voprosy Istorii*, nos. 5–6 (1995): 4.

4. *Pravda*, 5 March 1936.

5. Ibid., 10 March 1936.

6. See ibid., 7 and 8 February 1935 for the announcement and amplifications.

7. GARF, f. 3316, op. 40, d. 81, ll. 1–5.

8. GARF, f. 3316, op. 40, d. 5.

9. RGASPI, f. 558, op. 1, d. 3275, ll. 1–10.

10. Iurii Zhukov, *Inoi Stalin: Politicheskie reformy v SSSR v 1933–1937 gg.* (Moscow: Vagrius, 2003), 439.

11. Peter Solomon, *Soviet Criminal Justice under Stalin* (Cambridge: Cambridge University Press, 1996), 127.

12. RGASPI, f. 17, op. 2, d. 563, ll. 4–5.

13. A. Eliseev, *Pravda o 1937 gode: Kto razviazal "bol'shoi terror"?* (Moscow: Iauza, 2008), 82.

14. J. Arch Getty and Oleg V. Naumov, *The Road to Terror: Stalin and the Self-Destruction of the Bolsheviks, 1932–1939* (New Haven, Conn.: Yale University Press, 1999), 229–44.

15. Only two of the more than seventy first secretaries of republic and provincial committees wrote about the new constitution: Vareikis and Beria. But they adopted what would become the regional leaders' oppositional alternative to silence by pointing out that "enemies" could use the elections to weaken Soviet power. Zhukov, *Inoi Stalin.* 237.

16. For Akulov's communications from TsIK and the various telegrams in reply see GARF, f. 3316, op. 8, d. 222, ll. 37–39, 51–52, 94–106. List 92 is a memorandum to locals accusing them of "weakly organizing" the discussion. Fond 3316, op. 114 is one of many examples. It contains some of the records of the Orgotdel of the TsIK on the national discussion broken down by *oblast'*. Fond 1235, op. 114, d. 35 contains some of the records of the discussion in the Western *Oblast'* (Smolensk).

17. GARF, f. 3316, op. 8, d. 222, l. 36.

18. GARF, f. 3316, op. 8, d. 222, l. 92. For other examples, see GARF, f. 3316, op. 8, d. 222, ll. 51, 110–12, 135–36, and f. 3316, op. 41, d. 105, l. 1.

19. GARF, f. 3316, op. 8, d. 222, ll. 158–62.

20. GARF, f. 3316, op. 8, d. 222, ll. 26, 50, 62, and op. 41, d. 207, ll. 173–202, 230.

21. I. V. Stalin, *Voprosy Leninizma* (Moscow: Partizdat, 1939), 531–32.

22. See their speeches at the November meeting in *Pravda,* 27–30 November 1936.

23. "Materialy fevral'skogo-martovskogo plenuma TsK VKP(b) 1937 goda," *Voprosy Istorii,* no. 5 (1993): 3–14.

24. *Pravda* carried the resolution from Zhdanov's speech on 6 March and published his speech in full on 11 March. Speeches on enemies appeared in subsequent editions of the paper. Stalin's two speeches were not published until 29 March and 1 April.

25. "Materialy," no. 5 (1993): 12.

26. Ibid., 14. Eikhe was expected to speak because he was both a regional secretary and a candidate member of the Politburo.

27. Ibid., 17, 18, 27.

28. "Materialy fevral'skogo-martovskogo plenuma TsK VKP(b) 1937 goda," *Voprosy Istorii,* no. 7 (1993): 10–11. The third and fourth points on the agenda were about enemy penetration of the apparatus.

29. "Materialy fevral'skogo-martovskogo plenuma TsK VKP(b) 1937 goda," *Voprosy Istorii,* no. 7 (1995): 18.

30. "Materialy," no. 7 (1993): 13.

31. Getty and Naumov, *Road to Terror,* 49.

32. Recalling the June 1936 Plenum when the text of the new constitution was distributed only at the meeting itself.

33. "Materialy fevral'skogo-martovskogo plenuma TsK VKP(b) 1937 goda," *Voprosy Istorii,* no. 6 (1993): 16–17. Emphases mine.

34. "Materialy fevral'skogo-martovskogo plenuma TsK VKP(b) 1937 goda," *Voprosy Istorii,* no. 10 (1995): 21.

35. "Materialy fevral'skogo-martovskogo plenuma TsK VKP(b) 1937 goda," *Voprosy Istorii,* no. 6 (1993): 12.

36. "Materialy," no. 7 (1993): 20.

37. Kosior to Stalin and reply, 20 March 1937. RGASPI, f. 558, op. 11, d. 56, ll. 31–32.

38. "Ob organizatsii vyborov partorganov (na osnove resheniia plenuma)," 20 March 1937. RGASPI, f. 17, op. 163, d. 1141, ll. 68–69.

39. *Bol'shevik,* no. 7 (1937): 28–30.

40. Zhukov, *Inoi Stalin,* 424.

41. GARF, f. 1235, op. 76, d. 161, ll. 58–59.

42. GARF, f. 1235, op. 76, d. 161, ll. 60–65.

43. "O narusheniiakh poriadka oglasheniia rezul'tatov zakrytogo (tainogo) golosovaniia," Politburo postanovlenie. RGASPI, f. 17, op. 163, d. 1147, l. 98. See also the Politburo order of 5 August 1937. RGASPI, f. 17, op. 3, d. 987, l. 31.

44. GARF, f. 1235, op. 76, d. 157, l. 92: "Delo, no. S-52/20." GARF, f. 1235, op. 78, d. 159, l. 74.

45. GARF, f. 1235, op. 78, d. 159, l. 4. See also Kalinin's threatening 29 September 1937 letter on electoral districting: GARF, f. 1235, op. 76, d. 162, ll. 1–2, and f. 1235, op. 78, d. 159, ll. 121–22.

46. GARF, f. 1235, op. 76, d. 149, l. 13 (emphasis in original).

47. Vyshinskii to Stalin and Molotov. RGASPI, f. 82, op. 2, d. 888, l. 39.

48. Vyshinskii to Stalin and Molotov. RGASPI, f. 82, op. 2, d. 888, l. 17.

49. Vyshinskii to Stalin and Molotov. RGASPI, f. 82, op. 2, d. 888, ll. 21–23.

50. GARF, f. 3316, op. 8, d. 222, ll. 72, 73.

51. GARF, f. 3316, op. 8, d. 222, ll. 139–41, and f. 3316, op. 41, d. 126, l. 11.

52. GARF, f. 3316, op. 8, d. 222, l. 73. The legal right of republics to secede from the USSR was included in the Constitution.

53. V. Danilov, R. Manning, L. Viola, et al., eds., *Tragediia sovetskoi derevni: Kollektivizatsiia i raskulachivanie. Dokumenty i materialy v 5 tomakh, 1927–1939,* 5 vols. in 6 (Moscow: Rosspen, 2004), 5.1:247.

54. Ibid., 83.

55. GARF, f. 3316, op. 8, d. 222, l. 11.

56. Smolensk Archive, files WKP 111, pp. 14, 33, 75, and WKP 321, pp. 97, 216.

57. V. N. Khaustov, V. P. Naumov, and N. S. Plotnikov, *Lubianka: Stalin i VChK-GPU-OGPU-NKVD, ianvar' 1922–dekabr' 1936* (Moscow: Fond "Demokratiia," 2003), 775.

58. Danilov et al., *Tragediia,* 5.2:84–85.

59. "Protokoly i stenogramma IX plenuma Omskogo obkoma VKP(b)," 14–15 March 1937. RGASPI, f. 17, op. 21, d. 3294, l. 33.

60. "Protokoly i stenogramma IX plenuma Omskogo obkoma VKP(b)," 14–15 March 1937. RGASPI, f. 17, op. 21, d. 3294, l. 37.

61. Danilov et al., *Tragediia*, 5.1:524.

62. Ibid., 90.

63. Ibid., 150.

64. "Stenogramma VII Kara-Kalpakskoi oblastnoi konferentsii KP(b)UZ," 19–25 May 1937. RGASPI, f. 17, op. 27, d. 142, l. 369.

65. For these *svodki* and critical evaluations of them, see the volumes of *"Sovershenno Sekretno": Lubianka-Stalinu o polozhenii v strane (1922–1934 g.g.)*, ed. A. N. Sakharov et al. (Moscow: Akademiia Nauk, 2002).

66. "Spravka po delu esero-monarchicheskogo zagovora v zapadno Sibiri," V. N. Khaustov and Lennart Samuelson, *Stalin, NKVD i repressii: 1936–1938 gg.* (Moscow: Rosspen, 2009), 333–35.

67. "Protokoly i stenogramma IX plenuma Omskogo obkoma VKP(b)," 14–15 March 1937. RGASPI, f. 17, op. 21, d. 3294, ll. 34–37.

68. "Protokol II Omskoi konferentsii VKP(b)," 1–4 June 1937. RGASPI, f. 17, op. 21, d. 3277, ll. 206–8.

69. "Stenogramma zasedaniia pervoi oblastnoi partiinoi konferentsii g. Voronezha," 6 June 1937. RGASPI, f. 17, op. 21, d. 741, l. 210.

70. "Protokol II Omskoi konferentsii VKP(b)," 1–4 June 1937. RGASPI, f. 17, op. 21, d. 3277, l. 206.

71. Khaustov and Samuelson, *Stalin, NKVD i repressii*, 332.

72. In the interim, Stalin had apparently waited for a telegram from West Siberian party first secretary and candidate Politburo member Eikhe seconding Mironov's request, which formally had come through the NKVD line rather than the party. For the Politburo decision, see V. N. Khaustov, V. P. Naumov, and N. S. Plotnikov, eds., *Lubianka: Stalin i glavnoe upravlenie gosbezopasnosti NKVD, 1937–1938* (Moscow: Rosspen, 2004), 232. Eikhe's actual telegram has not been found in the archives. For indirect evidence of it, see "O vskrytoi v Zap. Sibire k.-r. povstanicheskoi organizatsii sredi vyslannykh kulakov." RGANI, f. 89, op. 43, d. 48, l. 1.

73. The documentary basis for the 1937–38 mass operation was NKVD Order No. 447: "Ob operatsii po repressirovaniiu byvshikh kulakov, ugolovnikov i drugikh antisovetskikh elementov," 30 July 1937. TsA FSB, f. 100, op. 1, por. 1, ll. 203–17. Order No. 447 and Stalin's telegram were first published in edited form in *Trud*, 4 June 1992, 1, 4. Order No. 447 has been published in full in *GULAG (Glavnoe upravlenie lagerei), 1917–1960*, ed. A. I. Kokurin and N. V. Petrov (Moscow: Fond "Demokratiia," 2000), 96–104. A partial English translation appears in Getty and Naumov, *Road to Terror*, 473–80.

74. J. Arch Getty, Gabor T. Rittersporn, and V. N. Zemskov, "Victims of the Soviet Penal System in the Pre-War Years: A First Approach on the Basis of Archival Evidence," *American Historical Review* 98, no. 4 (1993): 1017–49.

75. For differing views of the mass operations, see R. Binner and M. Junge, "How the Terror Became 'Great': Mass Execution and Camp Sentences on the Basis of Order 00447," *Cahiers Du Monde Russe* 42, nos. 2–4 (2001): 557–613; Getty, "'Excesses Are Not Permitted': Mass Terror and Stalinist Governance in the

Late 1930s," *Russian Review* 61, no. 1 (2002): 113–38; O. V. Khlevniuk, "Les mécanismes de la 'Grande Terreur' des années 1937–1938 au Turkménistan," *Cahiers du Monde Russe* 39, nos. 1–2 (1998): 197–207; O. V. Khlevniuk, "The Objectives of the Great Terror, 1937–1938," in *Soviet History, 1917–53: Essays in Honour of R. W. Davies,* ed. Julian Cooper, Maureen Perrie, and E. A. Rees (London: Macmillan, 1995), 158–76.

76. Some scholars believe that the lethal mass operations of 1937 were heir to the periodic police sweeps: P. M. Hagenloh, *Stalin's Police: Public Order and Mass Repression in the USSR, 1926–1941* (Baltimore: Johns Hopkins University Press, 2009); David R. Shearer, *Policing Stalin's Socialism: Repression and Social Order in the Soviet Union, 1924–1953* (New Haven, Conn.: Yale University Press, 2009). My argument here is obviously different.

77. Khaustov et al., *Lubianka 1922–1936,* 113.

78. "O komissii TsK VKP(b) po polit. (sudebnym) delam." Polozhenie Politburo. RGASPI, f. 17, op. 162, d. 3, ll. 120–22.

79. Danilov et al., *Tragediia,* 1:39.

80. Article 107 of the Russian Federation Criminal Code punished "speculation" in food by arrest and confiscation of personal property.

81. Letter from Stalingrad gubkom to TsK, 25 May 1928. RGASPI, f. 558, op. 11, d. 63, l. 34.

82. "'Soobshchenie tt. Sheboldaeva i Trilissera.' Postanovlenie Politburo," 23 September 1929. RGASPI, f. 17, op. 162, d. 7, l. 158; "Telegramma t. Sheboldaeva ot 2.10.1929." RGASPI, f. 17, op. 162, d. 7, l. 171.

83. "Direktiva Politbiuro TsK VKP(b) OGPU i NKIustam ob usilenii repressii," 3 October 1929. Danilov et al., *Tragediia,* 1:714.

84. "Spravka Kollegii OGPU ob ispolnenii direktivy Politbiuro ot 3 oktiabria 1929g.," 9 October 1929. Ibid., 732.

85. "Postanovlenie Politbiuro," 5 December 1929. RGASPI, f. 17, op. 162, d. 8, l. 17.

86. Danilov et al., *Tragediia.* 2:174.

87. Ibid., 313.

88. "'O zametke Kontr'revoliutsionnaia vylaska kulakov.' Postanovlenie Politbiuro," 20 April 1931. RGASPI, f. 17, op. 3, d. 822, l. 7.

89. "'Voprosy OGPU.' Postanovlenie Politburo," 10 July 1931. RGASPI, f. 17, op. 162, d. 10, l. 108.

90. "Protokol Komissii Politbiuro po Delam o vyschei mere sotsial'noi zashity," 26 March, 2 and 8 April, 13 May, 11 June, 10 July, and 10 August 10 1932. RGASPI, f. 17, op. 162, d. 12, ll. 69–70, 91, 71–74, 145–46, 190, and d. 13, ll. 27, 74.

91. "Postanovlenie Politbiuro," 22 November 1932, 10 and 20 March 1933. RGASPI, f. 17, op. 162, d. 14, ll. 48, 96.

92. "Postanovlenie Politbiuro," 9 February 1933. RGASPI, f. 17, op. 162, d. 14, l. 61.

93. "Telegramma Sredazbiuro TsK" and "Postanovlenie Politbiuro," 16 and 23 April 1933. RGASPI, f. 17, op. 162, d. 14, l. 123.

94. Stalin notes, 2 May 1933. RGASPI, f. 558, op. 11, d. 27, l. 63.

95. "Postanovlenie Politbiuro," 7 May 1933. RGASPI, f. 17, op. 3, d. 922, l. 16.

96. TsK/SNK decree of 3 May 1933. RGASPI, f. 17, op. 3, d. 922, ll. 50–55. Preliminary procuratorial approval was waived in cases of terrorism, bombers, arsonists, spies, those fleeing across borders, and bandits.

97. "Postanovleniia Politbiuro," 11 July and 11 August 1933. RGASPI, f. 17, op. 162, d. 15, ll. 2, 27.

98. "'Telegramma t. Molotova ot 19.IX.' Postanovlenie Politburo," 19 September 1934. RGASPI, f 17, op. 162, d. 17, l. 43.

99. "'O NKVD USSR.' Postanovlenie Politbiuro," 20 February 1934. RGASPI, f. 17, op. 3, d. 939, l. 2.

100. "'O rabote sudov i prokuratury.' Postanovlenie Politbiuro," 19 July 19 1934. RGASPI, f. 17, op. 3, d. 948, l. 95.

101. Telegrams from Kaganovich to Stalin and from Stalin to Kaganovich, Molotov, and Zhdanov, 9 October 1934. RGASPI, f. 558, op. 11, d. 86, ll. 51–52.

102. Report from Roginskii to Kaganovich and Molotov, 5 October 1935. RGASPI, f. 82, op. 2, d. 886, ll. 55–56.

103. Ezhov's speech to the February–March 1937 Central Committee Plenum, 2 March 1937. *Voprosy istorii*, no. 10 (1994): 15.

104. "Doklad N. I. Ezhova ob itogakh Plenuma TsK VKP(b). Stenogramma sobraniia aktiva GUGB NKVD SSSR," 19 March 1937. TsA FSB, uncatalogued folder, ll. 40–42.

105. Khaustov et al., *Lubianka 1937–1938*, 234–35.

106. Based on comparison of the limits first approved by the Politburo (Politburo protocols, RGASPI, f. 17, op. 162, d. 21, ll. 94–99) and the targets specified in Order No. 447 (TsA FSB, f. 100, op. 1, por. 1, ll. 203–17).

107. Mirkin (North Ossetia), Popashenko (Kuibyshev), Lavrushin (Gor'kii), Berman (Belorussia), Lomonosov (Dagestan), Mironov (West Siberia), Bulakh (Ordzhonikidze), Dement'ev (Chechnya-Ingushiia).

108. Feliks Ivanovich Chuev, *Sto sorok besed s Molotovym: Iz dnevnika F. Chueva* (Moscow: Terra, 1991), 296.

109. One of the mysteries of the field is how *limity* is routinely translated as "quotas." See, for example, Khlevniuk, "Objectives," 162–63, although the Russian version retains *limity*: Khlevniuk, *Politbiuro: Mekhanizmy politicheskoi vlasti v 1930-e gody* (Moscow: Rosspen, 1996), 190–91.

110. In 1930, a circular to procurators exhorted them to "merciless struggle" and "subordination of judicial policy to the general tasks of kolkhoz construction. Judicial organs should display in this work the maximum flexibility and class vigilance." Danilov at al., *Tragediia*, 2:178–79.

111. Ibid., 1:38.

112. Zhukov, *Inoi Stalin*, 438.

113. Khlevniuk, *Politbiuro*, 101.

114. Calculated from Politburo protocols (special folders): RGASPI, f. 17, op. 162, dd. 21–23; Kokurin and Petrov, *GULAG*, 97–104; V. M. Samosudov, *Bol'shoi Terror v Omskom Priirtysh'e, 1937–1938* (Omsk: OMGU, 1998), 160–61, 241; Nikolai Il'kevich, "Rasstreliany v Viaz'me: Novoe o M. N. Goretskom," *Krai Smolenskii* 1–2 (1994): 129–44; David Shearer, "Crime and Social Disorder in Stalin's Russia—a Reassessment of the Great Retreat and the Origins of Mass Repres-

sion," *Cahiers du Monde Russe* 39, no2. 1–2 (1998): 139–41; *Moskovskie novosti,* no. 25, 21 June 1992, 18–19; *Izvestiia,* 3 April 1996; Khlevniuk, "Les mécanismes," 204–6. Nikita Petrov believes that additional increase permissions were given orally or by telegram and puts the excess shooting figure at about 30,000 (personal communication). Such evidence is not currently available to researchers.

115. See Khlevniuk, "Les mécanismes," 204.

116. See Il'kevich, "Rasstreliany v Viaz'me," 138; Roberta T. Manning, "Massovaia operatsiia protiv 'kulakov i prestupnykh' elementov: Apogei Velikoi Chistki na Smolenshchine," in *Stalinizm v rossiiskoi provintsii: Smolenskie arkhivnye dokumenty v prochtenii zarubezhnykh i rossiiskikh istorikov,* ed. E. V. Kodin (Smolensk: SGPU, 1999), 239–42.

117. Khlevniuk, "Les mécanismes," 203.

118. Mikhail Shreider, *NKVD iznutri: Zapiski chekista* (Moscow: Vozrashchenie, 1995), 80.

119. Khaustov and Samuelson, *Stalin, NKVD i repressii,* 237–39.

120. For examples of "excesses" see A. G. Tepliakov, *Protsedura: Ispolnenie smertnykh prigovorov v 1920–1930-kh godakh* (Moscow: Vozvrashchenie, 2007).

121. Some scholars have argued that these mass operations were a prophylactic measure to remove potential enemies before war broke out. See, for example, O. V. Khlevniuk, "The Objectives of the Great Terror, 1937–1938," in Cooper et al., *Soviet History, 1917–53,* 158–76; and Khlevniuk, "Les mécanismes." Because we do not have at our disposal a single archival document connected to the mass operations that mentions a foreign policy motive, and dozens that refer to domestic causes, it is difficult to sustain the prophylactic interpretation.

122. A. F. Stepanov, *Rasstrel po limitu: Iz istorii politicheskikh repressii v TASSR v gody "ezhovshchiny"* (Kazan': Novoe Znanie, 1999), 14.

123. "'Ob antisovetskikh proiavlenniiakh v sviazi s vyborami v Verkhovnyi Sovet SSSR,' Spetssoobshchie UNKVD Orenburgskoi oblasti," 17 November 1937. Danilov et al., *Tragediia,* 5.1:525–26.

124. "'O khod operatsii po iz"iatiiu byvshikh kulakov, ugolovnikov i drugikh kontrrevoliutsionnykh elementov.' Dokladnaia zapiska UNKVD Ordzhonikidzevskii krai." Ibid., 343, 355.

125. "'Ob antisovetskoi aktivnosti vrazhdebnykh elementov v sviazi s vyborami v Verkhovnyi Sovet SSSR,' Spetssoobshchenie NKVD USSR," 5 November 1937, Ibid., 519–21.

126. For Bukharin's letter, see *Istochnik,* no. 0 [sic] (1993): 23–25, and an English version in Getty and Naumov, *Road to Terror,* 556–60.

127. "Plenum TsK VKP(b) 11–12 oktiabria 1937g., stenogramma." RGASPI, f. 17, op. 2, d. 625, ll. 1–10, 38, 49, 55, 63, 70.

128. "Polozhenie o vyborakh Verkhovnyi Sovet SSSR," *Pravda,* 2 July 1937, 1. "Ob antisovetskikh elementakh," Politburo resolution of 2 July 1937, *Trud,* 4 June 1992, 1.

129. He abandoned the contested elections in October, and the actual elections to the Supreme Soviet in December 1937 saw party candidates enter the elections in a "bloc" with nonparty candidates, effectively permitting only one candidate per

seat. See J. Arch Getty, "State and Society Under Stalin: Constitutions and Elections in the 1930s," *Slavic Review* 50, no. 1 (1991): 18–35.

CHAPTER 8. STALIN AND THE CLANS III

Epigraph: I. V. Stalin, *Sochineniia,* vol. 10 (Moscow: Partizdat, 1954), 329–33.

1. "Varangian" was the term applied by Russians to the Vikings who entered the Russian lands in the ninth century, subjugated the Slavic tribes, and set up the first Russian state.

2. T. H. Rigby, "Early Provincial Cliques and the Rise of Stalin," *Soviet Studies* 33, no. 1 (1981), 3–28.

3. Joint TsKK/Orgburo resolution. RGASPI, f. 17, op. 113, d. 622, l. 9.

4. Orgburo stenogram of 14 May 1928. RGASPI, f. 17, op. 113, d. 622, ll. 80–163. In particular, see Soltz's remarks, ll. 154–55.

5. For an example, see James R. Harris, *The Great Urals: Regionalism and the Evolution of the Soviet System* (Ithaca, N.Y.: Cornell University Press, 1999), 82ff.

6. Typically, before a new oblast or krai was formed, a temporary "organizational buro" was established to create and organize territorial party organizations and recruit new leaderships for them.

7. Susanne Schattenberg, *Die korrupte Provinz? Russische Beamte im 19. Jahrhundert* (Frankfurt am Main: Campus, 2008), 165–68, cited in Alexander Martin, "History, Memory, and the Modernization of 19th-Century Urban Russia," *Kritika* 11, no. 4 (Fall 2010): 856.

8. "Protokol zasedaniia biuro Iaroslavskogo oblastnogo komiteta VKP(b). 19 aprelia 1937g." RGASPI, f. 17, op. 21, d. 5985, l. 32.

9. "Stenogramma II plenuma Iaroslavskogo obkoma VKP(b) 14–15 marta 1937g." RGASPI, f. 17, op. 21, d. 5965, l. 19.

10. "Stenograficheskii otchet II-i Ordzhonikidzevskoi kraevoi partkonferentsii. 13–15 iuniia 1937g." RGASPI, f. 17, op. 21, d. 3425, l. 50.

11. For more on "tails," see Chapter 4.

12. "Stenogramma II plenuma Iaroslavskogo obkoma VKP(b), 14–15 marta 1937g." RGASPI, f. 17, op. 21, d. 5965, ll. 72–73.

13. "Zasedaniia 12-go plenuma Gor'kovskogo obkoma VKP(b), 13–15 marta 1937g. Stenograficheskii otchet." RGASPI, f. 17, op. 21, d. 878, l. 1080b.

14. "Protokol piatoi Gor'kovskoi oblastnoi konferentsii VKP(b). 5–11 iiunia 1937g." RGASPI, f. 17, op. 21, d. 872, l. 342.

15. "Stenogramma II Iaroslavskoi oblastnoi konferentsii VKP(b), 7–8 iuniia 1937g." RGASPI, f. 17, op. 21, d. 5954, ll. 130–31.

16. "Stenogramma II plenuma Iaroslavskogo obkoma VKP(b), 14–15 marta 1937g." RGASPI, f. 17, op. 21, d. 5965, l. 41–42.

17. "Zasedaniia 12-go plenuma Gor'kovskogo obkoma VKP(b), 13–15 marta 1937g. Stenograficheskii otchet." RGASPI, f. 17, op. 21, s. 878, l. 108, 1080b.

18. "Stenogramma VIII-go plenuma Azovo-Chernomorskogo kraikoma VKP(b). 14–16 marta 1937g." RGASPI, f. 17, op. 21, d. 2198, l. 241.

19. "Stenograficheskii otchet IX plenuma Ordzhonikidzevskogo kraikoma" (after January and before April 1937). RGASPI, f. 17, op. 21, d. 3319, l. 218.

20. "Stenogramma VIII-go plenuma Azovo-Chernomorskogo kraikoma VKP(b). 14–16 marta 1937g. RGASPI, f. 17, op. 21, d. 2198, l. 241.

21. "Stenogramma II Iaroslavskoi oblastnoi konferentsii VKP(b), 8–10 iuniia 1937g." RGASPI, f. 17, op. 21, d. 5955, l. 45.

22. "Stenograficheskii otchet II-i Ordzhonikidzevskoi kraevoi partkonferentsii. 13–15 iiunia 1937g." RGASPI, f. 17, op. 21, d. 3424, l. 88.

23. "Materialy k otchetu Stalingradskogo obkoma VKP(b) na II oblastnoi konferentsii VKP(b)." RGASPI, f. 17, op. 21, d. 4225, l. 40.

24. Stenotchet plenuma Azovsko-Chernomorskogo kraikom VKP(b). 6 ianvaria 1937g. RGASPI, f. 17, op. 21, d. 2196, ll. 48–49.

25. "Stenograficheskii otchet II-i Ordzhonikidzevskoi kraevoi partkonferentsii. 13–15 iiunia 1937g." RGASPI, f. 17, op. 21, d. 3425, l. 207.

26. Stalin's "Concluding Words" to the February–March 1937 TsK Plenum. *Voprosy istorii,* nos. 11–12 (1995): 13–14.

27. "Stenogramma 1-i Iaroslavskoi oblastnoi konferentsii VKP(b) i otchetnyi doklad o rabote Orgbiuro TsK VKP(b) s materialami. Tom 3. 30 ianvariia–4 fevraliia 1937g." RGASPI, f. 17, op. 21, d. 5951, ll. 88–108, 127.

28. "Stenograficheski otchet plenuma Azovsko-Chernomorskogo kraikoma VKP(b)." RGASPI, f. 17, op. 21, d. 2196, ll. 48–49.

29. "Stenograficheskii otchet pervoi Kurskoi oblastnoi partiinoi konferentsii. 4–14 iiuniia 1937g." RGASPI, f. 17, op 21, d. 2607, ll. 54–55.

30. "Stenograficheskii otchet II-i Ordzhonikidzevskoi kraevoi partkonferentsii. 13–15 iiunia 1937g." RGASPI, f. 17, op 21, d. 3416, l. 20.

31. "Stenograficheski otchet plenuma Azovsko-Chernomorskogo kraikoma VKP(b)." RGASPI, f. 17, op. 21, d. 2196ll. 100–101.

32. "Stenogramma zasedaniia pervoi oblastnoi partiinoi konferentsii g. Voronezh. 6 iiunia 1937g." RGASPI, f. 17, op. 21, d. 741, l. 189.

33. "Stenogramma zasedanii XII Dal'nevostochnoi kraevoi konferentsii VKP(b) 29 maia–5 iiunia 1937g." RGASPI, f. 17, op. 21, d. 5383, l. 5.

34. "Stenograficheskii otchet plenuma Azovsko-Chernomorskogo kraikoma VKP(b). 6 ianvaria 1937g." RGASPI, f. 17, op. 21, d. 2196, l. 241.

35. "Protokol 2-go plenuma Zapobkoma VKP(b) ot 18–20 iiunia 1937 goda." RGASPI, f. 17, op. 21, d. 4092, l. 4.

36. "Iaroslavskaia Oblastnaia Partiinaia Konferentsiia," *Pravda,* 5 February 1937, p. 2.

37. "Protokol biuro Iaroslavskogo oblastnogo komiteta VKP(b)," 2 February–2 March, 1937. RGASPI, f. 17, op. 21, d. 5984, ll. 2–49.

38. Provincial secretaries frequently tried to hide central reprimands from their party organizations. For example, the Kara-Kalpak buro had refused to forward the important TsK letter "To all party organizations . . ." (about the upcoming first show trial of Zinoviev and others) to its district organizations. "Stenogramma VII Kara-Kalpakskoi oblastnoi konferentsii KP(b) UZ. 19–25 maia 1937g." RGASPI, f. 17, op. 27, d. 142, l. 344.

39. "Materialy fevral'skogo-martovskogo plenuma TsK VKP(b) 1937 goda," *Voprosy Istorii,* no. 5 (1993): 7–13.

40. For Zhdanov's speech and the conflicts it provoked, see Chapter 7.

41. "Ne ushchemliat' prav chlena partii!" *Pravda,* 7 March 1937, p. 1.

42. "Protokol biuro Iaroslavskogo oblastnogo komiteta VKP(b), 8 marta 1937g." RGASPI, f. 17, op. 21, d. 5984, ll. 110–11.

43. *Voprosy istorii,* nos. 11–12 (1995): 14, and *Pravda* 1 April 1937, 1.

44. "O nepravil'nom podbore kadrov, podkhalimstve i chinopochitami," *Pravda,* 10 March 1937, p. 2.

45. "Stenogramma II plenuma Iaroslavskogo obkoma VKP(b), 14–15 marta 1937g." RGASPI, f. 17, op. 21, d. 5965, ll. 10–11.

46. Ibid., l. 79.

47. "Stenograficheskii otchet II-i Ordzhonikidzevskoi kraevoi partkonferentsii. 13–15 iiunia 1937g." RGASPI, f. 17, op. 21, d. 3425, ll. 48–49.

48. "Stenogramma II plenuma Iaroslavskogo obkoma VKP(b), 14–15 marta 1937g." RGASPI, f. 17, op. 21, d. 5965, ll. 10–11.

49. Ibid., l. 84.

50. Ibid., l. . 19.

51. Ibid., ll. 34, 94, 97.

52. Ibid., l. 147.

53. Ibid., l. 52.

54. Ibid., l. 41.

55. "Stenograficheskii otchet plenuma Azovsko-Chernomorskogo kraikoma VKP(b). 6 ianvaria 1937g." RGASPI, f. 17, op. 21, d. 2196, ll. 232, 249.

56. "Zasedaniia 12-go plenuma Gor'kovskogo obkoma VKP(b), 13–15 marta 1937g. Stenograficheskii otchet." RGASPI, f. 17, op. 21, d. 878, l. 154.

57. "Stenogramma zasedanii XII Dal'nevostochnoi kraevoi konferentsii VKP(b). 29 maia–5 iiunia 1937g." RGASPI, f. 17, op 21, d. 5382, l. 171.

58. "Zasedaniia 12-go plenuma Gor'kovskogo obkoma VKP(b), 13–15 marta 1937g. Stenograficheskii otchet." RGASPI, f. 17, op. 21, d. 878, l. 236ob.

59. "Stenograficheskii otchet plenuma Azovsko-Chernomorskogo kraikoma VKP(b). 6 ianvaria 1937g." RGASPI, f. 17, op. 21, d. 2196, ll. 266–70.

60. "Protokol piatoi Gor'kovskoi oblastnoi konferentsii VKP(b). 5–11 iiunia 1937g." RGASPI, f. 17, op. 21, d. 872, l. 345.

61. "Stenograficheskii otchet II-i Ordzhonikidzevskoi kraevoi partkonferentsii. 13–15 iiunia 1937g." RGASPI, f. 17, op. 21, d. 3424, l. 88.

62. Stenogramma II plenuma Iaroslavskogo obkoma VKP(b), 14–15 marta 1937g. RGASPI, f. 17, op. 21, d. 5965, l. 149.

63. Ibid., ll. 150, 156, 200.

64. Ibid., ll. 175, 176, 184.

65. Ibid., ll. 23, 198.

66. Ibid., l. 181.

67. "Protokol piatoi Gor'kovskoi oblastnoi konferentsii VKP(b). 5–11 iiunia 1937g." RGASPI, f. 17, op. 21, d. 872, l. 348.

68. "Protokol i stenogramma XVII Tatarskoi oblastnoi konferentsii VKP(b). 10–15 iiunia 1937g." RGASPI, f. 17, op. 1, d. 4348, l. 140.

69. "Stenogramma VIII-go plenuma Azovo-Chernomorskogo kraikoma VKP(b). 14–16 marta 1937g." RGASPI, f. 17, op. 21, d. 2198, l. 456.

70. "Stenogramma zasedaniia pervoi oblastnoi partiinoi konferentsii g. Voronezha. 6 iiunia 1937g." RGASPI, f. 17, op. 21, d. 741, l. 149.

71. "Stenograficheskii otchet II-i Ordzhonikidzevskoi kraevoi partkonferentsii. 13–15 iiunia 1937g." RGASPI, f. 17, op. 21, d. 3425, ll. 277–78.

72. "Protokoly i stenogramma XVII Tatarskoi oblastnoi konferentsii VKP(b). 10–15 iiunia 1937g." RGASPI, f. 17, op. 21, d. 4349, l. 177.

73. "Stenograficheskii otchet plenuma Azovsko-Chernomorskogo kraikoma VKP(b). 6 ianvaria 1937g." RGASPI, f. 17, op. 21, d. 2196, l. 239.

74. "Protokoly i stenogramma XVII Tatarskoi oblastnoi konferentsii VKP(b). 10–15 iiunia 1937g." RGASPI, f. 17, op. 21, d. 4349, ll. 110, 137.

75. "Stenograficheskii otchet II-i Ordzhonikidzevskoi kraevoi partkonferentsii. 13–15 iiunia 1937g." RGASPI, f. 17, op. 21, d. 3425, ll. 295–98.

76. "Protokoly zasedaniia biuro Iaroslavskogo oblastnogo komiteta VKP(b), 19 aprelia 1937g." RGASPI, f. 17, op. 21, d. 5985, l. 19. The transcript of the unusually lengthy buro meeting is on ll. 19–76.

77. "Protokoly zasedaniia biuro Iaroslavskogo oblastnogo komiteta VKP(b), 19 aprelia 1937g." RGASPI, f. 17, op. 21, d. 5985, ll. 87, 128.

78. "Protokol II Iaroslavskoi oblastnoi konferentsii VKP(b) s materialami. 7–12 iuniia 1937g." RGASPI, f. 17, op. 21, d. 5953, ll. 24–35. Because of the carefully crafted way this election report was written by the oblast leadership, here and in other provinces it is not possible to document the actual number of raikom secretaries removed.

79. "Stenogramma II Iaroslavskoi oblastnoi konferentsii VKP(b), 7–8 iuniia 1937g." RGASPI, f. 17, op. 21, d. 5954, l. 52. Iaroslavl"s elections mirrored those across the country, where at primary organization level, 50–70 percent of the committees were replaced, but above that the leading cadres were barely affected. See *Pravda*, 23 May 1937, and the discussion in J. Arch Getty, *Origins of the Great Purges: the Soviet Communist Party Reconsidered, 1933–1938* (Cambridge: Cambridge University Press, 1985), 157–60.

80. "Stenogramma II Iaroslavskoi oblastnoi konferentsii VKP(b), 7–8 iuniia 1937g." RGASPI, f. 17, op. 21, d. 5954, ll. 16–35.

81. Ibid., l. 130.

82. Ibid., ll. 150–51.

83. "Stenogramma II Iaroslavskoi oblastnoi konferentsii VKP(b), 8–10 iuniia 1937g." RGASPI, f. 17, op. 21, d. 5955, l. 127.

84. Ibid., l. 80.

85. "Stenograficheskii otchet pervoi Kurskoi oblastnoi partiinoi konferentsii VKP(b), 4–14 iuniia 1937g." RGASPI, f. 17, op. 21, d. 2607, l. 147.

86. "Stenogramma II Iaroslavskoi oblastnoi konferentsii VKP(b), 8–10 iuniia 1937g." RGASPI, f. 17, op. 21, d. 5955, l. 92.

87. "Rezoliutsiia vtoroi Iaroslavskoi oblastnoi partiinoi konferentsii po otchetnomu dokladu obkoma VKP(b)." RGASPI, f. 17, op. 21, d. 5957.

88. Ibid., l. 101.

89. RGASPI, f. 17, op. 21, dd. 3966–4092.

90. RGASPI, f. 73, op. 2, d. 19, ll. 1–106.

91. "Stenograficheskii otchet pervoi Kurskoi oblastnoi partiinoi konferentsii VKP(b), 4–14 iuniia 1937g." RGASPI, f. 17, op. 21, d. 2607, l. 147.

92. "Stenogramma Azovskogo-Chernomorskogo plenum VKP(b), 6 ianvariia 1937g." RGASPI, f. 17, op. 21, d. 2196, l. 279.

93. V. N. Khaustov and Lennart Samuelson, *Stalin, NKVD i repressii: 1936–1938 gg.* (Moscow: Rosspen, 2009), 141.

94. Feliks Ivanovich Chuev, *Tak govoril Kaganovich: Ispoved' stalinskogo apostola* (Moscow: Olma Press, 2001), 187–89.

95. Feliks Ivanovich Chuev, *Sto sorok besed s Molotovym: Iz dnevnika F. Chueva* (Moscow: Terra, 1991), 296–97.

96. For an analysis showing that although Old Bolshevik status and elite rank overlapped, the latter was a better predictor of risk of arrest, see J. Arch Getty and William Chase, "Patterns of Repression among the Soviet Elite in the Late 1930s: A Biographical Analysis," in *Stalinist Terror: New Perspectives,* ed. J. Arch Getty and Roberta Thompson Manning (Cambridge: Cambridge University Press, 1993), 225–46.

97. For works representing various interpretations, see J. Arch Getty and Oleg V. Naumov, *The Road to Terror: Stalin and the Self-Destruction of the Bolsheviks, 1932–1939* (New Haven, Conn.: Yale University Press, 1999); O. V. Khlevniuk, "The Objectives of the Great Terror, 1937–1938," in *Soviet History, 1917–53: Essays in Honour of R. W. Davies,* ed. Julian Cooper, Maureen Perrie, and E. A. Rees (London: Macmillan, 1995), 158–76; Peter H. Solomon, "Soviet Criminal Justice and the Great Terror," *Slavic Review* 46, nos. 3–4 (1987): 391–413; Robert Conquest, *The Great Terror: A Reassessment* (New York: Oxford University Press, 1990); Robert Thurston, *Life and Terror in Stalin's Russia, 1934–1941* (New Haven, Conn.: Yale University Press, 1996); William Chase, *Enemies Within the Gates? The Comintern and the Stalinist Repression, 1934–1939* (New Haven, Conn.: Yale University Press, 2001).

98. "Protokol 2-go plenuma Zapobkoma VKP(b) ot 18–20 iiunia 1937 goda." RGASPI, f. 17, op. 21, d. 4092, l. 4. Delo Sheboldaeva. RGASPI, f. 589, op. 3, d. 7542, ll. 1–2.

99. "Spiski arestovannykh rabotnikov Vostochno-Sibirshoi oblasti." RGASPI, f. 82, op. 2, d. 149, ll. 38–44.

100. For a different discussion of *krugovaia poruka* and the Terror, see G. Alexopoulos, "Stalinism and the Politics of Kinship: Practices of Collective Punishment, 1920s–1940s," *Comparative Studies in Society and History* 50, no. 1 (2008): 91–117. She argues that a Stalinist assault on the family in the 1930s made it the "basic unit" of terror, with *krugovaia poruka* as the method. Aside from the fact that Stalinist policy in the 1930s was to strengthen the traditional family, we note that *krugovaia poruka* was more often the justification for uprooting political clans, whose victims far outnumbered kinship family members.

101. For examples, see: "Protokol 2-go plenuma Zapobkoma VKP(b) ot 18–20 iiunia 1937 goda." RGASPI, f. 17, op. 21, d. 4092, l. 4. "Stenograficheskii otchet plenuma Azovsko-Chernomorskogo kraikoma VKP(b). 6 ianvaria 1937 g." RGASPI, f. 17, op. 21, d. 2196, l. 239. "Stenogramma zasedaniia pervoi oblastnopartiinoi konferentsii g. Voronezha. 6 iiunia 1937 g." RGASPI, f. 17, op. 21, d. 741, l. 149.

102. RGASPI, f. 73, op. 2, d. 19, ll. 1–106.

103. Stalin to Andreev, 19 September 1937. RGASPI, f. 73, op. 2, d. 19, l. 44.

104. See the various "Spetssoobshchenie N. I. Ezhova I. V. Stalinu" in V. N. Khaustov, V. P. Naumov, and N. S. Plotnikov, eds., *Lubianka: Stalin i glavnoe up-*

ravlenie gosbezopasnosti NKVD, 1937–1938 (Moscow: Rosspen, 2004); and Khaustov and Samuelson, *Stalin, NKVD i repressii.*

105. AP RF, f. 3, op. 24, d. 373, ll. 3–44.

106. RGASPI, f. 558, op. 11, d. 132, ll. 90–99.

107. Harvard Project on the Soviet Social System, Schedule B, vol. 1, case 101, p. 11 (seq. 9). Widener Library, Harvard University.

108. Harvard Project on the Soviet Social System, Schedule A, vol. 33, case 338/ (NY) 1390, p. 49.

109. Harvard Project on the Soviet Social System, Schedule A, vol. 19, case 385, p. 81.

110. Yoram Gorlizki, "Ordinary Stalinism: The Council of Ministers and the Soviet Neopatrimonial State, 1946–1953," *Journal of Modern History* 74, no. 4 (2002): 699–736; Yoram Gorlizki and O. V. Khlevniuk, *Cold Peace: Stalin and the Soviet Ruling Circle, 1945–1953* (New York: Oxford University Press, 2004).

111. Geoffrey Hosking, *Russia and the Russians: A History* (Cambridge, Mass.: Harvard University Press, 2001), 542.

112. Geoffrey Hosking, "Patronage and the Russian State," *Slavonic and East European Review* 78, no. 2 (2000): 317–18.

113. John Willerton, *Patronage and Politics in the USSR* (Cambridge: Cambridge University Press, 1992)

EPILOGUE

Epigraphs: David Ransel, "Character and Style of Patron-Client Relations in Russia," in *Klientelsysteme im Europa der frühen Neuzeit,* ed. Antoni Maczak and Elisabeth Mueller-Luckner (Munich: Oldenbourg, 1988), 216. Graeme Gill, *The Origins of the Stalinist Political System* (Cambridge: Cambridge University Press, 1990), 6. O. Cappelli, "Pre-Modern State-Building in Post-Soviet Russia," *Journal of Communist Studies and Transition Politics* 24, no. 4 (2008): 557.

1. "Tribal politics" is the felicitous phrase of Geoffrey Hosking, *Russia and the Russians: A History* (Cambridge, Mass.: Harvard University Press, 2001), 593.

2. In Transparency International's *Corruption Perceptions Index 2010,* Russia is among the most corrupt states in the world, ranking 154 of 178 in the "most corrupt" index. Russia shares that spot with such countries as Kenya, Congo, and Papua New Guinea.

3. Geoffrey Hosking, "Patronage and the Russian State," *Slavonic and East European Review* 78, no. 2 (2000): 319.

4. Hosking, *Russia and the Russians,* 612.

5. "Introduction," in *Russia as a Network State: What Works in Russia When State Institutions Do Not,* ed. Vadim Kononenko and Arkady Moshes (London: Palgrave Macmillan, 2011). 2, 6–8, 10.

6. Cappelli, "Pre-Modern State-Building."

7. See, for example, Vladimir Shlapentokh, *Contemporary Russia as a Feudal Society: A New Perspective on the Post-Soviet Era* (New York: Palgrave Macmillan, 2007); and R. D. Markwick, "A Discipline in Transition? From Sovietology to

'Transitology,'" *Journal of Communist Studies and Transition Politics* 13, no. 3 (1996): 255–76.

8. Michael Urban, "Forms of Civil Society: Politics and Social Relations in Russia," *International Political Anthropology* 1, no. 1 (2008): 93–111.

9. See references to Eisenstadt, Roniger, and others in the Introduction.

10. T. H. Rigby, "Russia's Clientelism, Cliques, Connections and 'Clans': The Same Old Story?" *Soviet and Post-Soviet Review* 25, no. 2 (1998): 119, 123; Cappelli, "Pre-Modern State-Building," 550.

11. Shlapentokh, *Contemporary Russia as a Feudal Society.* 171; Alena V. Ledeneva, "Can Medvedev Change 'Sistema'?' Informal Networks," in Kononenko and Moshes, *Russia as a Network State,* 46, 58.

12. Hosking, *Russia and the Russians,* 612.

13. Marina Litvinovich, *Vlast' semei: 20 klanov, kontroliruiushchikh ekonomiku Rossii* (Moscow: Eksmo, 2012).

14. Ledeneva, "Can Medvedev Change 'Sistema?'" 42, 44; Urban, "Forms of Civil Society," 99. On patronage in the state bureaucracy, see also Eugene Huskey, "From Higher Party Schools to Academies of State Service: The Marketization of Bureaucratic Training in Russia," *Slavic Review* 63, no. 2 (2004): 325–48, and his "Putin as Patron: Cadres Policy in the Russian Transition," in *Leading Russia: Putin in Perspective. Essays in Honor of Archie Brown,* ed. A. Pravda (Oxford: Oxford University Press), 2005.

15. V. Pribylovskii et al., *Vlast'-2010: 60 biografii* (Moscow: Panorama, 2010).

16. RGASPI, f. 17, op. 3, d. 961, l. 16.

17. Pribylovskii et al., *Vlast'-2010,* 1–9.

18. Mikhail Delyagin, ITAR-TASS (FRE/RL), 9 November 2007.

19. ITAR-TASS, 9 November 2007.

20. *Wall Street Journal,* 10 October 2007.

21. ITAR-TASS, 9 November 2007.

22. "Nel'zia dopustit, chtoby voiny prevratilis' v torgovtsev," *Kommersant,* 9 October 2007.

23. Edward Keenan, "Muscovite Political Folkways," *Russian Review* 45, no. 2 (1986): 119, 156. Russian sociologists have begun research on clientelism in Russia, a subject banned in Soviet times. Unlike members of the political elite, scholars are not under the traditional veil of secrecy. See, for example, M. N. Afanas'ev, *Klientelizm i rossiiskaia gosudarstvennost'* (Moscow: Moskovskii obshchestvenntyi nauchnyi fond, 2000).

24. *Kommersant,* 19 October 2007.

25. See Julie A. Cassiday and Emily D. Johnson, "Putin, Putiniana and the Question of a Post-Soviet Cult of Personality," *Slavonic and East European Review* 88, no. 4 (2010): 681–707, and Helena Goscilo. *Putin as Celebrity and Cultural Icon.* (New York: Routledge, 2012).

26. "'Twelve Moods of Putin' Hits Russia," BBC News, 6 December 2001.

27. "Ikona Vladimira Putina zamirotochila pered vyborami," *Kommersant,* 21 January 2012.

28. "Russian President Vladimir Putin Ruffled," Reuters, 6 August 2012. Video: http://www.guardian.co.uk/world/video/2012/aug/06/russian-president-vladimir-putin-priest-kiss-video.

29. Maureen Perrie, *The Image of Ivan the Terrible in Russian Folklore* (Cambridge: Cambridge University Press, 1987), 116–17.

30. For other effects of this change, see Moshe Lewin, *The Gorbachev Phenomenon: A Historical Interpretation*, rev. ed. (Berkeley: University of California Press, 1991).

31. "Putin's Plan for Former Moscow Hotel Site: A Park," *Reuters*, 20 January 2012; "Putin Says Replace Business-Center Plans for Rossia Hotel Site With Park," *Moscow News*, 20 January 2012.

32. *RIA Novosti*, 20 October 2008.

33. Because Novodevichii is a protected site of "federal importance," any changes to the ensemble require permission of an authority at that level. The convent ensemble is also listed as a UNESCO World Heritage site (the convention regarding which Russia ratified in 1992), so that any changes to the site are forbidden. But neither UNESCO nor Russian federal law can stand up against the tsar's patronage, and representatives of those bodies were not even invited to the planning meeting. "V Moskve priniali reshenie vozvesti khram v Novodevich'em monastyre, ne postaviv v izvestnost' IuNESKO," *Ekho Moskvy*, 11 June 2012.

34. "Lizost' k telu," *Vlast'*, no. 50 (803), 22 December 2008.

35. "Patriarkh vstal na zashchitu istorii," *Moskovskii komsomolets*, 2 October 2012.

36. *Russia and Eurasia Review* 1, no. 2 (18 June 2002).

37. Interfax, 16 December 2010.

38. Vladimir Isachenkov, "Russian Leaders Argue about Soviet Model," Associated Press, 27 December 2010.

39. Jan Plamper, *The Stalin Cult: A Study in the Alchemy of Power* (New Haven, Conn.: Yale University Press, 2012), 33.

40. R. W. Davies O. Khlevniuk, E. A. Rees, A. P. Kosheleva, and A. A. Rogovaia, eds., *The Stalin-Kaganovich Correspondence, 1931–1936* (New Haven, Conn.: Yale University Press, 2003), 349–50.

41. Dimitrov diary entry for 11 February 1937. Ivo Banac, ed., *The Diary of Georgi Dimitrov, 1933–1949* (New Haven, Conn.: Yale University Press, 2003), 51.

42. Stephen White, *Political Culture and Soviet Politics* (London: Macmillan, 1979).

43. Keenan, "Muscovite Political Folkways."

44. See Immanuel Wallerstein, *The Modern World System* (New York: Academic Press, 1974), and *The Modern World-System in the Longue Durée* (Boulder, Colo.: Paradigm Publishers, 2004).

45. "'Otets natsii' na dva sroka," *Nezavisimaia gazeta*, 24 May 2012, and *Russia Today*, 23 May 2012.

46. "Demontazh sistemy neformal'nykh institutov," *Nezavisimaia gazeta*, 16 April 2012.

47. S. A. Smith, "Bones of Contention: Bolsheviks and the Struggle against Relics 1918–1930," *Past and Present* 204, no. 1 (2009): 194. On neotraditionalism, see Kenneth Jowitt, *New World Disorder: The Leninist Extinction* (Berkeley: University of California Press, 1992), and T. Martin, "Modernization or Neo-Traditionalism? Ascribed Nationality and Soviet Primordialism," in *Stalinism: New Directions*, ed. Sheila Fitzpatrick (New York: Routledge, 2000), 348–67.

48. Kononenko and Moshes, *Russia as a Network State,* 10.

49. Eric R. Wolf, "Kinship, Friendship, and Patron-Client Relations in Complex Societies," in *Friends, Followers, and Factions: A Reader in Political Clientelism,* ed. Steffen W. Schmidt, James C. Scott, Carl Lande, and Laura Guasti (Berkeley: University of California Press, 1977), 174.

50. Afanas'ev, *Klientelizm,* 85.

51. Timothy Mitchell, 'The Limits of the State: Beyond Statist Approaches and Their Critics,' *American Political Science Review* 1 (1991): 94.

52. Oleg Kharkhordin, "What Is the State? The Russian Concept of *Gosudarstvo* in the European Context," *History and Theory* 40 (2001): 207–8.

53. Pierre Bourdieu and Loïc J. D. Wacquant, *An Invitation to Reflexive Sociology* (Chicago: University of Chicago Press, 1992), 111.

Index

Absolutism, 14, 183, 330n127
Akulov, I., 174–75, 209–10, 332n30
Aleksei II, 283
Aleksei Mikhailovich, 26
Alexopoulos, G., 27
Andreev, A., 94, 109, 165, 167, 169, 175, 212–13, 239, 262–63, 265, 276
Anna Ivanovna, 43
Arkhipov, V., 166, 195, 203–4, 333n53, 333n59
Artel, 167, 181, 240–41, 245, 248, 254–58, 260, 326n69. *See also* Clan
Avanesov, K., 59, 72
Awards, 3, 18, 25, 30, 35–38, 66,171

Balitskii, V., 171–72, 175, 329n105
Barsukov, V., 278
Beloborodov, A., 61, 63, 305n125
Berdyaev, N., 65
Beria, L., 55, 91, 93, 168–69, 171–72, 175, 177–78, 214–15, 263, 336n15
Berliner, J., 272
Blat, 7, 8, 187
blizkii, 93–94. *See also* Clan
Bolotnikov, I., 82
Bolshevik Party. *See* Communist Party
Bourdieu, P., x, 17–18, 66, 75, 271, 292, 297n50

Boyars: and collective responsibility, ix, 43; and political organization, 13–15, 18, 23, 45, 53–54, 55, 130, 132, 158, 169, 268, 285, 289, 291; and rank, 36, 297n41; and institutions, 65; and power struggle, 79, 82, 156, 169, 180, 205, 275, 281; decision-making practices of, 98–99, 146. *See also* Nobility
Brezhnev, L., 4, 10–11, 25, 95, 267–68, 275, 281
Bukharin, N.: on objective guilt, 40; show trial of, 41; kinship of, 46; condemnation of, 51, 203, 211, 275; on party expulsions, 59; on Lenin's funeral, 70; on oppositionists, 153–54, 157; on leadership, 214; on purges, 235
Bulbov, A., 278
Bureaucracy: rational vs. patrimonial, 2–3, 5–7, 18, 21, 24, 35, 83, 90, 127, 135, 139, 145–46, 269–72, 282, 286; and privilege, 17, 58, 297n44, 348n14; and the modern state, 21, 23, 86, 90, 96, 183, 269–70, 281, 290, 312n105; and personalization of power, 27–28, 96, 183; and letters of petition/appeal, 31, 33; purge of, 51, 194, 231; combat against, 63, 97, 99–100, 153, 186, 210, 257, 302n74; expansion of Soviet, 114; and

Zhdanov, A.: on "familyness," 23, 212–13; death of, 55; proximity to Stalin, 93–94; and firing of A. Nikolaev, 109; and *oprosom* decisions, 145; and Stalin's clan, 168–69; in Saratov, 198–99; and attack on regional party secretaries, 203; on elections, 211–13, 215–16; on demo-

cratization of regional party organizations, 247–59, 336n24

Zhukov, Iu., 233

Zinoviev, G., 40–41, 46, 51, 60–61, 63, 77, 108, 152–54, 156–57, 161–63, 222. *See also* Opposition, oppositionists: Zinovievists